Coasts for People

Issues of sustainability and increased competition over coastal resources are changing practices of resource management. Societal concerns about environmental degradation and loss of coastal resources have steadily increased, while other issues, such as food security, biodiversity and climate change, have emerged. This new form of resource management takes a local, community-based approach and looks not just at the ecological issues, but also at societal and human concerns. This interdisciplinary and unique text uses a series of vivid case studies from environments throughout the world to suggest how to achieve these new resource management principles in practical, accessible ways.

Fikret Berkes is Distinguished Professor and Tier 1 Canada Research Chair at the Natural Resources Institute, University of Manitoba, Canada. His studies on community-based resource management and the use of commons in a number of regions of the world have led to insights regarding the management of coastal and marine resources. Dr. Berkes has authored some 250 peer-reviewed journal papers and chapters and ten books, including *Sacred Ecology* (Routledge, 2012), *Navigating Social–Ecological Systems* (Cambridge University Press, 2003), and *Managing Small-Scale Fisheries* (IDRC, 2001).

Related Titles

Sacred Ecology
Third Edition
Fikret Berkes

Flood and Coastal Erosion Risk Management
A Manual for Economic Appraisal
Edmund Penning-Rowsell, Sally Priest, Dennis Parker, Joe Morris, Sylvia Tunstall, Christophe Viavattene, John Chatterton, Damon Owen

Coastal Systems
Second Edition
Simon Haslett

The Measurement of Environmental and Resource Values
Theory and Methods, Third Edition
A. Myrick Freeman III, Joseph A. Herriges, Catherine L. King

Constitutions and the Commons
The Impact of Federal Governance on Local, National, and Global Resource Management
Blake Hudson

Coasts for People

Interdisciplinary Approaches to Coastal and Marine Resource Management

Fikret Berkes

Routledge
Taylor & Francis Group

NEW YORK AND LONDON

First published 2015
by Routledge
711 Third Avenue, New York, NY 10017

and by Routledge
2 Park Square, Milton Park, Abingdon, Oxon, OX14 4RN

Routledge is an imprint of the Taylor & Francis Group, an informa business

© 2015 Taylor & Francis

Library of Congress Cataloging in Publication Data
Berkes, Fikret.
    Coasts for people: interdisciplinary approaches to coastal and marine
    resource management/by Fikret Berkes.—1 Edition.
    pages cm
    Includes bibliographical references and index.
    1. Coastal zone management. 2. Marine resources development.
    3. Social ecology. 4. Sustainable development. I. Title.
    HT391.B447 2015
    304.2—dc23
    2014029754

ISBN: 978–1–138–77980–8 (hbk)
ISBN: 978–1–138–77981–5 (pbk)
ISBN: 978–1–315–77103–8 (ebk)

Typeset in Adobe Caslon, Trade Gothic and Copperplate Gothic
by Florence Production Ltd, Stoodleigh, Devon, UK

Printed and bound in the United States of America by Publishers Graphics,
LLC on sustainably sourced paper.

CONTENTS

ILLUSTRATIONS

Figures

Photos

Tables

Boxes

PREFACE

The idea of writing this book came to me in 2009 with the chapter I prepared for Cochrane and Garcia's landmark *A Fishery Manager's Guidebook*, which expanded horizons from biological management to multidisciplinary governance. Perhaps, I thought, there was a need for a volume that built on some of that expanded scope. A series of marine-oriented articles published in 2010–11 assured me that I had the necessary material in hand: yes, I could try an interdisciplinary synthesis that looked like no other coastal management book. This synthesis would build on the topics I had been working on for years: commons and co-management, resilience, local and traditional knowledge, social–ecological systems and, to a lesser extent, community-based conservation, and livelihoods and development. It had been a great deal of fun writing on ecosystem-based management for *Fish & Fisheries* on the invitation of Tony Pitcher, the editor. So I knew I had something to say about that too.

Coasts have a special place in my life. I grew up in a coastal city (Istanbul), and then I spent about a decade of my life in Montreal, almost a coastal city. I did my PhD in Marine Sciences at McGill University, working on food webs in the Gulf of St. Lawrence. Marine Sciences was a science program, but it helped me understand that there really were no dividing lines between disciplines. You could not talk about plankton without knowing water movements and some oceanography. You could not understand contaminants in fish and shellfish unless you knew something about chemistry, geochemistry and food webs. So it was relatively painless after the PhD to extend my interdisciplinary horizons further, to the human dimensions of environment and resources. My formal training in social sciences was a postdoctoral year at Carleton University in Ottawa, and the start of my long-term work with indigenous fishers and hunters in the Canadian North, the subject of my other Routledge book, *Sacred Ecology*. A year in sociology and anthropology did not make a card-carrying social scientist out of me, but it helped shed some of my science blinkers.

In my early professional life, I ended up in that liminal space between natural sciences and social sciences. Some of my colleagues at that time warned me that I might be making it difficult for myself to get jobs and research grants and to find suitable journals for my work—basically committing professional suicide. (Fortunately, it did not work out that way.) Being an interdisciplinary scholar was an interesting experience. Science-oriented meetings did not often require the services of a social scientist, but social science meetings often did require natural science expertise. So, for example, in the 1985 National Research Council/ National Academy of Sciences meetings that redefined the field of commons, I found myself advising Elinor Ostrom about biological sustainability. I was in an unusual space: there weren't that many natural scientists in the world interested in commons.

Decades later, there are both natural scientists and social scientists extending their interests into each other's realm. Addressing the real problems of the world requires crossing disciplinary boundaries and, ultimately, eliminating the divides between science and management, resource user and decision-maker, and different kinds of knowledge. As the references in this volume indicate, there are now many authors and sources that cross various boundaries. These are the papers and books that would have been dismissed by specialist experts only a few years ago. They contain ideas "at the edge" of the various disciplinary areas—which is actually a good place to be if one is interested in paradigm change in the sense of Thomas Kuhn's *Structure of Scientific Revolutions*.

These paradigm changes are not only necessary, they are inevitable. In the 1970s, environment was "rediscovered," leading to a change in perspective: perhaps humans were part of the ecosystem too! The 1980s saw a great deal of interdisciplinary ferment and breaking down of disciplinary silos. It was at the first ecological economics meeting in 1990, Washington, DC, that I met Carl Folke. This led to international team projects based at the Beijer Institute, Royal Swedish Academy of Sciences, Carl's base. These were truly interdisciplinary projects exploring social–ecological systems, resilience, commons, and ecological economics, and led to two high-profile books, *Linking Social and Ecological Systems* (Cambridge University Press, 1998) and *Navigating Social–Ecological Systems* (Cambridge University Press, 2003).

In the meantime, my work on coastal environments and marine resources continued, with less emphasis on the Canadian North and more emphasis internationally. Projects and field research in the West Indies, Turkey, Bangladesh, India, Thailand, Cambodia, Philippines, Zanzibar, Mozambique, Brazil, Costa Rica, Indonesia and Sri Lanka gave me an appreciation of issues and conditions in many parts of the world. The Beijer-based group continued as the marine resilience working group, and our 2006 "roving bandits" paper in *Science* was, for me, one of the highlights. Despite this work and our 2001 book, *Managing Small-Scale Fisheries*, co-authored with two US colleagues (Bob Pomeroy and Richard Pollnac) and two West Indies colleagues (Robin Mahon and Patrick McConney), I was not concentrating on marine resources. Instead, I was discovering other kinds of commons, sometimes following the work of my graduate students, extending into forestry, protected areas and grazing lands. This work gave me new insights, but now I am glad to be back to marine and coastal commons.

With this book, I close the circle and return to my PhD roots in marine sciences, except that it is now interdisciplinary coastal and marine science, with a strong flavor of social science thinking from human geography, anthropology, political studies, international development and economics.

ACKNOWLEDGMENTS

I have been fortunate to work with groups of wonderful colleagues over the years. It is impossible to acknowledge all, but the following colleagues (all in alphabetical order) have been important for the development of many of the ideas in this volume:

- our original commons group (Jim Acheson, David Feeny and Bonnie McCay);
- the small-scale fisheries group (Brian Davy, Robin Mahon, Patrick McConney, Richard Pollnac and Bob Pomeroy);
- marine resilience working group (Carl Folke, Terry Hughes, Per Olsson, Bob Steneck, Jim Wilson and others);
- the Brazil project group (Alpina Begossi, Iain Davidson-Hunt, Natalia Hanazaki, Derek Johnson and Cristiana Seixas);
- Community Conservation Research Network and the east coast group (Derek Armitage, Tony Charles, John Kearney, Laura Loucks, Melanie Wiber and others);
- British Columbia and the west coast group (Mimi Lam, Rosemary Ommer, Ian Perry, Lyn Pinkerton, Tony Pitcher, Rashid Sumeila, Nancy Turner and others).

Some of my best teachers are fishers and coastal resource users in the communities I have worked with, too numerous to mention. My other teachers are my graduate students, and I acknowledge their contributions with great pleasure and satisfaction. Cited in this volume are: Tiago Almudi, Eleanor Bonny, Wolfgang Dressler, Helen Fast, Damian Fernandes, James (Jack) Frey, Eranga Galappaththi, Sandra Grant, Julian Idrobo, Dyanna Riedlinger Jolly, John-Erik Kocho-Schellenberg, Kenton Lobe, Andrés Marín, Melissa Marschke, Prateep Nayak, Luiz Chimello de Oliveira, Claude Peloquin, Lance Robinson, Cristiana Seixas, Jason Senyk, Ta Thi Thanh Huong, Micaela Trimble, Kate Turner and Melanie Zurba.

For permission to use previously published figures, I thank *Conservation Biology*, Earthscan, *Environmental Conservation*, *Human Ecology*, *Indian Journal of Traditional Knowledge*, *Journal of Environmental Management*, *Marine Policy*, National Academy Press, *PLoS ONE*, *Proceedings of the National Academy of Sciences*, *Science*, and *World Development*. For permission to use their photos, I thank Andrés Marín, Prateep Nayak, Micaela Trimble and Nancy Turner.

My sincere thanks go to Jacqueline Rittberg for secretarial assistance, Melanie Zurba for the figures, and Ron Jones for the web-links section. I am thankful for the advice and assistance of Stephen Rutter, Editor, Margaret Moore, Editorial Assistant, Social Sciences, and their team from the Routledge/Taylor & Francis Group, and James Sowden, Project Manager for the volume and the production team. I also thank the reviewers who provided feedback: Gerry Zegers, Patrick Christie (University of Washington), Rosemary Ommer (University of Victoria), Joshua Cinner (James Cook University) and Elise Granek (Portland State University).

As always, I acknowledge my wife, Dr. Mina Kislalioglu Berkes, for her continued support. My ongoing work has been funded by the Social Sciences and Humanities Research Council of Canada (SSHRC) and the Canada Research Chairs program, www.chairs-chaires.gc.ca

1
INTRODUCTION
THE ONGOING AGENDA

A new form of interdisciplinary and adaptive science is required
for the coast. Such a science requires both an understanding of global environmental processes and their regional and
place-specific manifestations, and also fundamental advances
in our ability to address self-organization, resilience and nature–
society interactions.

> (Brown et al. 2002, p. 2)

At the beginning of the 21st century, the management authority
faces a much more complex task than it did 60 years ago . . .
Bio-ecological objectives are broader. Social and economic
objectives, measures and constraints are more formally recognized . . . The extension of EEZs puts 90 percent of the
world resources under national jurisdiction, turning de facto
global commons into national commons ready for further
reallocation.

> (Garcia and Cochrane 2009, p. 452)

The Context

Almost half of the world's population lives in coastal areas and depends
directly or indirectly on coastal resources. Coastal ecosystems are among
the most diverse environments on the planet and are critically important
for their role in supporting human well-being (MA 2005a). Societal

concerns about environmental degradation and loss of coastal resources, livelihoods and values have steadily increased, and other issues, such as food security, biodiversity conservation and climate change, have emerged. Hence, management agencies face a much more complex task than they did in the middle of the last century, especially with the extension of national jurisdictions into the sea to incorporate Exclusive Economic Zones (EEZs). As a consequence, the education of resource managers is under revision and reorganization, to include the complexities of resource use and social considerations.

As well, there is much interest in civil society in resources and environment, as nongovernmental organizations (NGOs), user organizations and various interest groups have become part of governance. These organizations have a major say in decisions; citizen science is on the rise. Influenced by new fields and theories such as commons and resilience, management is no longer top-down, under the control of technical experts. It has become participatory, responding to multiple needs and problems and accommodating an increasingly broader set of objectives and interests. A full set of social, ecological and economic objectives are formally recognized, but there is little agreement on how to implement them.

Part of the context is that coastal resources are uniquely valuable and are coming under increasing pressures that lead to loss and degradation. Costanza and colleagues (1997, 1998) estimated the economic values and the net primary production (a measure of biological productivity) of different kinds of ecosystem. Based on these calculations, Figure 1.1 shows that economic values and biological productivity correlate well. The figure further shows that coastal ecosystems such as estuaries, seagrass beds, floodplains, marshes and mangroves tend to be high in both value and bioproductivity, compared with other types of ecosystem. Such data should be used with caution, as some of these environments intergrade into one another. Boundaries of coastal ecosystems are not simple but complex and forever changing. This volume interprets the "coast" rather broadly: we are dealing with a strip of water and a strip of land along this changing boundary (for detailed definitions, see Chapter 7). As well, the volume recognizes the commonalities of saltwater and freshwater environments and uses, to extend the concept of coast to include some major lake and river systems, such as the Mekong and the Amazon and their associated wetlands and floodplains.

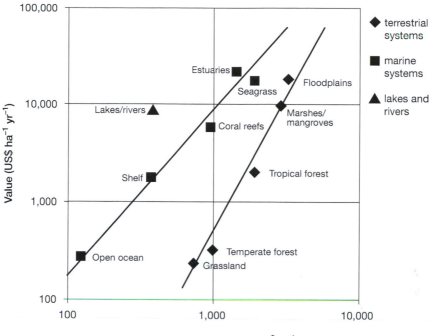

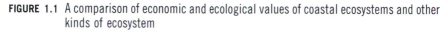

FIGURE 1.1 A comparison of economic and ecological values of coastal ecosystems and other kinds of ecosystem

Source: Brown et al. 2002; data from Costanza et al. 1998. Reprinted with permission

Everywhere in the world, coasts of saltwater, freshwater and mixed ecosystems (e.g., estuaries) have been coming under heavy use, with loss of social, ecological and economic value. The problems are so serious that we are often forced to talk about restoring these ecosystems, rather than managing them. Take, for example, the case of the Newfoundland cod, used by the Millennium Ecosystem Assessment (MA 2005a) to illustrate what a resource collapse may look like (Figure 1.2). Cod is not an isolated case. Myers and Worm (2003) have shown a worldwide decline in communities of large, predatory fish (but perhaps not as widely as reported; Hilborn 2006). This accelerating loss of populations and species adds up to a biodiversity decline that is thought to be resulting in declines, not just of sources of food, but of a range of ecosystem services (Worm et al. 2006).

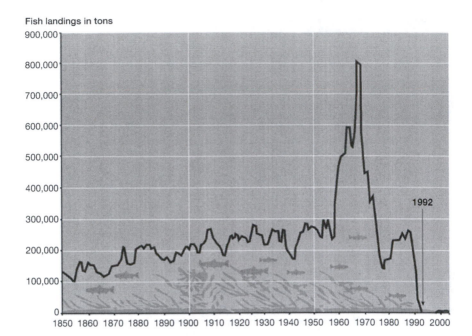

Fish landings in tons

FIGURE 1.2 Example of nonlinear change used by MA (2005a) shows the growth and eventual collapse of the Newfoundland cod fishery

The focus of the book is on coastal resources and their users. The major resource in question is fisheries, even though I deal with other resources (ecosystem services) as well. Of resource users, the major group worldwide is small-scale fishers. They are more numerous than large-scale fishers and other kinds of resource user. The numbers justify the focus. Globally, 158 million tonnes (mt) of fish were produced in 2012, 11.6 mt from inland fisheries, 79.7 mt from marine capture fisheries, 41.9 mt from inland aquaculture and 24.7 mt from marine aquaculture. Of these, 136 mt were used for human consumption, and the rest for other purposes such as reduction to feed (FAO 2014). Small-scale fisheries account for some 90 percent of more than 120 million *fisherfolk*, people who depend directly on fisheries-related activities such as fishing, processing and trading (HLPE 2014). Hence, the issues of small-scale fisheries, such as the changing picture of coastal resource use and rapidly increasing aquaculture production, cannot be ignored.

This book is uniquely designed to address some of these issues by contributing to the development of a new interdisciplinary science of

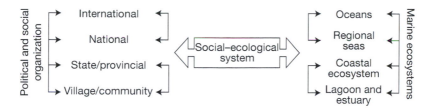

FIGURE 1.3 Matching social and ecological scales

coastal and marine resource management. To accomplish this, I develop four strategies.

The first is the use of a systems approach regarding interactions between human and environment systems, or social–ecological systems. The approach involves the consideration of social (human) and ecological (biophysical) subsystems together, rather than separately (Figure 1.3). The two subsystems are linked by mutual feedback and are considered to be interdependent and co-evolutionary (Berkes 2011). Second, I pay special attention to the human dimension of coastal and marine resource use. Most fisheries research focuses on fish rather than on fishers. This book dismantles the divide between natural sciences and social sciences and emphasizes the neglected human aspects of resource use, such as livelihoods.

Third, I emphasize community-based resource use, examining institutions and governance from the ground up. Small-scale fisheries and other resource use systems provide livelihoods and contribute to the food security of a far larger number of people worldwide than do industrial fisheries. Nevertheless, the discussion is relevant to all fisheries and some other resources. Fourth, I use an integrative approach to consider multiple theories to deal with the "big picture." The book offers a synthesis, bringing together several approaches such as social–ecological systems thinking, resilience, commons, co-management, use of fisher knowledge, sustainable livelihoods and ecosystem-based management.

Rethinking Coastal and Marine Resources

Resource management practices are constantly changing to deal with issues of sustainability and increased competition over coastal resources worldwide. Human impacts such as overfishing, habitat destruction, coral reef and mangrove losses, and pollution have damaged many coastal

TABLE 1.1 **Ten "public goals" or coastal and marine uses, according to Halpern et al. (2012)**

1. Food provision
    - Fisheries
    - Mariculture
2. Artisanal fishing opportunity
3. Natural products
4. Carbon storage
5. Coastal protection
6. Tourism and recreation
7. Coastal livelihoods and economies
8. Sense of place
    - Iconic species
    - Lasting special places
9. Clean waters
10. Biodiversity
    - Habitats
    - Species

ecosystems and eroded their capacity to provide ecosystem services. Yet oceans and coasts continue to support human needs physically (food), ecologically (biodiversity), economically (livelihoods) and culturally (sense of place). Fisheries and aquaculture continue to provide food, and coastal resources support economies based on tourism and recreation. Building on the Millennium Ecosystem Assessment (MA 2005a), Halpern et al. (2012) recognized ten "public goals" or major coastal and marine uses (Table 1.1), and the list can be expanded.

Coastal resource management has an unfinished agenda. Or perhaps it is more accurate to say, an ever-changing agenda. The setting and priorities for management are constantly evolving, addressed by a large number of books, reports and papers over the years. This book extends the debates initiated in several volumes, perhaps starting with the 1990 book by McGoodwin, *Crisis in the World's Fisheries,* and the 1998 book edited by Pitcher and colleagues, *Reinventing Fisheries Management.* The McGoodwin book was important in making the point that the fishery problem was not merely a biological problem, but a social problem as well. The Pitcher book took the bold step of questioning the management status quo. Charles's (2001) book, *Sustainable Fishery Systems*, charted one of the possible new directions: using systems approaches for sustainable fisheries. *Managing Small-Scale Fisheries*, by Berkes et al. (2001), argued for a broader, interdisciplinary view of management and attempted to provide new tools for managers of international coastal fisheries.

Coasts under Stress, by Ommer and team (2007), took a creative interdisciplinary approach to pursue parallels between coastal ecosystem health and coastal community health. *Fish for Life*, edited by Kooiman et al. (2005), brought together an international cast of writers addressing governance, as a broader setting for management. *A Fishery Manager's Guidebook*, edited by Cochrane and Garcia (2009), was prepared as a sourcebook, creating a new mix of interdisciplinary management practice, specifically targeting the Food and Agricultural Organization (FAO) community and international fishery resource managers. Both the Cochrane and Garcia (2009) book and the *World Fisheries* book edited by Ommer et al. (2011) explored the use of a social–ecological approach. The broader issues of coastal zone management were addressed by Cicin-Sain and Knecht (1998) in *Integrated Coastal and Ocean Management*. The Millennium Ecosystem Assessment evaluated the coastal ecosystems of the world in relation to ecosystem services and human well-being (MA 2005a).

With a rich literature base of books, articles, other publications and web sites to draw from, the present volume is written with two goals in mind. The first is to contribute to the field of coastal and marine resource management and offer alternative approaches that emerge out of recent developments in interdisciplinary fields such as commons and resilience. Here, the audience comprises scholars, management professionals and practitioners. The second goal is to produce a book that can be used as a text in environment and resource management programs, toward a better-educated civil society. The dilemmas of coastal and marine resource management are part of a larger debate on environmental sustainability. They have counterparts in other resource areas, such as forestry and wild-life management, and other environmental fields, such as conservation, international development and environmental planning.

Changes in coastal and marine resource management can be seen in the context of larger, historical conceptual shifts that have been occurring in ecology and resource management. Various fields of applied ecology seem to be in the midst of three paradigm changes: (1) a conceptual shift from reductionism to a systems view of the world; (2) a paradigm change in the way shared resources or commons are theorized and managed; and (3) a shift from expert-based, technical management, to a broader, participatory governance. These changes are not specific to coastal management but to environmental management in general. They provide the context and benchmarks in many areas of applied ecology, as they begin to incorporate human dimensions explicitly. Resource management is coming under critical inquiry, at a time when the science of ecology itself is undergoing major change. These ideas are explained further in the following three sections and developed in detail in Chapter 2, becoming cross-cutting themes for the rest of the book.

Paradigm Change from Reductionism to a Systems View

The environmental philosopher J. Baird Callicott (2003, p. 239) observed that, "for nearly half a century now, ecology has been shifting away from a 'balance-of-nature' to a 'flux-of-nature' paradigm." In Callicott's view, by the mid 1970s, the latter had begun to eclipse the former, and, by the 2000s, the shift was largely complete. It was a deep-seated change: from a conception of nature in a state of equilibrium, undisturbed by humans, to one in which nature is constantly changing and disturbed by many natural (and human) factors, a view of ecosystems as complex adaptive systems (Holling 1973; Chapin et al. 2009). It also made for a far messier kind of ecology: ecosystems as open, ill-bounded, disturbance-ridden systems, hardly stable.

Instead of possessing one equilibrium, ecosystems may temporarily settle into a domain of ecological attraction (or state) and may flip into other domains through various kinds of disturbance (Holling 2001; Levin 1999). These flips, however, are not at random; ecosystems respond to thresholds or tipping points (Walker and Meyers 2004). Some ecologists have been developing the idea that ecosystems are actually or potentially multi-equilibrium systems in which alternative states may exist over time, and that an ecosystem may flip from one state to another in some general, predictable ways, except that these regime shifts are not exactly predictable in space and time (Scheffer and Carpenter 2003).

There are some serious implications of this kind of thinking, and of the messier kind of new ecology. We can never possess more than an approximate knowledge of an ecosystem, and our ability to predict the behavior of multi-equilibrium complex systems, such as coastal ecosystems, is limited. Hence, models based on equilibrium thinking often do not work, not only because we lack data, but also because ecosystems are intrinsically and fundamentally unpredictable, and would continue to be so even if a great deal more data were available.

Recent practice in fisheries reflects the growing importance of recognizing complex adaptive systems thinking and the necessity of moving away from single-species stock assessment models to protecting the productive potential and resilience of the ecosystem as a whole (Holling and Meffe 1996; Cochrane and Garcia 2009). Once we put aside the idea of controlling nature, then we can then come to terms with the idea of dealing with resources through a learning-by-doing approach or adaptive management (Holling 1978). Adaptive management is the contemporary, scientific version of the age-old trial-and-error learning and knowledge production of traditional societies (Berkes et al. 2000). It starts with the assumption of incomplete information, and relies on repeated feedback learning in which policies are treated as experiments from which to learn.

One way to deal with uncertainty and complexity is to build local institutions that can learn from crises, respond to change, nurture ecological memory, monitor the environment, self-organize and manage conflicts. A complementary approach is to build working partnerships between managers and resource users. The use of imperfect information for management necessitates a close co-operation and risk sharing between managers and fishers. Such a process requires collaboration, transparency and accountability, so that a learning environment can be created and management practice builds on experience. Focus on institutions, partnerships, and learning to deal with uncertainty and complexity brings new social dimensions into applied ecology.

The understanding of ecosystems as complex adaptive systems stimulated attention to feedback relations, hallmark of systems thinking (Levin 1999). It also stimulated more attention to the various characteristics of complex adaptive systems, such as scale, self-organization, emergent properties, uncertainty, nonlinearity and irreversibility (or path dependence).

The importance of *scale* is well appreciated in ecology (Ahl and Allen 1996). A given fish stock may be used by coastal and offshore fisheries and by more than one nation. Can the fishery be managed by a centralized agency at one scale, or are there more appropriate structures of governance? A "one size fits all" kind of management is blind to scale issues and misses the point that scale matching is important in approaching a problem (Figure 1.3). A related point: issues may look quite different when viewed from (say) the local level as opposed to the national level. A fishing community will likely focus on livelihood resources, whereas export earnings may be the priority for the national government.

Self-organization is seen by Levin (1999, 2005) to be a key attribute of complex adaptive systems, with emphasis on the word adaptive, as related to feedback. Complexity emerges out of self-organization. Fishing communities have long been used as "laboratories" for investigating self-organization and self-governance (Ostrom 1990). Commons research over the last 30 years or so has documented in considerable detail the self-organization and self-regulation capability of communities to solve the commons problem. Relevant to coastal resources management, understanding of how self-organization arises has led to work on the evolution of co-operation (e.g., among a group of resource users) and the development of social norms (McCay 1998; Ostrom 2005).

Emergent properties are those properties of a system that cannot be deduced from the analysis of the parts of the system but can only be understood from the analysis of the system as a whole. For example, the brain is made up of neurons, but analyzing the sum of individual neurons will not be very informative about the brain's properties. Emergent properties follow the Anderson (1972) dictum that the whole is more than the sum of its parts. Coupled human–environment systems have a number of emergent properties, including resilience and vulnerability. Cumming (2011, p. 17) writes:

> all these system properties arise from the number and nature of system components, their interactions with one another and their external environment, and their ability to process information and respond to internal or external change through action, adaptation or learning.

Uncertainty is thought to be intrinsic to the system and essentially irreducible (Gunderson and Holling 2002). Our knowledge of social and ecological systems, and our ability to predict their future dynamics, will never be complete. Management science often makes simplifying assumptions about uncertainty, but assuming away uncertainty leads to problems by creating a disconnect between reality and scientific prediction. Charles (2001) refers to the "illusion of certainty" and the "fallacy of controllability" in fisheries. For example, it has been generally known that the maximum sustainable yield (MSY), as defined by stock assessment models, is in fact a meaningless target because of uncertainty. Having to deal with uncertainty has given rise to adaptive management that relies on learning-by-doing in an uncertain environment (Holling 1978; Lee 1993).

A *nonlinear system* is one whose output is not directly proportional to its input. Nonlinearity is often observed through threshold effects, as in the Newfoundland cod case (Figure 1.2). In general, ecosystem changes do not occur smoothly, but rather through thresholds that lead to ecosystem phase shifts (Walker and Meyers 2004). For example, in many coral reefs, the depletion of herbivorous parrotfish, beyond a certain threshold, can result in a phase shift in which macroalgae replace corals (Hughes et al. 2005). The depletion of fish and lobsters in kelp beds has led to explosions of sea urchins in various parts of the world, leading to phase shifts (Hughes et al. 2005). Resource management that uses linear thinking performs poorly in a world characterized by nonlinear processes and phase shifts.

Irreversibility (path dependence) explains how the set of decisions one faces for any given circumstance is limited or shaped by the decisions made in the past, even though past circumstances may no longer be relevant. As Ommer and Paterson (2014) point out, history matters. For example, co-management seems to be path dependent: its outcome is strongly influenced by the context and history of each case (Chuenpagdee and Jentoft 2007). To use the coral example above (Hughes et al. 2005), irreversibility means that the corals may not come back, even if the parrotfish are restored. Likewise, the depleted Newfoundland cod has not recovered, despite the cod-fishing ban since 1992 (Figure 1.2). This is presumably because the structure of the ecosystem has changed, perhaps through a phase shift.

Paradigm Change in Commons Theory

In his classic *The Structure of Scientific Revolutions*, Kuhn (1962) postulated that a dominant model or way of thinking (paradigm) in science persists until the accumulation of new evidence forces a reappraisal and rejection of the old paradigm and the formulation of a new one. In Callicott's view, the shift from a balance-of-nature to a flux-of-nature outlook was a paradigm change in ecology, and it happened relatively gradually. In the case of commons theory, the paradigm change occurred very quickly, between about 1975 and 1990.

With the paradigm change, Hardin's "tragedy of the commons" model (1968), with its negative prognosis, was replaced by a new commons theory based on the idea that resource users are capable of self-organization and self-regulation (Ostrom 1990). The "tragedy" does occur, however, under open-access regimes, in cases where commons are exploited under free-for-all conditions. Thus, the new theory opened the way to exploring the conditions that led to the resolution of the commons dilemma and drew attention to the importance of institutions for commons use. Here, I briefly reflect on the paradigm change, its cross-disciplinary context and policy implications.

As detailed studies were becoming available in the 1970s and the 1980s, scholars in various parts of the world were finding exceptions to the "tragedy" (Box 1.1). A consensus was building among scholars to the effect that Hardin's model applied to open-access exploitation of the commons, but was not valid for community-based resource use systems. In fact, Hardin's own example of the hypothetical English pasture was historically incorrect. Medieval English commons were generally used under locally devised regulations. For example, "stinting" rules limited the number of heads of animals that each owner was allowed to graze on the village pasture (Scott 1955). Medieval English commons operated successfully for many centuries, and several economic historians and other scholars have questioned whether a "tragedy" of the sort described by Hardin ever occurred widely (Dahlman 1980; Feeny et al. 1990).

Hardin had argued that users of a commons are caught in an inevitable (he called it "remorseless") process that leads to the destruction of the resources on which they depend. However, careful studies were showing that this was simply not so. More nuanced studies were showing the limitations of the Hardin model, covering various cultures and resource

BOX 1.1 NO "TRAGEDY OF THE COMMONS" IN CREE FISHERIES

I started my first study of community-based resource management in the mid-1970s in the indigenous Cree village of Chisasibi, James Bay, in eastern subarctic Canada. As a recent science PhD, I had no training to appreciate local resource management institutions. Worse, as a member of a generation of students under the influence of the "tragedy of the commons" concept, I started with the belief that resources had to be protected from the users by government resource management. This belief was shaken in the course of my studies of the Cree fishery. This was a subsistence fishery, with no commercial component, carried out under no apparent rules or regulations; as an indigenous subsistence fishery, it operated outside the sphere of government regulations. But as it turned out, there indeed was a management system. Fishers were self-organized and self-managed, contradicting the predictions of the "tragedy of the commons" (Berkes 2012b, Chapter 7, summarizes some ten years of this work, published 1977 onwards).

Until the 1980s, "tragedy of the commons" was the principal way in which commons were conceptualized. Hardin (1968) used the example of an imaginary pasture in Medieval England to which cattle herders had free and open access. Each herder received a direct benefit (say +1) from adding one more animal to graze in the pasture, and the costs of degrading the pasture were shared by all (a fraction of −1). Thus, each herder had the incentive to put as many cattle on the pasture as he could. Adding more animals was the economically rational choice; yet everyone exercising their rational choice led to the degradation of the pasture, hence the "tragedy"—in the sense of ancient Greek tragedies.

My James Bay Cree fishery did not fit this model at all. These fishers were far from the helpless actors in the Greek tragedy. They decided among themselves on the (unwritten) rules of conduct of the fishery, mutually agreed upon; they communicated and used social sanctions where necessary to get compliance among members. The Cree did not think of these as "rules" but simply the "way things were done."

Also of a great deal of interest to me, the locally designed fishing system was fundamentally different from management systems in use in commercial fisheries in subarctic Canada: fishing gear and mesh size restrictions, season and area closures, and catch quotas. By contrast, Cree fishers used the most effective gear available, a mix of mesh sizes that gave the high catch per unit of effort, and deliberately concentrated their effort on fish aggregations. In short, the Cree fishery violated just about every measure used by government managers. But the Cree fishers used a set of practices seldom seen in conventional fisheries: rotating areas; switching fishing areas according to declining catch per effort; and using a mix of mesh sizes that proportionately thinned out populations by size. They also keyed harvest levels to needs and followed a resource use leadership system in which fish were used under principles and ethics agreed upon by all.

(Berkes 2012b)

types—fisheries, wildlife, forests, grazing lands, protected areas, irrigation and ground water. Cases were brought together in several volumes (NAS 1986; McCay and Acheson 1987; Berkes 1989; Ostrom 1990; Bromley 1992), with a view to developing a new theory of the commons.

Constructing a new theory required a clarification of definitions and concepts. *Commons* (*common-pool resources*) share two characteristics: (a) exclusion or the control of access of potential users is difficult, and (b) each user is capable of subtracting from the welfare of all other users (Feeny et al. 1990; Ostrom et al. 1999). The new theory also needed to clarify property rights relationships and regimes (NAS 1986; Ostrom 1990; Bromley 1992). Commons could be held in one of four basic property rights regimes. Open access was the absence of well-defined property rights, with free access to all. Private property referred to the situation in which an individual or corporation had the right to exclude others and to regulate use. State property meant that rights to the resource were vested exclusively in government. Common-property regimes defined situations in which the resource was held by an identifiable community of users. These four regimes were pure analytical types; in practice, resources were usually held in combinations of property rights regimes.

Three of these property rights regimes (private property, state property and common property) may, under various circumstances, lead to sustainable resource use. No particular regime is inherently superior to the others, but one may fit a particular circumstance better than the others (e.g., private property for aquaculture; state property with quota systems for oceanic fisheries; common property for coastal fisheries). However, property rights cannot be prescribed; they need to fit the particular social, economic and ecological circumstances of a resource system. Further, no one particular regime guarantees sustainability. There are successes and failures under all three regimes. Regarding the open-access regime, however, there is general consensus that long-term sustainability is not possible (Feeny et al. 1990; Ostrom et al. 2002).

The paradigm change in commons theory has wide-ranging implications. Contrary to Hardin's assumptions, there is nothing inherent in commons that leads to resource degradation. Common property is analytically different from open access. This has important policy implications, as the "tragedy" has often been used by governments in various parts of the world to justify centralized resource management or to privatize resources. The paradigm change in commons theory indicated the viability of local solutions and opened the way for participatory approaches, co-management and the devolution of management power. The new theory also helped emphasize that commons management is not only about resources. It is about social and economic relations, for example, in making and enforcing rules. These social and economic relations often lead to management problem solving and the formulation of practical rules-in-use or institutions (Ostrom 1990).

Paradigm Changes in Resource Governance

Compared with the major shifts in ecology and commons, changes related to governance probably do not qualify as a paradigm shift, as there is no shift in theory but rather one in practice. However, the shift in practice is important enough to affect resource management in a major way, as governing is no longer considered only a task for government managers. Many governments are formally recognizing that public and private actors should also be involved, and the dividing lines between public and private sectors have become blurred (as in the phrase, "public–private partnerships").

Governance can be defined in different ways. Broadly, it refers to the collective efforts of society to define and achieve societal goals (Young et al. 2008). According to Kooiman et al. (2005), governance is the whole of public as well as private interactions taken to solve societal problems and create societal opportunities. It includes the formulation and application of principles guiding those interactions and care for institutions that enable them. Considering the broader arena in which institutions operate, governance covers some of the area previously captured by the terms policy and management. The trend is to use governance as the more inclusive term, followed by policy, and finally by management. Management is about action; governance is about politics—sharing responsibility and power and setting the policy agenda and objectives (Kooiman et al. 2005; Bavinck et al. 2013).

Several dimensions mark major changes occurring in resource governance. First, participation of users in governance is becoming the norm, rather than the exception, in various fields of environment and resources. Second, the role of technical expertise, along with centralized management, is being redefined. Third, there is a great deal of interest in capacity building to enable local institutions to engage in management, in part stimulated by the changes in thinking about commons governance. I discuss each in turn.

Regarding the first point, the governance concept has opened up management to nonstate actors. In a civil society, citizens are no longer treated as subjects but as participants in governance. This is part of a trend emphasizing horizontal processes such as collaboration, partnership and community empowerment in all areas of resource and environmental management. The literature on governance only developed in the 1990s, with emphasis on problem solving and opportunity creation as the joint responsibility of all parties—the state, the market and civil society. Viewed this way, governance is no longer considered to be the natural prerogative of governments but rather a broad responsibility to be shared, hence the expression "governance without government."

The rules of engagement are still being worked out, and the literature discusses good governance—governance that is participatory, consensus oriented, accountable, transparent, responsive, effective and efficient, equitable and inclusive, and follows the rule of law (UN 2008). Here, *transparency* refers to openness and the free availability of information in a language that stakeholders can understand. *Accountability* means that decision-makers should be available to answer to the people who are affected by the decisions. To this list, *legitimacy* may be added, the authority based on a democratic mandate (Pinkerton and John 2008). Legitimacy is important: do the stakeholders accept the authority of those making and enforcing the rules?

The second area marking major changes is the role of technical expertise in resource management. One of the characteristics of modern society is the important role played by professional and technical expertise. However, many of our environmental problems, including those related to fisheries and coastal governance (Jentoft and Chuenpagdee 2009), do not lend themselves to analysis by the conventional rational approach of defining the problem, collecting data, analyzing data and making decisions based on the results. There is too much uncertainty: targets keep shifting, and one often has to keep redefining the issue (Kates et al. 2001).

These characteristics make for a class of problems that have been called *wicked problems*, defined as those problems that have no definitive formulation, no stopping rule and no test for a solution (Rittel and Webber 1973). Many contemporary environmental problems, such as climate change, are wicked in the sense that they cannot be solved once and for all, but continue to pose an ongoing challenge, partly because it could not be known for sure when and if they were solved (Ludwig 2001). All wicked problems are unique and have no technical solution; they are difficult to define and delineate from other problems; they are persistent and tend to reappear; and they have no right or wrong solutions that can be determined scientifically (Jentoft and Chuenpagdee 2009).

Ludwig (2001) points out that wicked problems raise an important issue with regard to the notion of objective and value-free science. With wicked problems, "there may be as many approaches and purported resolutions as there are analysts. The role of experts in various specialties that approach such problems is diminished relative to the general public" (Ludwig 2001, p. 761). If experts have no special expertise with wicked problems, then how do we proceed? Kates et al. (2001) have argued that sustainability science must be created through a process by which researchers and local stakeholders interact to define important questions, relevant evidence and convincing forms of argument, basically a deliberative approach, in place of top-down technical expertise.

The third area marking major changes in governance concerns institutions and capacity building. Participatory management requires collaboration between managers and resource users, often across several levels of organization, from local to national. However, building such partnerships is not easy; it requires fishers and other stakeholders who are sufficiently well organized to carry out such a partnership with appropriate institutions. Of course, it also requires a favorable policy environment for participatory governance, and the presence of appropriate government institutions to interact with organizations of fishers and coastal resource users—because it "takes two to tango" (Pomeroy and Berkes 1997).

Here, *institutions* are defined as the sets of rules actually used or the working rules or rules-in-use (Ostrom 1990; North 1990). They are socially constructed codes of conduct (rules and norms) that define practices, assign roles and guide interactions. *Capacity building* is considered to be the sum of efforts needed to nurture, enhance and utilize the skills and capabilities of people and institutions at all levels, toward a particular goal, in this case, participatory management. The logic of capacity building is simple: involving fishers in the management process depends on their ability to self-organize to help in the making and enforcing of rules.

Some fishing communities have traditions of social organization and self-management. They may have their own resource use areas and a system for making rules of conduct (Wilson et al. 1994; Acheson 2003). However, in other cases, community self-organization may not exist at all. Certainly, not all fishing communities have the experience or capability to regulate themselves or to participate in management. It may take effort to organize and build institutions, often with the help of NGOs. Such institutional capacity building is widely recognized as a vital component of participatory management. It is not a rapid process. Case studies indicate a time frame on the order of ten years (Berkes 2007a; Seixas and Davy 2008).

There seems to be no blueprint or formula for building institutions. This is because context (history, politics, culture) is different in each particular case. A solution developed in one case cannot readily be transferred to another. For example, the community-based marine protected area approach, developed in one area of the Philippines and replicated throughout the country with little attention to local context, resulted in a high rate of failure (White et al. 2002).

These three paradigm changes, in ecology, commons and governance, are related. They all pertain to an emerging understanding of ecosystems as complex adaptive systems in which human societies are necessarily an integral part. Ecology is important as the basis of management. Commons is important because most coastal and marine resources are commons. Governance is important as it pertains to the rules of the game for decision-making. When Cochrane and Garcia invited experts and assigned them chapter topics, 7 of the 16 chapters in the book ended up addressing some aspect of governance (Cochrane and Garcia 2009, p. 453).

How likely are these major changes to have an impact on day-to-day practice? If we cannot entirely abandon the Age of Enlightenment assumptions of predictability and control, we should at least be very skeptical of them. Commons can be governed in more ways than one, including creative mixes of commons regimes. For example, aquaculture is often carried out under a private-property regime. But it can also be carried out under a mix of private-property, common-property and state-property regimes (Galappaththi and Berkes 2014). We need to recognize the limits of technical expertise and the advantages of participatory management. To move toward an interdisciplinary science of coastal and marine resources management, we need to learn from the lessons emerging from several recent interdisciplinary fields.

Elements of an Interdisciplinary Science of Coastal Resource Management

These historical developments in management philosophy regarding the adoption of a systems view, a new vision of commons and a shift to participatory governance are cross-cutting themes. In view of these changes, how do we build a new interdisciplinary science of resource management for the coastal environment? What are the elements of such a science? The key may be found in the lessons offered by emerging interdisciplinary fields that tackle coupled systems of humans and nature. Several fields or subdisciplines have been pursuing various aspects of human–environment relationships. Table 1.2 lists a large number of them. Of these, this volume is concerned with a smaller set: resilience, commons, co-management, coastal management, conservation and protected areas, livelihoods and rural development, local and indigenous ecological knowledge, and ecosystem-based management. These fields provide insights for coastal resource management and contribute to a better understanding of social–ecological interactions. They provide the grounding for a truly interdisciplinary science of coastal and marine resource management.

Chapter 2 is about the context of resource management science, in particular redefining the concepts of resource and management. Science is never static, and management practices have been changing rapidly, requiring a readjustment of concepts. The conventional ideas of resource and management are problematic because of the historical "baggage" that they carry. But this does not mean abandoning the two concepts; rather, they can be redefined in line with evolving theory and practice of a new interdisciplinary science.

If humans are an integral part of ecosystems, how do we define the system we aim to manage? Chapter 3 is about social–ecological systems, integrated complex systems that include social (human) and ecological (biophysical) subsystems in a two-way feedback relationship. The chapter discusses drivers and globalization and uses the development of

TABLE 1.2 Selection of subdisciplinary fields concerned with the interaction of nature and culture or human–environment relationships

Agricultural sustainability	Environmental law
Anthropology of nature	Environmental sociology
Biocultural diversity	Ethnobotany
Cognitive anthropology	Ethnoecology
Commons studies	Ethnolinguistics
Cultural anthropology	Ethnoscience
Cultural geography	Historical ecology
Cultural (landscape) ecology	Human ecology
Deep ecology	Human geography
Descriptive historical particularism	Indigenous knowledge
Development studies	Intercultural education
Ecofeminism	Landscape ecology
Ecological anthropology	Nature society theory
Ecological design	Political ecology
Ecological economics	Resilience (ecological and cultural)
Ecosystem health	Science and technology studies
Environmental anthropology	Social–ecological systems
Environmental education	Sustainability science
Environmental ethics	Symbolic ecology
Environmental history	Systems ecology

Source: Pretty et al. 2009, which includes definitions of each term

aquaculture to illustrate the interdependent nature of social and ecological subsystems.

Resilience is a key attribute of social–ecological systems. Chapter 4 develops the idea that the resource system needs to be managed, not for products and commodities, but for resilience, the capacity of a system to absorb disturbance and reorganize while undergoing change, but retaining its essential characteristics. Conventional resource maximization approaches tend to reduce natural variability, impairing the renewal capacity of ecosystems and the ability to absorb shocks and stresses. This makes them vulnerable to disturbance, hence the need for a new approach.

Chapter 5 expands on the fundamental topic of commons, with examples and analysis. Most coastal resources are fugitive: the fish you don't catch today may be caught by someone else tomorrow, hence the need for collective action. But who makes the rules for collective action? "When the users of a common pool resource organize themselves to devise and enforce some of their own basic rules, they tend to manage local resources more sustainably than when rules are externally imposed on them" (Ostrom 2000, p. 148).

Chapter 6 is about co-management, an important application of commons theory and an increasingly widespread practice worldwide. Managing resources often requires sharing management power and building linkages from local level upwards to involve multiple levels of organization. Purely community-based management has the same weakness as purely top-down management—they both ignore the multilevel nature of the problem. Focusing only at one level, whether local, national or international, is an inadequate design for governance. We have much practical experience to do better.

Chapter 7 expands the scope of analysis to examine the range of uses of the increasingly crowded coastal zone. It starts with an analysis of the complexity of the coast, which, according to McCay (2008), is liminal —an intermediate state that is neither water nor land. The historic sector-by-sector management of the coastal zone is problematic, because of interactions among resources and uses. The chapter deals with perceptions of coastal resources, their governance, and social–ecological restoration, examining the role of local communities and citizen science.

Coastal conservation and protected areas are increasingly important. Chapter 8 argues that increasing the effectiveness of marine protected areas (MPAs) can be achieved through reconnecting social and ecological systems. Conservation will ultimately depend upon a sense of place and strengthening local stewardship ethics (Chapin et al. 2012). MPA networks have been emerging, and conservation practices have been evolving to include local communities as partners. However, in line with commons theory, there needs to be local livelihood incentives for partnerships to be effective.

Chapter 9 argues that livelihoods are a key element in the multi-functional nature of coastal resources and an important management objective. The vast majority of fishers in the world are not full time. In developing countries, as well as in the small-scale fisheries of many industrialized countries, fishing is often part of a complex of livelihood activities (Béné and Friend 2011). For many fisheries, large and small, the ability to follow a seasonal round of activities and to switch gear, fishing grounds and target species is necessary for livelihood resilience, providing options and flexibility.

Dealing with problems of coastal management requires mobilizing a range of knowledge, including local and traditional ecological knowledge (Chapter 10). Local knowledge and traditional knowledge (if it is multigenerational) provide a practical and cost-effective way to understand resource status and environmental change. Using illustrations, the chapter explores practical contributions of local and traditional knowledge, and how to bridge such knowledge with Western science.

Chapter 11 focuses on ecosystem-based management, the holistic view of managing resources in the context of their environment. Such an approach involves moving from a single-sector (fisheries) to a multiple-sector approach and may include considerations of resilience, adaptive management and co-management. Adopting the broader frame of partici-patory governance (Cochrane and Garcia 2009) and interdisciplinary approaches helps to deal with coastal ecosystems as integrated social–ecological systems, rather than merely as ecosystems (Ommer et al. 2011).

Chapter 12 recaps some of the major points in the volume and reviews the eight elements of an interdisciplinary science of marine and coastal resource management. In conclusion, the chapter explores two divergent strategies for the way ahead: the neoliberal vision in which markets and economic considerations become increasingly dominant in decision-making, and the community-based vision in which social–ecological con-siderations become increasingly more dominant and coasts are managed for people.

2

NATURAL RESOURCES AND MANAGEMENT

EMERGING VIEWS

Ideologies of our time (economism, scientism, and technocracy) support the progressive view that experts, using scientific methods, can manage the world's problems by objective and efficient means . . . Several aspects of this view are no longer tenable. These include the notion of an objective and value-free natural science, and the idea that economics can be separated from ideology.

(Ludwig 2001, p. 758)

The nature and limitations of Western science are studied by historians and philosophers of science but, paradoxically, they remain ill-understood by many of the practitioners themselves. Scientific disciplines are often cocooned; scientific purity is assured by the assiduous avoidance of societal issues.

(Holling et al. 1998, p. 345)

The previous chapter considered some of the main reasons to develop an interdisciplinary science of coastal and marine resource management. To provide a historic and political context for the chapters to come, this chapter further explores one key consideration: the need to question and redefine the conventional view of *resources* and *management*. The argument is that the conventional concepts of natural resources and management are problematic, if not obsolete, because of their history and the "baggage" they carry (Berkes 2010c). These two terms can be replaced or, perhaps more reasonably, can be redefined in view of new perspectives and changing paradigms, as outlined in Chapter 1. In developing this argument, the chapter starts with an overview of some major shifts in perspective in resource management. The subsequent sections discuss the historic background and provide the rationale, both social and ecological, for redefining natural resources and management.

Changing Theory and Practice of Resource Management: An Overview

The contemporary theory and practice of fishery management evolved over the past century or so in response to a major restructuring of the relationship of humans with the environment. The history of the notion of natural resource management is closely associated with the emergence of several ideas in political economy and environmental philosophy. These include the following:

1. the separation of humans from the environment;
2. the commodification of nature;
3. the separation of the resource user from the manager and the rise of the managerial class;
4. the evolution of a tradition of positivistic science that assumes that the world is predictable and controllable; and
5. the predominant use of reductionism in science (Worster 1977; Bateson 1979; Callicott 2003).

However, over the last few decades, many of the basic views and assumptions that underpin the science of management in general, and classic fisheries management in particular, have been abandoned, one by one. Instead of the separation of humans from the environment, or the separation of mind and nature in Bateson's (1979) terminology, we are seeking ways to restore unity. This includes the recognition that the social and ecological aspects of the management are closely associated; these systems can be considered integrated social–ecological systems (Berkes and Folke 1998; Glaser 2006). Instead of production-oriented management objectives for fish-as-commodity, many are learning to appreciate the need to foster healthy fishing communities (Jentoft 2000) and healthy fish habitats and ecosystem processes as the basis for the fishery (MA 2005a; Francis et al. 2007).

Instead of entrusting resource decision-making entirely to managers and experts, the trend is toward user participation, public–private partnerships, governance (Kooiman et al. 2005), co-management (Wilson et al. 2003) and engagement with fisher knowledge (Haggan et al. 2007). Instead of positivistic science that assumes that the world is predictable and controllable, scholars are emphasizing the need to embrace uncertainty (Charles 2001; Gunderson and Holling 2002). Instead of reductionism that seeks to model, for example, individual fish species and fishing fleets separately, scientists are beginning to emphasize holistic approaches that consider complexity (Levin 1999, Lansing 2002) and fisher–fish–environment together (Cochrane and Garcia 2009).

Some of these elements of the shifting perspectives and assumptions in human–environment relations are summarized in Table 2.1.

TABLE 2.1 Some elements of the shifting perspectives in human–environment relations

	Conventional resourcist view	Emerging view	References
Human interactions with the environment			
	Human–environment (or mind–nature) dualism	Restoring unity of humans and environment	Bateson 1979
Use of the environment			
	Commodification of nature	Nature as providing ecosystem services and human well-being	MA 2005a
Role of expertise			
	Scientists and managers as independent, objective experts	Recognizing limitations of technical expertise; pluralism in management	Ludwig 2001
Uncertainty and the control of nature			
	Positivistic science that assumes the world is predictable and controllable	Recognizing intrinsic uncertainty of nature and the necessity to live with it	Charles 2001
Mode of analysis			
	Reductionistic science that treats individual species and fishing fleets separately	Holistic approaches that consider fish, fisher and environment together	See Table 2.2

What is labeled as the "conventional resourcist view" in Table 2.1 is a mix of Enlightenment Age or even older wisdom (e.g., human–environment dualism) and 20th-century science. "Emerging view" tries to capture the shifts that have occurred largely since the 1970s but are difficult to characterize in terms of the extent to which they have received acceptance. It is probably safe to say that each has good science behind it, but none has been fully incorporated into contemporary practice.

Several examples exist of attempts to develop an integrated, inter-disciplinary science of humans and environment (or fish and fishers, or coastal peoples and coastal environments). It is instructive to examine a set of these initiatives to see what these integrative approaches might look like, the shifts in perspective they may illustrate, and the theory base they employ. Several disciplines, such as geography, anthropology and development studies, and interdisciplinary areas such as ecological economics, have developed conceptualizations of integrated human–environment systems. The five examples in Table 2.2 are selected here because they represent a deliberate mixing of social science and natural science, two of them specifically about fish and fishers, and the other three more broadly about humans and environment.

McEvoy's (1986, 1996) conceptualization is based on a legal and historical study of California fisheries. He uses systems thinking to point out the feedback relations between the environment that sustains the fish stocks, the economy (including the social organization of user-groups) and management (including regulation and, more broadly, the legal system). For McEvoy, environment–economy–management constitutes a framework with which different fisheries can be characterized.

Francis and colleagues (2007) consider that a paradigm shift is under-way toward ecosystem-based management, and they seek to establish a set of principles and associated methodologies to help accelerate the shift. The emphasis is on the natural science of fisheries, with principles regarding population and spatial structure of fish stocks, conservation of habitat and critical food web connections. But they point out the necessity of interdisciplinarity and the need to integrate natural and social sciences. In addition to an eclectic mix of ecological theory, they use systems theory, complexity and resilience in the way they conceive the relationship of the ecological system and the social system.

TABLE 2.2 **Examples of interdisciplinary attempts to integrate human–environment systems**

The fishery consists of three interacting spheres: nature, the economy and the legal system. A systematic, mutually reinforcing relation exists between the social and cultural organization of harvester groups and the ecology of their target stocks. What we can manage for and sustain is the long-term health of the interaction among the three spheres	McEvoy 1986, 1996
To accelerate the ongoing paradigm shift in fisheries science toward ecosystem-based approaches, the authors offer ten principles ("commandments") for a holistic extension of conventional approaches that grapples with the complexity of social–ecological systems and incomplete knowledge	Francis et al. 2007
The concept of integrated social–ecological systems emphasizes the futility of dealing with the ecological or the social system separately, when the two subsystems are interactive and interdependent in resource management	Berkes and Folke 1998; Berkes et al. 2003
Sustainability science is a field that seeks to understand the fundamental character of interactions between nature and society. This is done through problem-driven interdisciplinary research, focusing on the interaction of global processes with the ecological and social characteristics of particular places	Kates et al. 2001; Turner et al. 2003
Millennium Ecosystem Assessment sought to assess the consequences of ecosystem change and informed various international conventions dealing with the environment. It focused on linkages between ecosystems and human well-being, and in particular on ecosystem services	MA 2005a

Resilience thinking and commons theory are the starting points of a team project reported in Berkes and Folke (1998). They develop the idea that the integrated social–ecological system must be the key analytical unit. This is because there is mutual feedback between the social subsystem and the ecological subsystem in any resource and environmental management situation. The key links between the two subsystems are ecological knowledge that people hold and the various kinds of management institution, both formal and informal, that establish the rules and norms by which humans interact with the environment. In a follow-up volume, Berkes et al. (2003) further identify complex adaptive systems as the setting (with its characteristics of scale, uncertainty, nonlinearity and self-organization), and resilience as the approach to deal with complexity and change.

Sustainability science (Kates et al. 2001; Turner et al. 2003) starts from the need to establish a methodology and principles to guide the sustainable development concept that emerged in the 1980s (Norton 2005). The sustainability science group is interdisciplinary, with expertise in various areas of social science, earth systems science, climate change and international scientific programs. The theory base is not explicitly given but leans toward complex systems, vulnerability and resilience. Key processes in nature–society systems are studied across a range of scales, from local to global. Research methodology emphasizes cases located in specific times and places, how they respond to stress, self-organizational phenomena, and different ways of knowing and learning.

A large team project with over a thousand scientists involved globally, the Millennium Ecosystem Assessment sought to evaluate the health of Earth's ecosystems and their ability to sustain human well-being (MA 2005a, 2005b, 2005c). Current conditions and trends in ecosystem services were assessed using various ecological theories and ecological economics. The MA (2005a) brought into the global environmental discourse the wide use of a vocabulary of drivers, policy responses and scenario planning. It expanded the scope of the interdisciplinary treatment of global environmental problems, and the methods by which national- and international-level policies could be developed and implemented.

These five attempts to develop an integrated science of people and environment help evaluate commonalities and differences. They are all interdisciplinary, combining social science with natural science concepts and approaches. They may involve a single scholar (McEvoy 1986), a small group of co-authors (Francis et al. 2007) or a large and loosely structured international team (MA 2005a). Each may emphasize a small-scale or a large-scale nature–society system, and many of them deal with multiple scales. They all use variations of systems approaches and emphasize feedback relations. Many of them use interdisciplinary fields as their theory base, such as commons, ecological economics, vulnerability and resilience. They pay attention to property rights, "including the familiar domain of privatized property, the still poorly charted territory of commonly held property, and the mythical terrain of no property or open access" (McCay 2008, p. 7). It is notable that resilience appears in four of these five examples, McEvoy's case being the sole exception. All five provide illustrations of the use of the suite of emerging views given in Table 2.2. In particular, all five deal with natural resources, not in the sense of commodification of nature, but in the sense of nature as providing ecosystem services and human well-being.

The "Intellectual Baggage" of Natural Resources and Management

Natural resources are assets for the creation of human satisfaction or utility. According to the classical view, they are not desirable in themselves, but rather they are a means to an end. They are of value only to the extent that they can be used to create goods and services—fishery resources to create human food and a fishing industry, for example, or coastal resources to satisfy human need for recreation. This view of resources is still found in most textbook and dictionary definitions. The idea of human-defined value is conveniently captured in Zimmerman's (1951) dictum: resources are not, they become. Not only is natural resource a socially constructed concept, it is also culturally defined. For example, European settlers in New England states and Atlantic Canada in the 1700s used lobsters as fertilizer in their fields. By contrast, in the 2000s, lobster was the most valuable species in the coastal fishery (Acheson 2003; Wiber et al. 2009; Steneck et al. 2011).

Traditionally, economists identified three broad categories of resource: natural resources, human resources and capital resources. Natural resources were referred to as free gifts of nature by the early economists, with the assumption that they were wholly replenished, without cost, after our use or consumption of them. The water we remove from a lake could be fully replaced by river flow and precipitation; the fish stocks we harvest could be fully renewed by growth and reproduction. As part of the freedom-of-the-seas concept, Hugo Grotius argued, around 1600, that the fish in the sea could not be exhausted. The concept persisted more or less into the 20th century. In fact, it was widely believed, as late as the 1930s, that fish in the sea could not be overfished (Eckert 1979).

Even though the idea that the environment is created for the use of humans, and human–environment dualism in general, goes back to the emergence of monotheistic religions, the early Industrial Age played a major role in the full development of these concepts. In pursuing individual wealth, people were taught to regard land, resources and their own labour as commodities for the market. "Natural resources were other-ized and objectified. They lost their identities as individuals, even as species, and became but raw material for human transformation into humanly useful commodities" (Callicott 2003, p. 245). Breaking human–environment bonds and separating people from nature allowed people to enjoy the fruits of industrialization without any undue obligations and concern for nature.

Worster (1988, p. 11) points out that this marked a shift in world-view so that everyone would treat the Earth, as well as each other, with a "frank, energetic self-assertiveness, unembarrassed by too many moral or aesthetic sentiments." Such commodification of nature as natural resources was strongly linked to the development of resource management, in which the use of reductionism, positivistic assumptions and the emergence of scientists and managers as independent, objective experts figure prominently.

In the history of American environmental philosophy, Callicott (2003) distinguishes between preservationism and resourcism. The first chief of the US Forest Service, Gifford Pinchot, who had been educated as a forester in Europe, articulated the elements of a resourcist philosophy that renewability required taking only the surplus, or the interest. The concept of nature developed by preservationists Thoreau and Muir became "natural resources" in Pinchot's terminolgogy. In case one missed the point about nature existing solely for human use, Pinchot declared: "there are just two things on this material earth—people and natural resources" (as quoted by Callicott 2003, p. 244). Pinchot brought resourcism into the then mainstream utilitarian ethic of the economists of the day, John Stuart Mills and others.

Efficiency was the hallmark of utilitarianism. The problem with the way that hunters, fishers, farmers and loggers used natural resources was that such uses were inefficient and destructive from the resourcist point of view. Renewable natural resources such as trees and fish could be consumed without their being depleted, but one could not depend on loggers and fishers to do this. Technical expertise was necessary to carry out such tasks as doing an inventory of the resource, finding out the growth rates of useful species, the age at which growth slowed down, and the age and size at reproduction, so that the harvestable surplus could be calculated. The idea of only skimming the interest off the natural resource capital required the development of various applied sciences, such as

forestry, wildlife management and fishery management, and the emergence of government agencies dedicated to the task of overseeing that
natural resources were managed productively and efficiently.

The master narrative of resource management, as Bocking (2004)
puts it, with nature as the source of raw materials, requires natural resource
professionals as arbiters of human–environment relations, pursuing
nature's efficient harvest. Efficiency could be achieved by making the
resource not only productive but also more predictable. Resource management is often said to be engaged in a quest for certainty, with precise
predictions of the future state of the resource, often involving the
simplification of the ecosystem (monoculture farming being an extreme
example). Variation is to be eliminated where possible in the quest for
factory-like harvesting, processing and marketing of these commodities.
The objective of efficiency was based on the best science available, using
reductionistic approaches and positivistic assumptions.

Since the 17th century, science has been dominated by positivism,
also called logical positivism or rationalism. It assumes the existence of a
reality driven by immutable laws based on universal truths. The role of
science is to discover these truths and put them to use for predicting
and controlling nature. Science is assumed to be value-neutral, and the
scientists themselves are thought to be operating in a value-free environment (Norton 2005). Hence, the nature and limitations of science are
rarely part of science education, and issues of values and objectivity are
rarely discussed by scientists and resource managers. For many, societal
issues are not part of science. Many scientific articles in ecology journals
are based on field experiments in which human influence is thought to
be nonexistent or insignificant (Holling et al. 1998).

The conventional scientific worldview is based on Newtonian physics
as the model for science. For two-and-a-half centuries, physicists used a
mechanistic view of the natural world. The general conception of reality
from the 17th century onward saw the world as a multitude of separate
parts assembled into a machine. It was thus believed that complex phenomena could be studied and controlled by their being reduced to their
basic components, and by identification of the mechanisms by which
they interacted. This approach, called reductionism, become an essential
part of Western science. Other sciences, including biology and economics, came to adopt the mechanistic and reductionistic approaches of

Newtonian physics as a model to describe reality. Generalizations and synthesis are made by seeing nature as clockwork, in which the pieces can be assembled or disassembled.

Such a summary of positivism and reductionism is no doubt simplistic. Few contemporary natural resource scientists and managers subscribe to all or most of the assumptions in these concepts. However, it is also true that the positivist–reductionist paradigm has historically dominated resource management science (along with most other scientific disciplines) and still remains influential (Worster 1977; Norton 2005). For example, most fisheries biology, economics and resource management throughout the world still use positivist–reductionist assumptions and methods and aim to calculate, species by species, the harvestable surplus in a predictable world. The terminology has changed. Instead of MSY (Larkin 1977), we use terms such as total allowable catch (TAC), individual transferable quotas (ITQs) and "catch shares" of those quotas, but the basic idea remains much the same (McCay 2012). However, the ground is shifting on many of the assumptions behind these mechanistic calculations, necessitating a reappraisal of conceptions of resources and management.

An Ecological Critique of Conventional Management

For several decades now, the science of ecology has been shifting from a balance-of-nature paradigm to a dynamic ecosystem paradigm, with major advances in the understanding of biodiversity, complexity and uncertainty. The shift was more or less complete in the field of ecology by the 1980s, and applied ecology disciplines such as fisheries management were beginning to grapple with the implications of the paradigm change. This chapter will touch upon two aspects of this change and their implications: biodiversity and species interactions, and the significance of natural variability.

Under conventional fisheries methodologies, it is implicitly assumed that the productivity and harvesting of a target species can be understood in isolation from other species. Thus, noneconomic species and other components of the ecosystem can be conveniently ignored. Such a focus on species of immediate economic interest works only if these resources are indeed "free gifts of nature," disconnected from their ecological roles. But, as ecologists know well, species are connected to one another through relationships such as predation, competition and symbiosis. Species are not discrete commodities in space and time, and harvesting one species has ecological implications for the rest of the ecosystem. The area of fisheries management is replete with examples of mismanagement through ignorance of ecological relationships (Francis et al. 2007).

A further complication is the issue of stocks. Genetic variation is part of biodiversity. Species tend to consist of genetically distinct sub-populations or multiple discrete stocks. The conservation of these subpopulations or stocks is part of conserving that particular species. In the case of commercial fish species, the more accessible stocks tend to get fished out first. Over a period of time, stocks may disappear, resulting in an erosion of the genetic integrity of the species, but the loss of these unit stocks may go unnoticed. Ames (2004) has produced evidence from interviews with old fishing captains that the disappearance of the Atlantic cod (*Gadus morhua*) from the Gulf of Maine may be explainable through some such mechanism (Chapter 10).

One of the major changes in ecological thinking, as mentioned in Chapter 1, is that ecosystems are seen as being in a state of contin-uous change, as opposed to hovering around an equilibrium point. This has resulted in the rejection of single equilibrium thinking ("balance of nature") and led to the development of multi-equilibrium thinking (Holling 1973; Gunderson and Holling 2002). Some of this change is related to uncertainty, thought to be intrinsic to the system and essentially irreducable (Charles 2001; Gunderson and Holling 2002). Assuming away uncertainty for so many decades has created public policy problems, especially where scientific predictions are contradicted by events reported in the media. It may become necessary to re-educate the public that uncertainty is part of the natural world, and that annual and other environmental variations are natural and to be expected.

A case in point is the salmon fishery of British Columbia, Canada. The fishery consists of many stocks, each of several species of salmon (sockeye being one), per river, and management agencies issue forecasts of the size of the larger stocks. When the actual salmon run differs greatly from the forecast, there usually is a public outcry. For example, in 1994, a major controversy broke out among the main user-groups (recreational, commercial and indigenous), accusing one another over the "missing" salmon in the Fraser River, as if the stock forecast were some sort of a guarantee of actual numbers.

Every few years, problems of missing salmon trigger newspaper headlines and sometimes may even trigger a judicial inquiry, as happened in 2009. It is not clear if the judicial inquiry helped anything, but, in the following year, a very large run of sockeye "clogged" the Fraser (Box 2.1). As reflected in the media, the small run of sockeye salmon in 2009 was a "disaster," and the large run in 2010 was a "great scientific mystery." Granted that the variation is rather large (fewer than 2 million fish in one year and 30 million in the next—same river, same species), the mass

---

BOX 2.1 PREDICTING SALMON RUNS IN BRITISH COLUMBIA, CANADA

"More than nine million sockeye have vanished from a BC river: How it happened remains a mystery"

Vancouver—The Fraser River is experiencing one of the biggest salmon disasters in recent history with more than nine million sockeye vanishing. Aboriginal fish racks are empty, commercial boats worth millions of dollars are tied to the docks and sport anglers are being told to release any sockeye they catch while fishing for still healthy runs of chinook. Between 10.6 million and 13 million sockeye were expected to return to the Fraser this summer. But the official count is now just 1.7 million, according to the Department of Fisheries and Oceans. Where the nine to 11 million missing fish went remains a mystery.

(The Globe and Mail, August 13, 2009)

"The salmon are back but the mystery deepens. The scientists said they were gone. Now 30 million sockeye are clogging the Fraser, raising the question: What happened?"

Steveston, BC and Vancouver—As fishermen haul in massive loads of sockeye salmon, the official estimate of this summer's near-record bounty has been upped to 30 million, the second increase in four days, deepening one of Canada's great scientific mysteries. It is the most sockeye that have returned to British Columbia's Fraser River in almost a century, and the Federal Department of Fisheries and Oceans responded to the new number Friday afternoon by increasing the total allowable catch for commercial fishermen by more than 60 percent to 10.2 million sockeye, from 6.2 million on Tuesday.

(The Globe and Mail, August 28, 2010)

media seem perplexed that the fish did not follow the scientific predictions, neatly illustrating lack of public appreciation of natural variation.

Unpredictability and change are part of natural variation. Holling and Meffe (1996) argued that natural variation is important for ecosystem resilience. Given the variability in such parameters as temperature and salinity in the physical environment, the diversity and variability in plant and animal populations provide the capacity to respond and adjust to change. Management that results in diminished genetic variation in hatchery fish, or major reductions in the population size of ecologically important species, erodes the resilience of the ecosystem. Conventional resource management that aims to reduce natural variation in an effort to make ecosystems more controllable, predictable and productive damages the very process that maintains resilience in a system. That leaves the system more susceptible to crises and less able to renew itself and self-organize in response to natural perturbations (Holling and Meffe 1996).

The implications of these points for the conventional concepts of natural resources management are quite serious, in fact fatal. All models based on equilibrium assumptions are suspect. Commodification of single species abstracted from the ecosystem and the conventional reductionist methodologies do not work, at least not for long-term sustainability. The uncertainty inherent in complex systems directly contradicts the positivist assumption that the world is predictable and, therefore, controllable. Furthermore, attempts to make nature predictable and controllable erode resilience.

Most natural and social scientists know that the Enlightenment Age analogy of a clockwork nature (or, for that matter, clockwork human body) has to be rejected. Nevertheless, mechanistic approaches are still common, and results of computer models are still presented as predictions, even when the assumptions behind the model are seriously flawed. Similarly, few contemporary ecologists would speak of a balance of nature, and yet the equilibrium-based concepts are still in use in ecology and resource management science. For example, the idea of maximum sustained yield is still used in fisheries management, disguised as TAC targets and "catch shares." In the short term, these quantitative targets may be appropriate for efficient resource exploitation. But, in the long run, fixed quantitative targets work against the maintenance of healthy and resilient ecosystems, because they ignore interactions within the system and because they reduce the natural variability of the system, including the ability of fishers to switch species flexibly.

A Social Critique of Conventional Management

Social critiques of conventional management align well with ecological critiques. For example, political ecology can help reveal the challenges in putting new ecology into practice and the contextual forces that make top-down management resistant to change (Armitage 2008). Historically, centralized government agencies have played a key role in carrying out the master narrative of resource management for a good reason. Making ecosystems more productive, predictable, controllable and economically efficient is a task for centralized institutions and command-and-control resource management. In the US, resourcism developed in parallel with the task of opening up the land taken away from indigenous peoples and establishing a whole new economic order—internal colonization (Cronon 1983).

In the industrialized world in general, centralized command-and-control resource management developed in the service of colonization and industrialization and was imposed on colonized lands (Gadgil and Guha 1992). It is, therefore, not surprising that long-term sustainability of local resources was never an overriding concern for conventional management, nor were equity and local livelihoods. Resource management, developed under a mechanistic worldview and inspired by the utilitarian ethics of John Stuart Mills, "had more to say about the human mission to extract rather than to conserve" (Worster 1977, p. 53). Such resource management was not geared for sustainability and social justice, but rather for efficiency and profit.

However, both then and now, resource management agencies frequently invoke the public interest as justification for their decisions. Gifford Pinchot is often credited with the classical formulation of the public interest in resource management: resources should be used for the common good, and not just for private gain. Pinchot's "the greatest good for the greatest number for the longest time" appears to be a rewording of John Stuart Mill's maxim, the greatest happiness for the greatest number (cited in Callicott 2003, p. 245).

In the case of resource management, the reference to the greatest number seems to be code for the government takeover of locally controlled or commonly held resources, for the benefit of society at large, with state agencies acting on behalf of the citizenry. It is the age-old distinction between *Gesellschaft* and *Gemeinschaft* of the German sociologist Ferdinand Tönnies, writing in the 1880s. *Gesellschaft* (society in an urban and capitalist setting) grabs control of rights of *Gemeinschaft* (the local society or community). As James Scott (1998) might put it, such a takeover not only generates revenues for the state, but also replaces the locally adapted but obscure local system with standardized scientific management that is transparent and intelligible to government.

Resource management by public agencies has continued to be justified in the name of public interest, and by the use of objective, rational science and decision-making. But the image of public-minded resource management is often met with skepticism. Critics note that, far from pursuing an idealistic notion of public interest, centralized resource management often privileges the interests of the resource industry (Regier et al. 1989). This is especially so in colonial and neocolonial resource extraction situations (Bocking 2004). A vivid example is the colonial takeover of indigenous fisheries in British Columbia, Canada, and in New Zealand (Turner et al. 2013a). A neocolonial example might be joint-venture fisheries, common in Africa and elsewhere, that provide some revenue for the central government, but often at the cost of damaging local, inshore, small-scale fisheries.

The disempowerment of the *Gemeinschaft* and the erosion of local control are two of the more serious consequences of contemporary resource management, with its standardized science and command-and-control practice. Prior to contemporary management, communities and tribal groups in many parts of the world managed their own resources. We have some idea about how these systems worked, mostly through locally designed commons rules (Wilson et al. 1994) such as reef and lagoon tenure systems (Johannes 1978). Command-and-control management did not fill a gap in the absence of management but rather replaced previously existing systems. Resource controversies in many parts of the world, for example in India, can be traced to centralized government management, loss of equitable access to resources, and damage to the livelihood systems of local people (Bavinck 2001).

Contrary to the assumptions of some, the national government's takeover of resources did not necessarily restore order or the rule of law,

PHOTO 2.1 Communities in many parts of the world manage their own resources. Fishing boats in the Bay of Bengal, Cox's Bazaar, Bangladesh

Source: F. Berkes

but often created open-access conditions that facilitated efficient exploitation, industrial-scale extraction and liberalized trade. Johannes's (1978) review from Oceania provides detailed documentation of the creation of open-access conditions that led to the demise of local management in the face of colonial pressures, the commodification of a whole range of species for export trade, and the subsequent decline of resources. The breakdown of local and indigenous commons management and their replacement by a government-backed free-for-all have been documented from the US Pacific Northwest, British Columbia and Alaska. The area was overrun by the "canned salmon stampede" between 1878 and the turn of the century, and tribal controls were replaced by an open-access system, before government management of some sort was eventually instituted (Rogers 1979).

The contestation of expertise is the other political aspect of resource takeover by government. Just as there is tension between government regulations and local commons rules, there is also tension between government technical expertise and local/indigenous knowledge (Berkes 2012b). Government scientists and managers in charge of the new management systems were not only the technicians who knew how to calculate the harvestable surplus, but also the high priests of the positivist–reductionist paradigm. They rejected local and traditional knowledge because it did not fit the paradigm and was not transparent to the state, and perhaps also because they did not want to share the legitimacy of expertise.

The role of expertise in management and the politics of legitimate knowledge is a large area; suffice to say that fisher knowledge has a potentially important role to play in fishery management (Neis and Felt 2000; Haggan et al. 2007; Lutz and Neis 2008). Ongoing poor relationships between indigenous groups and the government, and between fishers and fishery managers, not only in a few spots but in many parts of the world, can be ultimately linked to the disempowerment of the local (Bavington 2002). Rather than offering their knowledge and skills freely to assist government management, local and indigenous experts have generally stayed away from managers and scientists. One exception was the (unsuccessful) efforts of Labrador inshore fishers to warn managers of the impending collapse of the Newfoundland cod. In the Labrador community of Makkovik, only three codfish were caught in the entire summer of 1990, two years before the cod collapse was officially declared! However, fishers were unable to make themselves heard (Chantraine 1993).

The few indigenous groups that have seriously taken up scientific management and created their own tribal fishery management agencies were those forced to do so by law, the example being the establishment of tribal management agencies as a condition for salmon co-management under the Boldt decision in the US Pacific Northwest (Cohen 1986; Singleton 1998). For the most part, indigenous peoples' rejection of government management is not merely politics; it also has to do with their worldview. The notion of the separation of user from manager and the idea that a remote agency knows best what to do with a local group's resources just do not make sense to most local and indigenous knowledge holders (Berkes 2012b).

Interestingly, Ludwig (2001) comes to a similar conclusion about environmental managers and the limits to their expertise, but for somewhat different reasons. Noting that some of the really important environmental problems of our time cannot be solved by conventional management, he calls for a radical change in approach. He invites a re-appraisal of our unquestioned acceptance of economism (placing inordinate emphasis on economic values as opposed to other values), scientism (belief that science is inherently capable of solving almost all problems) and technocracy (achieving policy solutions by recourse to technological innovation). In seeking a new role for management experts, Ludwig (2001) proposes expanding the range of values to be taken into account and the range of knowledge used, including local and indigenous knowledge. As the really important issues are in the realm of ethics and environmental justice, he suggests that these considerations should be moved to the forefront, and a new kind of management style based on learning should be adopted.

Broadening Values and Objectives

As recognized by Malawi Principles (Folke et al. 2005), management objectives are a matter of societal choice and not a technical or scientific matter. As illustrated by the previous section, societal choice, in turn, can become quite political: a particular resource may be used for international trade to generate income for the nation-state, or it may be used for local food security. Who is to decide?

However, there is general scientific agreement regarding the larger goals of management: preventing the biological and economic extinction of resources and promoting their sustainable use. But the specific goals are more controversial and elusive. Benefits from a living resource can be measured in different ways, as the quantity harvested (biological) or as revenue (economic). Benefits can also be measured in many other ways than simply the weight or value, such as benefits to society in terms of sustainable livelihoods and sustainable communities. In the history of fisheries management, objectives have changed over time, from biological maximization objectives, to economic yield objectives, to some kind of optimum sustainable yield objective that includes trade-offs of different kinds of objective and built-in safety (precautionary principle) to account for uncertainty. The balance of opinion is that we should perhaps back off from "maximization" objectives. In the concluding chapter of a major book, Garcia and Cochrane (2009, p. 452) summarize the outlook at the beginning of the 21st century: "Bio-ecological objectives are broader. Social and economic objectives, measures and constraints are more formally recognized."

It is informative to look at the diversity of possible objectives in one coastal resources sector, the fishery (Clark 1985; Berkes et al. 2001). Most of the objectives commonly stated for fisheries management fall into three categories. The first set relates to resource sustainability, ensuring that the biological productive capacity of the resource is not exceeded.

TABLE 2.3 Some objectives of fishery management

Objective	Main purpose		
	Sustainability	Economic and social	
		Efficiency	Equity
1. Maximize catches		✓	
2. Maximize profit		✓	
3. Conserve fish stocks	✓		
4. Stabilize stock levels	✓		
5. Stabilize catch rates		✓	
6. Maintain healthy ecosystem	✓		
7. Provide employment			✓
8. Increase fisher incomes			✓
9. Reduce conflicts among fisher groups or with non-fishery stakeholders			✓
10. Protect sports fisheries		✓	✓
11. Improve quality of fish			
12. Prevent waste of fish	✓	✓	
13. Maintain low consumer prices			✓
14. Increase cost-effectiveness		✓	
15. Increase women's participation			✓
16. Reserve resource for local fishers			✓
17. Reduce overcapacity	✓	✓	
18. Exploit under-utilized stocks	✓	✓	
19. Increase fish exports		✓	
20. Improve foreign relations		✓	✓
21. Increase foreign exchange		✓	
22. Provide government revenue		✓	

Source: Adapted from Clark 1985

Photo 2.2 The choice of management objectives can privilege one use or one kind of fishery over another. Canoe fishers use handlines and short gillnets. Larger-scale, motorized boats use a variety of gear and participate in the tourism economy as well. Paraty, Rio de Janeiro State, Brazil

Source: F. Berkes

The other two sets are economic and social and relate either to the optimization of returns from the fishery (efficiency), or to the fair distribution of those returns among stakeholders (equity). Clark (1985) recognized some 22 fishery objectives, 6 of them related to sustainability, 12 related to efficiency, and 8 related to equity (Table 2.3).

Any one, or a combination of several, of these objectives may be a valid goal for a fishery, but it is not possible for a single fishery to achieve them all. Some of the objectives are incompatible with one another. For example, management can aim to maximize the biological yield or the economic yield, but not both simultaneously.

Similar considerations hold in the case of other marine and coastal resources. Benefits can be biological (e.g., biodiversity conservation in the case of a protected area) or economic (e.g., revenue from a national park), or both. In formulating management objectives more broadly for multiple sectors of ocean and coastal resources, scholars and practitioners are turning to the idea of ecosystem services. Mainstreamed by the Millennium Ecosystem Assessment, *ecosystem services* are the benefits people obtain from ecosystems. These include provisioning services such as food and water; regulating services such as natural hazard regulation; cultural services that provide spiritual and recreational benefits; and supporting services such as nutrient cycling (MA 2005a). Table 2.4 provides a listing.

TABLE 2.4 Ecosystem services: benefits people obtain from ecosystems

Each category has subcategories not shown here. A fourth category, Supporting services (nutrient cycling, soil formation, primary production), is not included in the table, as it is not used directly by people

Provisioning services	Food	Crops
		Livestock
		Capture fisheries
		Aquaculture
		Wild foods
	Fiber	Timber
		Cotton, hemp, silk
		Wood fuel
	Genetic resources	
	Biochemicals, natural medicines, pharmaceuticals	
	Freshwater	
Regulating services	Air quality regulation	
	Climate regulation	Global
		Regional and local
	Water regulation	
	Erosion regulation	
	Water purification and waste treatment	
	Disease regulation	
	Pest regulation	
	Pollination	
	Natural hazard regulation	
Cultural services	Spiritual and religious values	
	Aesthetic values	
	Recreation and ecotourism	

Source: MA 2005a

Given the list of possible objectives (Table 2.3) and the diversity of ecosystem services (Table 2.4) to be considered, the task of the resource manager is complex indeed. In a sense, it was much easier in the old days to aim for the maximum sustained yield and ignore all other objectives and ecosystem services. But there probably is no turning back to the old days, because simplistic objectives, with all the wrong assumptions behind them, are part of the reason we have a global resource and environmental crisis. The problem, however, is that dealing with multiple objectives requires addressing trade-offs and compromises. It necessitates a process of reaching consensus on the most appropriate objectives, and bringing people and multiple interests into the decision-making process.

Conclusions

Many of the assumptions of conventional management are in the process of being abandoned (Table 2.1). The emerging view rejects management in its deterministic sense: the manager operating by a fixed set of rules, measuring outcome in some quantitative way ("you can't manage what you can't measure") and exercising control over the system. Does this mean "the era of management is over" (Ludwig 2001)? Or do we redefine management?

It may make more sense to redefine "resource management" than to abandon it altogether, given that many of the elements of such a redefinition are, in fact, in place. First, we need to reformulate the term resource, which carries a sense of free goods, economism, strict human-centric use, and commodification of nature. The notion of *resource* can be revised to include production of ecosystem services for human well-being (MA 2005a), while maintaining biodiversity and social–ecological system resilience. Resources are needed and used by humans, but codfish and other species need their resources too, as the ecosystem-based approach reminds us. On the social side, de-emphasizing the market economics of resources would make us more sensitive to the political economy of resources. Some resources with little market value or global market demand may nevertheless be crucially important for local livelihoods, food security and local culture.

The term management, which as commonly used carries implications of domination of nature, efficiency, social and ecological simplification, and expert-knows-best, command-and-control approaches, similarly needs a makeover. The term *management* can be updated to emphasize steward-ship in place of domination and control of nature. Efficiency objectives need to be balanced against ecological (e.g., biodiversity) and social (e.g., equity) objectives (Cochrane and Garcia 2009). The conventional top-down, expert-knows-best management should be replaced by participatory approaches that are learning based (i.e., adaptive) and take a wider range of objectives into account. Resource management for multiple objectives, necessitating trade-offs and compromises, makes better sense when we consider integrated social–ecological systems as the unit of analysis, the subject of the next chapter.

3

SOCIAL–ECOLOGICAL SYSTEMS

In marine ecosystem management, people traditionally have been conceptualised by natural scientists as external agents who stress these systems (by for example fishing or altering habitats). By contrast, social scientists see people as recipients of management policies and practices that have been developed in response to changes in marine ecosystems. This artificial dichotomy fails to recognise that marine ecosystems and human societies are actually two inter-related parts of one marine social–ecological system.

(Perry et al. 2010, p. 356)

Introduction

Humans have been a part of marine ecosystems for a long time. In an age in which human activities have started to play a dominant role in natural systems at all levels, from local to global, it is high time to consider humans explicitly as part of the system. A consensus statement of high-profile scientists states that humans need to be reconnected to the biosphere, and a new social contract is required for sustainability based on a shift of perception—from people and nature seen as separate parts, to interacting, co-evolving and interdependent social–ecological systems (Folke et al. 2011). Reconnecting humans and nature is not a new idea (Chapter 2), but the statement helps emphasize that the paradigm change requires a shift of perception and perhaps worldviews.

Coastal and marine ecosystems have biophysical subsystems and human subsystems, including economic, political, social and cultural components, management and governance. In the last century, the study of biophysical subsystems became largely disconnected from the study of human subsystems, as fisheries science and other resource management sciences became specialized. Yet these two major components are highly interconnected and interactive, not only in the bioeconomic sense (e.g., Hilborn and Walters 1992), but also across the full range of biophysical and human subsystems (Kooiman et al. 2005; Cochrane and Garcia 2009).

Thus, one of the objectives of an interdisciplinary science of coastal and marine resources management would be to reconnect natural science and social science perspectives, and to get rid of this artificial dichotomy that Perry and colleagues (2010) refer to. Rather than treating the biophysical and the social as separate and distinct systems, the two should be considered together, both in theory and practice. This requires reconciling the various disciplines with largely different scholarly traditions (natural sciences vs. social sciences) to create the necessary space for such interdisciplinarity. Obviously, much of the research on marine ecosystems will continue to pursue disciplinary traditions. But understanding many of the complex global issues will require collaborations of multiple disciplines to interpret causes, deal with consequences and design policies for mitigation and adaptation.

As the Millennium Ecosystem Assessment demonstrated, driving forces of change are increasingly internationalized, and the impacts of these drivers emerge independent of the place where they are produced. Understanding these drivers requires interdisciplinary, international teamwork (MA 2005a). A number of approaches have been developed to carry out such work. One of these is sustainability science, in which understanding the impacts of drivers uses contextualized, place-based cases studied by interdisciplinary teams (Kates et al. 2001; Turner et al. 2003).

The approach to re-integrate social and ecological subsystems also needs to reconcile global environmental change (largely in the purview of natural sciences) with globalization (largely in the purview of social sciences and humanities). Both are important. Marine ecosystems are increasingly coming under the impacts of global environmental change. For example, climate-related changes have been occurring in marine ecosystems for some years. Biodiversity loss and habitat destruction, which used to be predominantly local and regional, are becoming global in nature.

In addition to these, global changes are taking place in human systems—*globalization*, sometimes defined as the compression of space and time scales with regards to flows of information, people, goods and services (Young et al. 2006). Such changes, including the globalization of trade in marine products, are also impacting marine ecosystems. Further, these two categories of major impacts (global environmental change and globalization) are actually themselves crucially interconnected and interactive.

The objective of the chapter is to explore the meaning of social–ecological systems with examples. The chapter has three parts. The first deals with the context and the basic concepts of social–ecological systems, exploring the significance and implications of the interconnected nature of the social and ecological subsystems. The second deals with globalization, developing a contextualized understanding of drivers of change, from local to global levels. The third is a case study of aquaculture as an example of a major transformation driven by an interaction of globalization and global environmental change.

The discourse on social–ecological systems does not end here but needs to expand into a discussion of resilience and property rights in commons, along with an exploration of the various ways in which the social subsystem interacts with the biophysical subsystem. The conceptual tools to do so include adaptive management, co-management, social and institutional learning, collaborative research and monitoring, partnerships for capacity building, and multilevel governance (Folke et al. 2005; Kooiman et al. 2005; Armitage et al. 2009). These topics are dealt with in the subsequent chapters of this book.

Context and Concept of Integrated Social–Ecological Systems

Fisheries are not purely biophysical systems free from human influence, nor are they purely social systems that function independently of ecosystem services. Although many studies have examined some aspect or another of human–nature interactions in fisheries, the complexity of coupled social–ecological systems has not been well understood or appreciated (Mahon et al. 2008; Berkes 2012a). This lack of progress is partly due to the disciplinary separation of ecological and social sciences in the study of fisheries.

A number of disciplines have traditions of human–environment integration. In geography, the human ecology school of the 1930s developed the idea that nature is the base for the activities of human society (Park 1936). In anthropology, the cultural ecology approach of Steward (1955) dealt with adaptive processes by which societies lived in and used their environment. Ingold's *dwelling perspective* elaborates this integrative concept of humans-in-nature. Seen as the basis for putting humans back into the ecosystem, it involves the "skills, sensitivities, and orientations that have developed through long experience of conducting one's life in a particular environment" (Ingold 2000, p. 25). Over the last few decades, a diversity of human–nature models has been developed in a number of disciplines (Glaser 2006). In effect, natural and social scientists have been rediscovering the unity of people and nature, but this intuitive idea was already well known to traditional and indigenous societies (Berkes 2012b).

Examples of traditional social–ecological systems have been documented from various parts of the world (Table 3.1). Some of these involve

TABLE 3.1 **A sampling of traditional integrated social–ecological systems for coastal management**

System	Description	Reference
Valli or *vallicoltura*	A dike-and-pond fishery management system of the Venice region, Adriatic Sea	Johannes et al. 1983
Acadja	A West African system in which cut branches (brush piles) are placed in lagoons and shallow waters to increase fish habitat	Johannes et al. 1983
Tambak	Indonesian brackish-water aquaculture systems combining fish and invertebrate culture with vegetables and tree crops	Costa-Pierce 1988
Pokkali rice–fish	A system in SW India for growing salt-tolerant *pokkali* rice with fish, invertebrates and wetland vegetation in coastal ponds stocked and cleared naturally by tidal action	Bhatta and Bhat 1998
Vanua and *puava*	Two of the many Pacific island systems of "corporate estate," signifying an intimate association of a group of people with a defined and named area of land and sea	Ravuvu 1987; Hviding 1990
Ahupua'a	A Hawaiian integrated system of wedge-shaped units of land and sea, extending from volcanic mountaintop to reef edge, and including zones of protection and use	Costa-Pierce 1987; Kaneshiro et al. 2005

coastal ponds and lagoons, such as *valli* of Europe and *cherfia* of North Africa. *Acadja* brush-pile fisheries are found in West Africa. Similar brush-pile systems, which are constructed by piling branches to increase fish habitat in shallow waters of lagoons, deltas and inlets, and which function as fish aggregating devices (Johannes et al. 1983), are found in many parts of the world, including South Asia.

Variations of Indonesia's *tambak* system of fishponds are widely found in South and East Asia. Some of these systems provide excellent examples of integrated management. In Indonesia, for example, one finds traditional rice–fish culture systems, with nutrient-rich wastes flowing downstream into brackish-water polyculture systems (*tambak*) and then into the sea, enhancing the coastal fishery (Costa-Pierce 1988). Various kinds of traditional integrated rice–fish system are found in India, Bangladesh, the Philippines, Vietnam, Laos, Cambodia and parts of China as well.

Some of these systems explicitly include humans in the definition of the ecosystem. The *vanua* in Fiji is a named area of land and sea, considered an integrated whole with its human occupants. Depending on the context, the term could be used to refer to the social group or the territory that it occupies, thereby expressing the inseparability of land and people (Ravuvu 1987). A number of Pacific Island societies have similar concepts, for example, *puava* in the Solomon Islands and *ahupua'a* in Hawai'i. Traditionally, land and reef–lagoon areas were not viewed as commodities to be sold or exchanged, but certain use rights might be granted by "custodians" or "guardians." There has been a revival of custodial institutions throughout the Pacific (Johannes 2002). For example, in New Zealand, Maori people (who are related to Polynesians) have initiated networks of MPAs to conserve their resources through Maori environmental guardians, *kaitiaki* (Stephenson et al. 2014).

Integrated people–environment systems are not new in human experience, but some of the terminology is new. Berkes and Folke (1998) used the term social–ecological systems to emphasize the integrated concept of humans-in-nature, and to stress that the delineation between social and ecological systems is artificial and arbitrary. *Social–ecological systems* may be defined as integrated, complex systems that include social (human) and ecological (biophysical) subsystems in a two-way feedback relationship. The term emphasizes that the two parts (social system and ecological system) are equally important, and they function as coupled, interdependent and co-evolutionary systems. Human actions affect biophysical systems, biophysical factors affect human well-being, and humans in turn respond to these factors.

The two subsystems are interconnected, but, until recently, the dominant discourse in global environmental change has tended to investigate how human activities are affecting ecosystem conditions and processes, with dimensions often limited to information on population change, economic growth, technology and development. However, to deal fully with the interconnections of the two subsystems, it is not sufficient to regard humans as merely stressors and/or managers of the ecosystem. Rather, the analysis needs to seek a detailed understanding of the mechanisms of this two-way relationship, with interacting, co-evolving and interdependent subsystems (Folke et al. 2011).

It has been argued that the most appropriate analytical unit for the study of sustainability is the social–ecological system, also called the socio-ecological system (Gallopin et al. 2001) or coupled human–environment system (Turner et al. 2003). The point about coupling is important. For example, the Millennium Ecosystem Assessment is not about ecosystem services only, nor about human well-being only, but about the relationships of the two (MA 2005a). The sustainability science approach is neither about the global biophysical system alone nor about social–economic–political systems alone, but uses place-based models that enable study of the interaction of people and their environment (Kates et al. 2001). The resilience perspective, which has proved to be valuable in understanding the dynamics of social–ecological systems, often focuses on biophysical and social subsystems together, because it is the interaction of the two that is particularly informative about nonequilibrium processes and surprises that account for the behavior of the system as a whole (Folke 2006; Liu et al. 2007).

Further exploring the concept, Figure 3.1 depicts social subsystems and biophysical subsystems as consisting of nested levels. Following Gibson et al. (2000) and Cash et al. (2006), *level* is defined as the unit of analysis located at different positions on a scale, and *scale* is defined as the spatial, temporal, quantitative or analytical dimensions used to measure a phenomenon.

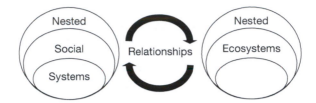

FIGURE 3.1 Social–ecological system consisting of nested social (human) and ecological (biophysical) subsystems, and integrated by two-way feedbacks. The links between the two subsystems may involve governance or ecological knowledge or institutions. Various versions of this concept have been offered by Berkes et al. (2003), Glaser (2006) and Kotchen and Young (2007)

Figure 3.1 shows the two-way interaction between the two subsystems of a coupled social–ecological system through some sorts of relationship. One may insert one of a number of alternative terms to highlight the different aspects of the relationship that may link social and ecological systems: ecological knowledge, institutions or governance, or even environmental values, culture and worldview. The important point remains that the system shown in Figure 3.1 is a coupled system with two-way feedback.

Nested ecosystems (e.g., Tampa Bay—Gulf of Mexico—North Atlantic . . .) are the obvious choice of scale for the biophysical subsystem. Ecologists are well familiar with the use of hierarchy theory in ecosystems (Ahl and Allen 1996). For example, to conserve sea turtles, one needs to look far beyond the beaches where turtles nest and consider a hierarchy of levels on a geographic scale that includes migration routes (Campbell et al. 2008). Local population trends of the sooty shearwater (*Puffinus griseus*) in New Zealand are likely affected by drivers originating far away. Long-term sooty shearwater harvest records by the Maori seem to be showing a possible link between adult survival and fecundity and the El Niño/La Niña Southern Oscillation (Moller et al. 2009b).

Nested social systems are less easy to define visually than are ecological systems. The dimensions can be institutions, jurisdictions or a hierarchy of resource management systems. A social system along an organizational scale is shown in Figure 3.2. Individuals and households make up the lowest level, followed by community, region, nation and international levels. Depending upon the particulars of a case, the levels could be different. For a given case, the ecological scale and the social/political

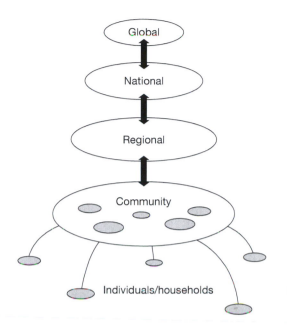

FIGURE 3.2 The social subsystem along a social/political organizational scale. The nested social systems may be depicted as a hierarchy of levels

organizational scale are unlikely to match exactly. However, the closer the match, the easier the fit between ecosystems and institutions (Folke et al. 2007).

The full implications of this two-way relationship are still being explored. Conventional resource management has in the past concentrated "on regulating the impacts of the volatility of biophysical systems on human welfare. What is new is the need to regulate the impact of human actions on large-scale biophysical systems" (Kotchen and Young 2007, p. 150). That is, the arrow connecting human systems to biophysical systems in Figure 3.1 is growing increasingly important. One might add that the arrow connecting biophysical systems to human systems is also increasingly important, but in different ways. Given the increasing recognition of the essential and irreducible nature of ecological uncertainty and variability (Charles 2001), the arrow is less and less about reducing the variability in the flow of resources for human welfare, and more and more about maintaining the structure/function or the biodiversity and resilience of the biophysical subsystem that provides those resources (Holling and

Meffe 1996; MA 2005a). This new emphasis, in turn, has led to a rethinking of resource management objectives, away from the conventional output-oriented fishery objectives and toward objectives that seek to maintain the health and integrity of the social–ecological system as a whole (Chapter 2).

Figure 3.1 serves to highlight the importance of rights, rules, decision-making systems, knowledge systems, research and communication, all of which are created by humans to mediate the two-way interactions between the two subsystems. This governance system is important to dampen the impact of humans on the global system. But it is also important for providing mechanisms, such as insurance schemes and emergency assistance programs, that help cushion the impact of biophysical factors (e.g., hurricanes and sea-level rise associated with climate change) on human systems (Kotchen and Young 2007). The social–ecological system at the global level, the "Earth system" in the terminology of international global environment change research programs, is not the only level of interest (Rockström et al. 2009). Consistent with hierarchy theory (Ahl and Allen 1996), complex systems function at several different levels, and all of the levels are important.

The implementation plan of the parties to the 2002 World Summit on Sustainable Development had 81 references to "at all levels" in just 50 pages (Cash et al. 2006), indicating the international recognition that we can no longer deal with global problems at only the planetary level. Social–ecological systems at all levels, from local to international, need to be considered. However, the links between social and ecological subsystems may be different at different levels. For example, the people of a fishing community may be primarily interested in their livelihood resources, whereas the national government may be primarily interested in stimulating the production of high-value export commodities such as aquaculture-produced shrimp. Driving forces for change that are operating at the level of the community or region may be quite different from those at the national level.

Drivers of change affect social–ecological systems in complex and unpredictable ways and offer the primary evidence that we are dealing with complex adaptive systems phenomena (Levin 1999). It is the inter-action of the two subsystems that is often responsible for some of the more puzzling kinds of complexity. In many sustainability problems, the investigation of the social subsystem or the ecological subsystem alone gives an incomplete (and sometimes misleading) understanding of the issue. To understand the behavior of the system as a whole requires an analysis at all levels, both social and ecological subsystems together. That is, many "socio-ecological systems are non-decomposable systems" (Gallopin 2006, p. 294).

Mathematical models of lake-and-manager systems based on the Northern Highland Lake District of Wisconsin (Carpenter et al. 1999) illustrate the idea of nondecomposability. The analysis of the behavior of these coupled social–ecological systems showed that unwanted collapse could occur even when ecosystem dynamics were perfectly known, and managers had perfect knowledge and control of human actions. Such insights could not have been obtained by analyzing social and ecological subsystems separately. Additional evidence comes from Liu et al. (2007), who studied the complexity of coupled human and natural systems across six well-documented cases of social–ecological systems. The authors found that the cases exhibited complex patterns and processes—nonlinear dynamics with thresholds, surprises, reciprocal feedback loops, time lags, legacy effects and resilience. Many of these patterns and processes were not evident when the cases were analyzed by social or natural scientists separately. They became apparent only when the full social–ecological system was taken as the unit of study.

All of these examples indicate that integrated social–ecological systems are complex adaptive systems (Berkes et al. 2003). The two-way feedback relations between the social and the ecological subsystems, the non-decomposability of the system, and the unpredictable ways in which drivers act all are all indicators of complexity. The following section illustrates these ideas further and expands on some of the complexities related to globalization.

Social–Ecological Systems and Globalization

There is a large and well-developed literature on global environmental change in such areas as biodiversity loss, habitat loss, pollution and climate change as related to ocean and coastal resources (Grafton et al. 2008). This literature examines both arrows in Figure 3.1, that is, both the impact of these changes on resources, and the ways and means by which the impact of human actions on the biophysical subsystem may be regulated.

By contrast, the literature on resources and globalization and on the interaction between global environmental change and globalization is poorly developed and often obscure (Leichenko and O'Brien 2008).

However, it is not that difficult to see that globalization (e.g., a cultural shift in international tastes toward considering shrimp as a desirable food item) can act as a driver (e.g., creating an international market demand for shrimp) affecting ocean and coastal resource use and contributing to global environmental change. One can also think of examples of global environmental change causing globalization. Leichenko and O'Brien (2008) have used the example of the Arctic Ocean to show that global environmental change (reduction of sea ice due to climate change) will stimulate oil, gas and mining activities, which will, in turn, have far-

TABLE 3.2 Examples of drivers of change related to globalization

Drivers	Comment	Reference
Globalized marine product trade for international markets	Globalized aquaculture technology for shrimp, salmon and other species; growth of reduction fisheries; rapid development and invasiveness of international markets for special products such as tuna and sea urchin	Deutsch et al. 2007; Berkes et al. 2006; Primavera 1997
Modernization and transformation of coastal fisheries	Small-scale coastal fisheries are under pressure from aquaculture, industrial fisheries and a variety of uses of coastal ecosystems	Chuenpagdee 2011; Nayak and Berkes 2010
Infectious diseases and fishers	Fishing communities are among the highest-risk groups in countries with high rates of HIV/AIDS, for a number of reasons related to their mobility and other factors of vulnerability	Allison and Seeley 2004
Certification, eco-labeling, "green" environmental activism	Fair trade and "green" environmental activism have potential impacts on technology used and the species and areas targeted; however, certification may also be subverted to favor large companies	Marine Stewardship Council 2014
Code of Conduct for Responsible Fisheries	International consensus on best practices, codes and ethics is beginning to shape the way fisheries are carried out worldwide, by drawing attention to wider environmental considerations	FAO 1995
United Nations Millennium Development Goals (MDGs)	MDGs draw attention to resource management policies (e.g., decentralization) as they may relate to poverty alleviation, sustainability, food security, equity and livelihoods	UN 2014

reaching social, economic, political and cultural impacts on the people of the Arctic (globalization). Table 3.2 provides some examples of drivers of change related to globalization.

Internationalization of the shrimp trade, one of the best-known examples of globalization of markets for marine products, is seen as a driver of both coastal habitat loss and biodiversity loss in many parts of the world (Naylor et al. 2000). Its impact on coastal mangroves has been particularly damaging (Kautsky et al. 2001). The loss of mangroves, in turn, has made people more vulnerable to coastal disasters. For example, the 2004 Asian tsunami was a natural disaster, and yet the devastation in countries such as Sri Lanka and Thailand was in part due to loss of mangroves and their buffering capacity, associated with the expansion of shrimp aquaculture for global markets (Adger et al. 2005). Another unintended effect of shrimp and other aquaculture was the diversion of a large part of the total marine catch from direct human food to aquaculture feed (Naylor et al. 2000; Deutsch et al. 2007).

PHOTO 3.1 Some of the mangroves lost in the shrimp aquaculture boom are coming back, thanks to mangrove restoration projects such as this one. Gulf of Thailand, south of Bangkok

Source: F. Berkes

The motivations for and the impacts of the globalization of shrimp are not seen only at national and international levels; they are also apparent at local and regional levels. The actual mechanisms may be understood as a mix of national economic policies (the desire to generate foreign exchange) and regional (economic development) and local-level decision-making. At the local level, factors at work may include the desire of coastal landowners to make quick profit and the ability of local influential people to seize control of government land by clearing mangroves and other coastal vegetation (Primavera 1997; Bhatta and Bhat 1998).

In Kerala, south India, shrimp (prawn in local terminology) was transformed from fertilizer for coconut palms to "pink gold" in the 1970s, as international demands and prices rose sharply (Kurien 1992). South India has a long tradition of coastal brackish-water aquaculture, using a rotation of salt-tolerant *pokkali* rice and a mix of fish and invertebrates. This system disintegrated with the advent of intensive shrimp aquaculture. The conversion of *pokkali* areas into permanent monoculture shrimp ponds resulted in irreversible change. Once the tide-operated water intakes of the traditional polyculture system fell into disuse, coastal ponds were excavated and the remaining natural vegetation was destroyed, the area was not easily restored to its natural state (Bhatta and Bhat 1998). However, the new system was not sustainable, because lack of tidal flushing resulted in the accumulation of salt in the ponds. Chemicals were needed to keep the system as a monoculture, and the imported seed stock brought shrimp disease into ponds. A recurring pattern of declining production and profits is common in intensive shrimp aquaculture throughout Southeast Asia. Some areas, such as the Gulf of Thailand, show a boom–and–bust cycle that travels around the coast, as intensive aquaculture runs its course, leaving behind a devastated coastal landscape, and moves on to another site (Huitric et al. 2002).

Some of the globalization drivers were hardly on the radar screen of fishery managers until recent years. For example, it came as a surprise, in the early 2000s, that HIV/AIDS infection rates among fishers in some countries were unexpectedly high. This high vulnerability has been explained in terms of fisher lifestyle and risk-taking, but the causes seem to be a great deal more complex than that. Allison and Seeley (2004) and Westaway et al. (2007) attribute high HIV/AIDS infection rates to a complex of interacting causes that include mobility, time spent away from home, periodic access to cash in an overall context of poverty, availability of commercialized sex in ports, as well as the fisher subculture of risky behavior. Other sectors in fisheries, such as fish vendors, who tend to be women in some countries, are also vulnerable owing to their daily inter-action with fishers. The problem is prevalent enough that some fisheries development programs in Africa and Asia have incorporated HIV/AIDS awareness in their planning (Allison and Seeley 2004).

The feedbacks involved in fishers and HIV/AIDS indicate a complex problem of social–ecological systems and globalization: they are driven by the dynamics of a shrinking world. For example, fishers from Bangladesh may seek employment across the Bay of Bengal in India, boom-and-bust incomes may follow the development of new marine products for lucrative markets, and the commercialization of livelihood resources creates vulnerability. As in the case of many African agricultural workers, HIV/AIDS-infected fisherfolk are often too sick to work, becoming dependent on others and further stressing local food security and the local social–ecological system as a whole.

Some of the globalization examples in Table 3.2 involve international movements, policies and programs. The use of certification and eco-labeling (Marine Stewardship Council 2014) is one of the ways in which market mechanisms may shape the conduct of international fisheries. As with fair-trade coffee, the agricultural counterpart, certification and eco-labeling have the potential to reward small producers who use environ-mentally friendly methods. However, data needs for certification make it prohibitively expensive for small producers to document sustainability and gain market advantage, making it likely that the benefits of certification will go to large companies. In a similar vein, consumer movements and environmental activism (e.g., the movement in Australia against illegal fishing) and organizations of scientists and citizens against bycatch of marine mammals and birds have potential to impact the way fishing is carried out.

Some international policies with potential to impact national fisheries policy and practice should also be considered as part of globalization, with drivers affecting marine social–ecological systems. A well-known example is the FAO Code of Conduct for Responsible Fisheries, which provides a comprehensive set of guidelines devised to guide marine social–ecological systems toward sustainability. The guidelines address (among other issues) ecosystem stewardship, dispute resolution, the precautionary principle, international law and international trade in fish products and they rely on the voluntary compliance of nation-states (FAO 1995).

Initiated formally by the FAO in 1991, the Code was developed in response to the management crisis in global fisheries. By the late 1980s, it had become clear that new approaches to fisheries management were needed, embracing conservation and environmental considerations and leading to responsible and sustainable fisheries. The Code and its technical guidelines were partly shaped by the UN Conference on Environment and Development (UNCED) and were intended to be consistent with the UN Convention on the Law of the Sea and other international agreements.

A number of other international agreements and conventions also fall under the category of international drivers. Among these is the Convention on Biological Diversity, with its stipulations on endangered and vulnerable species and about benefit-sharing rights of indigenous peoples and other rural communities (CBD 2014). Not directly involved in resource governance, but of potential impact, are the Millennium Development Goals (UN 2014). The program has eight major goals, including the eradication of extreme poverty and hunger, relevant for livelihoods, food security and fishing incomes. Targets regarding environmental sustainability include integrating the principles of sustainable development into country policies and reversing the loss of resources and loss of biodiversity. The strength of the Millennium Development Goals comes from the tracking of some 60 measurable indicators and the guidance they provide for development interventions.

Some of these international agreements and conventions result in policies that interact in influencing marine and coastal resource governance at various levels and create both new opportunities and new problems. For example, a key premise in the Code of Conduct for Responsible Fisheries is that marine resources, renewable but finite, need to be managed for their contribution to nutritional, economic and social well-being. To achieve this, states and other levels of management need to adopt measures for long-term sustainable resource use—but also need to give priority to human well-being. These measures are meant to meet a number of goals, including the Millennium Development Goal to reduce by half the number of poor people with food insecurity by 2015. Allison and

Horemans (2006) and Allison et al. (2012) show that achieving such international goals has implications for regional, national and local resource management policies.

For example, in the West Africa region, governments are committed to poverty reduction, decentralization and civil service reform through Poverty Reduction Strategy programs. These have led to the redefinition of the roles of central and local governments, with some of the responsibilities devolved to the local level. The premise here is that decentralization brings government planning closer to primary users and generates new opportunities for their participation in resource management (Allison and Horemans 2006). However, the experience is that newly devolved power, as a result of decentralization, tends to be captured by the local elite. Thus, making decentralization work as governance reform requires paying attention to factors such as the distribution of power (Béné and Neiland 2006).

Policy drivers such as Millennium Development Goals are relevant to marine social–ecological systems also because they interact with other social–ecological systems in agriculture and other livelihood systems. For example, reducing poverty in the overall system has an impact on resource management as well. High rates of HIV/AIDS impede the ability of fishing communities to escape from poverty and hunger. International market drivers transform small-scale fisheries into aquaculture in places such as Chilika Lagoon, increasing the export revenue from the fishery but creating livelihood and food security problems at a massive scale, making it difficult to implement Millennium Development Goals (Nayak and Berkes 2014). Such trade-offs and the broader social–ecological approach to fishery management are fundamentally different from treating management merely as stock assessment. Addressing complexity in marine and coastal social–ecological systems means paying attention to drivers and dealing with a number of complexities ignored by conventional resource management.

A Case Study on Transformations and Drivers: Aquaculture

The last three decades or so have seen a major global revolution that, some think, is comparable to the agricultural revolution that took place thousands of years ago. Global production of farmed fish and shellfish is now comparable to wild-caught fish and shellfish. Aquaculture produced only about 10 mt in 1987, reaching 66.6 mt (41.9 mt inland and 24.7 mt marine) in 2012, more than a sixfold increase in 25 years, whereas capture fisheries landings as a whole have remained around 85–95 mt per year (FAO 2014). The rise of aquaculture is often depicted as the natural progression from hunting to cultivation, a necessary modernization. The common perception of aquaculture is that it is an "add-on" to wild fish productivity. As Naylor et al. (2000, p. 1017) put it, "many people believe that aquaculture production will compensate for the shortfall in ocean harvests as ocean fisheries deteriorate, or that fish farming will restore wild populations by relieving pressure on capture fisheries."

A balanced look at the dramatic increase in aquaculture requires a serious consideration of the ecological and social costs of the transformation, followed by an examination of the belief quoted above. Some ecological costs have already been mentioned in the context of shrimp aquaculture; Naylor et al. (2000) summarize the main ecological impacts globally: the direct effect on wild fisheries to provide feed for aquaculture, and the indirect effect on wild fisheries by habitat modification, collection of wild seedstock, feed web interactions, introduction of exotic species and pathogens, and nutrient pollution. In terms of social costs, there may be equity problems (transformations tend to create winners and losers), displacement of coastal capture fisheries and other inshore resource uses, loss of resource control by local people, and livelihood and food security problems.

Where the fishers themselves become the aquaculturalists, there may be a rise in incomes and general improvement in the standard of life, even though some groups will be left at a disadvantage (Huong and Berkes 2011). In many cases, however, aquaculture development brings in new investors and their employees, displacing existing small-scale fishers and other coastal uses. Such a transformation may result in significant social and economic costs. A case in point is the fishery of Chilika Lagoon on the Bay of Bengal, India. Aquaculture development for the lucrative tiger shrimp (*Penaeus monodon*) in this large lagoon resulted in livelihood losses and food security problems for some 400,000 people, small-scale fishers and their families. They were basically strong-armed out of this valuable real estate, despite court decisions upholding their rights (Nayak and Berkes 2010).

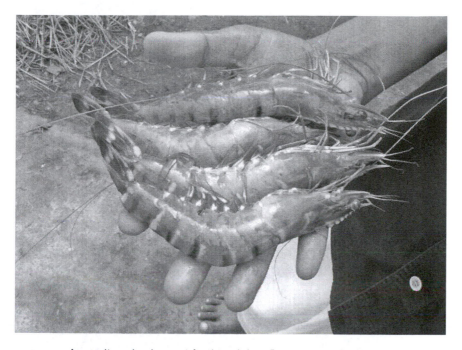

PHOTO 3.2 Aquaculture development for tiger shrimp *Penaeus monodon* has displaced large populations of fisherfolk in the capture fishery sector, Chilika Lagoon, Bay of Bengal, India

Source: Prateep Nayak

Some of the social impacts are really social–ecological impacts. Consider the case of the Bristol Bay fishery for wild sockeye salmon in Alaska. This fishery, monitored for some time and known to be biologically sustainable (Hilborn et al. 2003), has been in crisis in recent years. It is in crisis because of declining revenues, driven by the proliferation of salmon farms that produce a reliable supply of high-quality salmon, even though it is not sockeye salmon. It is ironic that international salmon aquaculture can negatively impact a well-managed wild salmon fishery in Alaska (which has no salmon aquaculture) and the livelihoods of the fishers (Robards and Greenberg 2007).

There is a common belief that the rapid growth of aquaculture relieves pressure on ocean resources, but the opposite is true for some kinds of aquaculture (Naylor et al. 2000). First, some background: Aquaculture can be distinguished from capture fisheries by two key criteria: ownership of stock and husbandry, and a deliberate intervention in the production cycle (Naylor et al. 2000). Fish and shellfish farming typically involves enclosing the fish in a secure system. The level of husbandry varies: excluding predators and competitors (extensive aquaculture), adding supplementary food (semi-intensive) or providing all food (intensive). Intensive systems imply increasing the density of individuals, resulting in higher production, but intensification also requires greater inputs and results in increased disease risk. Two somewhat distinct subsectors have emerged in aquaculture. The first subsector includes commercial farms that primarily use intensive and semi-intensive methods to produce high-value commodities for regional or international exports. The second subsector includes family or co-operative farms that rely on extensive or semi-intensive cultures to produce low-value species for local markets and household use.

Asia accounts for some 90 percent of the global aquaculture production, and China contributes some two-thirds of that total. Much of the Chinese production falls in the second subsector; it takes place in freshwater, involves carp species in low-intensity systems and serves low-income households. Extensive and traditional systems using herbivorous species do not require fishmeal but often add nutrient-rich materials to the water. Some of the more intensive systems based on herbivorous and omnivorous fish, for example US catfish and Vietnamese *basa* (*Pangasius bocourti*) catfish farms, rely on added feeds, but much less so than those that raise carnivorous species.

In the analysis of Naylor et al. (2000), the problem of impacting wild fish sources lies mainly with the first subsector, which primarily uses intensive and semi-intensive systems to produce salmon, shrimp and other high-value species for international markets. These intensive and semi-intensive aquaculture systems use between two and five times more fish protein as feed than is supplied by the farmed product. The fish protein used is in the form of fishmeal produced mainly from small pelagic ocean fish, such as anchovy and sardine species. According to the data used by Naylor et al. (2000), the top ten types of farmed fish required an average of 1.9 kg of wild fish for every 1 kg of fish raised on compound feeds, in which fishmeal and fish oil were dominant ingredients. Filter-feeding fish and shellfish are not fed compound feeds at all.

Among species that appropriate wild fish production in the form of fish meal, salmon and marine shrimp require some three times more fish as food input than is ultimately harvested. These ratios have been improving since the time of the Naylor et al. paper (2000), as much research has been going on to reduce the content of fishmeal and oils in aquaculture fish feeds and replace them with vegetable protein and oils (Pullin 2013; HLPE 2014). Nevertheless, it is clear that producing high-value species for the global trade is expensive ecologically, as well as costly in terms of social and environmental impacts. Observing that "the growing aquaculture industry cannot continue to rely on finite stocks of wild-caught fish," Naylor et al. (2000, p. 1019) propose a number of measures: expanding the farming of low-trophic-level fish; reduction of fishmeal and fish oil inputs in feed; higher use of integrated farming and polyculture; and promotion of environmentally sound practices.

The remarkable expansion of world aquaculture begs the question of drivers. Why did it happen, and why is it happening now? As with other cases of social–ecological transformation, there is no single answer. Multiple drivers are likely. Just about every paper on aquaculture starts with some sweeping statement about feeding the growing world population. However, the evidence suggests that food security or feeding the poor is not one of the major drivers, except perhaps in China. Even there, much of the research effort goes to developing aquaculture for high-value, carnivorous species.

Examining various kinds of aquaculture around the world, the primary motives seem to be: corporate profits, political influence and dispossessing low-caste fishers (case of Chilika, India, shrimp); corporate profits and indirect control over other coastal resources such as mangrove forests (Thailand, Philippines and Southeast Asia in general, shrimp); export earnings (Vietnam, *basa* and shrimp); corporate profits (France, Pacific cupped oyster, *Crassostrea gigas*); and corporate profits (Canada, salmon). There is some traditional aquaculture for local food and livelihoods, such as milkfish in the Philippines and carp polycultures in China. As well, there are some cases of relatively small aquaculture operations with local economic development in mind. Examples include community-organization-driven local aquaculture in India (De Silva and Davy 2010), household-level shrimp aquaculture in Sri Lanka (Galappaththi and Berkes 2014), Atlantic mussel culture in Brazil, and oyster (*Crassostrea virginica*) culture for indigenous economic development, Bras d'Or Lakes, Canada.

Aquaculture of high-value species for global markets, the first subsector in Naylor et al. (2000), is big business and shows all the characteristics of expansion-stage big business, such as secrecy, information control and a core of staff scientists to counter critics. Just as the pesticide industry attacked the critic Rachel Carson in the 1950s, Jurgenne Primavera, a Filipina scientist and one of the early critics of aquaculture, was marginalized and ostracized (Primavera 2005). Even as late as 2000, the Naylor et al. article came under attack by two scientists apparently employed by the Canadian aquaculture industry.

If profits are the big motive, why did aquaculture develop when it did? Here, there may be at least four drivers related to globalization and global environmental change. The first may be the prevailing neoliberal trade policies that may have facilitated international trade in marine products (Deutsch et al. 2011). The second may be a "globalization of tastes" that made Norwegian salmon desirable in Switzerland, Thai shrimp desirable in the US, and Vietnamese *basa* desirable in Uruguay (Trimble and Berkes 2013). The third may be related to global environmental change, the scarcity of certain luxury seafood products because of overfishing, and the opening up of new niche markets. The fourth may be related to developing technology and aquaculture know-how. Obviously, there are other factors as well and likely differences from region to region. The fact of the matter is that aquaculture for high-value species has attracted big business.

As industries mature, they tend to moderate and eventually become more responsible corporate citizens. Or perhaps those corporations that are more responsible survive better. Nevertheless, aquaculture has grown very rapidly and is occupying space that was formerly occupied by other sectors (HLPE 2014). There is no "free space" on the coast (Chapter 7). By definition, aquaculture is characterized by ownership of stock and, thereby, control of space on which the operation takes place. Hence, we are talking about a transformation that must include a reallocation of ocean and coastal commons (Chapter 5) and the granting of new spatial rights. Lam and Pauly (2010) pointed out that "rights" to fish and other coastal resources ought to imply ethical responsibilities of stewardship. They called for a "social contract for ethical fisheries that explicitly mandates collaborative governance and corporate responsibility" (Lam and Pauly 2010, p. 1). The time to press for a new social contract is when a major transformation is taking place and rights are being reallocated.

Conclusions

The chapter started with the idea that social and ecological systems are closely interconnected, and that integrated social–ecological systems are the logical unit of analysis. To perform such an analysis requires reconnecting natural science and social science perspectives. Human actions are responsible for many of the drivers that impact social–ecological systems, both in the area of global environmental change and globalization. However, there is a danger of thinking that the behavior of human systems can be equated with that of natural systems (Ommer et al. 2008). Human agency, including the role of individuals, leaders and institutions, is important and influences outcomes in major ways. This is part of the reason why sustainability science uses contextualized, place-based cases (Kates et al. 2001). Universal models do not serve understanding of local-level dynamics well.

In recognition of this, the Millennium Ecosystem Assessment included a volume on local and regional cases (Capistrano et al. 2005). It is the interplay between place-based cases and global trends that provides an understanding of the relationship between ecosystem services and human well-being at all levels (MA 2005a). The tools needed for such an analysis include the use of the concepts of scale and level (Cash et al. 2006), a vocabulary of interplay of institutions at different levels (Young 2002; Young et al. 2008), and the question of dealing with marine ecosystem dynamics across scales (Galaz et al. 2008). The examples in this chapter draw particular attention to scale issues, making the point that governance occurs at multiple levels, although not all levels are necessarily important in a given situation. The shrimp aquaculture example shows the interplay between global trends and local-level cases. The example of Poverty Reduction Strategy programs in the West Africa region show that a major problem in implementing decentralization is related to power relationships at the local level.

All levels are relevant and important, and the choice of scale or level is politically significant, as it may privilege one perspective over another (Reid et al. 2006), but there is no one "correct" perspective in a social–ecological system. A fishing community may focus on livelihoods, regional managers may focus on user-group conflicts, and the central government may focus on export earnings from shrimp aquaculture. The perspective depends on the interest of the observer, and it cannot be said that any one perspective is inherently superior to another. A social–ecological system cannot be captured using a single perspective; it can be best understood by the use of a multiplicity of perspectives.

The notion of drivers of change is one of the key ideas to deal with the dynamics of marine social–ecological systems and processes of change. The seeds of change are often not within the fishery but originate from outside the system, through market processes and policies at various levels. In such cases as the lake-and-manager systems in Wisconsin (Carpenter et al. 1999) and globalization of the shrimp trade (Adger et al. 2005) and salmon trade (Robards and Greenberg 2007), the analysis of drivers reveals that investigation of the social subsystem or the ecological subsystem alone would give an incomplete understanding of the behavior of the system as a whole. The social–ecological system has to be the unit of analysis, because it is not decomposable (Gallopin 2006).

Whereas the old-school fishery manager could carry out his/her trade by doing little more than stock analysis, the contemporary manager needs to look much farther afield to govern the marine social–ecological system, including such factors as the incidence of HIV/AIDS among fisherfolk. Part of the transition from conventional fishery management to social–ecological system management is the changing role of the manager to think in terms of drivers and globalization impacts. An interdisciplinary science of resource management that reconnects natural science and social science serves to maintain the productive capacity and resilience of the linked social–ecological system, including the well-being of fishers and communities. The next chapter expands on the resilience theme and its significance for marine and coastal resources.

4

RESILIENCE

HEALTH OF SOCIAL–ECOLOGICAL SYSTEMS

Introduction

Many decades ago, Aldo Leopold (1949 [1966]) proposed notions of environmental stewardship (which he called *land ethic*), productive use of ecosystems (*land*) and ecosystem renewal. He argued for a functional ecological norm for conservation that could be achieved when human use of land did not negatively affect ecosystem functions. Leopold's key perspectives are reflected in resilience thinking. His seminal concept of *land health* (and we might add water health) is a triangulation of stewardship, productive use and self-renewal. It can be reinterpreted through a resilience lens as the health of social–ecological systems (Berkes et al. 2012). This is the subject of Chapter 4.

Resilience concepts have already appeared in the preceding chapters in the context of changing paradigms, redefining management, and social–ecological systems. They appear in many of the forthcoming chapters as well, as resilience is one of the cornerstones of the arguments in this volume. Resilience thinking originates from systems approaches and complexity and is closely related to adaptive management as a way of dealing with uncertainty (Gunderson and Holling 2002; Norberg and Cumming 2008). This chapter starts by covering some of the basic concepts of resilience, followed by discussions of three areas of application: how resilience deals with social–ecological systems; the ability to help analyze change; and the exploration of policy options for uncertainty and change. Next, the chapter discusses assessing resilience and building resilience, followed by conclusions.

There are competing notions of resilience and many definitions. The Holling notion of *resilience* is the capacity of a system to absorb disturbance and reorganize while undergoing change, so as to still retain essentially the same function, structure, identity and feedbacks (Walker et al. 2004). There are other concepts of resilience, including one originally from the psychology of development that focuses on the ability of individuals to recover from adversity. It is used, among other areas, in community development and disaster research and shows many complementarities with Holling resilience (Berkes and Ross 2013). There is also a second resilience concept in ecology that focuses on bouncing back to a reference state after a disturbance. This definition is less useful for our purposes in discussions of resource management, as it presupposes an equilibrium state. In reality, there often is no such fixed reference state to bounce back to, as the reference state itself is subject to uncertainty.

Resilience started as an ecological concept, based on Holling's observations of the dynamics of the boreal forest ecosystem, its uncertainties and its renewal cycles. Recognizing that ecosystems often exhibit multiple states, Holling (1973) sought to characterize the capacity of a system to maintain itself in the face of disturbance. Resilience theory envisions ecosystems as constantly changing and focuses on renewal and reorganization processes rather than on stable states. It focuses on scale, nonlinear effects and thresholds. In its broader context, resilience is about managing ecosystems and people together, under the assumptions that there is no balance of nature but multi-equilibrium, complex, unpredictable social–ecological systems subject to continuous change, cycles, renewal and threshold effects (Berkes and Folke 1998; Berkes et al. 2003).

Resilience theory recognizes the nested character of social–ecological systems and the challenge of connectivity across levels (Gunderson and Holling 2002; Chapin et al. 2009). Through its conceptualization of nested levels and cross-scale interactions, the resilience approach helps analyze the effects of drivers originating at various levels, including the interplay among levels of governance. It can, therefore, generate insights regarding policies for resilience at appropriate levels (Brondizio et al. 2009).

Resilience has an interesting history of starting as an ecological idea and proliferating across disciplines and policy arenas concerned with crisis management, from pandemics to terrorism, and from financial (de)regulation to development economics. Resilience theory is being used (and overused) so extensively that, according to some critics, it is threatening to become "a pervasive idiom of global governance" (Walker and Cooper 2011, p. 144). It is probably best not to overextend the theory, and to take care to use resilience within its own limitations. In this volume, we confine ourselves to resilience as related to social–ecological systems in marine and coastal resource management.

When Holling wrote the seminal 1973 paper on resilience, he sought to define a complex notion that could account for the ability of an ecosystem to remain cohesive, even while undergoing perturbation. He sought to develop a theory of dynamic ecosystems that could deal with driving variables and change and that did not have deterministic outcomes, such as bouncing back to a predetermined equilibrium. The consideration of social variables gradually entered resilience thinking through the 1990s, and scholars started using social–ecological systems as the main unit of analysis (Berkes and Folke 1998). Thus, the inclusion of social science into resilience is relatively recent, and social–ecological resilience has not fully dealt with social science concepts such as power and agency (Brown and Westaway 2011).

The idea of alternative stable states is a key concept of resilience thinking. Many social–ecological systems have distinct, alternative sets of self-organized and self-stabilizing processes and structures recognized as *states* (Holling 1973). These states tend to be dynamic, responding to disturbances and changing conditions. As long as the system retains essentially the same function, structure, identity and feedbacks, it stays in one state, sometimes depicted as a ball moving around but remaining in the same cup (Gunderson and Holling 2002). However, in some cases, when conditions change too much (when the system no longer retains the same function, structure, identity and feedbacks), the ball can cross thresholds to an alternative state, depicted as a ball skipping the threshold of the first cup into a second cup. The recognition of periodic shifts in marine ecosystems did not start with the resilience idea; they have been known for some time, as in the decadal cycles of the North Sea, and the El Niño events of the South Pacific.

Holling developed the notion of an adaptive cycle, initially modelled on boreal forests, his area of expertise. In these forests, there is no end point or climax, as some classical ecologists assumed there was. Rather, renewal and regeneration of the ecosystem rely on a perturbation, often a fire event. The adaptive cycle, Holling argued, was characterized by four stages: (1) a rapid successional growth phase, followed by (2) a slow conservation phase in which the ecosystem (or forest) matures. These two phases are well known in classical ecology. The innovation of the Holling adaptive cycle was the contention that the mature ecosystem eventually disintegrates, called the (3) release phase, followed by (4) a spontaneous reorganization phase that leads to a new growth phase, and the cycle starts all over again. Timing is important in going from one phase to the other. These *windows of opportunity* also provide pathways to innovation and adaptation for the next cycle. Hence, each adaptive cycle is somewhat different within a given state. However, if the cycle spirals out of that state, it goes into a different state, with a different function, structure, identity and feedbacks (Walker et al. 2004).

The notion of *panarchy* refers to nested adaptive cycles. It extends the adaptive cycle idea in space and time and provides a way of thinking about different scales and levels. With panarchy, Holling and colleagues are arguing that all social–ecological system dynamics can be approached heuristically as iterations of an adaptive cycle with four distinct phases, and that a nested set of adaptive cycles may be used to represent nested systems, from large and slow ones to small and fast ones (Gunderson and Holling 2002). Extending the use of the panarchy idea to all social–ecological systems has been criticized by some social scientists (Walker and Cooper 2011).

Figure 4.1 shows a panarchy of three reclining figure eights representing the adaptive cycle, the white areas indicating growth and conservation phases, and the grey areas indicating release and reorganization phases. The adaptive cycle at the top may represent a large marine ecosystem, for example the Mediterranean, with a coastal economy dominated by tourism, shipping and fisheries and some resource-dependent communities. Social–ecological processes here tend to be slow: major economic changes and adoption of pollution control and fishing regulations system-wide may take decades. By contrast, the adaptive cycle at the bottom represents a small system, say a small bay in one of the Mediterranean

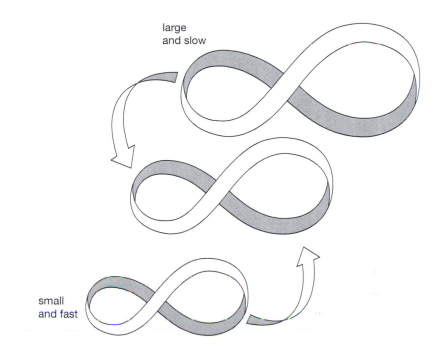

FIGURE 4.1 A panarchy consisting of a nested set of three adaptive cycles

countries, where social–ecological system processes may be much faster: the accidental release of untreated sewage from the local town may well end the tourism season for the year.

The panarchy concept provides a way to deal with interactions across levels and thresholds through system feedbacks. Two arrows in Figure 4.1 indicate two of the important interactions. The downward arrow (termed *remember*) indicates a stabilizing function, drawing from the accumulated experience of the higher level. The upward arrow (termed *revolt*) indicates a situation in which fast and small events overwhelm slow and large ones. There may be a series of revolt feedbacks in a system with multiple nested adaptive cycles, in which an action or event at the lowest level may *cascade* in a series of steps all the way up to the highest (Scheffer et al. 2005; Kinzig et al. 2006).

The levels in Figure 4.1 are conceptually distinct, and different principles and considerations may apply to each. In accordance with complex adaptive systems thinking (Anderson 1972), there are both similarities and differences among the levels. Some of the same principles may apply to building resilience at the local level as at the national level, but other factors and principles also come into play at each level.

Turning to the applications, the next section will touch upon three areas. First, resilience deals with coupled human–environment systems and contributes to an understanding of resource use systems by avoiding the artificial disciplinary divide between study of people and study of the environment. Second, resilience puts the emphasis on the ability to deal with change. It allows for the multiple ways in which a response may occur, including the ability of the system to buffer or absorb the disturbance, or to learn from it and to adapt to it, and to reorganize following an impact. These processes are often occurring simultaneously, across scale, in subsystems nested in larger subsystems, the panarchy (Holling 2001; Gunderson and Holling 2002). Third, resilience is forward-looking, which helps explore policy options for dealing with uncertainty and change. It is a way for thinking about policies for the future, an important consideration in a world characterized by unprecedented environmental change (Chapin et al. 2009; O'Brien et al. 2009). We deal with each in turn.

Social–Ecological Systems and Resilience

Some of the best illustrations of closely coupled social–ecological systems come from traditional societies. For example, *padu* systems in southern India provide rules of conduct for caste-specific, gear-specific and species-specific coastal and lagoon fisheries. They randomize fishing success, assigning fishing sites to members by lottery. This ensures that everyone gets a chance to fish the best bag-net sites (Lobe and Berkes 2004). These systems seem to be resilient, because they have persisted over time, despite increases in fisher numbers and declines in catch per unit effort (Coulthard 2008). *Padu* systems are important for managing resources as well as people: they help reduce conflict and provide social identity for members of the fishing caste. *Padu* rules are flexible: local observations of environmental change can be used to make adjustments to deal with siltation and may involve periodic reorganization of fishing sites (Lobe and Berkes 2004). At the same time, *padu* itself is based on an institution (the Indian caste system) that has persisted despite the inequitable social outcomes that it leads to and despite national laws against it—thus illustrating that resilience is not always positive.

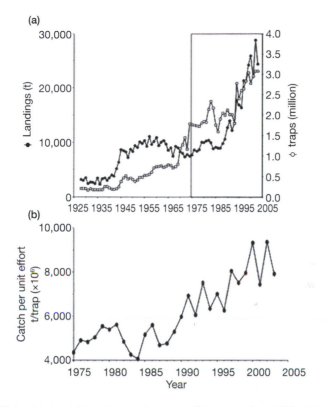

(a)

(b)

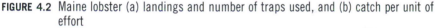

FIGURE 4.2 Maine lobster (a) landings and number of traps used, and (b) catch per unit of
effort

Source: Steneck et al. 2011. Reprinted with permission from Wiley

One intriguing story of interconnected social–ecological systems
concerns the Gulf of Maine, where a number of factors have come together
to result in a highly successful lobster fishery. In contrast to declining
stocks in many parts of the world, the Maine lobster fishery is more
successful than ever in its history. Even though the number of lobster
traps has increased more than tenfold since the 1930s, the catch per unit
of effort (an indicator of abundance) has also increased since the 1980s
(Figure 4.2).

However, the Gulf resembles a shellfish farm. Predators of lobster—
large bottom-feeding groundfish such as cod—are locally extinct, or nearly
so. Fishers feed the lobsters with herring bait and have devised management methods to maximize the number of large reproductive individuals
by placing them under permanent protection (Box 4.1).

BOX 4.1 THE GULF OF MAINE AS A LOBSTER POND: MONOCULTURES AND RESILIENCE

The commercial fishery of the Gulf of Maine relies very heavily on lobsters; in fact, some 80–90 percent of the value of the entire Gulf comes from this one species, *Homarus americanus*. It was not always like this. In the late 1800s, cod was the most valuable fishery. Archival photos show that extremely large codfish were captured. During the 1930s, the fishery developed the ability to target spawning aggregations of coastal cod and haddock; by 1949, these stocks were declared depleted by the State Government of Maine (Steneck et al. 2011). Oral history from retired captains indicates that these were distinct stocks of cod and haddock, many of them identified by name and location by the fishers (Ames et al. 2000). The harvest of more distant stocks of cod continued from the 1950s to the 1970s, and new fisheries for species such as monkfish, squid and sea urchins developed, increasing the diversity of the fishery for a few years.

By the 2000s, however, the Gulf of Maine had become "a highly simplified and domesticated ecosystem similar to many agricultural and aquacultural systems" (Steneck et al. 2011, p. 906). In many respects, the Maine lobster fishery does not look like a wild fishery, but shares many of the characteristics of aquaculture: control of predators (groundfish have disappeared); provision of food (herring, the second most abundant species in the Gulf, is used for bait in lobster traps); and a greatly simplified food web. The population density of lobsters at 20 m and less is 1–2 lobsters per square meter over hundreds of kilometers of coastline, higher than anywhere else in the world (Steneck et al. 2011). In some places, lobster traps are set so close together that the floats of the traps look like mooring buoys in a small-craft harbor.

The success of the Maine lobster fishery is in a major way due to effective management, partly designed and largely enforced by lobster fishers themselves. By law, fishers return undersized lobsters and egg-bearing individuals to the sea. But perhaps even more important, they have developed a technique called the v-notch, whereby "berried" (egg-bearing) lobsters are marked with a "v" cut into the tail. This marks these individuals as proven reproductive stock, and such v-notched lobsters cannot be landed or sold even when they are not carrying eggs. As well, fishers have developed their own rules of conduct, including territoriality in some areas (Acheson 2003). By all conventional resource management measures, this is a very successful fishery. But is it resilient and sustainable?

PHOTO 4.1 High lobster population densities in the Gulf of Maine: lobster traps are set so close together in places that the floats of the traps can be mistaken for mooring buoys in a small-craft harbor

Source: F. Berkes

However, from a resilience perspective, the Maine lobster fishery is notable as a "gilded trap," one in which the current state delivers lucrative short-term economic returns, but at increasing risk of resilience loss (Steneck et al. 2011). The problem is that, as with monocultures everywhere, the unnaturally high density of lobsters in the Gulf of Maine increases their susceptibility to disease. There is no disease in the Gulf (as of 2014). But only about 200 km south of the area, in eastern Long Island Sound, shell disease—lethal to some three-quarters of lobsters— was recorded in the unusually warm summer of 1998. Hence, Steneck et al. (2011) surmise that similar events can occur in the Gulf, as seawater temperatures continue to rise.

Some of the fishers themselves see the risk, but few want to return to the original stable state, a fishery that was ecologically and economically diverse, with an abundance of cod and other groundfish predators in the system. Many fishers carry high debt loads and see themselves as stuck in the current stable state, characterized by high profitability but lacking the economic and biological diversity required for long-term sustainability. Some fishers, in fact, seem to be ready for a system transformation—out of the fishery and into a recreation and tourism economy in which the Gulf becomes a playground. Some of these fishers are investing in guesthouses and other tourist amenities, toward an economy in which commercial fishery is perhaps not a major player.

Change, Drivers, Thresholds and Uncertainty

Resilience thinking provides an entry point for the study of uncertainty and change, including nonlinear effects and thresholds. Resilience is suitable for addressing the challenges of rapid change because it recognizes change as a central characteristic of social–ecological systems; because it considers drivers and their possible nonlinear effects in relation to thresholds; and because it has policy-relevant implications with respect to adaptive and transformative capacity. Many resilience applications regarding change are common sense and follow from the basic definition of the concept. For example, in the 2004 Asian tsunami, coastal devastation in Sri Lanka, Thailand and some other countries was explained in part as related to loss of mangroves and their buffering capacity along the coast (Adger et al. 2005). Following this line of thinking, the resilience approach has also made it possible to link tsunami devastation to coastal vegetation change for the expansion of shrimp aquaculture for global markets (Chapter 3), and the increasing vulnerability of coastal populations to cyclones and storm surges partly as a result of this globalization of shrimp.

Drivers may be related to local changes or may originate at different scales from the social–ecological system under consideration, as in the mangrove example. Extreme weather events, introduced species and "roving bandits," moving rapidly and targeting local stocks (Berkes et al. 2006), can all cause unexpected, abrupt changes in the local system. However, perhaps more common in coastal social–ecological systems, environmental and economic forces originating at a higher level may have major local impacts. To use two examples from Chapter 3, the expansion of aquaculture salmon production has devastated the local fishery in Bristol Bay, Alaska, based on wild salmon production (Robards and Greenberg 2007). The strong international market demand for large shrimp has led to the displacement of capture fisheries in Chilika Lagoon, India, by the high-value tiger shrimp aquaculture industry, and the loss of many livelihoods (Nayak and Berkes 2011).

What these examples have in common is that they involve a perturbation or change that leads to a nonlinear response, a response that is out of proportion to the size of the perturbation. Nonlinear responses are characterized by *threshold effects*, which are breakpoints or abrupt changes (Lyytimäki and Hildén 2007). Threshold is the point of shift from one stable state to another. In resilience terminology, such a flip is called a *regime shift*, as the nature of feedbacks in the system changes, resulting in a change of trajectory of the system itself (Walker and Meyers 2004).

Threshold effects are pervasive in both biophysical systems (e.g., the breaching of a seawall, for instance, in the Netherlands) and social systems (e.g., a relatively small perturbation in real estate markets leading to a global economic crisis). The relationships between drivers, nonlinear effects and thresholds are complex and subject to uncertainty. Most of the literature deals with effects after the fact and tends to focus on the ecological side of social–ecological systems. The large literature on resilience and thresholds deals mostly with biophysical systems, only a few with fully integrated social–ecological systems (Walker and Meyers 2004).

Box 4.2 tells the story of the Newfoundland cod fishery and explains that the collapse may be considered a shift in alternative stable states, from a groundfish-dominated ecosystem to one dominated by crustaceans. We can speculate on some of the elements of the failure of conventional management in the cod collapse. First is the assumption of control, even though the social–ecological system of the area had been neither predictable nor controllable. The social subsystem had been subject to drivers such as international markets and the 1982 Law of the Sea; the ecological subsystem had been subject to drivers such as climate change. Fishing technology had changed, and fishing pressure had increased over several decades.

Second, reductionistic science may in part be at fault. Ames et al. (2000) argued that conventional management models that approach overfishing with a single variable (fishing mortality), at a single spatial scale (range of the stock), and at a single temporal scale (one year), are not likely to work. This is because such models are omitting multiple-scale factors and complexity, such as the presence of multiple discrete

BOX 4.2 THE CANADIAN ATLANTIC COD FISHERY

Often known as the Newfoundland cod fishery in reference to the dominant stock, the Canadian Atlantic cod fishery, once one of the largest fisheries in the world, collapsed in 1992, forcing the closure of the fishery. It has not recovered, even though the closure has been maintained, except for some local use and sampling for monitoring. The case offers an illustration of the failures of conventional management and application of some concepts used in resilience analysis (Charles 2007). MA (2005a) uses the Newfoundland cod case as an example of nonlinear response and threshold effects, and the fact that depleted stocks may take many years to recover, or not recover at all (see Figure 1.2).

Until the late 1950s, the Newfoundland cod were caught by small-scale inshore fishers and migratory seasonal fleets from Europe. In the late 1950s, offshore trawlers began exploiting deeper waters, and catches increased sharply with the entry of offshore fleets into the fishery in the 1960s. Harvests reached a peak in the late 1960s, leading to internationally agreed quotas in the early 1970s. Despite quota management, however, catches declined sharply in the 1970s, followed by Canada's unilateral declaration of a 200-mile Exclusive Fishing Zone in 1977, ahead of the 1982 UN agreement on the Law of the Sea. This measure initially halted the decline, and the fishery seemed to be recovering in the late 1980s. Even though it was under a national quota system, using the best of conventional resource management, the fishery collapsed in 1992 (Walters 2007). What actually did happen to the fishery and why it has not recovered have been hotly debated ever since.

Regarding linearity and threshold effects, the verdict is fairly clear. In the 1960s, the sharp increases in harvest were in fact proportional to the increasing fishing effort. However, the sharp declines in the 1970s and the final collapse look like nonlinear effects. The prevailing level of fishing effort exceeded the threshold level of some controlling variable, resulting in stock collapse. Resilience theory would predict a regime shift from one stable state to another, and this is in fact what we find. Cod has collapsed, and the stable state characterized by groundfish has flipped into a different stable state. The new state is characterized by an invertebrate fauna of crab, shrimp and lobsters. These have increased, presumably because the predation pressure on them by the previously dominant groundfish has been lifted.

The aggregate value of the catch in Atlantic Canada, in fact, has not declined since the cod collapse. The increased value from the invertebrates has made up for the loss of groundfish—the real tragedy is a social one. The inshore groundfish fishers are the losers in this transformation, because they do not have the capital to enter the offshore, deep-water fisheries for valuable invertebrates. They do have access to lobster and, to some extent, crab, and these maintain the inshore fishery (Wiber et al. 2009). Both alternative states (groundfish vs. bottom invertebrates) are stable in the sense that small perturbations cannot flip them. Now that the invertebrates dominate, the system is resilient and will not easily flip back to a cod-dominated state.

PHOTO 4.2 Drastic reductions in cod and other groundfish in the Canadian Maritime provinces have left small-scale fishers largely dependent on lobsters and reduced their livelihood resilience. Port Mouton Bay, Nova Scotia

Source: F. Berkes

stocks. Third, conventional management was ignoring knowledge and observations that do not seem to fit the model, thus throwing out fisher knowledge and other useful information on trends (Chantraine 1993). This can have serious consequences. Walters (2007, p. 306) has commented that the cod collapse can be attributed "more or less directly to misinterpretation of inadequate monitoring data on trends in stock size."

The recognition of the pervasiveness of nonlinear responses and threshold effects is part of the revolution in ecology. The notions of stability and other positivistic assumptions that have guided ecosystem management for almost a century have given way to the idea of non-equilibrium systems, multiple steady states and surprises, necessitating management for resilience (Scheffer and Carpenter 2003). But further, many of the elements of uncertainty and surprise are social, economic and political, necessitating that resilience theory fully develop and elaborate the social subsystem of the social–ecological system (Berkes et al. 2003; O'Brien et al. 2009). This point can be expanded with regard to resource management policies.

Policy Options, Learning, Adaptation and Transformation

Resilience is forward looking and policy relevant regarding such areas as dealing with uncertainty and strengthening adaptive capacity. It can inform the policy process, but does not automatically plug into decision-making. There are often normative dimensions that include value judgments about priorities. "Whose resilience?" (Robards and Greenberg 2007) is often a pertinent question. The resilience of the social–ecological system in Bristol Bay has declined, whereas the resilience of the globalized system of salmon production and consumption has presumably gone up. When we enter the policy realm, it often becomes necessary to specify which social–ecological system is the focus, and ask the question, "resilience of what to what?" (Carpenter et al. 2001). Value judgments are involved in asking when it is desirable to focus on strengthening the adaptive capacity of a social–ecological system, and when it is appropriate to plan for transformative change.

Adaptive capacity is not the same as adaptation. Many resource management systems and societies may be well adapted to their ecosystems. Yet they may have little internal capacity to adapt to new kinds of global environmental change, stress or surprise (Folke et al. 2005). It has been suggested that *adaptive capacity* is in effect the capacity of actors in a system to influence resilience (Folke et al. 2010). It is possible to build adaptive capacity by increasing the ability of social systems (including institutions) to learn and adapt in response to change. In conventional educational theories, learning is about individuals, but, in resource management, learning theory is being extended to organizations and institutions (Pahl-Wostl 2009; Armitage and Plummer 2010).

Such *social learning* is a crucial element in the dynamics of participatory management (Armitage et al. 2007), adaptive governance (Folke et al. 2005) and interactive governance (Kooiman et al. 2005; Jentoft 2007). For the purposes of living with uncertainty, key issues include institutional learning that emerges out of society's response to previous crises, and the institutions and people that provide *social memory*

(McIntosh 2000). In many indigenous and traditional societies, the elders are the holders of social memory; in urban and industrial societies, this role is much less clear.

How does social learning work? Armitage and Plummer (2010) found that meaningful participation is key for social learning—but not just any kind of participation. The kind of participation needed is captured by the term *deliberation*: a process in which people confer, exchange views, debate the evidence and negotiate (Stern 2005). Even though the concepts of participation and deliberation cover some of the same ground, they are clearly distinct. A participatory process may or may not be deliberative. Participation without deliberation is static. Deliberation makes participation more conducive to learning, because it allows for the full consideration of stakeholder positions, and knowledge elaboration. Robinson and Berkes (2011) suggested that meaningful multilevel participation to increase adaptive capacity should have three features: deliberation, inclusivity of actors at multiple levels, and linkages and networks of actors and institutions connecting the various levels of governance.

For management agencies, learning in the resilience sense refers to social and institutional learning, as in adaptive management (Walters 1986; Lee 1993). This involves the development of flexible institutional and organizational arrangements to encourage reflection and innovation. Adaptive management is learning-by-doing; each new cycle of learning reflects on the results of the previous one and innovates in an attempt to deal with uncertainty. Hence, institutional learning is key to the adaptive management process, ideally one of systematic experimentation by trying different management policies and monitoring the results of these experiments. Without social and institutional learning, adaptive management cannot move forward and deal with uncertainty.

Building adaptive capacity can use the tools of adaptive management, preferably using a model of learning that accounts for the social context (conflict, power imbalances), pluralism, social memory and trust building (Armitage et al. 2009). In some cases, however, it may be deemed necessary to transform a social–ecological system into a different state, rather than perpetuating it (Folke et al. 2010; Wilson 2012). Such transformations or transformability have been defined in the resilience literature as "the capacity to create untried beginnings from which to evolve a new way of living" (Walker et al. 2004, p. 7). Much of the resilience literature seems to be discussing transformations at the global level, from unsustainable trends to more sustainable, resilient economies and ways of living (Rockström et al. 2009). However, transformations also apply to coastal and marine social–ecological systems at various levels.

Assessing Resilience and Building Resilience

Resilience is a future-oriented state and, strictly speaking, it cannot be measured directly. Carpenter et al. (2005) have used the notion of surrogates of resilience, a proxy used to assess resilience in a social–ecological system. Surrogates are different from indicators, because they are forward looking, rather than measures of the current or the past state. Surrogates and other indirect ways of measuring resilience are important for resilience assessment. Resilience Alliance (2010) has developed an analytical framework to analyze case studies as integrated social–ecological systems, and to evaluate the resilience of particular components of the system to shocks and stresses (abrupt and gradual change). Box 4.3 provides an outline of this approach. The first step requires the description of the system to be analyzed; the second requires choosing an analytical tool. The third step queries sources of resilience for adaptive capacity. This process bears some resemblance to vulnerability analysis (Hovelsrud and Smit 2010), but the Resilience Alliance (2010) framework goes further by considering transformative capacity as an alternative to building adaptive capacity.

The framework is particularly useful for investigating possibilities of thresholds, alternative states and their consequences, and focuses on critical components and likely thresholds. For example, some recent literature has focused on the loss of multi-year sea ice in the Arctic Ocean as a potential threshold for change into an alternative state in the Arctic ecosystem as a whole (Arctic Council 2013). The Resilience Alliance (2010) framework is suitable to explore such specified resilience (resilience to loss of sea ice). However, too much focus on a particular specified resilience may result in overlooking the resilience of the system to shocks and stresses other than the loss of sea ice. Similarly, increasing resilience of particular components of a system to specific disturbances may cause the system to lose resilience to other kinds of disturbance (Folke et al. 2010).

BOX 4.3 RESILIENCE ALLIANCE (2010) RESILIENCE ASSESSMENT WORKBOOK FOR PRACTITIONERS

A resilience assessment attempts to generate systemic and anticipatory knowledge about a particular social–ecological system to inform decision-making. An assessment typically involves participatory workshops with stakeholders and technical experts.

The first step answers the question, resilience of what to what? It describes the specific scale and components of the social–ecological system being assessed (resilience of what or whom?), and the specific threats to that system and those components (resilience to what?). It considers drivers of change, disturbances and potential thresholds.

The second step involves the development of a conceptual model of the dynamics of the social–ecological system, with a focus on thresholds, feedbacks and alternative states. The conceptual model may take a variety of forms. The assessment may choose to use historical timelines of change, may represent the system as an adaptive cycle, or may develop a state and transition model. The emphasis is on characterizing the threshold(s) of concern and on exploring alternative states.

The third step attempts to identify sources of resilience in the social–ecological system, and the capacity of the system for adaptation and/or transformation. Different approaches and analytical tools may be used, such as analysis of institutions or governance systems, social network analysis, and evaluation of opportunities for social learning and experimentation.

Turning to the question of building resilience, the identification of the system to be targeted is a starting point, as in assessing resilience. For example, building livelihood resilience at the household level is similar to, but somewhat different from, building resilience at the level of a fishing community (Marschke and Berkes 2006). Resilience at a regional level is likely to be different still, and resilience at the level of the Earth system will no doubt bring in new considerations (Rockström et al. 2009). In keeping with the basics of complex adaptive systems, each level might have its own principles, as well as some shared principles (Norberg and Cumming 2008). Folke et al. (2003) formulated four factors or approaches for building resilience that might be applicable to many levels: learning to live with uncertainty, nurturing diversity, combining different kinds of knowledge, and creating opportunities for self-organization. We deal with each in turn.

Learning to live with uncertainty is a difficult and unsettling idea for many who have grown up with positivistic science that assumes that the world is predictable and controllable. That is why it is so difficult for the mass media and the public to understand that the number of sockeye salmon returning to the Fraser River is perhaps not predictable (Chapter 3). Some decades ago, the science of ecology abandoned the idea of predicting and controlling ecosystems. But further, in the contemporary world, we are confronting a horizon of critical future events, such as the impacts of greenhouse-gas accumulation, impacts we are unlikely to be able to predict or prevent. Living with uncertainty requires adapting by building resilience and increasing options and flexibility to respond to future unfamiliar changes.

In the case of infrequent but known perturbations, living with uncertainty requires building and retaining a social memory of past events. For example, traditional societies in the South Pacific seem to retain a memory of extreme events, such as major cyclones (hurricanes), with a frequency of once in 20 years (Lees and Bates 1990); however, according to research done in Indian Ocean fishing communities following the 2004 tsunami, the retention of the memory of a once-in-60-years event appears much less likely (Berkes 2007b). Retaining social and ecological memory is essential for the adaptive renewal cycle—and for learning from mistakes (Finlayson and McCay 1998). Increasing the capacity to learn from a crisis and expecting the unexpected are also important. "Expecting the unexpected" may seem like an oxymoron, but it means having tools and codes of conduct to put into action when an unexpected event happens (Berkes and Folke 2002).

Nurturing diversity for reorganization and renewal is based on the idea that diversity provides the seeds for new opportunities (novelty) in the renewal cycle. Diversity increases the options for coping with change, making the social–ecological system less vulnerable. Diversification is the universal strategy for reducing risks, from agriculture to stock markets. Diversification spreads the risk and increases options in the face of change (Turner et al. 2003).

All kinds of diversity, and not only biodiversity, are relevant to building resilience. Biodiversity is obviously essential for providing a variety of resources for livelihood portfolios of coastal communities, for other ecosystem services for human well-being (MA 2005a), and for the functioning of ecosystems. Social diversity, including diversity of cultures, and culture-specific knowledge of ecological practices are also important (Berkes et al. 2000). The range of economic opportunities available has emerged as a major policy objective for building resilient communities and regions (Amundsen 2012). Often overlooked in the social–ecological resilience literature, infrastructure such as roads, harbors and communication facilities also appears to be crucial for healthy social–ecological systems (Berkes and Ross 2013).

Combining different kinds of knowledge is important for problem solving, and it tends to increase the capacity to learn. Interdisciplinary approaches require borrowing concepts and skills from an eclectic mix of natural sciences, social sciences and humanities (Ommer et al. 2011). As well, there are many potential areas and ways in which traditional environmental knowledge can enrich or complement Western scientific knowledge. Collaboration and communication between these two kinds of knowledge have been documented in detail, for example, in Johannes's (1981) work on Micronesian fisheries.

Creatively combining different kinds of knowledge to coproduce new knowledge is also possible and can help address knowledge gaps. For example, the biology and ecology of the Greenland shark (*Somniosus microcephalus*) are poorly known. Because the species is deep living, Inuit knowledge of the shark is also very fragmentary. However, deliberations based on existing knowledge enticed the Inuit to pool together their knowledge and to produce an informed speculation about the feeding ecology of the species (Idrobo and Berkes 2012, Chapter 10).

Combining different kinds of knowledge may also lead to social learning that broadens the scope of the issue in hand. Much of the early work on climate change was based on global models. However, from the point of view of the Inuit, the results of these models meant little, because "average" temperature or precipitation changes were meaningless in daily life. Inuit climate knowledge involves tracking a large number of variables qualitatively (fuzzy logic—more in Chapter 11). The key climate change observations made by the Inuit were that the weather was more variable and less predictable, with more frequent extreme events (Krupnik and Jolly 2002; Berkes 2012b).

Self-organization is one of the hallmarks of complex adaptive systems (Levin 1999). Thus, creating opportunities for self-organization, as well as facilitating it, is an important strategy for resilience building. The resilience of a system is closely related to its capacity for self-organization, because adaptive cycles involve renewal and reorganization. Community-based management involving multilevel linkages is used for illustration here (fuller discussion of these three topics to come in later chapters).

In many kinds of resource use situation, local-level, informal institutions arise spontaneously and play a role in the management of shared resources or commons (Chapter 5). These institutions are important, because communities respond best to change through their own institutions. However, community-based management is a necessary but insufficient condition to deal with resource management in a multilevel world. The local level is often at the mercy of drivers originating at higher levels, as we have seen in several examples earlier. Therefore, local institutions need to work with government agencies and NGOs to deal with many drivers that originate from outside. Such linkages may be horizontal (at the same level) or vertical (across levels of organization). Networks consisting of these linkages also tend to be self-organized and may lead to learning-by-doing (Berkes 2007a). Resource management power and responsibility may be shared through networks and take the form of iterative, collaborative, feedback-based problem solving (Olsson et al. 2004b). Such combination of time-tested collaborative management gives adaptive co-management (Armitage et al. 2007).

A summary of these four strategies for enhancing resilience is given in Table 4.1. There are overlaps among these strategies, and many other strategies are also possible. For example, resilience literature from the psychology of development and mental health indicates that resilience enhancing at the community level would include building on existing community strengths in areas such as people–place connections, values and beliefs, social networks and leadership (Berkes and Ross 2013).

Conclusions

The Newfoundland cod and the Gulf of Maine examples, along with some of the other examples in this chapter, can be used to generate some lessons from resilience thinking. The main message is to treat social–ecological systems as complex adaptive systems, characterized by cycles and uncertainty, and social systems and ecosystems as coupled and co-evolving. Table 4.2 summarizes some of these lessons, but it should not

TABLE 4.1 **Strategies for enhancing resilience**

Strategy	Description
Learn to live with uncertainty	An education and communication challenge, living with uncertainty requires mindset change. It also requires increasing options and flexibility to respond to future changes, learning from experiences and past mistakes, and building a memory of past events
Foster diversity in all of its forms: biological, social, economic	Diversity provides seeds for new opportunities and maximizes options for dealing with change. A resilient social–ecological system relies on biodiversity for ecosystem services. It also needs social diversity for a range of knowledge, capabilities and skills, and a range of economic opportunities for livelihoods
Foster ways of combining different kinds of knowledge for social learning	Communities, government agencies and NGOs can combine their knowledge and learn from one another. By working together, they can coproduce knowledge to fill gaps, solve problems and deliberate about policy options that show promise
Increase capability for self-organization	Resilient systems self-organize at all levels. The local level is key, because of the tight coupling of stimulus and response. Linkages among levels are a necessary part of the self-organization, because both problems and solutions can originate at multiple levels

Source: Folke et al. 2003

be taken to be an exhaustive list. For example, one can add items about thresholds and alternative stable states. If the Gulf of Maine lobster fishery collapses, and a groundfish fishery is not an option, then the system may be transformed from one state (a heavily lobster-dominated fishery) into another (a recreational economy). In such a case, not only would the species or technology change, but also the economy of the region and the social/cultural makeup of former fishing communities, that is, the whole social–ecological system.

Production objectives reduce natural variability, eroding resilience and leaving systems vulnerable in the face of change (Holling and Meffe 1996). Hence, it is necessary to manage resources and environment for resilience (instead of production) by protecting diversity, working with natural variation and maintaining social and ecological memory to enable self-organization. Consistent with adaptive management, resilience thinking obliterates the distinction between science and management. It is open

TABLE 4.2 Learning from resilience: some lessons for the management of marine and coastal resources

Management goals should not be framed in terms of stability but rather resilience	Social–ecological systems are rarely stable. Rather, they are nonequilibrium systems or systems characterized by multiple stable states, as in the Newfoundland cod and Gulf of Maine examples. Hence, stability, simplification and control are not realistic goals. Instead, maintaining variation, diversity, ecosystem processes and renewal makes more sense
Management should aim to retain and restore critical types and ranges of natural and social variation and diversity	Natural variation includes species and genetic variation, habitats and ecosystems. Different practices and methods of fishing add to diversity, and the ability to switch species and gear. Also important are the different livelihood strategies developed by different groups of fishers
Accommodate change, allowing for innovation and adaptation through windows of opportunity	Resilience theory focuses on systems characterized by cycles and constant change. Innovation and adaptation in these systems require diversity as raw material and system memory as the source of renewal. Timing is important to initiate change; for example, policy change can often benefit from "windows of opportunity"
Emphasize the importance of responding with flexibility and keeping options open	First and foremost, resilience is about flexibility and keeping options open, yet many government agencies have set ways of responding to resource problems, a possible reason for the collapse of the Newfoundland cod fishery. Management options are needed for the lobster monoculture in the Gulf of Maine, which is vulnerable to disease
Eliminate the various dichotomies that characterize conventional resource management	Eliminate distinctions between (1) the social system and the natural system and focus on integrated social–ecological systems; (2) science and management, as in adaptive management; (3) user and decision-maker, as in participatory management; and (4) different kinds of knowledge
Create learning institutions to provide flexible, multilevel governance	Learning-by-doing is important, because there are no set recipes for management in the face of uncertainty. Adaptive co-management, interactive governance and adaptive governance are some of the terms that capture related ideas of flexible management based on learning and experimentation

to user participation in management, and the recognition and use of users' knowledge. Social and institutional learning, based on a wider range of knowledge, enables better decision-making (Berkes and Folke 1998). The building of institutions that have the capability to learn from mistakes and retain that memory (learning institutions) is a major strategy for resilience enhancing (Folke et al. 2005; Armitage et al. 2009).

Human agency, including the role of individuals, leaders and institutions, influences outcomes. This collective capacity to manage resilience determines whether thresholds can be successfully avoided (Folke et al. 2010). Issues around power and conflict are also important, as they explain the persistence of top-down management and shape the ways in which partnerships and collaboration may take place (Armitage et al. 2009). These considerations are part of the shifting perspectives on resource management and the abandonment of many of the assumptions of conventional management (Chapter 2).

Resilience offers a contemporary theory to update Leopold's (1949 [1966]) insights. Just as Leopold's land health dissolves the dichotomy between ecosystem health and human health, resilience thinking offers insights regarding the health of the integrated social–ecological system, a nested system of many levels. If shared resources are not healthy at the local level, they are probably not going to be healthy at the regional and global levels either. In the next chapter, we turn to the idea of commons, an interdisciplinary field that has been dealing with resources along with the rights and responsibilities of the people and institutions that have been using them.

5

CAN COMMONS BE MANAGED?

Every year EC [European Community] communicates new
regulations. I don't know why. Because we have been managing
our own lagoon [Thau Lagoon, south of France] for centuries.
Our own rules are the rules we follow.

(Fisheries Association representative,
speaking at workshop with Resilience Conference
participants, Sète, France, May 2014)

Introduction

Tropical marine ecologist Bob Johannes made a major contribution to
the study of commons by showing that coral reef and lagoon resources
were regulated by "words of the lagoon," what commons researchers would
call *rules-in-use*. These rules, locally made and socially enforced with
"words," included closed areas/seasons and critical habitat protection,
among others (Box 5.1). Johannes was astounded by the sophistication
of these rules and the traditional ecological knowledge that supported
them. His findings (Johannes 1978, 1981) were only part of a series of
observations from many areas and resources around the world that
challenged the conventional wisdom of the "tragedy of the commons."

According to the tragedy of the commons metaphor of Garrett Hardin
(1968), based on the hypothetical example of a medieval English grazing
commons, collectively owned resources, such as coastal and marine

---

BOX 5.1 "WORDS OF THE LAGOON" AS LOCAL RULES-IN-USE

Known for his contributions on coral reef ecosystems, Bob Johannes worked for a time in the Pacific island state of Palau and showed how marine tenure at the community level worked. Reef and lagoon resources were regulated by "words of the lagoon," what commons researchers would call rules-in-use, informal rules devised by the community and enforced by social means. His 1981 book, *Words of the Lagoon*, documented the tremendous depth of local and traditional knowledge that underpinned these rules and practices. He argued that many of the traditional restrictions were intended to conserve shellfish and fish: "almost every basic fisheries conservation measure devised in the West was in use in the tropical Pacific centuries ago" (Johannes 1978, p. 352).

These measures included closed fishing areas, closed seasons, allowing escapement, a ban on taking pre-reproductive individuals, restricting the number of fish traps that can be used, a ban on habitat disturbance, and a ban on seabird and turtle egg harvesting in certain areas. Johannes (1978) noted that not all measures were used in all areas, and those that were used on a given island were tailored for that particular area. His work in Palau was supplemented by his deep knowledge of reef and lagoon traditional knowledge and management systems across Micronesia and Polynesia (Johannes 1978) and the broader Asia–Pacific region (Ruddle and Johannes 1990).

He wrote about the historic demise of these knowledge and management systems under colonial export-oriented regimes, and how resource after resource and area after area were opened up, often by force, for colonial trade (Johannes 1978). Some 20 years later, his pessimistic conclusions were replaced by optimism, as many of these local management systems were revitalized under neotraditional reef and lagoon tenure systems (Johannes 2002), supplementing conventional science for fishery management (Johannes 1998b).

---

resources, inevitably face decline and depletion. If all users restrained themselves, the resource could be sustained. But, if you limited your use and your neighbors did not, the resource would still collapse, and you would have lost your share of the benefits. So the economically "rational" decision is to maximize your benefits. However, as other users are also rational decision-makers, everyone loses in the long run; hence the "tragedy." The earliest theories of the commons were formulated more than a decade before Hardin. Two fishery economists (Gordon 1954; Scott 1955) are usually credited with the first statements of the theory of the commons. Long before Hardin, fishery economists were already modeling the attraction of excess labor into fisheries, and the income dissipation and the resource depletion that often followed.

Commons (or common-pool resources) share two characteristics: *excludability* and *subtractability*, meaning that the control of access of potential users is difficult, and each user is capable of subtracting from the welfare of all other users. Thus, Ostrom et al. (1999, p. 278) defined *common-pool resources (commons)* as those "in which (i) exclusion of beneficiaries through physical and institutional means is especially costly, and (ii) exploitation by one user reduces resource availability for others." Advances in the notion of commons, along with the principles that could be used to solve (or avoid) the tragedy of the commons, and in particular her 1990 book, *Governing the Commons*, were the reasons that Elinor Ostrom became the 2009 Nobel Laureate in Economic Sciences.

Common-pool resources are ubiquitous. Many of the world's sustainability questions concern common-pool resources, and they need to deal with the excludability and subtractability problems that characterize these resources. Common-pool resources are not *divisible*, that is, not separable into commodities in space and time. Hence, privatization is often not an option. Rather, these resources are interrelated, and their users are interdependent, paralleling the interdependence of ecosystem components. Hence, using social–ecological systems as the unit of analysis (Chapter 3) for commons management helps deal with these interdependencies.

Managing common-pool resources calls for *collective action*, any action taken together by a group of people whose goal is to enhance their status and achieve a common objective (Olson 1965). In practice, this may require making operational decisions within a set of rules and enforcement of these agreed-upon-rules among the community of users, whether that "community" is a Japanese fishery co-operative association or the group of countries that have a coastline on the Mediterranean. Locally, a community of fishers may get together to manage their coastal fishery. Regionally, countries of the Baltic Sea basin may get together to reduce nutrient flows into their sea. Internationally, the countries of the world can get together to agree on a number of multilateral conventions and set up the Intergovernmental Platform on Biodiversity and Ecosystem Services (IPBES) to reduce the erosion of global biodiversity.

In the examples above, individual fishers cannot act alone to solve the problem, neither can individual Baltic states, nor one nation concerned with biodiversity loss. There has to be collective action. In some cases, some members of the "community" work toward the common objective, but others get the benefits without contributing to collective action. In the economic theory of public goods, someone who benefits from resources or services without paying for the cost of the benefit, or otherwise obtains the benefits without working for the public good, is known as a *free rider* (Olson 1965).

This chapter is about commons theory, community-based management institutions, and principles for collective action. The chapter concludes with the "roving bandits" case of a globalized tragedy of the commons. The chapter is closely linked to Chapter 6, as co-management is one of the applications of commons theory. Chapter 7 takes a broader view and considers the coastal zone as a whole, with its complex of interacting uses and users. Such complex commons usually comes under the rubric of coastal zone management. Even though principles of commons still apply and practices of co-management inform coastal zone management, additional tools and concepts come into play as well.

Property Rights: Ownership or Not?

Fishers often talk about "owning" their resources. For example, lobster fishers of the Gulf of Maine often refer to their fishing spots and their lobsters, as if they owned them (Acheson 2003). In reality, no one owns that lobster until it is caught. The fishing area itself is owned by the government, which has the jurisdiction to make and enforce rules. The harvesters have the skills and knowledge, boats and gear, and the licenses granted by the government. But they do not own the lobsters, nor do they own the fishing grounds.

However, participatory mapping of fishing grounds reveals an intricate knowledge of such things that only a community member would know, for example, the details of the coast and fishing banks, fish distributions by season, and spawning areas (St. Martin and Hall-Arber 2008). Such intimacy with the area and resources illustrates the commons notion of "ownership" based on community sharing and transmission of knowledge.

It is not just the ownership that one takes to the bank or loses in a divorce court; it is the ownership that leads one to protest abuses (such as oil and gas exploration on fishing grounds) and to claim compensation or privilege, and a seat at the table in management or conservation decision-making.

(McCay 2008, p. 20)

Multiple meanings of ownership create confusion in policy and practice. Commons scholars discuss ownership and property in terms of a *bundle of rights* and responsibilities that individuals or groups may hold in the use of a resource system. Property rights are not a simple yes/no dichotomy. Schlager and Ostrom (1992) defined a property rights schema ranging from authorized user, to claimant, to proprietor and to owner (Table 5.1). Owners are not the only resource users capable of making long-term investments in the improvement of a resource (Schlager and Ostrom 1992). Proprietors may also have incentives for similar long-term investments. Both proprietors and claimants may have expectations of future returns. Hence, they may partake in making resource use rules and, under some conditions, have incentives to act as the stewards of the resource. The nature of rights and length of tenure (relative to the renewal rate of the resource) affect incentives for stewardship (Costello and Kaffine 2008).

Also fundamentally important for understanding property rights in commons, scholars have focused on *property rights regimes*. Commons may be held in one of four basic property rights regimes. *Open access* is the absence of well-defined property rights. Access is free and open to all, the condition that is assumed in the tragedy of the commons, but in reality the medieval English grazing commons were not open to all (Scott 1955; Feeny et al. 1990). *Private property* refers to the situation in which an individual or corporation has the right to exclude others and to regulate the use of a resource. This is the "owner" in Table 5.1. *State property* or *state governance* means that rights to the resource are vested exclusively in government, which controls access and regulates use, typically top-down. In *common-property* regimes, the resource is held by an identifiable community of users who can exclude others and make rules to regulate their own use. These four regimes are ideal, analytical types. In practice,

TABLE 5.1 A conceptual schema for distinguishing among diverse bundles of rights that may be held by users of a resource system

	Owner	Proprietor	Claimant	Authorized user
Access and withdrawal	✗	✗	✗	✗
Management	✗	✗	✗	
Exclusion	✗	✗		
Alienation	✗			

Source: Schlager and Ostrom 1992

resources are usually held in combinations of property rights regimes, as in the case of co-management (Chapter 6).

The evidence accumulated over the last few decades indicates that three of these property rights regimes (private property, state property and common property) may, under various circumstances, lead to sustainable resource use. No particular regime is inherently superior to the others, but one may fit a particular situation better than the others. No one particular regime guarantees sustainability; there are successes and failures under all three regimes. Regarding the open-access regime, however, consensus is that long-term sustainability is not possible. Open-access conditions are a historical anomaly; they do not persist for long. In time, property rights become established, and authority is exercised over the resource, a process that may or may not involve the government—there often is commons governance without government (Kooiman et al. 2005). That said, however, even short periods of open-access conditions can lead to resource depletion, before rights can be established and protected.

Much fishery and coastal resource management in the world uses mixes of property regimes and use rights. For example, most aquaculture is managed as private property, but it is the state that normally leases aquaculture rights and enforces various government regulations. There are also cases where aquaculture is carried out by individual farmers, with rule-making by co-operatives and rules enforced by the government (Galappaththi and Berkes 2014). In the case of capture fisheries, many developed countries use quota management (e.g., ITQs) to privatize commons rights through the use of market-based approaches. In developing countries, ITQs are not often used, mainly because small-scale fisheries with many landing points and diffuse marketing links do not lend themselves to government quota management. As well, resources often have multiple values, and privatizing use rights runs the risk of damaging livelihoods of rural people (Chapter 9).

In both aquaculture and ITQ fisheries, there are many regulatory measures developed and enforced by governments, and they continue to be important. However, pure state-property regimes, in which the government makes and enforces *all* the rules and regulations, are rare. More common are governance partnerships: government regulations that use input from fisher organizations, with enforcement that is aided by community and market processes (Pinkerton 2009; Cochrane and Garcia 2009).

Similarly, pure common-property regimes, in which the community controls the commons and all fishers have equal rights and equal say, probably exist only in theory. It is the state that allows/empowers (or not) the community to control its fishing area. Most common-property arrangements depend on government recognition of local rights, as in Japan (Makino 2011) and elsewhere in Asia–Pacific (Johannes 2002). These fisheries may include simultaneous, multilayered sets of rights and authority, both communal and individual. Such mixed-regime fisheries may further come under increasing international market influence in the globalized world, with rapid exploitation through "roving bandits" to meet distant market demands (Berkes et al. 2006).

Figure 5.1 shows a hypothetical coastal zone in which several property rights regimes are found together in one area. Private aquaculture areas, leased from the government, share the coast with fishing spots and set-net sites controlled by communities. The coastal fishery within the territorial sea (12 miles) and the offshore fishery in the EEZ (to 200 miles) are under state property. Beyond the EEZ, there may be an international regime in force on the high seas, such as ICCAT, the International Commission for the Conservation of Atlantic Tunas. However, areas not enclosed by EEZs often have many of the characteristics of an open-access regime, with fishing fleets opportunistically targeting various stocks.

Further, resources may be effectively open access within the territorial sea and the EEZ, if the state is unable to make effective regulations or

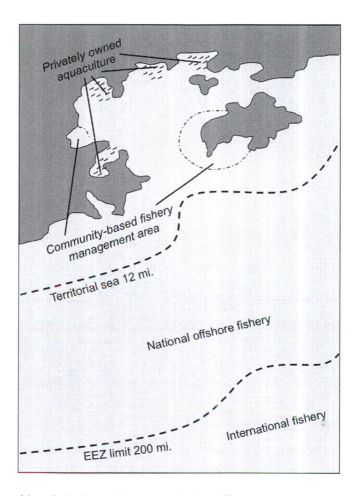

FIGURE 5.1 A hypothetical coastal commons showing different property rights regimes within the territorial sea (12 miles), the national offshore fishery (within 200 miles) and the international fishery beyond the 200-mile EEZ

enforce them. This is a common situation in many developing countries, and not all that uncommon in developed countries either. Even some apparently well-regulated fisheries can fail. A case in point is the Gulf of St. Lawrence snow crab fishery in Canada, where government and market institutions failed to prevent overfishing, whereas nonmarket institutions succeeded: economic behavior was co-ordinated by various mechanisms such as negotiation, horizontal (user-to-user) communication and co-management contracts (Loucks 2007).

PHOTO 5.1 Fishing spots and net sites controlled by communities: the pound net, *cerco flutante*, in the photo is in the community fishing area of Ponta Negra, Paraty, Brazil. *Cercos* have fixed sites and are owned by individuals in the community (Idrobo and Davidson-Hunt 2012). Sea tenure in the form of community fishing spots is found in many parts of the Brazil coast (Begossi 1995)

Source: F. Berkes

The tragedy of the commons analysis assumes that resource users are self-centered utility maximizers, unrestrained by community and social relations. This is simply not so (Ostrom 1990; Jentoft 2000). Even the most selfish and individualistic fishers respond to social pressures. The social environment tends to shape human behavior. Communities are not merely aggregations of individuals but networks of people guided by social values and norms (Crona and Bodin 2006). For example, the fishers of the eastern Caribbean, long known for their individualism, have longliners' information exchange and mutual assistance networks (McConney et al. 2007). Communication through networks is key to community-based resource management, but some groups have more incentives to conserve than do others (Crona and Bodin 2006). Locally crafted rules help express fishers' social values and norms, for example, the principle of fairness in making a livelihood (Berkes 1986), and create control mechanisms enforced socially, as Johannes observed decades ago (Box 5.1).

Bringing Decisions Close to Resource Users: Communities and Institutions

How do we bring the government closer to the governed, so that the people whose livelihoods and well-being are affected by decisions can have a say in those decisions? Effective user participation and problem solving at the lowest feasible level of organization is known as the *subsidiarity principle* (Kooiman 2003; O'Brien 2008). Advocated by Agenda 21 of the 1992 UNCED, the subsidiarity principle was incorporated into Article A of the Maastricht Treaty of 1992 establishing the European Community. It specifies that "decisions [should be] taken as closely as possible to the citizen" (McCay and Jentoft 1996).

The effectiveness of subsidiarity policies is highly suspect in some cases. As the quote at the top of the chapter indicates, some EC policies seem to be getting in the way of customary self-governance, such as the centuries-old *confrérie* (brotherhood) system in the French Mediterranean and the Catalan *cofradías* (Alegret 1996). However, by the 1990s, governance focus worldwide had shifted to the local level, with many developing countries undertaking decentralization reforms (Ribot 2002). In place of top-down management, principles of grassroots or bottom–up planning and management, such as public participation and co-management, became entrenched in various areas of environment and resources governance, in both developing and industrialized countries (Wilson et al. 2003; Borrini-Feyerabend et al. 2004; Brunner et al. 2005).

Some of these subsidiarity policies and devolution appeared to be, in effect, "top-down co-management" (Berkes 2010a) and may have been designed to serve the neoliberal agenda to privatize government services, rather than to facilitate local-level empowerment (Dressler et al. 2010). Nevertheless, the international interest in subsidiarity and devolution brought local-level governance and communities to the forefront. Commons approaches are often characterized by an interest in the community, emphasis on governance institutions, and a search for principles of effective collective action. First, we deal with communities and institutions, before we turn to the question of principles.

According to Singleton and Taylor (1992, p. 315), *community* involves a set of people with some shared beliefs and stable membership, who expect to interact in the future and whose relations are direct and over multiple issues. A sense of community is helped by trust, a history of social ties and a history of commons use, for example, of coasts and coastal resources (McCay 1998). The common-property element in resource use by a community is found in notions of social equity and the inalienability of use rights, not only historically but also (for example) in contemporary United States (McCay 2008).

Agrawal and Gibson (1999) consider that the literature on resource management and conservation frequently uses the concept of community, but rarely analyzes it. They find this strange, given the popularity of the concept and the large amounts of funding directed toward community-based conservation by international agencies. As pointed out with regard to subsidiarity and devolution, this interest is relatively recent. For a long time, scholars of social change considered that community was being replaced by other forms of social organization. Modernization theorists often regarded community as limiting and an impediment to "progress." Agrawal and Gibson (1999, p. 630) point out, "A strong correlation exists between those who view progress positively and community negatively."

In the 1950s and the 1960s, the state was often seen as the engine of modernization. As discussed in Chapter 2, top-down government decision-making in resource management was the norm for a long time. However, in the 1980s, critics from various fields (commons, international development, city planning and others) started to question top-down management and to analyze the disappointing performance of central governments (Chambers 1983; Manor 1999). As a consequence, more attention came to be directed at increasing user participation in decision-making, the sharing of management responsibilities through partnerships, as well as community-based resource management, trends that accelerated in the 1990s.

However, in implementing subsidiarity and user participation in decision-making, simplistic views of "community" have become a barrier to effective community-based management (Brown 2002; Berkes 2004). Agrawal and Gibson (1999) criticize what they call the conventional view of community as a small spatial unit, as a homogeneous social structure and as shared norms. They proceed to show that, in fact, none of these assumptions is correct. To move forward, they suggest a focus "on the multiple interests and actors within communities, on how these actors influence decision-making, and on the internal and external institutions that shape the decision-making process" (Agrawal and Gibson 1999, p. 629). To do so would effectively change the emphasis from "communities" to "institutions."

It is probably true in most cases that external institutions (for example, global market demands) shape the resource management behavior of resource users and communities. In effect, Agarwal and Gibson's critique shifts the focus from communities to institutions in seeking sustainability in the commons. However, it does not quite solve the problem: the focus on communities may be misplaced, but are commons institutions up to the challenge? *Institutional capacity building* entered the lexicon of management around the same time as community-based management (Berkes 2009a). It was useful in helping draw attention to institutions at the community level, as well as institutions at other levels, prompting some to question whether government capacity building may also be necessary, as "it takes two to tango" (Pomeroy and Berkes 1997).

Consistent with the economics literature, commons literature uses the term institutions to refer to rules-in-use, rather than to agencies (North 1990). Institutions are used to regulate the actions of humans in particular situations, such as harvesting fish. In its broadest sense, the term *institution* refers to the regularized rules, norms and strategies that people use in making decisions (Ostrom 1990). By contrast, *governance* involves the crafting of rules in an effort to improve incentives to do something, people's behavior, and outcomes over time, such as achieving sustainable resource use or establishing a protected area. Ostrom (1990, 2005) makes a distinction between rules that operate at three different levels: operational level, collective choice level and constitutional level.

Resource users are acting at the *operational level* in their day-to-day decisions about where, when and how to harvest resources. For example, a fisher may decide to follow the rules and not fish within the boundaries of an MPA, if he or she knows the rules defining the protected area and considers them legitimate (Pinkerton and John 2008). The operational level is important, especially with respect to how resource users may or may not follow rules, both internal and external. And their behavior is shaped by the next level of institution.

Collective choice level refers to the rules that affect the incentives that actors face at the operational level. Who is involved in making the rules at the collective choice level depends on the particular resource management context. If resource users themselves have the authority and capability to decide how the resource is to be governed, they may make the collective choice rules. They may also decide to modify the rules from time to time, discussing and deliberating on what may be needed, and making decisions about changing the rules as needed, a common practice in real life. Government agencies may make collective choice level rules, if resource users themselves are not able to make them.

Constitutional level rules are the ones that affect the structure of collective action. They include rules regarding who the legitimate resource users are (that is, members of the group using the commons), how they enter or exit the group, and which rules can be adopted or changed at the collective action level. For example, a fishing co-operative in most countries would typically have a charter or constitution that specifies membership rules and the mandate of the membership in terms of the kinds of rule they are permitted to make. Within the parameters specified by their constitution, co-op members make rules at the collective choice level, which in turn shapes the day-to-day decisions they make at the operational level.

Much of community-based resource management is about the collective choice level, in the sense that many communities of commons users operate like co-ops. Even though they are not formal co-ops, they make rules among their members, and these (often unwritten) rules are just as real as those of a chartered co-operative. Of course, communities differ greatly in their capabilities for collective action and rule-making. Some have highly complicated, formal rules (Takahashi et al. 2006); some have complex, enforceable but informal rules, with (Berkes 1986) or without (Lobe and Berkes 2004) government backing; and even apparently disorganized/unorganized communities have some kinds of rule (Trimble and Berkes 2013). The extent to which communities can make and enforce their own rules has a strong bearing on their ability to manage their resources.

Principles for Collective Action and Commons Use

Some management works, and some does not. It is, therefore, important to analyze conditions for success. In her 1990 book, *Governing the Commons*, Elinor Ostrom formulated eight principles that facilitated collective action for commons use. These principles were used to evaluate various resource systems, including forests, water and fisheries. Throughout the 1990s, other scholars also attempted to identify conditions for success. By the time Agrawal (2002, p. 65) reviewed this literature, the total number of factors that affect successful management of commons appeared to be greater than 30 and closer to 40. This is an unwieldy number and makes it rather difficult to research conditions for success.

Cox et al. (2010) went back to the original eight design principles and analyzed some 91 cases that implicitly or explicitly evaluated these principles. They found that the principles were well supported by the empirical data, some more strongly than others. However, Cox et al. (2010) also concluded that a reformulation by splitting of three of the principles (1, 2 and 4) into their component parts would be warranted, as these individual components often made important contributions to the outcome of cases. For example principle 4, regarding monitoring, was divided into principle 4A, regarding users monitoring one another's behavior, and principle 4B, regarding users monitoring the condition of the resource (Table 5.2).

It is unlikely that any single set of design principles could capture all the relevant variables of a particular case. Cox et al. (2010) recommend that the design principles be used with a probabilistic, rather than deterministic, interpretation. As well, it is questionable that the design principles may apply to systems at various levels. Young (2002) in particular has been critical of the use of principles derived at one level (e.g., community) to be applied at another (e.g., global level). A diagnostic process that deals with clusters of variables, as a medical doctor would, is a possible way to eliminate groups of variables to focus on the most important ones in a given case. Ostrom was moving in a diagnostic direction as well: "We need to recognize and understand the complexity to develop diagnostic methods to identify combinations of variables that affect the incentives and actions of actors under diverse governance systems" (Ostrom 2007, p. 15181).

The design principles are mainly about collective action and, therefore, deal mainly with internal, rather than external, factors. In the search for universal applicability, one of the major criticisms of the design principles has been that they omit external factors or forces, such as population growth, commons enclosures or global market influences. For example, Klooster (2000) pointed out that development and market forces can

TABLE 5.2 Modified Ostrom (1990) design principles for long-enduring commons institutions

Principle	Description
1A	User boundaries: clear boundaries between legitimate users and nonusers must be clearly defined
1B	Resource boundaries: clear boundaries are present that define a resource system and separate it from the larger biophysical environment
2A	Congruence with local conditions: appropriation and provision rules are congruent with local social and environmental conditions
2B	Appropriation and provision: the benefits obtained by users from a common-pool resource, as determined by appropriation rules, are proportional to the amount of inputs required in the form of labor, material or money, as determined by provision rules
3	Collective choice arrangements: most individuals affected by the operational rules can participate in modifying the operational rules
4A	Monitoring users: monitors who are accountable to the users monitor the appropriation and provision levels of the users
4B	Monitoring the resource: monitors who are accountable to the users monitor the condition of the resource
5	Graduated sanctions: appropriators who violate operational rules are likely to be assigned graduated sanctions (depending on the seriousness and the context of the offense) by other appropriators, by officials accountable to the appropriators, or by both
6	Conflict-resolution mechanisms: appropriators and their officials have rapid access to low-cost local arenas to resolve conflicts among appropriators or between appropriators and officials
7	Minimal recognition of rights to organize: the rights of appropriators to devise their own institutions are not challenged by external governmental authorities
8	Nested enterprises: appropriation, provision, monitoring, enforcement, conflict resolution and governance activities are organized in multiple layers of nested enterprises

Source: Cox et al. 2010

destabilize commons arrangements that used to work well when the community and resource were isolated. In an analysis of overfishing in small-scale coral reef fisheries in Papua New Guinea, Cinner and McClanahan (2006) found that communities in close proximity to markets tended to overfish the higher-value species, whereas those far from markets did not.

The "roving bandits" example in the next section provides a detailed look at the dynamics of external factors that pose challenges for commons management.

Roving Bandits: Globalized Tragedy of the Commons

The roving bandits example can be used to illustrate some of the issues and complications of commons problems in the globalized world. *Roving bandits* are highly mobile fishing enterprises that can move around the globe, exploiting resources in response to global market opportunities. Typically, they proceed by mining out a specific resource from one area and then moving on to the next, in a worldwide, marine version of the tragedy of the commons (Berkes et al. 2006). Depending on the fishery, the operation may consist of fishing boats working their way across a geographic region, or of local fishing and diving enterprises supplying roving buyers and/or processors. In some cases, fleets are only mobile within certain regions; the buyers may or may not be mobile, but the product certainly is.

The term roving bandit was coined by the economist Mancur Olson (2000), who argued that local governance created a vested interest in the maintenance of local resources for local harvesters (as in Box 5.1). However, the ability of mobile harvesters to move on to other areas and resources severed local feedback and the motive to conserve. Distant-water fleets and mobile traders for marine products often operate like roving bandits, because global markets do not generate stewardship incentives, the self-interest that arises from attachment to place, the *sense of place*. Harvesters have no incentive to save for tomorrow, if whatever they do not take will soon be taken by others.

The classical solutions to local commons problems operate largely through local institutions, but roving bandits at once create problems of geographic scale and timely response. Local marine tenure alone is insufficient to deal with roving bandits: the threat is local, regional and global. As well, solutions must address temporal as well as spatial scales, because the *speed* of market development often outstrips the ability of national or international institutions to deal with roving bandits. In the case of small or highly localized stocks, the resource may vanish even before the problem is detected.

In the case of widely distributed and relatively abundant species, serial depletion of local stocks, one after another, may be masked in the catch statistics by spatial shifts in exploitation, as in the case of sea urchins (Andrew et al. 2002). Local depletions could be detected if spatially explicit harvest data were available, but they are not. So the catch statistics in the FAO data for a particular country may mislead researchers, who may think that relatively stable harvest data for a given species over several years indicate sustainable catches, whereas, in reality, the numbers may be showing serial depletion of one area after another, with the data aggregated in the statistics.

The global sea urchin fishery provides an illustration of the dynamics of roving banditry by consideration of the historical context of the fishery and noting of the geographic expansion of harvests (Figure 5.2). Sea urchin is a valuable resource in Japan for sushi production. Commercial sea urchin harvests began in Korea, largely for export to Japanese markets, after Japan's own resources declined around 1960. After the depletion of resources in Korea, the coasts of Washington and Oregon States came under exploitation in 1971, followed by Baja California and California in 1972–3. Next in line (1975) was Chile, with its long coastline. Alaska and British Columbia came under exploitation in 1980, followed by Russia in 1982 and then the northwest Atlantic (Maine, New Brunswick and Nova Scotia) in 1987–9. With continuous expansion of the fishery to new regions, the global harvest peaked in about 1990, but declined after that, because no frontiers remained to be exploited (Berkes et al. 2006).

The sea urchin case illustrates that the geographic expansion of harvests by waves of exploitation around the globe may be accompanied by sequential depletion of stocks. This phenomenon was originally formulated as the *staples theory* by the economic historian Harold Innis (1930), and was termed *fishing-up sequence* by Regier and Loftus (1972) and *sequential exploitation* by Berkes (1985). The general phenomenon involves the exploitation of the resource from areas closest to markets first and then from distant grounds, and from the highest-valued species to the less valued. Geographic expansion masks local depletions, and species substitutions mask biodiversity loss, common characteristics of sequential exploitation.

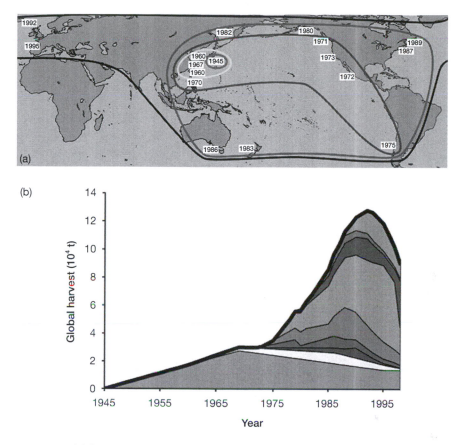

FIGURE 5.2 (a) Sequential exploitation of sea urchin resources: initiation year by location of major commercial fishery. (b) Global sea urchin harvests over time. Color-coded by region in chronological ascending order: Japan; Korea; Washington and Oregon; Baja, Mexico; California; Chile; NE Pacific (Alaska and British Columbia); Russia; NW Atlantic (Maine, Nova Scotia, New Brunswick)

Source: Berkes et al. 2006; data from: Andrew et al. 2002

Roving banditry has both ecological and social implications. Ecologically, the depletions of species that have major roles in the ecosystem may result in the simplification of food webs and loss of biodiversity. This may erode the resilience of marine ecosystems and increase their vulnerability to regime shifts (Hughes et al. 2003). Regarding social impacts, the quest for quick profits in roving banditry can destroy local resources, livelihoods and local economies, and the long-term resilience of social–ecological systems in resource-dependent areas.

Roving banditry poses serious challenges for conventional marine resource governance. Rapid market development and the resulting high-speed resource exploitation often overwhelm management institutions. National-level regulation is often too slow to respond, and international response is even slower. At the international level, CITES, the United Nations Convention on International Trade in Endangered Species, bans and controls trade in species placed on CITES Appendices I and II, respectively. However, the CITES process is too slow to protect against rapid depletions; the meetings at which members vote to place species in CITES appendices take place every two years.

Sea urchins are not the only marine resource that comes under roving banditry. Similar patterns have been observed with regard to several other species or types of resource: the live reef food-fish trade (Scales et al. 2006); the live aquarium-fish trade (LAFT) (Hughes et al. 2003; Shuman et al. 2004); seahorses, for mainly "medicinal" use (McPherson and Vincent 2004); sea cucumbers (Anderson et al. 2011); abalone (Prince 2010; Raemaekers et al. 2011); and others. The bleak outcome of the roving bandit phenomenon repeats itself with many species in many places. However, there is some evidence of learning from experience in the case of the live reef-fish trade (LRFT) and the LAFT.

The LRFT supplies luxury seafood restaurants, mainly in Hong Kong (Scales et al. 2006). It started around Hong Kong and spread to other places at an accelerating pace from the 1970s, reaching 19 exporting nations by the late 1990s. Harvests in 10 of these 19 countries clearly showed a boom-and-bust pattern. Species were depleted serially in order of value. However, some of the exporting nations did not show the boom-and-bust pattern. Scales et al. (2006) found a surprisingly promising outcome in parts of the Pacific region. Observations of wholesale depletions of valuable species led several Pacific island states to introduce small-scale trial fisheries for LRFT and management plans. These developments occurred along the edge of the serial depletion wave. The response seemed to be originating at two political levels: the island states themselves and the Secretariat of the Pacific Community, a regional body. Within the Secretariat region, national and regional organizations had important roles. The role of local commons institutions was unclear, but the region had strong traditions of community-based reef and lagoon management (Johannes 2002).

Some cases of the live LAFT also provide promising examples of dealing with roving banditry. Global markets for marine ornamental fish developed as a result of the spread of saltwater aquarium technology. Fishers from Olango Island, Philippines, who had been carrying out cyanide fishing since the 1960s, started harvesting for LAFT. The practice of cyanide use spread to other parts of the Philippines, and then to Southeast Asia regionally (Rubec et al. 2001). LAFT has received a great deal of international attention because of coral reef damage from cyanide, at a time when coral reef ecosystems are coming under a variety of other environmental pressures (Hughes et al. 2003).

Research carried out in Bali, Indonesia, provides insights into the dynamics of LAFT (Berkes 2010b; Frey and Berkes 2014). LAFT started in Bali in the 1980s, and local harvesters initially used cyanide. However, they found, after a few years, that all reef fish, along with the ecological health of the reef, started to decline. By the mid 1990s, many fishers in the community of Les on the north coast of Bali were seriously concerned and receptive to change when an NGO showed up in 2000 offering potential solutions. Cyanide-free harvesting techniques were introduced shortly after 2000, along with reef restoration measures.

Harvesters established a community association and agreed among themselves to stop using cyanide and, instead, adopted the dip netting technique from the NGO. This required more skill than using cyanide, but also reduced postharvest mortality and produced a better product (Rubec et al. 2001). Reef restoration was initially run by the community association, with help from local NGOs and an Indonesian national NGO, with funds from the Global Environmental Facility Small Grants Program. Cyanide kills live coral and often causes a rot-like condition in which dead areas spread from the top coral heads down. Once the use of cyanide was stopped or reduced, active restoration was carried out in partnerships with NGOs, later switching to natural regeneration (Frey and Berkes 2014).

The harvest of LAFT at Les has been cyanide-free (or nearly so) since the mid 2000s. This transformation was accomplished through a strong community institution, good leadership and timely NGO support. Other LAFT harvesting communities in Bali seem to be only partially cyanide-free (Frey and Berkes 2014), and the environmental problem of cyanide use probably continues in much of Southeast Asia.

PHOTO 5.2 Fishing boats in Les, Bali, Indonesia. Collective action in Les was successful in reversing the decline of cyanide-damaged coral reefs and helped improve the coastal economy

Source: F. Berkes

Roving banditry creates management challenges. The ability of the local fishers to self-organize for collective action is important, and so is the ability of local and national institutions to learn. In the sea urchin case, the speed with which roving banditry developed left little chance for self-organization, and even less for social learning. Institutions involved in the management of sea urchins must be able to learn from the *experience elsewhere*, an interesting twist on adaptive management. In the LRFT case, the regional institution seemed to be learning and reacting (Scales et al. 2006), putting in place a co-management system, with a learning loop through trial fisheries and local linkages. The LAFT case seems to be characterized by both social learning and adaptive management. Collective action and consensus building at Les were stimulated by capacity building with NGO support. However, many of the other LAFT communities were not able to do this (Frey and Berkes 2014). Some harvesters may never learn from the damage of cyanide use, especially if they are roving bandits who keep moving on. Rubec et al. (2001) mention that many of the LAFT collectors at the point of origin of cyanide fishing are third-generation users!

Conclusions

We know a great deal about the conditions under which commons management may or may not work (Dietz et al. 2003; Ostrom 2005). Commons is not the same as open access, and coastal resources are rarely used in an open-access regime. In most coastal areas of the world, commons institutions develop in a self-organized way. As problems develop, communities discuss the issue and seek solutions. There is nothing inherent in commons that would lead to resource degradation. Commons theory is sufficiently well developed to enable prediction at the local level, with a set of principles that have been verified against empirical data (Cox et al. 2010). However, this does not mean that all problems are easily solved. Commons are embedded in a multilevel world. Local people are never in complete control of their resources; indeed, neither are nation-states. Globalization, characterized as the collapse of space and time scales, has major impacts on commons management.

Roving bandits provide a testing ground for the commons problems of the 21st century. In an era of trade liberalization, roving banditry probably cannot be completely prevented (Deutsch et al. 2011). As well, each case is likely to have its own special problems, such as the presence of organized-crime syndicates in the South African abalone fishery case (Raemaekers et al. 2011). We do know that the usual measures in the management toolbox, such stock assessments and regulatory controls, are insufficient to deal with roving banditry. Although MPAs, an indirect measure, can help, possible solutions need to go beyond biological management. They may include enforcing and protecting resource rights and marine tenure; local monitoring with regional co-ordination; developing stewardship and a sense of place; and using flexible management approaches that can adapt to rapid change.

As well, market mechanisms can be added to the mix of solutions, as markets are a key driver in many cases of resource overexploitation (Cinner et al. 2013). In the ornamental fish trade case, for example, a serious impediment is that no appropriate pricing incentives exist for cyanide-free fish. The supply chain is murky, and the middlemen who purchase the fish from fishers and sell to international traders mix cyanide-caught fish and cyanide-free fish. Thus, a buyer in the United States or Europe does not have the option of purchasing sustainably harvested fish. As well, there is no economic incentive for the fisher at the point of sale to fetch a higher price for cyanide-free fish. There is, of course, economic incentive for smart communities to keep their marine environment healthy and productive. However, that requires secure rights to the resource and the ability to enforce the cyanide ban by social means (Frey and Berkes 2014).

Potential solutions to commons problems need to address the dilemmas of a complex world: Can commons theory, originally based on local-level cases, be scaled up to deal with complexity at multiple levels? How do we link local controls to a multilevel governance system? How do we design governance systems that are well matched to the speed at which globalized market demands and the resulting waves of resource exploitation emerge? Cases in this chapter offer a number of lessons for commons management in general.

First, commons management, with or without roving bandits in the mix, has to address the two essential characteristics of commons: the problems of excludability and subtractability—a well-defined community of users with an ability to take collective action and to make and enforce rules among themselves. Ostrom's principles of collective action provide a useful benchmark to evaluate collective action but do not guarantee sustainability (Ostrom 1990; Cox et al. 2010).

Second, the ability to address problems of excludability and subtractability is intimately connected to the issue of who has use rights and ownership of resources. For example, roving bandits operate best under open-access conditions and rely on their ability to exploit resources rapidly, before authorities can restrict access. Hence, governance must protect the spatial rights of local users and empower them to address problems quickly. The costs of resource depletion are borne mainly by local people; governance that strengthens community-based resource management, with commons rights and multilevel spatial planning, will help tighten the feedback loop between observation and response (Levin 1999).

Third, sustainability requires the ability to monitor the health of social–ecological systems. This not only applies to marine and coastal systems but also to other kinds of commons (Nagendra 2007; Chhatre and Agrawal 2008). Effective institutions must have mechanisms to detect change, follow up and act upon it. This process starts with monitoring at the local level, but it is in fact needed at multiple levels. The LRFT case in particular underscores the importance of monitoring and co-ordinating at the regional level. Further, at the international level, monitoring vessel flag history, for example, may improve the ability to track potential roving bandit problems before they occur (OECD 2004).

Fourth, the issue of environmental knowledge is crucial. Local resource users, whose livelihoods may be affected by resource depletion, pollution and other problems, also happen to be the people most knowledgeable about their resources. They can read signals from the environment and note changes in the course of their day-to-day livelihood activities. The key to timely response to threat, and commons violations in general, is a sense of local ownership and stewardship to exercise the responsibility to detect change, communicate it rapidly and take action.

Fifth, too much government regulation is a threat to common-property systems, because it stifles the local ability to solve problems (Ostrom 2000). As well, privatization and commons enclosures are a threat to the management of resources that fall under the definition of commons and that are not divisible. Some resources need to be managed collectively. For example, quota systems, whereby fishing rights by species are pri-vatized, make more sense in offshore, large-stock fisheries, but less sense in inshore multi-species ones. With other kinds of coastal resource, the creation of new rights (e.g., aquaculture sites, tourism development) constrains established commons rights of rural coastal communities (McCay 2008).

Finally, social learning and adaptive management are key to long-term sustainability. Social–ecological systems being complex adaptive systems, it is difficult to predict the outcomes of management interventions. Most management situations should therefore include deliberative processes of learning by experimentation. Many situations of resource governance, whether by communities or by governments or by both, require adaptive management, rather than blueprint solutions or *panaceas* (Ostrom 2007). Multilevel adaptive management that starts at the community level has the advantage of bringing decisions closer to the resource user.

Local fishers and other resource users need to have incentives to exercise stewardship for their resources and be a partner in governance. In many areas of both the developed and the developing world, resource managers are increasingly recognizing resource users as part of the solution, rather than as part of the problem. Communities are key to making and enforcing rules for managing the commons. This does not mean the end of management (Ludwig 2001) but the beginning of collaborative problem solving. The next chapter is about such collaborative problem solving, dealing with the multilevel world, paying attention to social and institutional learning, and engaging with management as a *process*, rather than searching blueprint outcomes.

6

CO-MANAGEMENT

SEARCHING FOR MULTILEVEL SOLUTIONS

Introduction

Complex contemporary resource problems require appropriately complex solutions. Coastal and marine resources often require partnerships, and building linkages from the local level up, to involve multiple levels of organization. As cases in Chapter 5 show, the task may be to build multilevel institutions, from local to global, that can learn from experience. In building theory, commons research of the 1980s and 1990s focused on community-based resource management and local institutions (Ostrom 1990). However, purely community-based management has the same weakness as purely top-down government management—they both ignore the necessity of multilevel institutional linkages (Dietz et al. 2003).

Co-management is by far the most widely known arrangement for dealing with multilevel linkages, but there is in fact a diversity of institutional forms for dealing with multilevel commons (Berkes 2002). These other forms include epistemic communities (Haas 1990), policy networks (Carlsson 2000) and polycentric systems (McGinnis 2000). Each of these concepts provides an approach to understand institutional interplay. Following the terminology of Young (2002), institutional interplay involves institutions that may interact *horizontally* (across the same level) and/or *vertically* (across levels of organization).

By definition, *co-management* provides vertical linkages between at least two levels. It involves the sharing of power and responsibility between the government and local resource users. It may be about a particular resource, a set of resources, or an area. The hallmark of co-management is the presence of at least one strong vertical linkage involving the government and a user-group, as well as some formalized arrangement for sharing power and responsibility (Pinkerton 1989; Berkes 2009b). Many cases of fisheries co-management are backed up by law, as in Japan (Takahashi et al. 2006; Makino 2011) and Chile (Castilla and Defeo 2001). There is no single, universally accepted definition of co-management, because there is a continuum of co-management arrangements with different degrees of power sharing and joint decision-making (Armitage et al. 2007), but most authors do not regard mere consultation as co-management (Pinkerton 2003).

Early representations of co-management focused on a two-link relationship between the government and local resource users, as shown in many of the chapters of Pinkerton's 1989 fisheries co-management book. Over the years, it has progressively moved from such simple two-party interactions to ones that examine multiple linkages and social relationships, in the form of networks, as the essence of co-management (Carlsson and Berkes 2005). Detailed case studies of co-management show a wide array of actors and relationships and illustrate the ways in which these relationships evolve and deal with a series of problem over the years (Armitage et al. 2007). Much of this problem solving occurs through informal learning networks (Olsson et al. 2004b). These networks may constitute *learning communities*, which are groups of people with a shared interest, learning through partnerships (Armitage et al. 2008). Learning communities are similar to Wenger's (1998) *communities of practice*, emphasizing learning-as-participation, and to *skunkworks*, informal working groups used by some organizations for generating innovative thinking (Goldstein 2008). Various studies have identified the importance of leadership roles and key individuals in these networks (Olsson et al. 2004a; Seixas and Davy 2008).

The argument in this chapter is that, not just participatory management, but fully-fledged adaptive co-management is possible and feasible in many cases. Following a note on terminology, the chapter first discusses the origins of co-management and some of the purposes that it serves, touching upon the role of co-management in four areas: practical problem solving, indigenous rights, collaborative research and decentralization reforms. Second, the chapter explores some of the mechanisms that make co-management work: relationships and networks, use of different kinds of knowledge, bridging organizations, leadership, capacity building and social learning. Third, the chapter discusses the emergence of adaptive co-management from time-tested co-management and develops a model to capture some of the essential processes and feedback relationships in building adaptive co-management.

Networks and social learning are important parts of this discussion. In the context of co-management, *social learning* may be defined as "the collaborative and mutual development and sharing of knowledge by multiple stakeholders (both people and organizations) through learning-by-doing" (Armitage et al. 2009, p. 96). It is a key element in turning co-management into adaptive co-management that combines elements of both co-management and adaptive management. Proper adaptive man-agement requires learning by design (Walters 1986), but even learning by trial and error is a powerful mechanism for creating social learning.

Three commonly used terms are associated with co-operative environ-mental management: partnership, collaboration and co-management (Plummer and FitzGibbon 2004). There are many similarities, some differences and considerable overlaps among these terms. Each of the three areas has its distinct but overlapping technical literature.

Partnership "is a dynamic relationship among diverse actors, based on mutually agreed objectives, pursued through a shared understanding of the most rational division of labour based on the respective compara-tive advantages of each partner" (Brinkerhoff 2002, p. 21). There seem to be three different perspectives in the partnership literature. The normative perspective critiques top-down practice on the basis of equity, empowerment and democracy, calling for local involvement in govern-ance. The second perspective, taken by government and business, uses partnership terminology in advancing neoliberal policies and programs in which government responsibilities may be privatized, as in public–private partnerships. The third perspective is instrumental, focusing on the function of partnerships, as in capacity building (Brinkerhoff 2002).

Collaboration involves the pooling of resources by multiple actors or stakeholders to solve problems (e.g., Ostrom 1990). Although often used as a synonym for partnership, collaboration emphasizes the process of interaction among actors. Central to collaborative interaction are issues of inclusion, power sharing and joint decision-making, as in collaborative research that is about an interaction of equals, rather than researchers dealing with people as "subjects" (Davidson-Hunt and O'Flaherty 2007). Collaborative management is often used as a synonym for co-management. However, in some circles, for example in some Canadian federal government departments, collaborative management is used to indicate an informal (nonlegal) relationship, whereas the term co-management is reserved to denote a formal relationship of power sharing.

Why Co-management?

The term co-management is relatively recent, if the practice is not. Pinkerton (2003) traces the earliest use of the term to the late 1970s, in salmon management under the Boldt Decision regarding the US Treaty Tribes in Washington State. The practice of power sharing in management goes back to earlier times. In fisheries, the earliest documented legal arrangement seems to be the Lofoten Islands cod fishery in Norway in the 1890s (Jentoft and McCay 1995). Nearly as old, co-management-like arrangements existed in Japanese inshore fisheries under the 1901 Fisheries Act and its subsequent revisions (Lim et al. 1995; Makino 2011). Co-management exists in other resource areas as well—forests, wildlife, watersheds, river basins and protected areas (Borrini-Feyerabend et al. 2004; Armitage et al. 2007; Berkes 2009b).

Co-management can help accomplish a number of management tasks. Pinkerton (1989) discussed several tasks that can be carried out more easily under a well functioning co-management system, including data gathering and enforcement, allocation and logistical decisions, such as who can harvest and when, and better long-term planning and decision-making. Table 6.1 summarizes some of the major tasks and functions (Carlsson and Berkes 2005). Illustrations will be provided throughout the chapter.

Experience since the 1970s indicates that many co-management systems have been generally helpful in accomplishing these tasks, but, of course, not every case is successful (Pinkerton 1989; Wilson et al. 2003; Armitage et al. 2007). In fact, many cases of co-management have not worked at all. However, systematic studies are beginning to demonstrate beneficial effects of co-management and the conditions under which co-management is successful (Gutiérrez et al. 2011). For example, the

TABLE 6.1 What is co-management good for?

1.	**Allocation of tasks**	Management systems need to operate at both the small scale and at the large scale, and there are different kinds of skill and knowledge necessary for each scale. Allocation of tasks enables specialization to increase efficiency. Cash and Moser (2000) refer to this as utilizing scale-dependent comparative advantages
2.	**Exchange of resources**	Local groups may need certain types of resource that they are themselves unable to provide, such as technology and scientific expertise, but they may possess resources needed by government managers, such as information about harvests. If co-management involves multiple partnerships, there often is a web of resource dependences
3.	**Linking different types and levels of organization**	In Max Weber's image of bureaucracy, different layers of organization are linked to one another in a framework of coherent hierarchy. Co-management cuts across this hierarchy. It is a process by which representatives from different levels of organization and types of organization co-ordinate their activities in relation to a specific area or resource system
4.	**Reducing transaction costs**	Transaction costs are the costs of doing business. Early phases of co-management may be costly in both time and money, but co-management can reduce transaction costs in the long run through better data collection, monitoring, enforcement and conflict reduction. Government managers do not have to dedicate as much time and resources for these functions, thus reducing costs
5.	**Risk sharing**	Decision-making involves risks, and monolithic decision systems are vulnerable. Webs of relations that have evolved over time in co-management lead to diversified management arrangements. These webs serve the purpose of spreading the risk among the parties
6.	**Conflict resolution mechanism**	Co-management systems may function as a means of conflict resolution between communities and the state. The processes of negotiation and setting up agreements that codify the rights and responsibilities of the parties function as a long-term conflict reduction mechanism

Source: Adapted from Carlsson and Berkes 2005

standing biomass of fish in co-managed coral reef areas is demonstrably higher than that in open-access areas—but lower than in no-take protected areas (Cinner et al. 2012). A meta-analysis by Evans et al. (2011) indicates that fisheries co-management in 90 sites in developing countries delivers benefits to end-users through improvements in process indicators (e.g., participation) and outcome indicators (e.g., income).

However, before suggesting co-management as a panacea for all commons problems, it must be pointed out that most co-management arrangements fall short of accomplishing these various tasks. As well, a critical approach would require asking if power sharing in some cases might be an attempt by state authorities to legitimize taking over previously community-managed resources (Nayak and Berkes 2008). Co-management might, in fact, be a means of perpetuating an existing unjust situation, or it might be an attempt by the government to offload a regulatory function that is proving too costly to manage (Carlsson and Berkes 2005). On the other hand, it can bring mutual benefits to co-managers in a number of areas. Hence, co-management can facilitate a degree of power sharing in several ways, without necessarily eliminating injustices and power relations.

Co-management arrangements originated for a number of different reasons, to serve a variety of purposes. In this chapter, we will touch upon four of these: management problem solving, power sharing for indigenous rights, collaborative research and decentralization reforms.

For practical purposes, co-management is a good way to solve management problems, especially in cases involving conflicts. Co-management in the Lofoten Islands cod fishery falls in the problem-solving category. A highly lucrative fishery that has supplied southern Europe since the 15th century, Lofoten was often an area of bitter conflict among groups of fishers using different gear. Unable to resolve the conflicts, the Norwegian government formulated legislation to let the fisher gear groups solve their own problems, and the arrangement has persisted to date, with periodic adjustments (Jentoft and McCay 1995).

In some co-management cases, problem-solving skills were progressively refined over the years. In others, problem solving seems to enable parties to transfer learning from one situation to another. Examples from Sweden and Canada, tracked over a time span of two to three decades, show that such problem solving may enable parties to tackle increasingly complex problems as they learn, develop problem-solving skills and accumulate experience. For example, in Lake Racken, Sweden, co-management that started in the 1970s with a "liming group" (to reduce lake acidity from acid rain) expanded into a fishing association, to a network of associations, and to linkages with municipal, county and higher levels. Tackling crayfish rehabilitation, trout management and habitat restoration, the network developed adaptive co-management for problem solving, with an ever-expanding scale of capabilities (Olsson et al. 2004a).

Each round of problem solving can be depicted as a loop, and successive loops of learning-as-participation can be shown as expanding circles over time (Figure 6.1). Each cycle starts with observation and problem identification (Downs 1998). The identification of problems and opportunities leads to planning for the formulation of solution(s). Participants need to monitor the outcomes of the plan to evaluate the effectiveness of the action, followed by reflection that leads to the next cycle (Colfer 2005; Fisher et al. 2007). Each iteration provides new information that can be incorporated into the next round of solutions, the basis of adaptive management. At the same time, each cycle is a learning step for the problem-solving network, leading to co-management at successively larger scales over time (Olsson et al. 2004a).

Such a depiction may give the impression of an idealized unity and harmony among co-management partners. However, even the facilitation of co-operation among the actors can be a major challenge in itself, given power asymmetries (Wollenberg et al. 2007). Furthermore, each actor is far from homogeneous. Within a given user-group, there can be elites who speak for the group but often ignore the interests of the less powerful. Hence, the distribution of power among the co-management partners is further complicated by the need to empower marginalized groups internally, within the user-group or community (Béné and Neiland 2004, 2006).

A second area in which one finds co-management arrangements is indigenous land and resource rights. There is a relatively large literature from the United States, Canada, Australia and New Zealand concerning indigenous co-management with coastal and other resources. In the United States, salmon co-management with the tribes of the Pacific

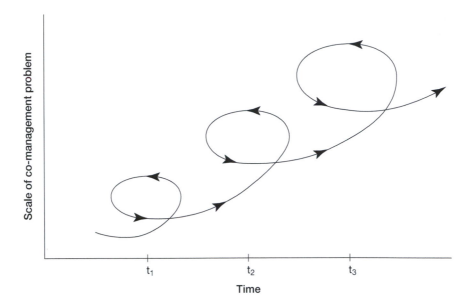

FIGURE 6.1 Learning-as-participation in co-management, resulting in increasing levels of trust and the ability to tackle more complicated problems. Each loop in the figure goes through observation–planning–action–outcome phases, followed by a period of reflection

Source: Berkes 2009b. Reprinted with permission from Elsevier

Northwest is relatively well known (Singleton 1998). The 1974 Boldt Decision (*US v Washington*) was a US Supreme Court decision that recognized the rights of western Washington State Indian tribes to up to a 50 percent share of the salmon that passed through their customary fishing sites. The tribes had been unable to exercise these rights, because the vast majority of the stock was fished out in the open sea, before the migrating salmon finally reached the bays, estuaries and rivers that were the customary Indian fishing sites. Judge Bolt reasoned that only by their participating in the management decisions for the overall salmon harvest could the allocation rights of the tribes ever be exercised.

Pinkerton (2003) showed how co-management under the Boldt decision evolved through a series of stages, consistent with Figure 6.1. The protocols for salmon harvesting, that is, making and agreeing on harvest regulation and allocation, had been completed within the first decade of the court decision, and the co-managers were ready for the next set of problems. These included issues of habitat protection, regional

planning and international allocation. The initial co-management agreement, which was about the sharing of salmon, set the stage for a complex
multi-stakeholder exercise and multijurisdictional integrated resource
management (Pinkerton 1992; Pinkerton 2003).

In Canada, each of the recent (from the 1970s to present) comprehensive land claims agreements, now covering the entirety of the Canadian
North, contains a chapter on fish and wildlife co-management. Agreements establish management boards, with indigenous and government
representation, that jointly determine rules and procedures for the sustainable use of living resources (Berkes and Fast 2005; Ayles et al. 2007).
Australia's co-management arrangements with indigenous groups go
back to the 1970s with the Kakadu National Park; Australia is a world
leader in indigenous peoples' protected area management (Ross et al.
2009). Although many of these indigenous co-management arrangements
are impressive in their reach and supposedly empower indigenous groups,
critics have pointed out that they have not been very successful in reversing
historic depletions of coastal resources that indigenous peoples used to
depend upon, in areas such as New Zealand and Canada's British
Columbia (Turner et al. 2013a).

A third area in which one finds co-management arrangements is
collaborative research, in particular, participatory action research (Moller
et al. 2009a). The principle here is that participatory approaches are central
to learning by groups, because they create the mechanism by which
individual learning can be shared by other members of the group and
reinforced (Diduck 2004; Sims and Sinclair 2008). Collaborative research
as co-management relies on learning-by-doing and operates on the
assumption that power sharing can be regarded as the result, rather than
the starting point, of co-management (Carlsson and Berkes 2005).

There are many barriers to carrying out participatory research with
fishers. In a four-year participatory fishery research project in the Scotia-
Fundy region of Atlantic Canada, Wiber et al. (2004, 2009) sought to
revise standard participatory research approaches (those involving fishers
in biological sampling) in favor of research for community-based management. They turned their research budget over to five small-scale fisher
communities and provided technical support for the resulting fishery
social science research projects. The results indicated that participatory
research in support of community-based management can be a powerful

tool. However, it must deal early in the research process with power imbalances, should strive for empowerment through collaborative learning or coproduction of knowledge, and should involve political engagement.

The approach developed in the Canadian study was applied to Uruguay, where there is no tradition of collaborative management. In a small-scale coastal fishery in Piriápolis, Uruguay, university researchers facilitated the formation of an informal group, POPA (Spanish acronym, "For Artisanal Fisheries in Piriápolis"). After two years of trust building, a small number of fishers, NGO people, university researchers and a government manager came together to discuss problems and possible solutions. They prioritized the problems of the artisanal fishery (conflict with sea lions that damage the gillnets; loss of markets to cheap, imported *basa* catfish from Vietnam), held an artisanal fisheries festival to mobilize public support, made plans for a collaborative research project to address issues, and were actually successful in obtaining funding from the government to carry it out. Perhaps equally important, the deliberative process followed throughout

PHOTO 6.1 Kick-starting co-management by mobilizing public support: the photo exhibition at the Artisanal Fisheries Festival, Piriápolis, Uruguay

Source: Micaela Trimble

this action research project created the beginnings of a co-management arrangement by sharing knowledge and views, making linkages and building trust. In Uruguay, as well as in the Canadian experiment, collaborative learning was a key process, and persisting power imbalance was a major impediment (Trimble and Berkes 2013).

Finally, decentralization reform can be considered a special case of co-management. Following the global fiscal crises of the 1980s and the collapse of socialist economies after 1989, many countries of the developing world were encouraged by international bodies such as the World Bank to institute decentralization reforms (and perhaps pave the way to neoliberal policies) in several areas, including development, environmental management, health care and education (OECD 1997; Manor 1999). Decentralization experience in the areas of environment and development has given rise to a large body of literature, much of it on forest resources (Colfer and Capistrano 2005; Larson and Soto 2008).

Devolution is generally considered a kind of governance reform to bring the decision-making process closer to the citizen. More specifically, one can distinguish between *devolution* (transfer of rights and responsibilities to local groups, organizations, and local-level governments that have autonomous decision-making powers) as opposed to *decentralization* (transfer of rights and responsibilities from the center to branches of the same government ministry) (Brugere 2006). Figure 6.2 captures this distinction. However, in Ribot's (2002) terminology, *administrative decentralization* refers to transfer of power to local branches of the same ministry of the central state, and *democratic decentralization* refers to any act of the central government formally ceding power to actors and institutions at lower levels.

Perhaps best characterized as "top-down co-management," many decentralization reforms seem to have failed to meet their objectives of participatory development and administrative efficiency. Many of them involved insufficient transfer of powers to local institutions (Ribot 2002), and off-loading was common; local jurisdictions were not given the resources commensurate with their new responsibilities (Pomeroy and Berkes 1997). Actions of central governments themselves and local elites often undermined decentralization reform in many countries (Ribot et al. 2006). Findings in the area of fisheries were generally consistent with those from other resource and development fields (Béné and Neiland 2006).

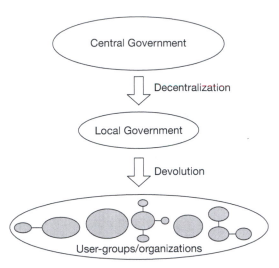

FIGURE 6.2 Decentralization and devolution in resource and environmental management
Source: Berkes 2010a, adapted from Brugere 2006; reproduced with permission

However, there were some cases linked to decentralization policies that showed demonstrable positive outcomes. Pomeroy et al. (2010) found that the decentralization reforms of 1991 and 1998 for coastal and marine resources management in the Philippines facilitated co-management in the 1990s and integrated management in the 2000s. Based on a communitarian tradition and successful implementation of community management in various areas in the 1980s, decentralization in the Philippines helped improve fisheries management at the ecosystem and multijurisdictional level. Maliao et al. (2009) further showed that community-based coastal resource management programs in the Philippines (and not necessarily decentralization itself) were perceived by coastal populations to be effective in empowerment and participation in management—but not to any extent in livelihood improvement.

The role of different approaches to governance in regard to resource management and co-management is a large and active area (Kooiman 2003; Kooiman et al. 2005). One of the governance approaches that has received close attention from commons scholars is polycentric governance (McGinnis 2000; Ostrom 2005). Box 6.1 expands on the relevance of polycentric systems for co-management, using the example of an MPA.

BOX 6.1 POLYCENTRIC SYSTEMS FOR CO-MANAGEMENT

Polycentric systems cut across different levels of authority. Governance is said to be polycentric in structure if it has multiple and overlapping centers of authority (Folke et al. 2005). Such structures are inefficient in the narrow sense (because of redundancy and overlaps) but robust. They allow for experimentation and contribute to the creation of an institutional dynamic important for adaptive management. The distribution of authority across overlapping institutions has significance for reducing decision-making risks. Trial-and-error learning by overlapping institutions does not reduce the probability of error with any one resource, but greatly reduces the probability of disastrous errors for all resources in a given area or setting (Ostrom et al. 1999). Overlapping institutions also help connect different levels of governance by providing communication channels for the various parties in multilevel arrangements (Wilson 2006). Polycentric and multilayered institutions improve the fit between knowledge and action in a social–ecological system in ways that allow societies to respond adaptively to change (Lebel et al. 2006).

An example of polycentric arrangement is the governance structure of the Papahānaumokuākea Marine National Monument in Hawai'i, a very large MPA. The 2006 proclamation establishing the Monument requires two federal agencies, the National Oceanic and Atmospheric Administration Agency (NOAA) and the US Fish and Wildlife Service, and the State of Hawai'i to manage the Monument collaboratively as co-trustees. It is a novel arrangement for US MPA governance, where typically a "lead agency" is named. In the present case, the three agencies are meant to function as co-equals, breaking agency barriers to work in an integrative way. In the analysis of Kittinger and colleagues (2011), the arrangement shows promise but has faced some early challenges, such as differences in "agency cultures."

What Makes Co-management Work?

The literature on commons and co-management provides insights on how to proceed from the devolution of power toward participatory management. Over the years, the analysis of co-management has progressively moved from one that considers simple interactions to one that considers social relationships of multiple players in the form of networks (Crona and Bodin 2006). Co-management is essentially about managing relationships, not resources (Natcher et al. 2005). Networks help bring together the different kinds of knowledge and skill needed for joint management. Combining or, better still, bridging different kinds of knowledge is a major consideration, especially if local knowledge is based on a different epistemology and worldview than government science (Reid et al. 2006). Bridging organizations facilitate relationships, help make sense of the diversity of actors and kinds of knowledge among co-management partners, and play a key role (Crona and Parker 2012). Leadership often makes the difference between success and failure (Olsson and Folke 2001; Seixas and Davy 2008). In a study of 130 co-managed fisheries, Gutiérrez et al. (2011) identified leadership as the single most important attribute contributing to success. Finally, social learning is important in turning co-management into adaptive co-management (Armitage et al. 2007, 2009). We expand on some of these points.

The consideration of multiple players and a wide array of relationships is a major development in the history of co-management. The "state" is not monolithic; there are different actors on the government side, with different tasks and agendas (Carlsson and Berkes 2005). There may also be different leaders, some facilitating co-management and others hindering (Pinkerton 2007; Seixas and Davy 2008). On the side of user-groups and communities as well, there are often distinctly different groups and interests. In addition to these, a number of different kinds of organization, such as those involved in funding, marketing and research, may impact co-management in various ways.

A striking example is the co-management system for *loco*, the "Chilean abalone" *Concholepas concholepas*, an economically important gastropod. *Loco* co-management was set up in law in 1991 as a "triumvirate" of fisher associations, state institutions and technical assistance institutions (Castilla and Defeo 2001; Gelcich et al. 2010). However, the three-player characterization may be a rather limited view of the actual diversity of the players as co-management evolved. Thirty-eight fisher organizations in two *loco* management zones were surveyed regarding their linkages with other actors in the co-management system, and the responses were mapped using social network analysis (Marín and Berkes 2010). The results (Figure 6.3) indicate that fisher organizations interacted with no less than seven functional groups: fisher associations (umbrella groups for fisher organizations); power sharing and enforcement (government); funding (mostly government); territorial authorities (various levels of government); monitoring, research and development; marketing; and "other" (private sector and civil society).

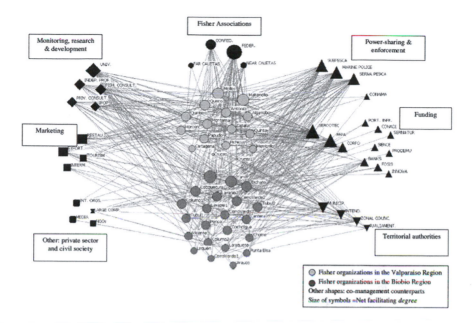

FIGURE 6.3 Network linkages as the essence of co-management in Chile, based on Management and Exploitation Areas for Benthic Resources

Source: Marín and Berkes 2010. Reprinted with permission from Elsevier

As pointed out in Table 6.1 in the allocation of tasks, there are different kinds of skill and knowledge necessary at different levels, and the challenge is to use the full range of available knowledge for the management task in hand (Berkes and Folke 1998). When Reid et al. (2006) explored how science and local knowledge could be best brought together, the most robust bridges were those constructed by combining complementary knowledge and capabilities at different levels. Local people are experts at the local level (e.g., status of the local fishery and abundance trends of different species), whereas the state has a regional and national vantage point and a repertoire of tools and techniques (e.g., scientific databases, remote sensing) not normally available to local groups. Co-management enables different partners to bring to the table knowledge that is acquired at different levels in space and time scales. This is part of the allocation of tasks, using scale-specific comparative advantage of co-management partners (Cash and Moser 2000). An example is the long-standing case of the Arctic Borderlands Ecological Knowledge Co-op in Alaska and Yukon, where local observations are often followed up by government research and environmental monitoring (Eamer 2006). What kinds of arrangement enable co-management partners to bring their comparative strengths in knowledge and skills?

Accumulating cases in the co-management literature show that part of the answer lies in bridging organizations and leadership. Bridging organizations provide an arena for such tasks as knowledge coproduction, trust building, sense making, learning, collaboration and conflict resolution. They can respond to opportunities and serve as catalysts and facilitators between different levels of governance and across knowledge systems (Folke et al. 2005; Hahn et al. 2006). They are similar to boundary organizations, as originally described for the science–policy interface (Cash and Moser 2000).

An example of a bridging organization is the Ecomuseum of the Kristianstads Vattenrike Biosphere Reserve, a coastal wetland in southern Sweden. The Ecomuseum provided the forum for trust building, conflict resolution and accessing knowledge. By linking existing networks concerned with different objectives (bird conservation, water quality, cultural heritage), the Ecomuseum provided leadership to produce a comprehensive vision and goals. For example, when the wetland area in Vattenrike was set aside for conservation and cattle grazing stopped, it became overgrown. The Ecomuseum co-ordinated the deliberation over this unintended impact, leading to the coproduction of new knowledge. A consensus was reached to the effect that grazing was indeed essential for the ecological health of the wetland, and a management decision was taken to restore grazing (Olsson et al. 2004b). The director of the Ecomuseum played the key leadership role in solving the management problem.

Olsson et al. (2007) have pointed out the dual importance of bridging organizations and leadership. The case of Maine lobster co-management is informative in this regard. Success of the Maine lobster fishery case was attributed to two factors: the existence of the Maine Fishermen's Forum, a neutral discussion forum, and the leadership of the Marine Resources Commissioner. The Commissioner was a skilled networker and the founder/editor of the *Commercial Fisheries News*, which had an important role in communication and co-ordination (Acheson 2003). Beem (2007) analyzed why co-management developed successfully in the Maine case but not in the Chesapeake Bay blue crab fishery, noting that the two cases had many similarities. The Chesapeake case had a formally constituted bridging organization, the Bi-State Crab Advisory Committee, and other ingredients seemingly favorable for co-management success. Beem (2007) concluded that the failure of the Chesapeake Bay case might have been due to the top-down nature of the proposed co-management arrangement and the poor networking of leadership with the fishing community.

Bridging organizations, especially when coupled with good leadership, provide a package of services and facilitate linkages. Figure 6.4 summarizes the many potential roles of bridging organizations, such as bridging institutions and knowledge; building trust; strengthening local institutions; building the ability to use local knowledge; and accessing outside knowledge, technology and resources. Where bridging organizations do not exist, some key partners may still provide the needed support for *capacity building*, the sum of skills and capabilities that enable a group to achieve its goals.

Brazil's fishery co-management is instructive here. Historically, co-management developed in the Amazon region through the use of "fishing agreements" (Castro 2002). Each agreement was tailored to the specifics of a given case, establishing use rights by community, zoning for commercial and subsistence fisheries, and establishing conservation rules in

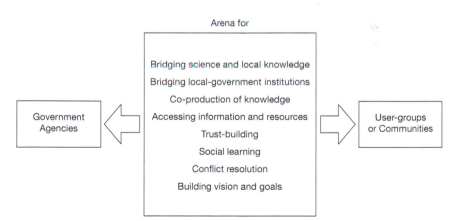

FIGURE 6.4 The many possible roles of bridging organizations in co-management. No single bridging organization is likely to supply all of these functions. In some cases, a number of different organizations may share the various roles of a bridging organization

Source: Adapted from Berkes 2009b

these river and lake systems (Castro and McGrath 2003; McGrath et al. 2008). The agreements do not seem to have had the benefit of bridging organizations, but the Catholic Church was instrumental in capacity building. (By contrast, rural areas dominated by evangelical religious movements were nonparticipants, as these churches do not seem to believe in sustainability planning—God gives resources or takes them away!) Some of this co-management experience is being put to use on the Brazil coast, in areas such as Paraty (Begossi et al. 2012; Begossi 2014), including the use of ecological economics approaches in designing incentives for stewardship (Begossi et al. 2011).

International experience shows that sources of capacity building are diverse (Berkes 2007a). Figure 6.5 shows some of the various ways that

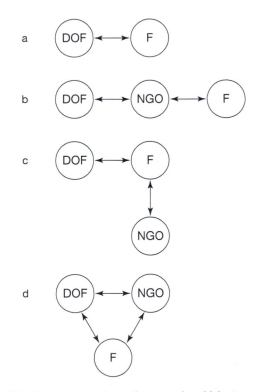

FIGURE 6.5 Capacity building: some alternative ways in which capacity building can be delivered to fishing communities (F) by nongovernmental organizations (NGOs) and/or the Department of Fisheries (DOF) or other branch of government

Source: Berkes 2002. Reprinted with permission from the National Academy of Sciences, Courtesy of the National Academies Press, Washington, DC

capacity building can be delivered to fishing communities. For example, NGOs may play a supportive role for fisher communities or an intermediary role between fishers and managers. The models were based

---

BOX 6.2 A CAMBODIAN VILLAGE MANAGEMENT COMMITTEE PONDERS OVER MANAGEMENT OPTIONS

We conducted a brainstorming session with the Kompong Phluk village resource management committee to examine alternative solutions to the problem of protecting their fishing area, and whether some of these might be viable in their opinion. Brainstorming was conducted around three alternative solutions or options. Given that the community was unable to harvest its allocated fishing ground fully and control large-scale fishers, were there ways to make deals with these fishers? Would a joint-venture option, enabling community members to sell their rights to outsiders, work? The committee mulled over this idea and eventually rejected it for two reasons. First, they did not think that their resource rights were secure enough to sell or rent, as in transferable fish quotas in some countries. Second, if they invited large-scale fishers into their community area, it might be even more difficult to get rid of them later.

A second option followed the practice in some Philippines lagoon fisheries in which armed guards protect valuable fishing areas. How did they feel about giving community members guns to patrol the area? This option was not seen as viable or desirable, given the experience in Cambodia with Khmer Rouge violence in the 1970s. A committee member commented that violence does not solve problems, and, besides, big fishers are likely to have bigger guns than the community patrol. A third option was to use the power of the temple, blessing the fishing grounds through a ceremony, as done in some community fisheries (for example in Brazil), and discouraging potential poachers through religious sanctions. How about using Buddhist teachings to stop illegal practices? This idea received considerable discussion and many smiles, but, ultimately, it was not seen as plausible: "This cannot work. Every fisher kills fish, and this already goes against Buddhist teachings. Killing an animal is bad karma. So as fishers we don't have the moral authority to use religious sanctions against anyone else."

The discussion highlights the multiple factors that resource management committees actually do consider. The responses to the options are indicative of extensive community discussions on planning and action, an understanding of management practicalities, and the legal and ethical context of options.

Source: Edited and abridged from a longer narrative in Marschke and Berkes 2005, pp. 30–1.

PHOTO 6.2 "As fishers we don't have the moral authority to use religious sanctions against anyone else." The village management committee meets at the courtyard of the local *wat*, the Buddhist temple. Kompong Phluk, Tonle Sap, Cambodia

Source: F. Berkes

on actual observations of capacity building in floodplain fisheries of Bangladesh, where NGOs helped implement development projects and programs supported by donor agencies (Berkes, unpublished).

Many capacity-building efforts involve local and national NGOs and university personnel working with development agencies and NGOs. Box 6.2 illustrates development work involving a local commons institution, a village management committee in Cambodia. The committee is faced with the problem that large-scale fishers from the outside have been using their government-allocated fishing area (Marschke and Berkes 2005). The committee ponders over their options: in the face of resource appropriation by powerful people, can they still manage their area? Can they count on co-management with the government and protection of their legal rights? (Marschke 2012).

Building Adaptive Co-management

As many of the examples in the previous sections (such as the Boldt case) illustrate, co-management is often not a static arrangement; it evolves through practice and learning. Increasingly, scholars and practitioners have been recognizing the significance of adaptive learning as part of co-management. Adaptive management, or learning-by-doing, was originally formulated as a way to deal with uncertainty and complexity in manage-ment (Holling 1978; Walters 1986). Adaptive management has been becoming collaborative in practice, while time-tested co-management increasingly relies on learning-by-doing.

Thus, co-management and adaptive management have been evolving toward a common ground: adaptive co-management, which merges the principles and practices of co-management and adaptive management (Olsson et al. 2004a; Armitage et al. 2007). Other authors have used the terms *adaptive collaborative management* (Colfer 2005) and *adaptive governance* (Folke et al. 2005; Brunner et al. 2005) to capture versions of the same idea. However, adaptive co-management is not the simple sum of adaptive management and co-management. It differs from the two in substantive ways, for example, with respect to the kinds of linkage, organ-izational levels and capacity-building focus (Table 6.2).

The following model is an attempt to understand the major processes in adaptive co-management. It is roughly based on the conceptual model of Prabhu, McDougall and Fisher (2007) for adaptive collaborative management, patterned after Habermas (1981). It is further informed by Pahl-Wostl (2009), Goldstein (2009) and Plummer (2009). The model is meant to be explanatory rather than predictive. The objective is to explore plausible building blocks, or some of the key factors and considerations, on how to proceed to adaptive co-management. The model is based on the assumptions that there are no blueprints or packaged strategies that can be used for all cases, and that it is futile to look for some small number of key explanatory factors. Plummer (2009) and Plummer et al. (2012) have shown that there are a great many variables that can be important in a given case. The task, therefore, is to understand underlying com-plexity.

There are three phases of the model that Prabhu et al. (2007) based on the three forms of action of Habermas (1981): (1) *communicative action*, aimed at the generation of understanding; (2) *strategic action*, aimed at

TABLE 6.2 Similarities and differences between co-management, adaptive management and adaptive co-management

Co-management	Adaptive management	Adaptive co-management
Linkages		
Primary focus: vertical institutional linkages	Linking science and management for learning-by-doing	Horizontal and vertical linkages for joint learning-by-doing
Temporal scope		
Short to medium: tends to produce snapshots	Medium to long: multiple cycles of learning and adaptation	Medium to long: multiple cycles of learning and adaptation
Organizational level		
Bridging between local and government levels	Focus on managers' needs and relationships	Multilevel, with self-organized networks
Capacity-building focus		
Resource users and communities	Resource managers and decision-makers	Needs and relationships of all partners

Source: Adapted from Berkes et al. 2007

dealing with relationships and self-organization; and (3) *instrumental action*, dominated by rules-in-use for collective action that produces results. Although this conceptualization suggests a linear progression from communicative to strategic to material action, the three phases are not meant to be mutually exclusive, but rather overlapping, interconnected and cyclic, with many causal feedback loops among the three phases and within each phase.

Communicative Action

The first phase of the model is about processes of communication aimed at reaching a common understanding of issues and the creation of a shared vision among stakeholders (Figure 6.6). It starts with the articulation of goals, objectives and values for resource use by each stakeholder, and the sharing and clarifying of worldviews and *mental models*, that is, the cognitive frameworks that people use to interpret and understand the world (Biggs et al. 2011). This is not a top-down, superficial participation process, as sometimes mandated by governments. Rather, it is a locally controlled, deliberative process organized to help think through the

FIGURE 6.6 A conceptual model of how a case might proceed from decentralization to adaptive co-management, through the phases of Habermasian communicative action, strategic action and instrumental action. The phases are overlapping, interconnected and cyclic, with causal feedback loops among and within phases

Source: Revised from Berkes 2010a, adapted from Prabhu et al. 2007 and others

objectives, and to reflect on values and knowledge that pertain to resource management (Stern 2005). It requires good leadership. It may also involve dealing with conflicts among stakeholders. As a person who has a clearly articulated vision communicated with passion, the leader embodies certain values and can set standards for others. He/she has the capacity to inspire and empower others, without telling them what to do (Olsson et al. 2004a; Seixas and Davy 2008).

Effective communication requires co-ordination. Sharing of the world-views and knowledge of the participants will help co-ordinate the group and set the stage for the coproduction of new knowledge that might be needed for management (Davidson-Hunt and O'Flaherty 2007). In many cases involving aboriginal co-management, the ability to bring together government science and indigenous knowledge is key for co-management success (Eamer 2006).

The creation of a shared vision is important for at least two reasons. First, adaptive management requires an understanding of the system being managed and an explicit vision of the management goals (Walters 1986).

Second, a sense of purpose and shared meaning provides empowerment. Communicative planning is a search for meaning and vision (Goldstein 2012). In some situations, a resource crisis is helpful as a trigger to bring management vision into focus, clarifying objectives and galvanizing action (Seixas and Davy 2008). Some of the most robust cases of co-management were precipitated by crises. For example, the Lofoten Islands cod co-management case, which incorporates more than a century of learning, was the consequence of a particularly intense user-group conflict that the government was unable to resolve by top-down measures (Jentoft and McCay 1995).

Strategic Action and Self-organization

The second phase of the model, strategic action, turns visions into actionable plans. It involves relationships development for the emergence of communities of practice and social networks. Wenger's (1998) communities of practice concept is particularly appropriate for describing self-organization for social learning. Co-management cases followed through time show that effective co-operation develops through learning-as-participation in a variety of resource contexts, such as wetlands (Olsson et al. 2004b), fisheries (Napier et al. 2005), wildlife (Fabricius et al. 2004), water (Pahl-Wostl et al. 2007) and integrated management (Pahl-Wostl and Hare 2004). Participatory approaches create the mechanism by which individual learning can be shared by the larger group and reinforced to become social learning and, sometimes, transformative learning (Sinclair et al. 2011; Diduck et al. 2012). Such learning may proceed from simple, single-loop learning to double-loop learning (Armitage et al. 2008).

Participatory learning helps the theory–practice linkage, or praxis, depicted in Figure 6.1 as a spiral of action–reflection–action processes that results in a continual reinforcement of strategic action through feedback. Each cycle starts with observation and identification of problems and potential solutions, leading to action, followed by reflection. Outcomes are monitored and evaluated, followed by reflection, to lead to the next cycle. Each cycle provides new information for the next iteration and serves as a learning step. Social learning can emerge from the experiences of influential individuals or of the group itself (Agrawal 2005). It can also be triggered by action research, as in the Canadian Maritime provinces (Wiber et al. 2004, 2009) and Uruguay artisanal fishery cases (Trimble and Berkes 2013). Networks are important as the site of social learning, coproducing knowledge (Davidson-Hunt and O'Flaherty 2007), combining resource management and development (Wilson et al. 2006) and capacity building (Berkes 2007a).

Instrumental Action

Communicative action and strategic action set the stage for the third phase of the model, which is dominated by collective action that produces material results, such as a healthy social-ecosystem and human well-being. This phase is characterized by the emergence of new or revised rules-in-use, that is, institutions (Ostrom 1990, 2005). Institution-building goes hand in hand with social capital, a concept that captures four interrelated features of networks: trust; reciprocity; shared rules, norms and sanctions; and connectedness (Pretty and Ward 2001). Social capital lowers the transaction costs of working together and facilitates co-operation. It gives people incentives to invest in collective activities, with the confidence that others will do so as well.

The dynamics of the process are such that, as collaboration becomes widespread, new possibilities come into focus beyond solving the original problem (Goldstein 2009). Each round of problem solving leads to another. Olsson and Folke (2001) found that, in Lake Racken, Sweden, experience in dealing with lake acidification led to knowledge-building and learning regarding a range of issues, enabling the group to deal with one problem after another over a period of several years. Social learning resulted in expanding the scope of problem solving and increasing the capacity to experiment (Olsson et al. 2004a).

The expertise needed for capacity building can be accessed through networks and often involves multiple partners (Wilson et al. 2006). Partners interact with the community to provide a range of support functions related to capacity. These might include fund-raising, facilitating self-organization, business networking and marketing, innovation and knowledge transfer, technical training, research, legal support, infrastructure, and community health and social services (Berkes 2007a). Capacity building and institution-building require an enabling environment in the political, social and economic context. Political space is needed by local actors to practice and develop their approaches (Prabhu et al. 2007). The ability to exercise power is particularly important and is often limited by the willingness of the central government to devolve appropriate powers to the local level (Ribot et al. 2006). Ostrom (1990) emphasizes the rights of resource users to devise their own institutions, without being challenged by government (the minimal recognition of rights to organize), as one of the principles for successful commons management.

Conclusions

As a solution to the problem of commons, co-management involves the sharing of power and responsibility between the government and local resource users, often in the form of government-agency and local-community partnerships, with each side contributing what it does best. Partners agree on joint rules, essential for commons management, and build problem-solving networks. These networks are the key sites of social learning that are essential for building co-management that works and, ultimately, adaptive co-management. Many of the principles for successful commons management (Ostrom 1990; Cox et al. 2010) also apply to successful co-management. Cinner et al. (2012) provide empirical evidence that co-management can help sustain fisheries and the people who depend on them. This seems to occur through improvements in key process indicators, such as participation and rule compliance, and outcome indicators, such as access to resources, well-being and income (Evans et al. 2011). The review by Gutiérrez et al. (2011) suggests the importance of leadership, consistent with the model developed in this chapter.

Co-management is not one thing. It can include a diversity of ways of sharing management power and responsibility, as the examples show. Key conditions vary by case, and capacity building may be delivered in a variety of ways, as Figure 6.5 indicates. A number of different pathways can be used to get to co-management, some more difficult than others. For example, cases with a history of conflict between users and managers may require some extra effort of trust-building (Chuenpagdee and Jentoft 2007) and may take a long time, even with a formal co-management agreement in place (Kocho-Schellenberg and Berkes 2014).

To identify some of the major processes in moving toward adaptive co-management, the chapter develops a Habermasian framework or conceptual model adapted from Prabhu et al. (2007). Without attempting to account for every possible variable, the model summarizes some of the essential considerations: deliberation for visioning; building social capital, trust and institutions; skills acquisition and capacity building through networks and partnerships; and action–reflection–action processes leading to social learning (Figure 6.6). Such adaptive co-management is not simply a theoretical possibility, but is a working reality in a number of resource management contexts, in both developed and developing nations (Olsson et al. 2004a; Colfer 2005; Pahl-Wostl 2009; Armitage et al. 2007). This is despite the fact that government decision-making realities often pose challenges to Habermasian ideals (Jones 2013).

Three points can be offered in conclusion. First, making co-management work takes time (Napier et al. 2005; Kocho-Schellenberg and Berkes 2014). Co-management evolves into adaptive co-management, shaped by interactions among the actors and feedback learning. Partnerships and social learning help an adaptive response to change and allow social–ecological systems to be resilient in the face of uncertainties in a world in flux (Folke et al. 2005; Armitage et al. 2007). Second, sharing of governance responsibilities and ability to learn from experience are relevant to institutions at all levels, from local to international. Interactions occur, not only among actors, but also among decision-making levels. Third, traditions of top-down rule are likely to lead to top-down co-management as well. Democratic institutions develop slowly, but can be nurtured and facilitated through capacity building. Enabling environments for co-management, or retention of existing community-based management, are likely to be found in countries with strong civil society traditions.

These conclusions are relevant also for Chapter 7, dealing the broader issue of coastal zone management with multiple sectors, and often involving social–ecological restoration initiatives in which local people and groups take the lead.

7

COASTAL ZONE

RECONCILING MULTIPLE USES

A fundamental notion in managing the commons is that one needs clear, agreed-upon, defensible and socially and ecologically acceptable boundaries, boundaries that mark off who has rights, who has responsibilities, who has jurisdiction, where and for what. However, littoral boundaries are liminal; they are complex, contextually contingent, and changing.

(McCay 2008, p. 8–9)

Introduction

Looking at the coastal zone as a whole, the management picture becomes more complicated than managing coastal fisheries only or sharing commons rights and responsibilities in co-management. This is because boundaries in the coastal zones are complex and forever changing, as McCay (2008) noted. However, the governance of coastal areas is segmented and rarely matches the complexity of coastal uses and their inter-relationships. The mismatch is due to historic reasons: coastal management has been carried out sector by sector, often with little regard to interactions (Crowder et al. 2006). Separate regimes govern fisheries, aquaculture, marine conservation, shipping and transportation, oil and gas, and mining. In the United States, at least 20 federal agencies implement over 140 statutes. These regimes are designed to manage conflicts within sectors —but not across sectors. Crowder et al. (2006, p. 617) point out that,

"This is like a scenario in which a number of specialist physicians, who are not communicating well, treat a patient with multiple medical problems. The combined treatment can exacerbate rather than solve problems."

The services provided by coastal ecosystems, such as food production and storm protection, are vitally important to a large number of people everywhere in the world (Brown et al. 2005). Halpern and team (2012) identified ten major uses or services provided by ocean and coastal ecosystems, expressed as human goals, chosen to reflect both human needs and ecosystem sustainability (Chapter 1, Table 1.1). The Halpern et al. (2012) list is shorter than the Millennium Ecosystem Assessment list (Table 2.4), which has four categories and many subcategories of ecosystem services (MA 2005a). In addition to obvious goals such as food production from fisheries and marine aquaculture (mariculture), the Halpern list includes some composite items such as "natural products" and "sense of place." As the authors themselves point out, many of the goals are interlinked. For example, coastal habitat loss affects the multiple goals of carbon storage, coastal protection and biodiversity. Conversely, the restoration of mangroves, salt marshes and coral reefs would significantly improve the provision of multiple goals.

Integrated coastal zone management is one of the four priority areas recognized by the Millennium Ecosystem Assessment for *integrated responses* (i.e integration of ecosystem management goals within other sectors and within broader development planning frameworks) to improve the condition of ecosystems and human well-being. The other three priority areas are sustainable forest management, integrated conservation and development, and integrated river basin management (Brown et al. 2005). Given the significance of the problem, and the inappropriate governance structures created by the sector-by-sector approach, integrated coastal zone management has become a widely accepted response to sustain coastal ecosystems (Cicin-Sain and Knecht 1998; Kay and Alder 2005). Several journals and annual conference series are devoted to integrated coastal zone management.

There are two major reasons for using the integrated coastal zone management approach. First, the various ocean and coastal uses have impacts on the environment. Second, these various uses have impacts on one another (Cicin-Sain and Knecht 1998). *Integrated coastal zone management* deals with these problems and seeks to address multiple

PHOTO 7.1 Integrated coastal zone management deals with problems from multiple drivers of change originating from processes at various levels: beach erosion in the tourist zone of Cancùn, Mexico. Beach erosion is an increasingly common sight in many parts of the world

Source: F. Berkes

drivers of social–ecological system change originating from processes at various levels. It seeks to address conflicts between different uses, improve coastal planning to regulate demands on resources, and promote institutional change (Brown et al. 2005).

However, integrated coastal zone management is only one of several possible strategies for managing the coastal zone (Table 7.1). Community-based and co-operative management is another (Chapters 5 and 6, respectively). Another alternative, privatizing coastal areas and resources, will be discussed briefly in the present chapter and again in Chapter 12. Learning-based coastal zone management applies principles of adaptive management, or learning-by-doing (Lee 1993; Olsen et al. 1998). Finally, creation of MPAs is the topic of Chapter 8. These categories are, of course, overlapping. One can have integrated coastal zone management with privatization and MPAs, for instance, or protected areas with different shades of local control and co-operation.

TABLE 7.1 **Coastal zone management strategies**

Approach	Summary and objectives
Integrated coastal zone management	A continuous and dynamic process that unites government and communities, science and management, private and public interests in preparing and implementing integrated plans for the protection and development of coastal ecosystems and resources
Co-operative coastal zone management or community-based management	A framework that guides diverse and conflicting individual interests into co-operative collective decisions that draw maximum support and enhance stakeholders' willingness to co-operate voluntarily in the implementation (Crance and Draper 1996)
Allocation of private or state property rights	Privatizing commonly owned resources or bringing them under government control to prevent overuse
Learning-based coastal zone management	Management initiatives are implemented as experiments that must be subjected to ongoing revision in terms of developing hypotheses for testing, use of control sites, documentation of the experiment and analysis (Olsen et al. 1998)
Creation of exclusive MPAs or restrictive zones	MPAs are reserved by law or other effective means to protect part or all of the enclosed environment. They are often part of fisheries management strategies, as coastal areas can act as spawning grounds for important fish species

Source: Adapted from Brown et al. 2002

This chapter aims to discuss these various possibilities for a broader conceptualization of the coast as a multiple-stakeholder, multiple-sector setting. The chapter starts with some concepts of horizontal and vertical linkages and moves on to a consideration of some characteristics of the coastal zone, followed by examples of applications. Restoring coastal ecosystems and social systems is a major topic, given the sorry state of many coastal ecosystems (MA 2005a), and is followed by a discussion of grassroots action and citizen science in the context of restoring coastal social–ecological systems.

Horizontal and Vertical Integration of Multiple Uses

Part of the complexity of the coast is that there are multiple jurisdictions. Some of these are at the same level of political, social and economic organization, and some are at different levels. To address multiple jurisdictions and multiple levels, political scientists have developed the language of horizontal and vertical relationships first introduced in Chapter 6 (Young 2002; Young et al. 2008). *Horizontal relationships* are those within a local or regional context; by definition, they involve institutions at the same level—for example, among government departments managing different, and potentially conflicting, sectors such as shipping, tourism and infrastructure development. Interactions among national governments are horizontal relationships. For example, in semi-enclosed seas such as the Mediterranean and the Baltic, negotiated solutions must be found among nation-states for pollution control and for sharing fish resources.

Vertical relationships are about different levels of government; by definition, they are those that occur across levels of organization (Young 2002). The different levels of government play different roles and address different needs. These differences may pose challenges to harmonized planning and policy development, as in the southern California case (Crowder et al. 2006). Vertical relationships are not only about levels of government; they may involve communities, tribal governments and NGOs as well.

Figure 7.1 shows a hypothetical coastal zone management case, illustrating the linked multilevel nature of resource management at local, regional and national levels. Many real life examples exist, for example, management of Japanese fisheries (Makino 2005). Local decision-making (for example, the municipal regulation of beach water quality) is appropriate but not independent of the other levels that may impact water chemistry and health standards. Drivers originating at various levels, including international, may have a profound impact on the local environment and local options. Such interactions are of the vertical kind. An example is the serial depletion of sea urchin resources in one area after another, driven by international market demand (Chapter 5).

In integrated coastal zone management, the objective is horizontal and vertical integration, and integration of different institutions and stakeholders into the decision-making process. Stakeholder inclusion is a central feature of integrated coastal zone management. Examples include the Regional Fishery Management Councils of the United States.

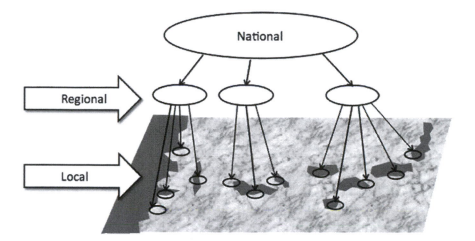

FIGURE 7.1 Multilevel organization for coastal management. Land shown by dark shading. The local level may involve associations representing various sectors and the local government. There may be horizontal (within the same level) interactions at each level, as well as vertical (across level) interactions. Multilevel governance would connect local, regional and national levels

Source: Berkes 2010a. Reprinted with permission from Elsevier

The Magnuson-Stevens Fishery Conservation and Management Act (MSA) created eight regional fishery management councils responsible for the fisheries that require conservation and management in their region. The councils are composed of both voting and non-voting members representing the commercial and recreational fishing sectors in addition to environmental, academic, and government interests.

(NOAA 2014)

How do these councils work? McCay and Jentoft (1996) point out that the councils are consultative. Governments consult with user-groups through public hearings and advisory boards, but there is no joint decision-making. This is the case with the Regional Fishery Management Councils and other coastal advisory councils in countries such as Norway, Denmark and New Zealand. Such consultative systems provide a relatively weak form of participation, as compared with co-management. As discussed in Chapter 6, co-management is (or should be) more than advisory (McCay and Jentoft 1996).

In Canada, the *Oceans Act* that came into force in 1997 provides for both horizontal and vertical integration. It designates one federal department (Fisheries and Oceans) as the lead agency to co-ordinate and integrate the various federal departments that have jurisdiction in the coastal zone (DFO 2002). It also directs this federal department to build partnerships with stakeholder groups, communities and aboriginal land claims agencies (Berkes and Fast 2005). However, the Canadian system is also consultative or advisory, except with aboriginal land claims agencies that have legally binding co-management arrangements with the government (Berkes and Fast 2005; Berkes 2009b).

In the case of international jurisdiction, there is no formal mechanism for stakeholder inclusion in decision-making, but, in some cases, NGOs are involved in discussions. Formal negotiation takes place between sovereign nations. However, there may be policy networks in play (Carlsson 2000). Haas (1990) identified a particular kind of institution that provides linkages between local issues and regional and international agencies. These *epistemic communities* have members who share principled beliefs, notions of validity and policy goals that cut across political boundaries (Haas 1990). An example is the group of scientists, government representatives and NGO people who put together the Mediterranean Action Plan. Haas pointed out that the Plan was jointly signed by a number of countries that are often in conflict, indicating that epistemic communities were able to override political differences among nations. More broadly, all policy issues bring together a community of players, *policy communities*, and some scholars consider epistemic communities as a subset of these policy communities (Coleman and Perl 1999). To the extent that they enhance horizontal and vertical interplay (Young 2002), one can also consider epistemic communities as a kind of co-management institution (Berkes 2002), perhaps similar in function to bridging organizations (Chapter 6).

Coastal zone jurisdictions have been reorganized by UNCLOS, the United Nations Convention on the Law of the Sea. Until the mid 20th century, the seaward boundary of coastal states was typically 3 miles, the range of a cannon shot, as allegedly determined by Thomas Jefferson (McCay 2008). The limit of this territorial sea subsequently expanded to 6 miles and later to 12 miles. Further, most nations of the world chose a 200-mile EEZ to define the area of their coastal interest. This was

TABLE 7.2 Jurisdictions under UNCLOS. The territorial sea extends to 12 miles, and the EEZ to 200 miles

Internal waters	EEZ		High seas
	Territorial seas		
Sovereign territory. All activities under state jurisdiction (including navigation rights)	Most marine activities under jurisdiction of coastal state Exclusive fishing zone can be established, open only to coastal state citizens Right of innocent passage available to all	Coastal state has automatic juris-diction over seabed & subsoil resources; can also claim juris-diction over fisheries & other activities (i.e., pipe & cable laying) Access to fisheries may be restricted Fishing to take account of impacts on non-target species	No sovereignty; accessible to coastal & non-coastal states All states must act reasonably; have regard to conserva-tion; regulate their citizens. Any state may exercise freedom of the sea (i.e., weapon testing) Fishing to take account of impacts on non-target species
Coastal state jurisdiction	Coastal state jurisdiction	Coastal state; UNCLOS & treaties	Flag state; UNCLOS & treaties

supported by the multilateral agreement signed by most nations, the 1982 UNCLOS (Table 7.2). Under UNCLOS, the territorial sea is 12 miles, but the coastal state has additional jurisdiction within the 200-mile EEZ, beyond which is high seas.

The 200-mile EEZ is a historically significant development. It provides a major redefinition of coastal commons, perhaps comparable to the enclosure and privatization of common lands throughout the world. Eckert (1979) considered the EEZ extension as an enclosure of ocean resources, bringing under the nation-state a huge amount of additional ocean space, no longer open access but under national jurisdiction. Thus, it simplifies (but does not quite solve) the assignment of national controls over many uses of the coastal zone: transportation; oil and gas development; mining; wind, wave and tidal power development; recreation; and protected areas.

Of these uses, oil and gas development is already a reality in coastal waters, with the industry now beginning to drill in deeper waters and in the increasingly ice-free Arctic (Leichenko and O'Brien 2008). Wind farms are common in the coastal waters of some European nations, such as Denmark. Tourism has dominated development within both the landward boundary and the seaward boundary of the coastal zone. In some of the seasonal tourist destinations, population increases manifold during a few months of the year. Coastal tourism has expanded with the phenomenon of "second homes," as many fishing communities have been gentrified into picturesque villages for the benefit of urban dwellers. As McCay (2008, p. 13) puts it, "These days, throughout the world, coastal 'development' is more likely to mean building resorts and expensive housing than the enhancement of the socio-economic welfare of traditional coastal water-dependent communities."

In many parts of the world, including the Mediterranean, the Caribbean and some other tropical destinations, and parts of the United States and Canada, coastal economies that used to be based on fishing have transformed into coastal economies based largely on tourism (Hall 2001; Fabinyi 2010). Commercial fishers have lost ground to recreational fishers in many parts of the US coast and in the Great Lakes. Barbados fishers have to look for deeper waters to set their fish traps (fish pots) to avoid recreational divers. Uruguay reserves 300 m of the coastline for recreational boaters and fishers, displacing artisanal gillnetters. With the development of deep-sea recreational fishing and whale watching in many parts of the world, tourism activities have been expanding toward the seaward boundary of the coastal zone.

MPAs have shown rapid growth in recent decades and will be discussed in more detail in Chapter 8. The intensification of use of the coastal zone brings with it the necessity of conservation. However, the establishment of MPAs has been slow. The movement of waters, and the organisms within, and problems of enforcement have been barriers to MPAs trying to catch up with terrestrial protected areas. Networks of MPAs are part of a vision of the coastal waters carved into functional zones for various uses, from conservation to energy production. Designating waters for recreational and commercial fishing, with transportation corridors running through MPAs, boating and diving areas, can produce a complex interlacing of uses (Crowder et al. 2006).

TABLE 7.3 Advantages and disadvantages of some decision-support techniques

Conceptual basis/method	Description	Advantages	Disadvantages
Cost–benefit analysis	Evaluates options by quantifying net benefits (benefits minus costs)	• Considers the benefits and costs of management options • Translates all outcomes into commensurate monetary terms • Reveals the most efficient option	• No direct consideration of the equity distribution of costs & benefits • Ignores non-quantifiable costs and benefits • Assumes that all stakeholders have equal incomes and well-being levels
Cost-effectiveness analysis	The least-cost option that meets the goals of the decision-maker is preferred	• No need to estimate the benefits of different management options • Cost information is often readily available	• The relative importance of outputs is not considered • No consideration given to the social costs resulting from side-effects of different options
Multi-criteria analysis	Uses mathematical programming techniques to select options based on objective functions with explicit weighting	• Allows quantification of implicit costs • Permits the prioritization of options • The model can reflect multiple goals or objectives for the resources	• Is an unrealistic characterization of decision-making • Difficulties associated with aggregating preferences for use in weighting • Large information needs
Risk–benefit analysis	Evaluates benefits associated with a policy in comparison with its risks	• Framework is flexible • Consideration of all benefits and costs • No automatic decision rule	• Framework is too vague • Factors considered to be commensurate are not

Source: Adapted from Pearce and Markandya 1989

All of this complexity of uses creates decision-making problems. How would one go about deciding on one use over another? The decision-making process is usually thought to have three steps: (1) identify the problem, (2) establish options for the course of action, and (3) select an option from those available and account for the decision. Sometimes, the preferences of the decision-maker are implicit rather than explicit, and may not be based on clearly defined criteria. Hence, there is a need for decision-support tools that can make the decision process clear, transparent and inclusive. These tools help generate information about the problem, generate alternative solutions, and provide the context and criteria to account for the decision made. A number of tools or techniques have been developed and used for decades, including cost–benefit analysis, cost–effectiveness analysis, multi-criteria analysis and risk–benefit analysis. Brown et al. (2002) consider that the complexity of coastal zone management problems necessitates the use of a mix of techniques appropriate to the context. Pearce and Markandya (1989) have reviewed a number of decision support techniques with their advantages and disadvantages (Table 7.3). Understanding the liminal nature of the coast helps put the decision-making issue in perspective.

The Liminal Nature of the Coast

Both the landward boundaries and the seaward boundaries of the coastal zone are complex, and they are subject to events that change the boundaries in unpredictable and sometimes devastating ways. One can think of the inundation of New Orleans in the Hurricane Katrina event, or the amazing images of the wall of water sweeping through the countryside in the 2011 Japanese tsunami. In countries with coastal zone management, such as the United States, Canada and Norway, both landward and seaward boundaries are established administratively, reflecting political, legal and geographic considerations (Cicin-Sain and Knecht 1998; Jentoft and Chuenpagdee 2009). For example, in the State of New Jersey, the landward boundary varies according to a number of different factors. In some parts of New Jersey, it is a very narrow zone, extending only to the first road or property line. In other parts, it extends inland by 0.5–24 miles, depending largely on the extent of coastal wetlands and existing development.

Interestingly, not only the state but also the market, such as insurance companies, may have a role in defining landward boundaries. To insurers, the "coastal area" is the area of uninsurable risk. In much of the mid-Atlantic region of the United States, this area used to extend from the shore to 1,000 feet landward. However, in 2006, one of the largest insurance companies in the United States changed the definition of the "coastal area" to 1 mile, rather than 1,000 feet, widening it about five-fold. According to newspaper reports, this was in response to increasing damage claims from hurricanes and storms (McCay 2008). The example illustrates the dynamism of the coastal zone, in terms not only of the impacts of climate change but also of the significance of costs of perceived environmental change in the business decisions made by large corporations.

From other perspectives as well, there may be good reasons to extend the landward boundary far inland. For example, much of marine pollution originates on the coast, but many point sources of pollution are not directly on the shoreline. Rather, much of the pollution load arrives by river discharge. Hence, to control marine pollution, it becomes important to control pollution at the watershed level, whether it is industrial pollution or nutrient and sediment pollution. For example, given the eutrophication (nutrient over-enrichment) problems of the Baltic Sea, much effort has gone into the control of nutrients in agricultural watersheds throughout the nine-country Baltic region (Österblom et al. 2010). Similarly, much of the oxygen-free dead zone of the Gulf of Mexico is being blamed on the nutrients and sediments arriving by the major river of the Gulf, the Mississippi (NOAA 2014). The situation has been further complicated by the impacts of the Gulf oil spill of 2010.

In this regard, estuaries and lagoons merit special mention. An *estuary* is defined as a partly enclosed coastal body of brackish water, with one or more rivers or streams flowing into it, and with a free connection to the open sea (Pritchard 1967). Estuaries are an important part of the coastal zone and provide a microcosm that exhibits all the complexities of that zone. Estuaries are the first areas to be affected by pollution carried down by the rivers. They are the first areas to be affected by hurricanes and changes in water levels. Think of Bangladesh as one giant flood-plain when river discharges peak seasonally, converting much of that country's land into a coastal zone where freshwater mixes with saltwater. Like estuaries, *lagoons* (shallow bodies of water separated from a larger body of water by barrier islands or reefs) are part of that liminal space (McCay 2008) that is neither freshwater nor saltwater but both, a transition that straddles the threshold. The coastal environment is complex, and human activities are intense; conflicting relationships among users (Nayak and Berkes 2010; Huong and Berkes 2011) and environmental changes that impact uses are likely to carry a large price tag.

The seaward boundary is just as complex as the landward one and brings with it the issue of the competing and overlapping uses and property rights regimes of the marine coastal zone, as sketched earlier in Figure 5.1. It is not that property rights on the landward side are simple, but at least they follow the solid land model: private ownership, individual and corporate, and government land, some of which is public land or shared land, "owned" by the citizens and held in trust by the government (McCay 2008). The complications in property rights are those related to the uncertainties and complexities of the liminal. However, in the case of the seaward side of the coastal zone, property rights are poorly developed and uncertain, as compared with the landward side.

Hence, an often-cited solution is to assign property rights to the seascape and resources on the seaward side. Property rights have in fact been assigned, for example, in the coastal commons rights of Japanese commercial fishers, or in the government-assigned leases and concessions for aquaculture and offshore oil and wind farms. Even though experts in the field of marine spatial planning advocate extending property rights to all the various uses (e.g., Norse and Crowder 2005; Crowder et al. 2006; Norse 2010), this is not so easy to do. That is because the various uses are interdependent. Unlike the terrestrial realm, where resources are largely spatially fixed, marine resources, as well as the marine and coastal waters in which they reside, tend to move around. Using commons terminology, the phenomenon of subtractability looms large: not only does each user potentially affect all the others, but also some kinds of use are mutually incompatible. For example, "some pairs of activities—spearfishing and underwater fish-watching, bottom trawling and pot fishing, or wind farms and parasailing—cannot occur in the same place at the same time" (Norse 2010, p. 185).

Coastal Zone Concepts and Application

Not all societies see a sharp distinction between land and sea. For example, for the rural people of Bangladesh, who every year obtain as many as two crops of rice, one crop of dry land produce and one crop of fish from the same, seasonally flooded piece of land–water, solid land is an ephemeral concept (Haque 1998). Likewise, for the traditional Inuit, sea ice (especially shelf ice attached to the coastline) is an extension of land, even though it may disappear seasonally (Freeman 1984). More than an anthropological footnote, this concept was legally recognized by Canadian authorities in the negotiation of Inuit land claims.

Some integrated human–environment concepts and the traditional "ridge-to-reef" social–ecological systems practiced in many Pacific island societies were mentioned in Chapter 3 (with more detailed discussion to come in Chapter 11). These systems illustrate ecosystem-like ideas where humans are part of a particular piece of land–sea, from mountaintop to the edge of reef and lagoon. Many other traditional societies have concepts of the coast and coastal resources that cut across the rigid divide between land and sea. The indigenous people of Australia are among them.

The term *caring for country* refers to indigenous Australian stewardship values for both lands and waters (Ross and Innes 2005; Rose 2005). The value of coastal resources to Girringun people, in northern Queensland, was explored using a participatory art project (Zurba and Berkes 2014). Artists from the Girringun Aboriginal Arts Centre were asked, "What does caring for country mean to you?" Starting with a moderated focus group exploring this question, 14 members of the Centre worked collaboratively on one canvas for some six weeks on the question, capturing the various elements of the costal environment and their practical and cultural values. The resulting canvas is shown in Figure 7.2.

As explained by the artists themselves, the individual panels of the painting explored a range of themes, from important species of the coast, to *Dreamtime* (the spiritual domain in which ancestral totemic beings created the physical and spiritual world), to current conservation issues. The center of the canvas includes some iconic species, such as sea turtle, stingray, saltwater crocodile and dugong. All four of these species are important in spirituality and traditional ways, they are involved in the Dreamtime, and they are special foods used in ceremonies. The shape

FIGURE 7.2 Girringun art, "Caring for Country," 1.5 × 1.25 m acrylic on canvas

Source: Property of the indigenous Australian artists from Girringun who painted it (Zurba and Berkes 2014). Reprinted with permission from Taylor & Francis

at the top left-hand corner of the painting is about the land–saltwater–freshwater interface from the point of view of the Girringun people of Warrgamay country:

> The participant chose to paint his country from both a spiritual and environmental perspective. The *Girimore* (snake) is a *dreamtime* creature which carved out the features of the land. The fine lines and background work are the geographic features found on Warrgamay country such as *Garrgul* (rivers) running through *Wabu* (rainforest). The blue waves represent *Warrangan* (ocean) and the green waves represent freshwater.
>
> (Zurba and Berkes 2014, p. 830)

Many of the 23 panels of the canvas refer to cultural stories, landforms, food species, spiritually powerful creatures, medicinal plants and material culture. Some panels deal with contemporary issues. For example, the panel at the bottom right-hand corner of the canvas expresses concern for the disappearance of cassowary habitat due to land clearance for urban development. In the words of the artist:

> This speaks about the tree clearing for development and how this affects the cassowary (*Gunduy*) conservation area on tribal lands. It is getting to the point that in the future there will be no rainforest left for this endangered animal to inhabit.
>
> (Zurba and Berkes 2014, p. 831)

Some of these traditional ways of seeing the coast have been inspiring contemporary applications. In Japan, *sato-umi* refers to marine and coastal land and waterscapes that have been formed and maintained by prolonged interaction between humans and ecosystems (Figure 7.3). Japan Satoyama

FIGURE 7.3 *Sato-umi* is a mosaic of coastal ecosystems comprised of seashore, rocky shore, tidal flats, coral reefs and seaweed/grass beds, with an emphasis on the aquatic ecosystems

Source: Japan Satoyama Satoumi Assessment 2010

Satoumi Assessment (2010) defines *sato-yama* (*sato* = where people live, *yama* = forest) and *sato-umi* (*umi* = sea) landscapes as dynamic mosaics of managed socio-ecological systems producing a bundle of ecosystem services for human well-being. The original managed environment concept known for centuries is *sato-yama*, and these landscapes occupy about 20 percent of the forest area of Japan. *Sato-umi* is a new concept for sustainable use of the coastal environment and was recently "invented" by Japanese scholars, based on the concept of *sato-yama* (Yanagi 2008).

These social–ecological productive land and waterscapes, *sato-yama* and *sato-umi*, are being explored to assist with post-disaster rebuilding from the Great East Japan Earthquake and tsunami (Takeuchi 2013). The emerging issue is how to create a resilient society and economy that can respond to disasters and gradual environmental transformations such as climate change. As applied to Sado Island, *sato-yama* and *sato-umi* land and waterscapes are used to create a new business model whereby coastal resources are used in an integrated way to create livelihoods, conserve biodiversity and build synergies between tourism and bioproduction industries (Takeuchi 2013).

Social–Ecological Systems-based Restoration

Pitcher and Lam (2010) assessed ten broadly conceived fisheries management strategies against various performance criteria and found that historically based restoration came out as the best, ahead of ecosystem-based management. Some of the conventional approaches (stock assessment, privatization and MPAs), along with *laissez-faire* freedom from government interference, finished at the bottom of the list. Although the details of the results can be debated, the findings are significant in drawing attention to the significance of environmental restoration. As coastal environments perhaps support the most heavily used ecosystems, they probably also support the most heavily damaged ecosystems (MA 2005b). Hence, in most cases, the issue is not development but ecological restoration. As in *sato-umi*, we are referring largely to peopled landscapes and waterscapes, and therefore the challenge is not merely ecological restoration but social–ecological restoration.

A good example comes from the Kristianstads Vattenrike Biosphere Reserve, a coastal wetland south of Stockholm, Sweden. Discussed earlier in Chapter 6 in the context of co-management and the role of bridging organizations, strengthening the ecological integrity of the Biosphere Reserve required restoring wetland functions. That, in turn, necessitated reversing long-standing practices to drain the wetland. Interestingly, the restoration effort included the decision to *resume* cattle grazing, which had earlier been prohibited with the declaration of the Biosphere Reserve. However, grazing was found to be ecologically useful: it reduced the choking of waterways by vegetation and helped water circulation. Another key action was to change the mindset of local inhabitants and resource users, from regarding the area as "water-sick" to regarding it as "water-rich" (Olsson et al. 2004b; Hahn et al. 2006).

Some of the best examples of restoration come from indigenous areas, because the social and cultural aspects of restoration are often at the forefront, and people's livelihoods tend to be closely related to the health of local ecosystem services. Sinkyone Wilderness, said to be the first intertribal wilderness area in the United States, was created in an area where "the genocide of the Sinkyone people came with the ecocide of the ancient forests of *kahs-tcho* (redwood)." The *kahs-tcho* was considered by local tribes as sacred: "destroy these trees and you will destroy the Creator's love" (Rosales 2010, p. 9). The Wilderness area is relatively small, only a small portion of the original Sinkyone territory, but it supports a remnant coastal redwood forest and has an integrated restoration program focusing on culturally important places and species (Box 7.1).

Web sites indicate a number of restoration projects initiated by, or partnered with, tribal groups. For example, the Seminole Tribe of Florida developed their own Everglades initiative, restoring (in partnership with the US Army Corps of Engineers) close to 1,000 ha of the original Big Cypress wetlands. The plan consisted of constructing water control and treatment facilities. Contributing to the rehabilitation of the western Everglades, the project restored water storage capacity and native vegetation. It had a major role in supporting the Seminole Tribe of Florida's water entitlement and enabling sustainable agriculture (US Army Corps of Engineers 2014).

The Nisqually River and delta restoration project near Olympia, Washington State, has a history of accomplishments in integrated coastal restoration (Nisqually Delta Restoration 2014; Washington Tribes 2014). It also has an interesting story behind it, intertwined with treaties and the Boldt Decision of 1974 regarding salmon fishing rights (Cohen 1986;

BOX 7.1 INTERTRIBAL SINKYONE WILDERNESS COUNCIL, MENDOCINO COUNTY, CA

With significant support from Lannan [Foundation, a family foundation dedicated to cultural freedom, diversity and creativity], the nation's first intertribal wilderness has been created on a 3,845-acre parcel of redwood forestland located along the Lost Coast north of Fort Bragg. The InterTribal Sinkyone Wilderness land is only a small portion of the original indigenous Sinkyone Indian territory.

From the mid-1800s to the early 1900s, the Sinkyone people were massacred and driven from their land. Some Sinkyone survivors became members of neighboring tribes. This land has great cultural significance for Indian peoples of the region who in the mid-1980's helped stop the further clear cut logging of the land's last old growth redwoods and then formed the InterTribal Sinkyone Wilderness Council to acquire and conserve the property. Comprised of ten federally recognized North Coast tribes, the Council is a nonprofit land conservation consortium that owns and manages the InterTribal Wilderness land. The Council worked with TPL, the Pacific Forest Trust, the State Coastal Conservancy, and other conservation groups to reestablish indigenous peoples' control of the land and to place protections on it that ensure permanent conservation and stewardship of its sensitive cultural and ecological values.

The Council's management includes a preservation and restoration program focusing on stewardship of forest, salmon, and other culturally important resources. The Council has completed a plan for limited public access that calls for low-impact campsites and backcountry hiking trails linking to the Lost Coast Trail in the adjacent Sinkyone Wilderness State Park. The Council collaborates with conservation organizations, local communities, and state agencies to address conservation and restoration needs for the InterTribal land, the Sinkyone State Park, and the aboriginal Sinkyone Indian territory at large.

(Lannan 2014)

Grossman 2010). The Stevens Treaties of 1854–5 extinguished Native claims to the area in return for exclusive tribal use of reservation lands located near prime fishing areas at the mouths of salmon rivers, with tribal rights to fish in all the accustomed fishing grounds. However, after Washington entered the Union in 1889, and canning technology gave rise to a lucrative salmon fishing industry in the late 1800s, salmon stocks and the Native share of the fishery started to decline sharply. State officials blamed Natives who continued to fish (calling them "poachers") for the decline of fish stocks.

Tribal fishers started to contest state regulations and harassment in the early 1960s and held "fish-ins" on the Nisqually and other rivers. Severe disputes eventually led to a court case. A 1974 decision by Federal Judge Boldt affirmed treaty rights and recognized the Native right to a share of the state fishery (Cohen 1986). However, open ocean fishing fleets, hydroelectric dams that blocked or reduced salmon migrations, and clear-cut logging that silted up spawning rivers had already reduced salmon runs to levels much below the historic norms. Politicians and "white backlash" groups continued to blame tribal fisheries as the central culprit (Grossman 2010).

This led to the next phase of the Boldt decision, in which tribes demanded a voice in regulating the various impacts on salmon populations and in the decision-making process. The state and the tribes instituted co-management and eventually got it working after about ten years, leading to a number of positive outcomes (Singleton 1998). The North-west Indian Fisheries Commission so established became a model for other tribal natural resource agencies around the United States. The co-management arrangement established tribal groups as "legitimate" players in management, helping normalize relations with other user-groups. It also fostered a wave of stewardship activity, protecting and restoring salmon habitat.

The Nisqually Tribe started restoring salmon habitat on the Nisqually River and bought out, piece by piece, the wetlands where the river joins the sea. As with the Everglades initiative of the Seminole, the various phases of the Nisqually River and delta restoration projects have multiple partners, with state and federal agencies and other groups. Along with environmental restoration, the Nisqually people and other tribal nations of Washington have been in a state of cultural and economic revitalization, restoring ceremonies and engaging youth in tribal programs. "In the 21st century, Washington's tribal nations are going through an unprecedented revitalization, rooted partly in the treaties they signed in the 19th century," concludes Grossman (2010, p. 1).

Citizen Science or Civil Empowerment?

In many parts of the United States, Canada and many other countries, citizen groups participate in monitoring the environment. For example, birdwatchers everywhere collect data that are combined to reveal trends in bird numbers, distributions and change, for instance, in first egg dates; stream watchers collect data on water quality and stream biota. Some of these programs can be very large. For example, tens of thousands of volunteers are involved in the Christmas Bird Count run by the National Audubon Society in the United States. Some are sophisticated, involving the use of technology such as remote sensing and GIS. Many have a strong public education component, for example, programs run by the Cornell Lab of Ornithology (Shirk et al. 2012). The COASST (2014) project at the University of Washington works in partnership with state, tribal and federal agencies, environmental organizations and community groups. The project trains volunteers to monitor marine ecosystem health, mainly by recording details of dead birds on the beach over large areas of the US Pacific coast, in five states.

These kinds of activity are broadly referred to as citizen science. The term is normally understood to mean the involvement of citizens as volunteers in the collection of scientific data, mostly survey data. Citizen science is a way of collecting large volumes of data cheaply; at the same time, it serves science education and fosters stewardship by connecting people to their ecosystems. However, some civil society groups are engaged in activities of monitoring, managing and restoring their local ecosystems in ways that go beyond the usual definitions of citizen science. Ecological restoration efforts of tribal groups, such as the Niqually River restoration, fall in this category. Collaborative monitoring of salmon aquaculture wastes by Kwakwaka'wakw clam harvesters of the Broughton Archipelago, northern Vancouver Island, British Columbia (Heaslip 2008), is also in this category. Other examples can be given from different parts of the world.

Citizen action in Lake Racken, western Sweden, started with a local resident who was a water quality technician and concerned with lake acidification from acid rain. He started a liming group in the early 1970s and actually reversed acidification trends in his area before the Swedish national monitoring program was established. The local response at Racken started a knowledge accumulation process that resulted in the tackling of a series of environmental problems. The liming group self-organized into a fishing association in 1986 and dealt with crayfish disease in the lake, crayfish overexploitation and brown trout habitat management (Olsson and Folke 2001; Olsson et al. 2004a).

In India, "people's science movements" have a history that goes back to the 1960s in the southern state of Kerala. Village-level resource mapping programs emerged in the 1980s, and the People's Biodiversity Registers (PBRs) program developed in the mid 1990s in a number of states, involving hundreds of rural communities. It documented the local knowledge of useful biodiversity, ongoing environmental change and local development aspirations, how rural people would like to see resources managed. The PBR program was decentralized, with different groups focusing on different issues. Technical support was often provided by local post-secondary institutions. The PBR used participatory rural appraisal-type methodologies, widely applied in development research and useful in bridging local knowledge and science (Gadgil et al. 2000, 2003).

Such programs go beyond citizen science, because the citizen participants are no longer carrying out value-free science but are engaging in policy-relevant questions. In many cases, they are also initiating their own projects. In the Lake Racken case, the impetus came from the local community. In the PBR case, communities were running their own projects and connecting biodiversity to livelihood needs. Both cases involved participatory research and the empowerment of the citizens. The Kwakwaka'wakw clam harvesters in British Columbia raised questions about salmon aquaculture waste at a time when research and media attention was concentrating on the spread of parasites from escaped aquaculture salmon. The clam harvesters had an advantage: they knew their waters for many generations. They had a baseline of what was normal and what was not and knew how to tell when something was wrong. Their efforts were able to get the attention of government researchers and resulted in participatory research (Heaslip 2008).

The origins of participatory research or participatory action research go back to the 1970s, with the development of research methodologies that combined theory, action and participation to further the interests of exploited groups in Latin America and other regions (Fals-Borda 1987). The Brazilian scholar Paulo Freire (1970) advocated redressing power imbalances through learning approaches that included an equitable teaching and learning environment, where learners were teachers and teachers were learners. The assumption was that those who were most affected by decisions should have a say in those decisions, that they should be empowered to participate in the direction of research and application of results (Jentoft 2005; Trimble and Berkes 2013).

In some cases where government research is lacking, citizen groups are finding their own partners to carry out their own research. Port Mouton Bay is a fishing community south of Halifax in Nova Scotia, Canada (Photo 4.2 in Chapter 4). With the collapse of cod stocks, lobsters became the mainstay of the fishery. In 1994, an aquaculture company anchored three temporary cages in the Bay. Initially, fishers observed crabs and lobsters in the vicinity of the cages and thought that they were benefiting from aquaculture feed settling on the bottom. Their views changed in 1997 when the aquaculture site expanded, and lobsters began avoiding the part of the Bay with salmon cages. Fishers also observed the disappearance of eelgrass and invertebrates such as mussels and excessive growth of algae spreading throughout the Bay and even blocking lobster trap entrances. The company applied for a second lease in 2002, to be located in an area that the fishers considered to be a critical habitat for lobsters. The fishers became very concerned and formed, in 2006, the Friends of Port Mouton Bay (FPMB) (Loucks et al., in prep.).

Not getting a favorable response from the government regarding aquaculture expansion, FPMB set out to show that the Bay was not suitable for salmon aquaculture, and that aquaculture was damaging local livelihoods. Two local oceanographers attended FPMB meetings and asked the fishers how the Bay worked. The siting criteria for aquaculture leases stipulate the need for high flushing rates, but the fishers' knowledge of currents and the bathymetry (bottom contour) map of the Bay showed that the proposed aquaculture site was a semi-enclosed area, with a deep basin that trapped sediments and aquaculture waste, and was, therefore, not suitable for aquaculture. A series of scientific studies was undertaken by the community and its science partners. The FPMB has posted over 26 scientific and local ecological knowledge reports on its web site, documenting the negative impacts of aquaculture on the Bay's ecosystem and loss of livelihood benefits (Loucks et al., in prep.). The research, as guided by independent scientists and university researchers, was proper science, but the questions were formulated jointly, and the whole project was initiated by the community—very different from conventional citizen science.

Conclusions

Managing the coastal zone is more complex than managing a particular commons, because of multiple uses and users. A non-communicating group of specialist physicians treating a patient with multiple medical problems is an apt analogy (Crowder et al. 2006). The patient's problems may worsen, despite expert treatment. Coastal zone management is ecosystem-based management; it is also adaptive management (Brown et al. 2005). It is both an art and a science, involving learning, user-group participation/deliberation and trade-offs. Balancing various uses is a necessary part of decision-making but involves value judgments. A number of decision-support tools are available to help with the clarity, transparency and inclusiveness of the decision-making process (Table 7.3).

The co-management experience indicates that the usual three-step decision-making process (identify problem, develop options, select one option) can be improved by use of decision-support tools. It can also be expanded to include explicit consideration of linked social–ecological systems and capacity building, followed by evaluation and returning to step one, the adaptive management cycle (Table 7.4).

One of the exciting developments in coastal management involves the proliferation of community-driven ecosystem restoration projects, presumably a response to the degraded state of many coastal environments. It is probably not possible to return to the original "pristine" condition of an ecosystem, as resilience theory might argue. However, many projects such as the one in Nisqually River and coastal wetlands seem to be doing well in restoring ecosystem function, as well as cultural and economic values. A second kind of exciting development is the proliferation of citizen science projects, many of which are going beyond conventional citizen science to address complex issues of science and society and are serving to increase political participation and social networking (Shirk et al. 2012).

Port Mouton Bay is an example of a community taking matters into its own hands to carry out the needed research with its own science partners. Port Mouton Bay also serves as an excellent example of participatory education (Freire 1970) and transformative learning (Diduck et al. 2012). With livelihoods threatened and the government silent, the community took matters into its own hands and carried out the necessary

TABLE 7.4 **A six-step process for problem solving**

1.	*Define the social–ecological system*, i.e., the resource system, the people, the action arena and how it is structured
2.	*Map the essential management tasks* to be performed and the problems to be solved. What management decisions must be made, and who makes them?
3.	*Clarify the participants* in co-management activities and related problem-solving processes. Who participates? How is management organized? What is the web of relations, and how is power shared?
4.	*Analyze linkages.* How and to what extent do the identified relations connect central levels of decision-making to those of the local level? What are the historical and political contexts of the system?
5.	*Evaluate capacity-building needs.* What efforts are needed to nurture, enhance and utilize the skills and capabilities of people and institutions at all levels?
6.	*Prescribe remedies.* The analyst can communicate the results of research to relevant groups. What can be done better? Evaluate outcomes and return to the first step, completing the adaptive management cycle, using policies as experiments from which managers can learn

Source: Adapted from Carlsson and Berkes 2005

research, empowering itself in the process (Jentoft 2005). However, the example also shows that the government was not responding to community concerns and had perhaps lost the capability of delivering relevant science for this particular coastal zone conflict. In an era of declining government services and increasing coastal resource privatization, this is cause for concern.

8

CONSERVING BIODIVERSITY
MPAS AND STEWARDSHIP

Marine Protected Areas, or MPAs—ocean zones limiting human activity—cover little more than 2 percent of the world's oceans, despite an internationally agreed target of 10 percent by 2020. And thousands of those that do exist are little more than "paper parks," many scientists have found. Entering these choppy waters is geographer Peter Jones, who shows, through some 20 case studies, how and how not to govern MPAs effectively. Jones compellingly concludes that a diversity of incentives, from economic to social, is as essential as the diversity of the ecosystems MPAs are designed to protect

(Anon. 2014)

Introduction

The above quote appeared in a book review of Jones's (2014) *Governing Marine Protected Areas*. It is insightful in capturing in a nutshell the dilemmas of coastal and marine conservation. We have international consensus on the need to do a better job of conserving coastal ecosystems and have established a conserved area target of 10 percent of the world's oceans. The problem is that we are not anywhere near that target, and the hastily established MPAs in various parts of the world seem to exist mainly on paper. In short, there is a gap between policy and on-the-ground reality, and that is mainly because of the complexities of limiting human activity in large areas of heavily used coastal waters, not an easy thing to do, as the previous chapter argued.

The need for conservation has been well documented. Human exploitation of coastal and marine resources has resulted in: species declines, especially of predatory species (Myers and Worm 2003); degradation of key ecosystems and habitat types such as coral reefs (Hughes et al. 2003); regime shifts in ecosystems (Hughes et al. 2005); and loss in ecosystem services (Worm et al. 2006). On the other hand, scholars such as Hilborn et al. (2005) caution about overgeneralizing species declines, pointing out that we need to acknowledge the many stocks that appear to be managed well. However, habitat degradation and loss throughout the coastal areas of the world are well established (MA 2005b).

Protected areas have been the primary means by which biodiversity is conserved. The International Union for Conservation of Nature (IUCN) co-ordinates and categorizes marine and terrestrial protected areas. Different protected area categories have different management objectives. In addition to the well-known category of national parks, several other categories tend to achieve conservation by excluding human uses. However, the two relatively recent IUCN categories, V and VI, embrace certain kinds of sustainable human use and cultural values (Table 8.1).

The argument in this chapter is that conserving biodiversity in marine and coastal environments is obviously necessary and important. However, the conservation models used are often inappropriate for a given case. First, not all biodiversity can be conserved through protected areas. Most of the world's biodiversity is not in protected areas but on lands and waters used by people for their livelihoods. Second, there may be too much emphasis on people-free protected areas and perhaps not enough on sustainable use areas. If so, long-term biodiversity conservation in much of the world can be achieved most effectively in partnership with the people making a living in that area. This, in turn, depends on understanding the interactions of societies with their environments and what motivates people to conserve. Thus, the chapter holds that, in most cases, local people, communities and their institutions have to be involved in conservation. As Murphree (2009) argued in the African context, this may be the only viable option for an effective human stewardship of landscapes and seascapes.

TABLE 8.1   IUCN categories of protected areas

Protected area category	Management objectives
Ia Strict nature reserve	Strictly protected areas set aside to conserve biodiversity and, possibly, geological/geomorphological features, where human visitation, use and impacts are strictly controlled and limited to ensure protection of the conservation values. They serve as indispensable reference areas for scientific research and monitoring
Ib Wilderness area	Large, unmodified or slightly modified areas, retaining their natural character and influence, without permanent or significant human habitation, which are protected and managed so as to preserve their natural condition
II National park (ecosystem protection; protection of cultural values)	Large natural or near-natural areas set aside to protect large-scale ecological processes, along with the complement of species and ecosystems characteristic of the area, which also provide a foundation for environmentally and culturally compatible spiritual, scientific, educational, recreational and visitor opportunities
III Natural monument	Areas are set aside to protect a specific natural monument, such as a landform, sea mount, a cave or even a living feature such as an ancient grove. They are generally quite small areas and often have high visitor, historical or cultural value
IV Habitat/species management	Areas dedicated to the conservation of particular species or habitats. Many Category IV protected areas need regular, active management interventions to meet their objective
V Protected landscape/ seascape	An area where the interaction of people and nature over time has produced a distinct character and significant ecological, biological, cultural and scenic values, and where safeguarding the integrity of this interaction is vital to conserving nature and sustaining other values
VI Protected area with sustainable use of natural resources	Protected areas that conserve ecosystems and habitats, together with associated cultural values and traditional management systems. They are generally large, with most of the area in a natural condition and part under sustainable natural resource management. Low-level nonindustrial use of natural resources compatible with nature conservation is seen as one of the main aims of this type of protected area

Source: Borrini-Feyerabend et al. 2013, p. 9

The chapter starts with some concepts and definitions. Then it turns to a consideration of different models of biodiversity conservation. The people-free protected area approach is under criticism, but models of community-based conservation are under debate as well. The chapter then discusses some innovative approaches in various parts of the world, showing a diversity of conservation models, from the Great Barrier Reef of Australia, which includes large no-take zones, to Fiji's locally managed marine areas designed to restore fishery values. Emerging out of this analysis is the need to consider multiple objectives of conservation and human well-being. Ways of reinforcing the stewardship ethic and reconnecting social and ecological systems may help think through multiple objectives. Finally, the chapter considers some possible directions in the way protected areas are conceived and implemented.

The chapter is in part about *community-based conservation*, which "includes natural resources or biodiversity protection by, for, and with the local community," according to the original definition by Western and Wright (1994, p. 7). The authors noted that defining it more precisely would be futile, as community-based conservation includes a diverse mix of activities practiced in various parts of the world. The central idea of the concept should hold everywhere: "the coexistence of people and nature, as distinct from protectionism and the segregation of people and nature" (Western and Wright 1994, p. 8). However, to focus merely on the "local community" is not adequate, given our current understanding that community-based conservation extends beyond communities to include linkages and multiple levels of institutions that shape outcomes at the local level, as argued in Chapters 6 and 7. Hence, the seminal community-based conservation definition of Western and Wright (1994) needs to be extended, so that it "includes natural resources or biodiversity protection by, for, and with the local community, taking into account drivers, institutional linkages at the local level, and multiple levels of organization that impact and shape institutions at the local level" (Berkes 2007a, p. 15193).

Some kinds of community-based conservation project are referred to as *integrated conservation–development projects* (ICDPs). Also called *people-centered conservation and development* and *eco-development*, ICDPs typically refer to biodiversity conservation projects with rural development components (Brown 2002). The approach tries to combine social development with conservation goals, often seeking alternative resources or sources of income to release pressure on the resource to be conserved. The conservation impetus is often exogenous, coming from the outside.

By contrast, in *indigenous and community-conserved areas* (ICCAs), another kind of community-based conservation, the conservation impetus is endogenous. It involves community (and not government or outside NGO) control and implementation. Close connection of a group of people to the local ecosystem, local control of the area, and management decisions leading to conservation of both the ecosystem and associated cultural values are the defining characteristics of ICCAs (ICCA 2014). Typically, ICCAs support multifunctional cultural landscapes and seascapes (Martin et al. 2011). These are not people-free conservation areas, but rather humanized environments that tend to support cultural values, as in IUCN Categories V and VI protected areas (Table 8.1). Combining

TABLE 8.2 IUCN governance types for protected areas

Type A: Governance by government
- Federal or national ministry or agency in charge
- Sub-national ministry or agency in charge (e.g., at regional, provincial, municipal level)
- Government-delegated management (e.g., to an NGO)

Type B: Shared governance
- Transboundary governance (formal arrangements between one or more sovereign states or territories)
- Collaborative governance (through various ways in which diverse actors and institutions work together)
- Joint governance (pluralist board or other multi-party governing body)

Type C: Private governance. Conserved areas established and run by:
- individual landowners
- non-profit organizations (e.g., NGOs, universities)
- for-profit organizations (e.g., corporate landowners)

Type D: Governance by indigenous peoples and local communities
- Indigenous peoples' conserved territories and areas—established and run by indigenous peoples
- Community conserved areas and territories—established and run by local communities

Source: Borrini-Feyerabend et al. 2013, p. 29

considerations of both biodiversity and cultural diversity has led to the concept of *biocultural diversity*, which Maffi and Woodley (2010, p. 5) define as comprising "the diversity of life in all its manifestations— biological, cultural and linguistic—which are interrelated (and likely co-evolved) within a complex socio-ecological adaptive system."

The IUCN recognizes the existence of multiple governance types for protected areas. In addition to the familiar "governance by government," protected areas may show shared governance, private governance or community governance (Table 8.2). Protected areas are not always administered by governments. There are many large, privately run protected areas, for example in Africa. Shared governance includes conservation regimes in transboundary areas. It also includes co-management regimes involving stakeholders, as in Australia's Indigenous Protected Areas (Smyth 2006). As well, indigenous peoples and local communities may govern their own protected areas, including ICCAs. Many biodiversity-rich areas are under multiple and competing claims, including nominally government-owned coastal land and seascapes that are under community control.

Competing Models of Biodiversity Conservation

In a symposium paper in 1974, conservation ecologist Raymond Dasmann made a distinction between *ecosystem peoples* (those who depend for their livelihoods primarily on the ecosystem(s) in which they live) and *biosphere people* (those who have the whole biosphere at their disposal). Although all dualisms are risky, his point was that there were some peoples who have managed, in one way or another, not to bring about changes in the local ecosystem that were deleterious to their continued existence (Dasmann 2002). To the extent that the dualism holds in the contemporary world (yes, ecosystem peoples also have cellphones and other technology), one could say that it is the biosphere people who create national parks; ecosystem people have always lived in the equivalent of national parks, areas rich in biocultural diversity:

> It is characteristic of wealthier biosphere people that they do not want to stay at home. They wander the globe always searching— searching for something they seem to have lost along the way in their rush to capture the resources of the world and accumulate

its wealth. Thus they give rise to the tourist industry, and this in turn provides a financial justification for creating and maintaining national parks. In these parks the wanderers can see some of the wonders that they left.

(Dasmann 2002, p. 158)

People who are dependent on local ecosystems need to be able to control their resource base. This follows from the commons literature that shows that the creation of property rights is crucial for commons management (Chapter 5). Thus, the logic of community-based conservation is to create a stake for the local community to conserve a particular resource or resources. The community level in conservation is important precisely because it is the interface of ecosystems and rural livelihoods —ecosystem services and human well-being. Historically, livelihoods depended on ecosystem services used as a portfolio. Maintaining biodiversity was crucial for maintaining livelihoods. This was so, not only in terrestrial ecosystems (Gadgil et al. 1993), but also in marine ones, and not only in the developing world, but also in parts of the industrialized world. For example, lobster fishers in Nova Scotia, Canada, can make a good living only if they have access to quotas of other species such as groundfish (benthic species) and crabs that help fill in the seasonal cycle and provide the flexibility to switch species, without putting too much fishing pressure on any one of them (Wiber et al. 2004, 2009). Thus, modern quota management, which tends to force fishers to specialize in a small number of stocks and which constrains flexibility, works against biodiversity-maintaining portfolios (McCay 2012).

The people-free protected area approach has come under criticism for a variety of reasons (Brechin et al. 2002), including human rights (Dowie 2009). IUCN's 1975 Kinshasa Resolution on Protection of Traditional Ways of Life, the Durban Accord of the Vth IUCN World Parks Congress, which agreed to a new approach to protected areas and their role in broader conservation and development agendas, and the Convention on Biological Diversity (CBD 2014) were all steps toward integrating human considerations into conservation, somewhat of a paradigm change (Phillips 2003). In recent decades, many countries have discontinued the practice of displacing resident populations from newly created protected areas (Mascia and Claus 2008). Will this hamper the effectiveness of conservation measures? With commons considerations in mind, one can argue that just the opposite may be the case.

It is very difficult to create a stake for the local community to conserve resources in human-free protected areas. Lack of attention to human well-being invites encroachment and poaching, especially in MPAs, where monitoring and enforcement are particularly difficult. The outcome of encroachment may be resource degradation and conflict, in turn reinforcing the assumption that communities cannot conserve (Figure 8.1). With increased population pressures and other drivers such as market demands, the stage is set for conservation failure (Roe et al. 2000). The solution is to break the vicious cycle by creating incentives to conserve, linking conservation to better livelihoods. For more than two decades, researchers and practitioners have been searching for models to implement this approach, often against overwhelming trends for centralization and neoliberalization (Lele et al. 2010).

One possible model is integrated conservation–development, which seeks to substitute other resources and income sources to reduce the pressure on the resources to be conserved. Salafsky and Wollenberg (2000)

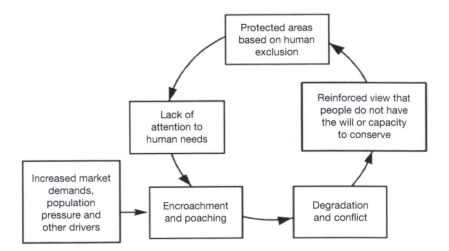

FIGURE 8.1 Lack of attention to human rights and livelihoods invites encroachment and poaching. This leads to degradation and conflict, in turn reinforcing the assumption that people do not have the will or capacity to conserve. Coupled by other drivers that exacerbate encroachment pressures, the stage is set for failure of both conservation and livelihoods

Source: Modified from Roe et al. 2000

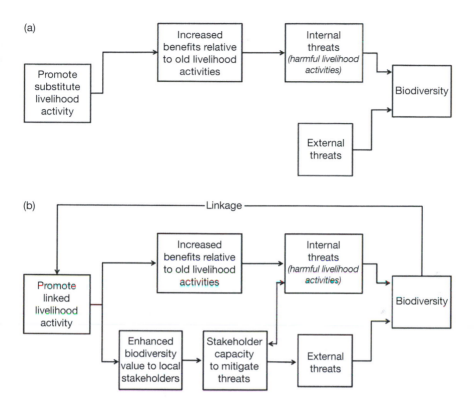

FIGURE 8.2 Two models for connecting livelihoods and biodiversity: (a) indirect linkage: substitution strategy, and (b) direct linkage: linked incentive strategy

Source: Adapted from Salafsky and Wollenberg 2000. Reprinted with permission from Elsevier

consider the substitution strategy of ICDPs to be an indirect linkage between biodiversity conservation and livelihood, and not very effective (Figure 8.2a).

They suggest that a more effective strategy would be to seek a direct linkage between biodiversity conservation and livelihood as a way to strengthen incentives. Under this model, improved conservation would lead to increased livelihood benefits relative to old livelihood activities, giving further incentives to mitigate internal and external threats to conservation (Figure 8.2b). The logic of this direct linkage model seems to be robust, but problems are likely to emerge out of the details (Roe et al. 2013). For example, does conserving livelihood resources give a close correspondence to conserving biodiversity? Who reaps the increased benefits? What kind of capacity building and legal protection would local people need to counter internal and external threats?

International Experiments with MPAs

Here we examine a number of international "experiments" with MPAs, as these are less well developed and often more experimental than terrestrial protected areas. The examples come from Australia, the United States, New Zealand, Oceania and Canada. The section starts with a consideration of Australia's Great Barrier Reef Marine Park and the Papahānaumokuākea Marine National Monument (originally, the Northwestern Hawaiian Islands Marine National Monument) of the United States, both very large MPAs. It continues with ICCAs and co-managed MPAs; these are often small players in the international network of protected areas, but they are important to understanding of the characteristics of alternative conservation pathways. What are the drivers of success or failure in protected areas? What policy mechanisms work? The brief descriptions hide the fact that many of these cases have gone through periods of trial and error, often with more failures than successes. Various problems and obstacles no doubt remain in all cases. Hence, these examples should be considered as innovations and experiments to learn from, rather than blueprints to follow (Berkes 2007a).

Australia's Great Barrier Reef Marine Park, which is almost the size of Japan, is considered a globally significant demonstration of the effectiveness of large-scale networks of marine reserves (McCook et al. 2010). Established in 1975 and covering an area of 345,000 km^2, more than 33 percent of the Park as of 2004 is in no-take areas (previously 4.5 percent). The new zoning implements many of the design principles in the literature. For example, the network of no-take areas has at least 20 percent protection per bioregion, minimum levels of protection for all known habitats or unique features, and minimum sizes for no-take areas of at least 10 or 20 km across at the smallest diameter (Fernandes et al. 2005). Some of the key success factors may have global applicability. They include: problem focus; applying the precautionary principle; using independent experts; seeking input into decision-making; conducting participatory consultation; having appropriate legislation; mobilizing broad public support; and having the ability to address issues of displaced user-groups, such as commercial fishers (Fernandes et al. 2005; Olsson et al.

2008). The transformation process toward ecosystem-based management relied on the ability to mobilize support at critical times, triggered by a sense of urgency in the face of land runoff, overharvesting and climate change. This helped shift the focus of governance from protection of individual reefs to stewardship of the large-scale seascape (Olsson et al. 2008).

At 360,000 km^2, larger than Greece, the Papahānaumokuākea Marine National Monument is larger than the Great Barrier Reef Marine Park. Created in 2006, it is an IUCN Category V protected area (protected landscape/seascape) in the UNESCO (2014) World Heritage listing. It includes ten islands and atolls of the Northwestern Hawaiian Islands and is internationally recognized for both its cultural and natural values. According to the web site:

> The area has deep cosmological and traditional significance for living Native Hawaiian culture, as an ancestral environment, as an embodiment of the Hawaiian concept of kinship between people and the natural world, and as the place where it is believed that life originates and to where the spirits return after death.

It has the advantage that the area is sparsely populated, and the IUCN Category V status permits interaction of people and nature, minimizing problems of human displacement. The governance model for the park involves two federal agencies and the State of Hawai'i working collaboratively in a polycentric arrangement (Box 6.1; Kittinger et al. 2011). This one, very large heritage site adds up to about 3 percent of US territorial waters—but constitutes some 95 percent of all US MPAs (as of 2014), meaning all the remaining US MPAs are small and do not add up to much in terms of total area.

Turning to a consideration of smaller MPAs, some informative examples come from New Zealand. Māori communities have traditionally relied on access to coastal resources for food and ceremonial purposes. For example, in some areas, treating guests to a meal of abalone was important for showing hospitality. Since the Treaty of Waitangi 1840, which established New Zealand as a British colony, Māori have tried to maintain their rights to manage coastal fisheries, but the growth in commercial fishing, combined with increased pressure from multiple uses of coastal areas, has made this difficult. New Zealand government reports on the health of fisheries do not match the observations of indigenous people. Whereas the government consistently claims that New Zealand is a world leader in sustainable fisheries, Māori environmental guardians (*kaitiaki*) report ongoing declines in the health and abundance of coastal resources, especially of inshore species, since the 1970s (Dick et al. 2012; Stephenson et al. 2014).

The Treaty of Waitangi Fisheries Settlement Act 1992 introduced an obligation on the New Zealand government to develop, in partnership with Māori, a set of measures for management of customary Māori fisheries. This resulted in three key management tools: *Taiāpure* are gazetted areas in which local Māori can be involved in the conservation and management of the fishery, aquatic life and seaweed. They can be set up at the request of the local tribal group for an area that has customarily been of special significance to them as a source of food or for cultural reasons. Another class of Māori-led MPA, *māitaitai* reserves can be established to protect traditional fishing grounds to provide for customary practices and food harvesting. *Kaitiaki* can request the government to provide bylaws to control fishing for noncommercial purposes. *Temporary closures* of fisheries, based on the Māori traditional management practice of *rāhui*, and similar to taboo closures in Oceania (Johannes 2002), are meant as a tool to respond to local depletions.

There are important differences between these three kinds of measure. *Taiāpure* cannot exclude commercial fishing except by regulation, but *temporary closures* and *mātaitai* reserves can. *Taiāpure* committees have representatives of all local stakeholders, whereas *mātaitai* can be directly managed by *kaitiaki*, although in practice they often involve a wider stakeholder group and are essentially co-management-type arrangements (Taiepa et al. 1997; Stephenson et al. 2014). Since the 1990s, a substantial network of these ICCA-like *taiāpure* and *māitaitai* reserves has developed around New Zealand, with a total area of about 700 km^2 (as of mid 2012). Discounting two large offshore reserves, this area is about twice that of New Zealand's coastal marine reserves (Stephenson et al. 2014) and is increasing at a faster rate (Figure 8.3).

Oceania has a rich heritage of indigenous reef and lagoon tenure systems with prohibitions, and species, season and area taboos (Johannes 1978). Some of these systems are still functional, and some have been

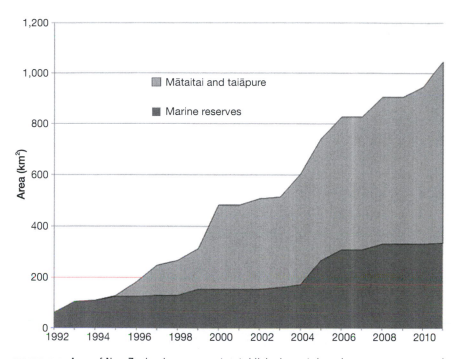

FIGURE 8.3 Area of New Zealand government-established coastal marine reserves compared with indigenous co-managed *taiāpure* and *mātaitai* marine reserves

Source: Stephenson et al. 2014

revitalized (Johannes 2002). Oceania and some other Pacific island states, such as the Philippines, are world leaders in community-conserved MPAs. Some of these MPAs have been organized into networks of locally managed marine areas (LMMA Network 2014). The average size of these ICCAs tends to be small, but numbers are impressive; more than 500 marine ICCAs were found in the Philippines alone by the early 2000s (Kothari 2006). Christie et al. (2009) analyzed the rich database of Philippines examples and showed that their positive impacts could be documented. They found that biological measures of success were positively correlated with low populations, remoteness and threats from external forces such as illegal fishing.

Many of these locally protected areas emerged out of practical needs. For example, the people of Ucunivanua village, Fiji, noticed in the early 1990s that their marine resources were becoming scarce. Working with the University of the South Pacific, villagers set up a small closed area (*tabu*) for the clam *kaikoso* (*Anadara antiquate*), an important subsistence and commercial species. This was the site of the first locally managed marine area in Fiji, and the results were dramatic: the *kaikoso* clam became abundant once more, and village incomes increased (WRI 2005). The experience changed the mind-set that only experts knew best and only governments could carry out conservation and development planning. It showed that the people most dependent on the resource for their livelihoods were the appropriate people for making the decisions. The success in Ucunivanua led to the adoption of locally managed marine areas for a variety of species throughout Fiji (Figure 8.4). MPA networks have been elaborated in various parts of Fiji (Clarke and Jupiter 2010), in neighboring island states such as Vanuatu (Johannes 1998a) and elsewhere in the Asia–Pacific region (WRI 2005).

Typically, communities set aside part of their LMMAs as a restricted area. The location and size of this *tabu* area, usually 10–15 percent of a village's fishing waters, is determined by the community. Often, they are

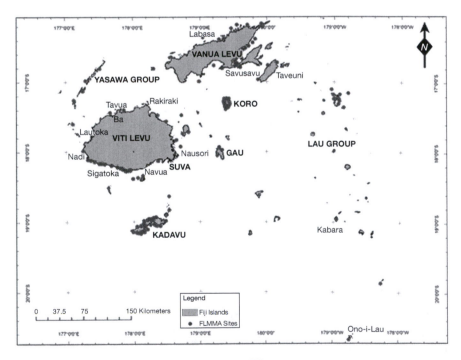

FIGURE 8.4 Locally established MPA networks in Fiji

Source: LMMA 2014; www.usp.ac.fj/index.php?id=4334

supported by the government through legislation that recognizes tradi-tional use rights. They are based on revitalized traditional systems, com-plete with ceremonies (Johannes 1998a), and they may use biological monitoring methods. However, they are significantly different from MPAs. In an MPA, the government makes the decisions, often from afar and with little or no local input, often with poor results, and sometimes with counterintuitive outcomes (Lejano and Ingram 2009a).

Enforcement is a major problem in government-protected areas, espe-cially in developing countries such as those in Asia–Pacific. Often MPAs depend on the ability of communities in the area to enforce conserva-tion rules in a way such that they themselves can derive social and economic benefits from them, consistent with commons theory (Berkes 2004). For example, in the Roviana Lagoon, Solomon Islands, Aswani and Hamilton (2004) found that there were marked differences among neighboring villages with respect to conservation. Villages that held strong commons rights could protect the "corporate sea estate" (village fishing territory) against poaching, but other villages, which had weak rights (and thus little conservation incentive), could not or did not.

The Province of British Columbia on the Pacific coast of Canada has a concentration of MPAs. This is a part of Canada with complicated legal disputes over land and resource rights of indigenous peoples referred to as First Nations (Turner at al. 2013a). Many of these disputes have been over threats to resources and ecosystems used by First Nations. In some cases, negotiations have resulted in power sharing, producing a diversity of different models of co-managed protected areas. Examples include government-designated parks, such as Pacific Rim National Park Reserve and Gulf Islands National Park Reserve, which has some level of co-management with tribes in the area. There are also First Nations-designated parks, such as Meares Island and Ha'uukmin Tribal Parks, established by the Tla-oqui-aht Nuu-chah-nulth First Nation. As well, there are Conservancies, the first designated class of protected area in Canada to be established with legal incorporation of First Nations' inter-ests (Turner and Bitonti 2011; Murray and King 2012).

Perhaps the best known of these is an ICCA, Gwaii Haanas National Park Reserve and Haida Heritage Site. The Park is on Haida Gwaii (formerly Queen Charlotte Islands), an archipelago of over 200 islands off the north coast of British Columbia, the homeland of the Haida

PHOTO 8.1 Gwaii Haanas National Park Reserve and Haida Heritage Site, northern British Columbia. The first fully co-managed national park in Canada, it was established to maintain and restore both cultural and ecological heritage

Source: Nancy Turner

Nation. It was established in 1993 as the first fully co-managed national park in Canada, with equal representation by the Council of the Haida Nation and Parks Canada on its governing board. The trigger for the establishment of the park was concern over destruction of Haida ancestral village sites and Haida dissent over logging on one of the islands of Haida Gwaii in 1974. The intent of the Park was "to maintain and restore the rich cultural and ecological heritage of Gwaii Haanas for the benefit, education and enjoyment of present and future generations." In 2010, a final piece was added to the original protected area; the Gwaii Haanas National Marine Conservation Area Reserve and Haida Heritage Site was established as Canada's first national marine conservation area, extending the original 1,500 km² park out to a zone 10 km offshore, covering 3,400 km² of ocean and coastline.

Park management uses both scientific knowledge and Haida traditional knowledge, including *yahguudang*, the Haida concept of "respect for all living things." Management is aimed at balancing biodiversity conservation with sustainable use by the Haida for food, economic and cultural purposes. A key provision is the caretaker and monitoring role of the Haida Gwaii Watchmen. This program had been established by the Haida earlier and was formally integrated into protected area management. It has served as a model for the development of a wider network of coastal First Nations Guardian Watchmen programs to monitor, steward and protect First Nations lands and waters throughout the central and northern British Columbia coast (Jones et al. 2010; Murray and King 2012; Turner et al. 2013a).

Issues of Multiple Objectives and Community Benefits

Returning to the question of what motivates conservation and environmental stewardship in general, control of landscape/seascape by the group in question and their ability to benefit from the resources are key elements. Consistent with commons theory and consistent with findings from terrestrial, marine and freshwater protected areas (Kaimowitz and Sheil 2007; Castello et al. 2009; Roe et al. 2013), this conclusion emerges out of the experience with the locally initiated MPAs in New Zealand, Oceania and Canada in the previous section. It is not applicable to the two large MPAs in Australia and the United States, although the objectives of Papahānaumokuākea Marine National Monument do include a strong component of local Hawaiian cultural values.

However, there are, of course, additional considerations in environmental stewardship. For example, Chapin et al. (2012) emphasized the following factors: commitment to long-term sustainability of a place (sense of place); collective engagement of all stakeholders for the collective good; priority of long-term solutions; government recognition of local rights to organize and manage; consensus on sustainability goals and the ability to renegotiate these goals over time; monitoring that informs progress (or not) toward goals; and good leadership. Many of these are again consistent with commons principles (Ostrom 1990; Cox et al. 2010), although most commons scholars would probably place more emphasis on institutions and their capability for collective action (Agrawal and Gibson 1999) and not merely on rights to organize.

The upshot of these considerations is that effective conservation planning would require an integration of human well-being-oriented objectives and biological conservation objectives. Many conservationists support the integration of social and conservation objectives; some oppose it, arguing that it dilutes the conservation agenda. Yet others point out that a realistic approach deals with multiple objectives and compromises between objectives, and that trade-offs are necessary in most cases and should be made explicit (McShane et al. 2011). It is true that contemporary society often does deal with the reality of multiple objectives ("integrated responses" in Millennium Ecosystem Assessment terminology) in many areas of environmental management. Multiple objectives are found not only in biodiversity conservation but also in forest management, integrated coastal zone management, watershed and river basin management (Brown et al. 2005) and fisheries management (Chapter 2).

Biological conservation objectives are relatively clear: we need to conserve biodiversity at the level of ecosystems, species and genes (e.g., Sodhi and Ehrlich 2010). But what are the social objectives? The examples in the previous section suggest a suite of objectives related to well-being, including those related to economic benefits, and social, cultural and political considerations, such as indigenous rights. However, many of these objectives are both interrelated and connected to biological objectives through the provision of ecosystem services. For example, in the Canadian case, the indigenous people of British Columbia see a close connection between their loss of control of resources and resource declines and degradation (Jones et al. 2010; Murray and King 2012; Turner et al. 2013a). In New Zealand, Māori perceive a close relationship between biological and cultural aspects of conservation (Wehi 2009; Wehi et al. 2013; Stephenson et al. 2014).

In cases involving indigenous peoples, the single most important factor for conservation is the recognition of indigenous rights. Indigenous land/ water and resource claims are strongly in the background of the Canadian and New Zealand cases, as well as in Brazil (Schwartzman and Zimmerman 2005; Oviedo 2006), Australia (Ross et al. 2009; Davies et al. 2013) and elsewhere. Indigenous people of the Pacific Northwest had tribal systems of control of coastal resources (Williams and Hunn 1982). The new arrangements described in the New Zealand and Canada cases do not recreate these historical controls but use negotiation processes to restore some indigenous control over lands/waters and resources. But there is more going on here than simply indigenous claims in a legal sense. For example, New Zealand MPAs borrow in part from the Polynesian heritage of reef and lagoon tenure systems (Johannes 2002), as in the use of temporary closures, which are similar to Polynesian taboo systems. So there is a cultural revitalization issue as well.

Table 8.3 provides a closer look at what communities themselves consider as their objectives. The first four of the eight cases come from studies designed to follow up on United Nations Development Program (UNDP) Equator Initiative conservation–development cases (Berkes 2007a; Seixas and Davy 2008; Seixas and Berkes 2010), and the other four are cases with comparable information. Although the five categories (economic, environmental, political, social and cultural) are interrelated and often overlapping, there is additional complexity within categories. For example, economic objectives include future income from fisheries (Guyana), current jobs and commercial income (Thailand, the two Brazil cases, Indonesia), and future income from ecotourism/cultural tourism (the two Canadian cases). Environmental benefits include reversing resource declines (Guyana, Thailand), restoring habitats that are important for livelihood resources (Thailand, Indonesia), and maintaining environmental integrity (the two Canadian cases). Political benefits include participation in decision-making (Guyana) and human rights (Peixe Lagoon, Brazil), and control of traditional resources in the face of powerful developers (Thailand and James Bay, Canada). For indigenous groups, control of traditional resources is of key importance, because it is seen as the first step to social and economic development.

Social and cultural benefits include improvements in social, educational and health services; community pride and cohesiveness; strengthening or revitalizing cultural traditions; protecting traditional values; cultural identity; and protecting heritage values. Cultural aspects tend to be stronger in indigenous cases. Both Canadian indigenous groups in Table 8.3 articulated cultural values to shape economic and environmental objectives. The Gitga'at of British Columbia proposed that "environmental integrity" and "responsibility to the environment" objectives should be considered as integral to "community integrity" and "cultural integrity" objectives (Turner et al. 2012). The James Bay Cree of Quebec emphasized attention to *miyuupimaatsiiun* (living well), within a total community of life, *pimaatsiiun* (Scott 2014).

Based on the case studies in Table 8.3, a number of conclusions may be offered and they are consistent with a larger set of examples from

TABLE 8.3 The nature of community objectives and local benefits

Case	Economic	Environmental	Political	Social	Cultural	Reference
Arapaima conservation in the North Rupununi, Guyana	xx	xxx	xxx	xx	xx	Fernandes 2004
Pred Nai community forestry group mangrove restoration, Trat, Thailand	xx	xxx	xxx	xx	x	Senyk 2006
Cananeia Oyster Producers Cooperative, São Paulo State, Brazil	xxx	xx	x	xx		Haque et al. 2009
TIDE Port Honduras marine reserve, Belize	xx	xxx	xx	x		Fernandes 2005
Gitga'at Nation ecotourism development, British Columbia, Canada	xx	xxx	xx	xxx	xxx	Turner et al. 2012
Proposed Tawich (Marine) Protected Area, Cree Nations of James Bay, Quebec, Canada	x	xxx	xxx	xx	xxx	Scott 2014
Peixe Lagoon National Park, Rio Grande do Sul, Brazil	xxx	xx	xxx	x	x	Almudi and Berkes 2010
Coral reef restoration, Les, Bali, Indonesia	xxx	xxx	x	x	x	Frey and Berkes 2014

Notes: xxx = very strong, xx = strong; x = present

Source: Adapted from Berkes 2013

PHOTO 8.2 Grassroots protected area planning with the James Bay Cree of Quebec and university researchers. Cultural heritage and the control of traditional lands–waters–resources in the face of development were priorities, with attention to Cree notions of living well within a community of life. Wemindji, Quebec, Canada

Source: F. Berkes

land-based conservation–development projects as well (Berkes 2013). Community objectives that create incentives for biodiversity conservation are complex. Even though economic objectives are often in the forefront, the conception of local incentives purely in terms of cash benefits is too narrow, too simplistic, and potentially counterproductive (Berkes 2013). In many cases, political, social, cultural objectives are very important—more important than money. Empowerment as a political objective is ever present in the form of participation in decision-making. As many rural livelihoods are based on mixed strategies of wage employment and resource use, access to resources is almost always important. Hence, any conservation measure that closes access to an area or a resource is likely to be opposed, at least by some members of the community. There is almost always a mix of community objectives, but the mix is case-specific, making it impossible to design "blueprint" solutions that can be applied universally.

Biodiversity conservation can be treated as a multilevel commons problem. Biodiversity is a global commons, important for humanity as a whole. It is a regional commons, important for ecotourism and other benefits. It is also a local commons that produces ecosystem services for human well-being. The multilevel nature of biodiversity defies simple solutions for conservation. International standards and co-ordination are obviously important, and so are national-level policies. However, when it comes to the day-to-day operations of an MPA and the enforcement of conservation rules, the role of local people and communities comes to the forefront.

Prospects and Conclusions

At the Tenth Conference of the Parties to the CBD, it was agreed that 17 percent of the global terrestrial and inland water area and 10 percent of the global coastal and marine area should be conserved through protected area designations by 2020 (CBD 2014). The number of MPAs has been increasing rapidly in the recent decades, but the CBD resolution would mean near doubling of the area under MPAs over only a decade. We are, therefore, likely to see many new areas brought under protected area legislation over a short period of time. We are also likely to see a change in the kinds of MPA. Many of the early MPAs have been discrete, small ones. New MPAs are likely to be characterized by the use of marine spatial planning (Chapter 7) and rely increasingly on ecosystem-based management for relatively large marine areas that incorporate MPA networks (McCay and Jones 2011). Some parts of the world, such as the Philippines, have accumulated considerable experience regarding what such networks might look like, along with the remaining institutional issues regarding access and compliance (Lowry et al. 2009; Pollnac and Seara 2011).

These developments imply an intensification of academic debates over conservation versus sustainable use, as well as an intensification of on-the-ground conflicts over seascapes and resources. There are no unused coastal areas, and many of the biodiversity-rich prime sites for conservation are also seascapes where resource-dependent communities make a living. Human displacement from MPAs is a very controversial matter (Mascia and Claus 2008). Decisions about MPAs are politically difficult, and governments have often been insensitive to social and political issues related to MPA decisions (Christie et al. 2009; Mascia et al. 2010). Perhaps the issue of conservation versus sustainable use stems from a basic ideological dichotomy: should humans be viewed as intruders in marine systems? Or should we consider seascapes as essentially inhabited by humans (McCay and Jones 2011)?

Another way to pose the issue is to consider whether conservation and sustainable use are incompatible or compatible objectives. Jones (2013) argues that there is an essential divergence of objectives between marine biodiversity conservation and resource use, even if it is sustainable resource use. Part of the argument is hinged on government's legal obligations for biodiversity conservation, and it challenges the idea that government managers may best be facilitators of management partnerships, allowing considerable local autonomy for commons governance. "As the state has a duty to ensure fulfillment of these obligations, so [it] must maintain a degree of control," which means that the state "cannot shift from being a controller to a facilitator" (Jones 2013, p. 44). Further, "it must be recognized that the state has important roles to play in protected area governance and that these roles will often be more strategic, instrumental and to a degree, controlling in nature" (Jones 2013, p. 48).

These are the kinds of practical considerations that pose barriers for community-based conservation, "the coexistence of people and nature, as distinct from protectionism and the segregation of people and nature" (Western and Wright 1994, p. 8). Considering the bigger picture of conservation in a historical context, Folke et al. (2011) observed that modern society seems to have disconnected itself from nature and has to find a way to reconnect. Folke et al. (2011) argued that reconnecting humans to the biosphere requires a new social contract for sustainability based on a shift of perception—from people and nature seen as separate parts, to interacting, co-evolving and interdependent social–ecological systems.

There are mechanisms for reconnecting nature and culture, and they seem to involve governments as facilitators rather than controllers. The protected area classification of the IUCN includes categories of multiple-use landscapes and seascapes that accommodate such reconnection (Table 8.1; Phillips 2003). One way to reconnect nature and culture is to create conservation incentives through conservation–development projects or other ways to involve local communities in the process of conservation (Salafsky and Wollenberg 2000). Conservation that helps meet human needs is a powerful way of serving the purpose of linking biodiversity conservation and poverty reduction (Roe et al. 2013).

A second way to reconnect is to think of conservation as biocultural conservation and protect the diversity of life in all its manifestations (Maffi and Woodley 2010). ICCAs are prime examples of a biocultural approach to conservation. Here, protected areas are parts of dynamic landscapes in which human activity is an integral part (Stephenson and Moller 2009). ICCAs are under discussion for their potential to contribute to protected area networks, as well as to serving local needs (Kothari 2006; Martin et al. 2011). Such multiple-use protected areas may be seen as coupled social–ecological systems in which the needs of the local people are a central component of conservation, providing local communities with incentives to maintain biodiversity in the long term.

Involvement of local communities is important for tailoring conservation to local circumstances through the use of local and traditional knowledge (Turner 2005, 2014; Moller et al. 2009b; Stephenson and Moller 2009). Bawa et al. (2004) note the efforts to develop regional conservation models by large international conservation organizations, models that seek unifying conservation principles, driven by a need for general application. However, such science-based, generalized, global models tend to view the world through relatively coarse filters and may be at odds with the emergence of fine-grained models adapted to local conditions. Bawa et al. (2004) argue that the best hope for conservation is to focus on locally driven approaches that (1) draw on local and traditional practices as well as science, (2) are locally adaptive, and (3) seek to increase human and social capital in addition to natural capital.

The diversity of social–ecological marine conservation examples in New Zealand, Oceania and Canada considered in this chapter seem to bear out the call of Bawa et al. (2004) for locally driven approaches. These approaches have a key role to play in conservation, along with large MPAs such as Papahānaumokuākea Marine National Monument and the Great Barrier Reef Marine Park. It must be noted, however, that these two reserves are unusual in having relatively low human pressure. In many of the coastal areas of the world, establishing MPAs will require dealing with local resident populations and heavy demands on livelihood resources.

However, if MPAs can serve livelihood needs as well as biodiversity conservation, then the local communities may help enforcement and contribute in terms of their local and traditional knowledge.

One of the lessons from the cases in this chapter concerns the importance of local knowledge for conservation. Many of the Canadian indigenous-controlled protected areas are based on the use of indigenous knowledge, as in Haida Gwaii. Many Australian protected areas use indigenous knowledge (Ross et al. 2009), and the documented success of Mamirauá Sustainable Development Reserve in Brazil is based on the integration of local knowledge with science and the use of local knowledge for monitoring the iconic endangered fish species, *Arapaima* (Castello et al. 2009). The mobilization of local and traditional knowledge for conservation also has implications for governance, as use of knowledge at different levels (local knowledge and scientific knowledge) helps bridge scales (Reid et al. 2006).

In both New Zealand (Stephenson et al. 2014) and Canada (Turner et al. 2013a), national-level jurisdiction provides key legislation. However, the governance structure of these protected areas is anything but flat. There is local and indigenous jurisdiction in the mix, municipal and provincial governments in some cases, and the possibility of an international level, through IUCN's incipient category of ICCA. Is this too complex? Multi-level governance may be a good fit for conservation where the mix of local objectives is likely to be different from the regional, national and international ones. Consistent with complex adaptive systems thinking, there is no one correct level of governance. Both local- and national-level governance should be in the mix, possibly along with some other levels as well.

At the international level, policy mechanisms include flexibility under IUCN Categories V and VI, recognition of ICCAs as a governance type (Table 8.2), and recognition of local and indigenous knowledge and ways to combine such knowledge with science. The relatively new IUCN categories V and VI are consistent with ICCAs and biocultural conservation. In fact, Brazil's Extractive Reserves served as the basis for the development of IUCN Category VI protected areas (Oviedo 2006). Not all ICCAs are going to be suitable for national conservation networks, and not all local and indigenous groups that control such areas will want to become part of national networks (for reasons of loss of local control).

Nevertheless, ICCAs are significant for the potential expansion of MPA networks. All of this assumes that conservation and human well-being can be made into compatible objectives. As most of the world's biodiversity is not in protected areas but on lands and waters used by people for their livelihoods, we turn to the subject of development and livelihoods in the next chapter.

Coastal Livelihoods

Resources and Development

Introduction

Over the last two decades or so, ecological economists have shown that coastal resources are unique in being both productive and valuable, as pointed out in Chapter 1 (Figure 1.1). Coasts have historically attracted people and provided the resources to make a living. Coastal environments such as estuaries, marshes, wetlands, floodplains, coral reefs and mangroves provide a rich array of ecosystem services for human well-being. Following ecological economics terminology used in the Millennium Ecosystem Assessment, these ecosystem services are the benefits that people derive from ecosystems. They include supporting services such as nutrient cycling, provisioning services such as food production, regulating services such as water purification, and cultural services such as heritage and spiritual values (Figure 9.1).

Together, these ecosystem services provide the various constituents of human well-being, such as the basics for a good life (including livelihoods), health, security and good social relations. They also provide a framework for valuation of nature's services (Costanza et al. 1997, 2014). For example, coastal wetlands have a storm protection value that can be calculated from information on historical damage, storm tracks and probability, wetland size and location, built infrastructure location, population and other factors. Valuation helps decision-making. However, valuation in monetary

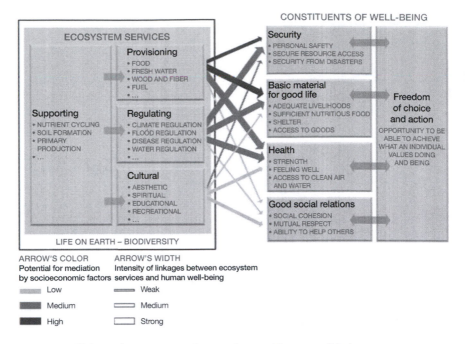

FIGURE 9.1 Linkages between ecosystem services and human well-being
Source: MA 2005a

terms is not so readily applicable to all types of ecosystem service, for example, cultural services (Chan et al. 2012). Ecological economics sees people and economy as embedded in nature. Ecosystem services are the relative contribution of natural capital to human well-being. As Costanza et al. (2014) pointed out, ecosystems cannot provide benefits to people without the presence of people (human capital), communities (social capital) and their built environment (physical capital).

The Millennium Ecosystem Assessment considers a range of human benefits from ecosystem services, including social and cultural ones. This is an improvement over conventional resource management, which has generally emphasized biological and, to a lesser extent, economic objectives. Social objectives do come up for discussion (Chapter 2) but are rarely given equal weight compared with biological and economic objectives, even when issues around livelihood are often acknowledged as important. This chapter argues for the significance of social objectives, with focus on livelihoods, and explores ways to include them in management. The argument builds on the points made about multiple objectives in Chapter 7 and the need to reconcile conservation and livelihoods in Chapter 8.

Following some background, first I examine some of the historic context of development thinking. Next, I discuss issues of poverty among coastal resource users and make the point that livelihood diversification is one of the most common adaptive strategies. After that, I discuss some areas in which social objectives can be incorporated into management, assisted by community-based development and social enterprises as alternatives to conventional economics of resource development.

The social dimension and livelihood concerns are particularly important in the case of small-scale fisheries, which account for more than half of the world's food-fish harvest and employ more than 90 percent of the people engaged in fishing (Béné et al. 2007; Cochrane et al. 2011). Using figures from BNP (2009), Béné and Friend (2011) point out that 56 million people are directly involved in fish-related activities in *inland* small-scale fisheries in the developing world. This number (which includes people in fish processing and trading) is comparable to the estimated 50 million people who depend on the same types of activity in coastal and marine fisheries. A network, "Too Big to Ignore," has been devoted to the human dimension of fisheries, mostly small scale fisheries (TBTI 2014).

For many development practitioners, "freedom of choice and action" in Figure 9.1 brings to mind several concepts. One is *empowerment*, defined by Chambers (1983: 11) as, "the process through which people, and especially poorer people, are enabled to take more control over their own lives, and secure a better livelihood, with ownership of productive assets as one key element." Another is *equity*, or fairness in distribution of benefits. A third is the *capabilities approach*, namely the development theory concerned with the capability of people "to achieve outcomes that they value and have reason to value" (Sen 1999, p. 291).

The term livelihood has been used widely since Agenda 21 of the 1992 UNCED Earth Summit held in Rio de Janeiro. Livelihood is considered a better descriptor than the term employment for resource-dependent rural communities. According to Ellis (2000, p. 10), "a *livelihood* comprises the assets (natural, physical, human, financial and social capital), the activities, and the access to these (mediated by institutions and social relations) that together determine the living gained by the individual or household." The livelihood approach was considered important for the discussion of sustainability in UNCED, because it helped bring people issues to the foreground.

In a seminal paper, Chambers and Conway (1992, p. 6) proposed that, "a livelihood is sustainable when it can cope with and recover from stresses and shocks, maintain or enhance its capabilities, assets and entitlements, while not undermining the natural resource base." This *sustainable livelihoods* approach has resulted in the creation of elaborate frameworks; dominant themes have included the consideration of the assets of the poor, dealing with them as clusters of interrelated capitals (human, natural, financial, social and physical capital) and as livelihood strategies used by people (Bebbington 1999; DFID 1999) (Figure 9.2). The notion of coping with and recovering from stresses and shocks lies at the heart of the Chambers and Conway definition and indicates the importance of options and flexibility, in effect livelihood resilience (Chapter 4). Resilience is a key concept in this book and is relevant to development; we note, however, the cautions about the misuse of resilience ideas in development (Béné et al. 2014).

Resilience may be thought of as "insurance" in the livelihood system (Coomes et al. 2010). Sustainable livelihoods can provide "layers of resilience" to overcome "waves of adversity," as Glavovic and Boonzaier (2007, p. 2) put it. Resilience may be incorporated into management

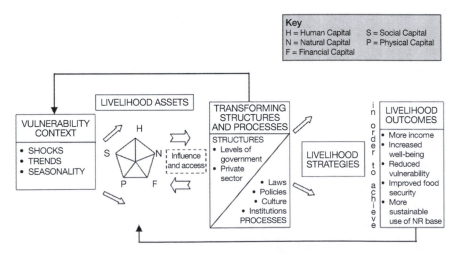

FIGURE 9.2 Sustainable livelihoods and the five capitals
Source: DFID 1999

objectives, for example, as part of the "primary fisheries management" of Cochrane et al. (2011), whereby social and ecological resilience is considered an integral part of ensuring food security and planning poverty reduction. Sustainability of livelihoods depends on the ability of people to deal with natural variations in the environment, such as fluctuations in resource abundance, seasonal cycles of resource use, extreme weather events and sometimes natural disasters. Livelihood sustainability also depends on the ability to deal with the interactions between global forces and local contexts, including economic drivers such as global market demands and policy drivers such as government programs.

Context of Development Thinking

The topic of livelihoods brings together the fields of resource management and international development; the emergence of participatory processes in these two fields is closely coupled. Back in the 1950s and 1960s, central governments were widely seen as the main vehicle for the implementation of the development agenda to raise living standards and incomes. Both resource management and development were considered as technical matters, and central governments were seen as the repository of the technical expertise to carry out the various tasks required (Béné and Neiland 2004). By the 1980s, however, there was a general disillusionment in the ability of central governments to plan and administer development. They often seemed to be too remote from the people they were supposed to be serving (Chambers 1983). Meanwhile, in the resource management area, scholars were beginning to question the wisdom of policies that assumed central governments should be solely in charge. In particular, concerns were raised regarding the suitability of central governments for the sustainable and equitable management of shared resources, such as marine and coastal commons (McCay and Acheson 1987; Berkes 1989).

In both development and resource management areas, there was great interest in community-based approaches and the ability of local and traditional institutions to manage local resources and to help set development goals. "Putting the last first," in rural and agricultural development (Chambers 1983), stakeholder participation, community engagement and decentralization came to be considered as essential components of planning. The idea behind decentralization was to bring the decisions from the central government down to the local government. There were strong arguments to go further and devolve powers to institutions at local levels, in the form of democratic decentralization (Ribot 2002) or devolution (Brugere 2006) (Chapter 6).

In the commons management area, a strong case was being made for the involvement of local institutions and the use of collective action in the management of local resources. Such devolution seemed to be a good fit with commons, in both the developing and the industrialized worlds (Chapter 5). The Nobel Prize winner in Economic Sciences, Elinor Ostrom, argues, not so much for the devolution of governance to local institutions, but rather for the recognition of local institutions that already govern the commons. In cases where government decision-making powers could be shared but not effectively devolved, co-management became the policy objective (Chapter 6).

The logic of this new thinking was compelling: bringing government closer to the governed, and enabling people whose livelihood and well-being would be affected by policy decisions to have a say in those decisions. Widespread recognition of the notion of user participation and problem solving at the lowest feasible level of organization, the subsidiarity principle, even resulted in the incorporation of this principle in the 1992 treaty establishing the European Community (Chapter 5). Instead of top-down planning and management, "grassroots" and bottom–up planning became entrenched in various areas of environment, resource management, planning and development in both developing and industrialized countries (Wilson et al. 2003).

Thus, by the 1990s, governance focus in development had shifted to the local level, with many countries undertaking decentralization reforms as part of "good governance" (Ribot 2002). The majority of national governments in Africa, Asia and Latin America, encouraged by international bodies such as the World Bank, instituted decentralization reforms in a broad range of areas, including development, environmental management, health care and education (Manor 1999).

However, decentralization has not lived up to the original expectations and shows a mixed record at best (Ribot 2002; Béné and Neiland 2004, 2006). Although decentralization was defined and implemented in different ways around the world, findings have been consistent in showing a gap between the promise and the practice (Capistrano and Colfer 2005). As summarized in Table 9.1, decentralization reforms were

TABLE 9.1 **The gap between the promise and the practice of decentralization**

Promise of decentralization	Practice of decentralization
Participatory development and greater attention to local priorities	Local jurisdictions not receiving sufficient powers or resources
Increased voice for local communities, empowerment and democratization	Elite capture of resources, as the powerful locals take advantage of uncertainties
Poverty reduction through equitable access to resources	Marginalization of the extreme poor and the disadvantaged groups
Greater accountability in local governments	Lack of representativeness of decentralized bodies
Tailoring resource management objectives to local contexts	Fragmenting management responsibility for ecosystems (such as a mangrove area)
Local conflict resolution and more sustainable resource management outcomes	Creating more local conflicts and social tensions, some leading to resource overuse

Sources: Colfer and Capistrano 2005; Ribot 2002; Béné and Neiland 2006; Larson and Soto 2008

undertaken to achieve participatory development and greater administrative efficiency, with benefits in terms of local empowerment, democratization and accountability, and, to some extent, poverty reduction and resource sustainability.

Detailed studies internationally show that few of these promised benefits were achieved. A number of reasons have been offered to explain the gap between the promise and the practice. Most decentralization reforms were characterized by insufficient transfer of resources and powers to local institutions, the phenomenon of "off-loading." Central governments were often the main reason for the failure of decentralization reforms. According to Ribot et al. (2006), central governments used two main strategies to undermine the ability of local governments to make meaningful decisions: limiting the kinds of power that were transferred, and choosing local institutions that served and answered to central interests.

A number of other factors are also involved. Uncertainties over the control of resources precipitated new conflicts, rather than resolving old ones. *Elite capture* was a common experience: local elites took advantage of the power vacuum, while decentralization was in progress, to consolidate their controls over resources. This worked against equity and poverty reduction goals, especially with regard to the extreme poor and marginalized groups who tend to be underrepresented in local decision-making bodies (Béné and Neiland 2006).

Lack of representativeness of decentralized bodies tends to work against accountability goals. As Ribot (2002, p. 1) put it, "Transferring power without accountable representation is dangerous. Establishing accountable representation without powers is empty." A key recommendation from critics is that the policy objective should be democratic decentralization, with *downward* accountability of local institutions to the local people, and not just the usual upward accountability that bureaucracies are good at (Ribot 2002; Colfer and Capistrano 2005; Béné and Neiland 2006).

Regarding the objective of sustainable resource management, the record is mixed, but some countries showed promising outcomes. As noted in Chapter 6, the decentralization reforms of the 1990s in the Philippines led to coastal resources co-management and integrated management. Evidence shows that community-based coastal resource management programs, which originated in part from decentralization reforms, were effective for user participation and empowerment (Pomeroy 1994; Pomeroy et al. 1997, 2010). It appears that, once participation starts, it can generate its own momentum; however, progress tends to be slow. Results from a large number of cases indicate the importance of the time scale for learning, adapting and capacity building:

> Decentralization takes time and thus is better implemented gradually, allowing for institutions and stakeholder groups to learn and to adapt. It requires building consensus through an open, transparent and inclusive process; participatory decision-making; institutional, technical and human capacity-building; provision of adequate financial resources and incentives for investment; tailoring objectives to local contexts; and developing the flexibility to adapt to different situations and changing circumstances.
>
> (Capistrano and Colfer 2005, p. 311)

Further, Capistrano and Colfer (2005) point out that successful decentralization often goes hand in hand with secure resource tenure of users or local traditional rights. The point is consistent with the co-management experience (Chapter 6) and commons in general (Chapter 5). It becomes particularly important when dealing with social–ecological restoration projects, such as those in Chapter 7 and the coral reef restoration case in Bali (Frey and Berkes 2014).

Coastal Resource Users and Poverty

What kinds of livelihood do marine and coastal resources provide in developing countries? Fishers are often perceived as poor, and the small-scale fishery is perceived as "an activity of last resort." Béné (2003, p. 967) and colleagues contest these generalizations, pointing out that the two common narratives about fishers, "they are fishermen because they are poor" and "they are poor because they are fishermen," make a circular and self-reinforcing argument. Neither has empirical basis.

> Fishers are often presented or perceived as the "poorest of the poor" . . . and their poverty as the consequence of the open-access nature of the fisheries, a situation which allows more and more people to enter the fishing sector, leading to the economic (and possibly biological) overexploitation of the resources, dilapidation of the economic rent and finally, impoverishment of the fishing community (for example, Gordon 1954; Hardin 1968 . . .). This systematic equation between fisheries and poverty has contributed to create and maintain a "paradigmatic trap" where poverty in fishing communities is taken for granted and no real analytical effort made to go beyond this simplistic Malthusian narrative.
>   (Béné and Friend 2011, p. 120)

As livelihood and well-being issues are part of the mix of resource management objectives, it is rather important to get out of this trap and offer an analysis that may lead to a more satisfactory understanding of poverty. A review of the literature does not help much, Béné (2003) argued, as, perhaps surprisingly, there was an absence of references to fisheries case studies in the current poverty literature. Nevertheless, it is "particularly urgent to correct the simplistic and ill-conceived views presenting poverty in fisheries as a consequence of the tragedy of the commons" (Béné and Friend 2011, p. 120). Before reviewing the arguments and alternative interpretations, the notion of poverty needs to be examined.

All concepts evolve, and the concept of poverty is no exception. As reviewed by Béné (2003), the most important measure used in the 1960s in various areas of development economics was income. Poverty was also measured in terms of income, as the ability to purchase food and other necessities of life. This income–poverty model was replaced in the 1970s by the basic needs model that recognized that poverty was not only about income, but that it was multidimensional and included material requirements to meet minimally acceptable human needs such as health and education. After a series of refinements over the years, there seems to be consensus on the multidimensional nature of poverty. According to the OECD (2001, p. 8), "*poverty* encompasses different dimensions of deprivation that relate to human capabilities including consumption and food security, health, education, rights, voice, security, dignity and decent work."

One of the influential voices in understanding poverty was Amartya Sen, with his 1981 book, *Poverty and Famine*. Sen observed, in post-Green Revolution India, that famine could occur in the midst of food surplus, and he developed the idea of food entitlement. Lack of resources was only one reason people might starve; starvation could also occur owing to food entitlement failure, that is, a failure of means of command over food because of a range of economic, political and social factors. This view brought about a dramatic change in the way famine was perceived. Once seen as a Malthusian crisis of too many people, too little food, famine was thereafter seen as a breakdown in the rights of access to food, bringing into the debate issues of power/empowerment and political voice.

Sen also developed the capabilities approach. Originally formulated to broaden the understanding of development economics, it was a reaction to utilitarian models that focused entirely on income growth. The capabilities approach in his *Development as Freedom* (Sen 1999) considers the notion of "freedom" as both the outcome and the instrument for development. That is, freedom from poverty (in its multidimensional sense, above) is the ultimate goal of development, but it is also the essential means by which it is achieved (Sen 1999).

Sen's concepts were extended into the area of natural resources as environmental entitlements (Leach et al. 1999). This led to the recognition that there was no simple linear relationship between population, resource availability and poverty. Béné (2003) argued that it also led to a growing realization that, to understand poverty more fully, it was necessary to redirect part of our attention away from the biology and economics of resources themselves, and to put greater emphasis on the role of political, economic and social factors regarding access, control and redistribution of natural resources.

Béné (2003) further contributed to this effort by constructing a typology of processes leading to the denial of people's access to resources. His typology included four processes: economic exclusion (due to financial inability of the poor to enter a productive activity); social marginalization (denial based on social criteria such as gender, caste or ethnicity); class exploitation (where the poor are not denied access but do not receive their fair share); and politics of disempowerment (the poor are left out of decisions that affect their livelihoods and their command over resources).

Béné (2003) considered the four mechanisms in the framework to be analytically separable, even though they are interdependent and, in some cases, reinforce one another. These mechanisms were proposed as part of the effort to refocus poverty research away from natural resource limitations per se, and toward political, economic and social factors regarding entitlements. The framework thus excludes mechanisms that directly bear on resource supply issues. However, issues of resource supply often interact with the four mechanisms proposed, indicating interdependence and feedback reinforcement. For example, cases from Brazil and India indicate that a diminishing resource supply has two-way feedback relationships with some of Béné's mechanisms, in some cases triggering economic or social marginalization. It is proposed, therefore, that bringing back some resource-related or ecological factors into Béné's framework may provide a fuller picture of poverty in coastal resource use (Nayak et al. 2014).

A further contribution to understanding poverty comes from a consideration of *vulnerability*. In human geography and development fields, vulnerability is presented as a function of the risks to which people are exposed (*exposure to risk*), their sensitivity or susceptibility to risks (*sensitivity*) and the extent of their capability to adapt to or cope with change or to recover from its impacts (*adaptive capacity*) (Adger et al. 2005), such that:

$$\text{Vulnerability} = f(\text{exposure to risk, sensitivity}) - \text{adaptive capacity}$$

One can talk about exposure sensitivity (the degree to which people may be exposed to a stress and their susceptibility to it) and adaptive capacity (the ability to cope with, adjust to, or recover from, that stress) (Hovelsrud and Smit 2010). Béné and Friend (2011) used this notion of vulnerability and looked specifically at livelihoods and the sensitivity of particular livelihoods to the risks to which people are exposed. They found that the exposure and sensitivity of fisher livelihood risks are relatively high in comparison with non-fishers, and their adaptive capacity is generally low. This is because fishers' sensitivity is not only related to their dependence on fishery resources, but also to other factors, such as debt and dependence on other capitals (Figure 9.2) over which they have little control. Their adaptive capacity is limited, because many of the risks of fishing cannot be avoided. They can, however, try to increase their adaptive capacity (and resilience) by diversifying and increasing their options. Thus, for many fishers and fishing communities, their vulnerability to shocks and stresses (Chambers and Conway 1992) increases if they are unable to diversify their activities.

There appears to be no systematic or clear relationship between fishing and poverty. Fishing households are no worse off than other comparable socioeconomic groups and are often better off. In any case, poverty is a relative concept, open to misinterpretation and overuse. There are cases, of course, where fishers are clearly destitute, but often this is related to livelihood shocks such as loss of access to fishing areas (e.g., Nayak and Berkes 2010). In such cases, fishers themselves can give an account of what poverty means to them, for example, by using the methodology that Narayan et al. (2000) developed, based on narratives and direct quotes from the poor themselves. Diversification of livelihood is important in the context of poverty, because diversification is a universal response to dealing with vulnerability by spreading the risk (Turner et al. 2003).

Livelihood Diversification

Diversification is a response to the limited adaptive capacity that Béné and Friend (2011) allude to. In the narrow sense, it refers to diversity in the use of natural capital in the DFID (1999) framework. However, in the broad sense, livelihood diversification is not one strategy but many. Some of the strategies used by coastal people include: occupational pluralism (e.g., combining fishing and agriculture) to widen the income portfolio; flexibility in fishing activities, using different types of gear; geographic mobility, fishing in different areas or migrating seasonally;

specialist–generalist alternation, operating in one or multiple fisheries; supplementing fishing with shellfish and aquatic/coastal plant collection; seasonal wage labor or sending a family member away for wage work; and seasonal dependency on government programs (mostly from Allison and Ellis 2001). Livelihood strategies may be analyzed as attempts to add options and to build buffering capacity to deal with perturbations. In many parts of the world, fisher households make their livelihood in diverse ways.

> Both in Africa and Asia, communities that are dependent on fishing extend far beyond the usual stereotypes of the full-time "fisherman." Reference to this stereotype . . . denotes a very poor understanding of the economy of households and communities living close to water bodies . . . Usually for these households, fishing like dry season cultivation, small-scale irrigation of vegetables, or seasonal migration, is a complementary but critical activity that generates additional cash . . . [to ensure] household economic viability, and with this, fishing provides important nutritional as well as cash-economic benefits.
>
> (Béné and Friend 2011, p. 137)

Why aren't more coastal people full-time fishers? An underlying reason for livelihood diversification is in the nature of the resource, as Allison and Ellis (2001, p. 383) explain:

> fishing is a high-risk occupation, and one prone to seasonal and cyclical fluctuation in stock size and location . . . Diversification reduces the risk of livelihood failure by spreading it across more than one income source. It also helps overcome the uneven use of assets (principally labor) caused by seasonality.

Diversification reduces vulnerability in the face of widespread market failures and uncertainties, and includes the ability to switch activities as necessary (Chambers 1997). Examples from Brazil and the Caribbean illustrate the point.

Brazil's fisheries are dominated by the artisanal sector, both inland and coastal (Begossi 2010). The mixed-heritage Caiçara people of the southeastern Brazil coast traditionally combined fishing with small-scale agriculture and forest resource use (Hanazaki et al. 2007). In recent decades, they have added wage labor, tourism and commerce to their portfolios. These compensate for declines in resource abundance, mainly due to incursion of large-scale fisheries into their area, and loss of access to some coastal areas due to enforcement of MPAs (Lopes et al. 2013). Nevertheless, the small-scale fishery has continued to be important both for food and for income. Surveys by Hanazaki et al. (2013) showed that fishing was a livelihood activity of 70 percent of Caiçara households in the Paraty area, even though it was the declared main activity of only 16 percent (Figure 9.3).

The fishery of Gouyave, Grenada, in the Eastern Caribbean is dominated by high-value pelagic species. The fishers caught four major species with surface long-lines, their main gear. But not every species was available every month (Figure 9.4). In September, when none of the four pelagic species was normally available, the fishers switched gears and went mainly for benthic species and small coastal fish. Or they switched to non-fishing livelihoods, including agriculture and wage work. Even though long-line fishing provided a good livelihood relative to other options, many fishers chose to maintain a diversity of activities. Fishing was the sole source of income for only 21 percent of Gouyave fishers (Grant et al. 2007).

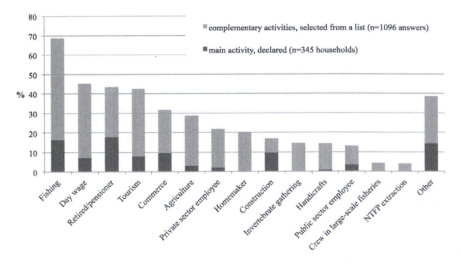

FIGURE 9.3 Main livelihood activities (self-declared) and complementary livelihood activities (chosen from a list) of 345 rural households in Paraty, Brazil

Source: Hanazaki et al. 2013. Reprinted with permission from Springer

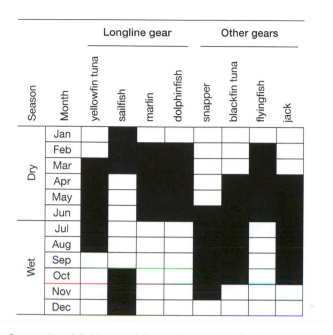

FIGURE 9.4 Seasonality of fishing: peak harvesting periods for the main species, Gouyave, Grenada, West Indies

Source: Grant et al. 2007

The above examples come from marine costal fisheries, but inland fisheries show similar patterns. For example, clam harvesters in the Backwaters (a lagoon system) of Kerala, south India, are also farmers and opportunistic fishers. They have even diversified marketing opportunities for their clam harvests. Clam meat goes to the market, and the large piles of clamshells left behind (which are almost pure calcium carbonate) are sold to a company that produces fine cement (Berkes, unpublished). "Indeed, a large proportion, if not the great majority, of rural farming households who live close to . . . any type of water bodies . . . in the developing world are effectively engaged in some form of fish-related activities" (Béné and Friend 2011, p. 120). This phenomenon is well documented from many parts of the world, for example from West Sumatra, Indonesia, where the title of an article says it all: "Fishing farmers or farming fishers?" (Yuerlita et al. 2013). These examples emphasize small-scale fisheries in developing countries, but, in fact, fishers in industrial fisheries almost never work full time year-round either.

PHOTO 9.1 Clam harvesters going to the market in town, Backwaters, Kerala, India

Source: F. Berkes

Many developed countries have small-scale fisheries; the Gulf of Maine lobster fishery discussed in Chapter 4 is one of them; traditional inshore fisheries in England are another (Reed et al. 2013). Small-scale fisheries on the Atlantic coast of Canada have livelihood diversification issues very much in common with the developing country examples above (Wiber et al. 2004; Kearney and Berkes 2007). Mixing of livelihoods in coastal areas of the world is nearly universal. For example, resource management in Japan seem to be taking livelihood diversification into account in *sato-umi* seascapes (Chapter 7). These seascapes produce a bundle of ecosystem services for human well-being, not just traditional coastal and marine products, but also a mix of tourism, biodiversity conservation and certified products (Japan Satoyama Satoumi Assessment 2010).

Incorporating Social Objectives into Management

What are the prospects for managers to design appropriate social objectives for marine and coastal resources? There are several points to consider. To begin with, resource managers and development planners need to appreciate the needs and livelihood strategies of fishing households. Opportunities exist in a number of areas to develop appropriate policies to incorporate social objectives into management. These include what Cochrane et al. (2011) call "primary fisheries management," human rights-based fisheries governance, food security, and gender. Strengthening community-based development and fostering social enterprises can help facilitate the incorporation of social objectives into management.

Some of the earlier livelihood studies regarded poor people as passive victims. However, more recent studies focus on livelihood strategies and the lived experience at the levels of households, social networks and the community (de Haan and Zoomers 2005). The literature on fisher livelihoods does not show passive victims but indicates a great deal of creativity in terms of livelihood strategies (Jentoft and Eide 2011). In some cases, where livelihood diversification and fishing diversification are feasible, fishers may be considerably better off economically than other groups (Grant et al. 2007). However, fisher households are at a disadvantage (as compared with other groups) because of political and economic marginalization and their vulnerability to livelihood shocks (Béné 2003; Béné and Friend 2011). Appreciating livelihood characteristics of fishers is not easy for managers and policymakers who have been taught that all fishers should be full-time fishers. They are not.

Internationally, there is some evidence of changing national policies. South Africa has adopted the sustainable livelihoods approach to underpin policy development (Glavovic and Boonzaier 2007). South Africa's draft small-scale fisheries policy of 2010 makes special provisions for subsistence and small-scale fishers. This includes such measures as incorporating human dimensions into an ecosystem-based fishery management approach, increased user participation (and co-management in some cases), and expansion of interdisciplinary research into such areas as food security (Sowman 2011). Although fishers and policymakers are still grappling with implementation, these developments do indicate a shift in attitude and governance approaches (Sowman 2011). The recognition of the socioeconomic rights of the small-scale fishery sector through the Equality Court Ruling was a key factor in this shift. Sowman and Cardoso (2010) compared food security strategies and the legal framework to recognize and protect small-scale fisheries in three southern African countries, Angola, Namibia and South Africa. They found that, in Angola, local food security needs have been given priority, whereas, in the other two, fisheries are mainly export oriented. Further, only in Angola, subsistence and artisanal fishers are fully recognized by law, with measures in place to support and develop the small-scale sector (Sowman and Cardoso 2010).

Focusing on entitlements and socioeconomic rights is the logical approach in improving livelihoods of fishers and other coastal resource users. A review of small-scale fisheries in the developing world concluded that a major impediment to development "is the inability of fishers to secure and exercise rights and responsibilities over fisheries resources" (Andrew et al. 2007, p. 228). Rights are always contested, and protecting the commons rights of rural users of coastal resources is not an easy matter, in light of multiple demands on valuable coastal resources such as aquaculture and protected areas (Nayak et al. 2014). However, even where governments have seriously attempted to assist small-scale fisheries, the efforts have often been misplaced.

The earlier productivist thinking had emphasized increasing fishing capacity, for example, by subsidizing mechanization and larger fishing boats; this often resulted, not in increased production, but in overfishing. Béné and Friend (2011) argue that fisheries managers, donors and researchers need to embrace a fundamental change in the way they conceive development in small-scale fisheries. In light of entitlements thinking and the multidimensional model of poverty, interventions aimed at improving access to health facilities, public services such as transportation, education, drinking water and electricity, and economic institutions such as financial credit may have deeper impacts on livelihoods than interventions aiming at improving productivity.

Some of these points have been articulated as primary fisheries management. This is the idea that, where adequate management does not exist, the aim should be a minimum management goal that includes social–ecological resilience (to minimize risks of fishery systems crossing undesirable thresholds), food security and poverty reduction (Cochrane et al. 2011). Using a concept developed in health care, primary fisheries management is basic needs oriented. It may involve "barefoot ecologists" as on-site fishery development workers and co-managers, a take-off from "barefoot doctors" in China (Prince 2003). The entitlements approach is recognizable also in the calls for human rights-based fisheries governance

COASTAL LIVELIHOODS   213

(Charles 2011; Allison et al. 2012). Some advocates of privatization have been using the term "rights-based" approach. But fishing rights are human rights and should not be commodified (Kumar 2008). Hence, supporters of social objectives have made the argument that human rights are first priority, favoring basic entitlements: access to food, social services, decent work, freedom from oppression and right to a dignified livelihood (Allison et al. 2012).

Food security, as in international issue with a growing profile, is related to local-level food production. It was defined by the 1996 World Food Summit as, "a condition when all people, at all times, have physical and economic access to sufficient, safe and nutritious food to meet their dietary needs and food preferences for an active and healthy life" (Béné et al. 2007). Thus, food security is more than just freedom from hunger. Often overlooked by government decision-makers and resource managers, the harvest of small-scale fisheries can be sold, consumed in the household or shared within the community. The sharing of food provides a social safety net within a well-functioning community; it is often overlooked, perhaps because it is rarely quantified in studies.

Table 9.2 gives the distribution of the fish catch in seven Caiçara communities in Paraty, Brazil, where fishing was one of the livelihood activities of 70 percent of the households. Ninety-seven percent of the households that reported a catch indicated that at least some of it was consumed within the household, 75 percent shared with relatives, and 69 percent shared with neighbors and friends. Fish sold commercially represented smaller percentages. Many households distributed their catch in multiple ways, both commercial and noncommercial. These results indicate the importance of the community fish catch for local food security, and the role of fish-sharing as part of community exchange networks and social capital (Hanazaki et al. 2013). Studies elsewhere in Brazil have shown the continued importance of local fish in community diets (Hanazaki and Begossi 2003).

Other supporting evidence can be given, showing that the amount of fish going into community networks can be substantial. In Gouyave, Grenada, 93 percent of fishers reported giving away a mean of 16 kg of pelagic fish per fisher to community members after each trip (Grant et al. 2007). Further, beach seining operations left behind some lower-value fish to be gleaned and used by poorer members of the community. Often,

TABLE 9.2 Distribution of fish catch in households that reported fishing activity in seven communities in Paraty, Brazil (data in percentage of households)

	Total	PN	PS	PG	TR	BG	IA	TA
Consumed by the household	97	96	100	82	100	100	98	100
Share with relatives	75	74	79	82	90	43	71	82
Share with neighbours/ friends	69	70	79	64	93	21	63	64
Sell to fish markets/ middlemen	55	83	59	45	10	21	83	55
Sell to restaurants	34	48	48	36	40	0	22	36
Sell to others in the community	21	17	21	27	13	29	22	27
Other	29	22	34	9	37	7	37	27
N	159	23	29	11	30	14	41	11

Notes: PN = Ponta Negra; PS = Praia do Sono; PG = Praia Grande; TR = Trindade; BG = Barra Grande; IA = Ilha do Araújo; TA = Tarituba

Source: Hanazaki et al. 2013

there was no expectation of direct compensation, but fishers assumed that their generosity would be remembered if they fell on hard times. Cash income earned, as well as fish for food, was channelled back into the community, creating an economic multiplier effect and keeping the community going. Grant et al. (2007, p. 121) observed that:

> It is possible to tell by walking down the street in Gouyave if fishers are catching fish. If the streets are relatively quiet, with a number of shops closed, one can tell that no fish has been caught lately. However, if people are in the streets, the bars are open late, and there is merriment, then the fishery is doing well.

In assessing social objectives of management, the area of gender needs more attention. Often overlooked is the role of women in the fishing community. It is true that, in many fisheries, women do little fishing. For example, in the Gouyave study (with 169 interviewed, 51 of them female), only 1 female fished regularly with her partner, 1 was an investor/boat owner, and 12 were involved as fish vendors (Grant et al. 2007). However, numbers can be misleading. For example, in Paraty, very few women would

PHOTO 9.2 Small fish deliberately left behind from beach seining being gleaned by some of the poorer members of the community, an example of artisanal fisheries contributing to local food security. Gouyave, Grenada, West Indies

Source: F. Berkes

self-identify as "fisher," but it is well known that almost all women (and children) in the smaller coastal communities take part in the squid (*Loligo plei* and *L. sanpaulensis*) jigging season (Hanazaki et al. 2013). Chapman (1987) wrote a groundbreaking review of gender division of fishing in Oceania. Women's fishing was primarily carried out in intertidal waters (lagoons), and men's fishing was carried out in deeper water. Because fishing was gendered and occurred in different habitats, it was necessary to include the fishing of both women and men to understand the full fishery. A great deal of women's harvesting goes unreported. Women shellfish harvesters in Pemba Island, Zanzibar, did not call themselves "fishers," and neither did the fishermen. Nevertheless, women gathered and sold substantial amounts of shellfish, as evidenced by roadside stalls (Berkes, unpublished notes).

There are very few well-documented cases of women-dominated fisheries and fishing-related industries, such as the lagoon fisheries of

Asia–Pacific and fish vendors of the Eastern Caribbean and West Africa. However, international statistics indicate large numbers of women fisherfolk. The first comprehensive attempt to estimate the number of fishworkers found that 47 percent of the 120 million people who work in the capture fisheries sector and its supply chains were women, the vast majority of them in small-scale fisheries in developing countries. Post-harvest workers (84 million), many of whom are women, outnumbered fish harvesters (35 million). In small-scale inland fisheries and large-scale marine fisheries, women outnumbered men, in the latter case because of the number of women in processing (HLPE 2014, p. 680).

Harper et al. (2013) provide a review of women in fisheries and emphasize the importance of the gender dimension in food security and local economy. Jentoft (1999, 2000) explored the social and economic role of women in sustaining fishing communities, as Box 9.1 explains. It is often women who keep a fishing community together, a point usually missed by managers. He argued that the community has a key role in coastal resource management; therefore resource rights should be vested in communities, and not in individuals, as many quota systems tend to do. As Johnson (2006) pointed out, the real significance of small-scale community-based fisheries may be in promoting socially just and eco-logically sustainable fisheries.

Communities themselves are the best authorities on the question of appropriate management objectives for marine and coastal resources, and how to incorporate these objectives into development planning. Local development, grassroots development (Chambers 1983) and community-based development (Berkes and Davidson-Hunt 2007) are some of the terms that refer to local-level development planning that follows com-munity priorities, rather than some other development agenda. Can communities have priorities? Communities are not homogeneous entities, and most have different social groups with different interests (Agrawal and Gibson 1999). Nevertheless, most communities have distinct ident-ities and leadership that can articulate community aspirations and objectives.

Chapter 8 (Table 8.3) examined community objectives with respect to conservation–development projects and found that communities usually had not one but a range of objectives that were economic, environmental, political, social and cultural in nature. Many of the cases in Table 8.3 can

BOX 9.1 WOMEN, FISHING COMMUNITIES AND FISHING RIGHTS

It is now well established that women provide a whole range of services that are key to the viability of the fishing household as well as the fishing enterprise of their spouses. This, of course, is a phenomenon that is not unique to Norwegian fisheries ... Here, it is women's efforts, partly channeled through their local association Helselaget that keep the community together and maintain the spirit and life's meaning during times of crisis. In other words, women's contributions are not restricted to the household and their husbands' fishing enterprise. They also take on a responsibility for the whole community, also as community spokespersons vis-á-vis the society at large. Again, this is not unique to women in Norwegian fisheries communities.

The irony is that these contributions are mostly disregarded by fisheries managers who have their eyes fixed on the fish and the fishermen. Had they adopted the functional system model of fishing communities rather than the interdependent model, they could not have avoided noting that fishing enterprises could only work within the larger context of the community, in which women play crucial roles. Then, they would have had to also recognize that women are stakeholders in fisheries management and that they also could legitimately claim to be holders of resource rights, a status which current management systems do not grant them, in fisheries less so than in other primary industries ...

Not only are healthy fish stocks necessary for healthy communities, but the reverse also holds true. Overfishing is not always a result of market failure, as the interdependent system model would have it, but a community failure. This is the community that fails to instill self-restraint, high normative standards, social solidarity and cohesion among community members, and not least among the young fisher recruits ... Norwegian newspapers have reported that quotas are deliberately being exceeded, rules are ignored, and that a culture of cheating is spreading within the fishing industry, at the expense of the resource. I argue that this is what to be expected of a fisheries management system that has no appreciation of community as a functional system, where the roles and contributions of men and women are equally important, for the material as well as moral well-being of communities.

(Jentoft 1999)

be characterized as development projects of a particular kind—they did not have the sole objective to maximize profits, but included multiple objectives instead. The cases may be characterized as social enterprises.

Social enterprises by definition are not based on the familiar utilitarian–economic models but rather on an economic model in which resources provide for broader goals—economic, political and social/cultural (Anderson et al. 2006). Social enterprises are a good fit with the idea of multiple objectives, because they tend to respond to the multiple needs of a community, such as job creation, resource access, empowerment and environmental health. Whereas global enterprises focus on providing growth in capital to shareholders, social enterprises strive to provide social dividends to community members and play a role in maintaining economically and socially viable communities. Often, they involve collective action, depend on the local resource base, and require partnerships and networks to make them work.

Network-like partnership arrangements with linkages across levels seem to be common in many cases, for example, the conservation–development projects from the UNDP Equator Initiative. A sample of nine cases showed that partnerships typically spanned four levels of organization (local, regional, national, international) and involved 10–15 partnerships each (Berkes 2007a; Seixas and Berkes 2010). The partners assist communities with a variety of tasks, such as capacity building for business management, raising capital and technology transfer (Berkes 2007a). Networks of partnerships are clearly important in ecological restoration projects as well (Chapter 7) and in co-management (Pinkerton et al. 2014).

Conclusions

Coastal and marine resources everywhere are under pressure from over-fishing, habitat loss and global environmental change. Coastal, and mainly small-scale, fisheries are under pressure also from urban and industrial expansion, pollution, incursions of large-scale fisheries, and loss of productive fishing grounds to tourism, recreational fishing, energy and mining development, protected areas, aquaculture and other uses (Chuenpagdee 2011). The expansion of these other uses inevitably means a loss of coastal space and resources for traditional users. The livelihood implications of these losses to the millions of fisherfolk and other coastal users are potentially very serious.

Chapter 5 argued that the control of fisheries and other coastal resources by the people who use them is a key consideration. Chapter 6 further discussed how commons institutions of coastal resource users can become part of coastal governance. Small-scale fisheries cannot very well be eliminated; they are part of the fabric of coastal communities and produce income and food for these communities. Nor can they be replaced whole-sale by large-scale fisheries or aquaculture, which use different technologies (some not so suited for coastal sustainability) and tend to produce different kinds of product than do small-scale coastal fisheries. Hence, resource managers and policymakers need to address the needs of the coastal fishery sector.

Examples in this chapter show that many small-scale fisheries have social enterprise characteristics. For example, food sharing within the community is common (Hanazaki et al. 2013), providing a social safety net for the poorer community members, as in Gouyave (Grant et al. 2007). Many community-based management programs are beginning to resemble community-based development. For example, Wilson et al. (2006) pointed out that co-management programs in Asia are increasingly characterized by networks that mix management power sharing with local development. One co-management case in the Philippines began with a small aquaculture project, but expanded into other resource management and development activities, such as ecotourism and livelihood enhance-ment, through alliances with local government agencies and NGOs (Wilson et al. 2006).

Fishing is not merely a job or source of income and food; it is also the basis of social relationships that hold the community together. Fishing is often part of a livelihood complex, which may include agriculture and other part-time occupations, and part of a seasonal round of activities that enable households to make a living. This is so, not only in low-income countries, but also in many middle-income countries of the world, such as Brazil, Turkey and Thailand, and regionally in many high-income countries, such as Canada, Japan and the United States. A livelihood is sustainable when it can cope with and recover from stresses and shocks; hence, resilience of livelihoods is the basis for sustainability. Coastal livelihoods require access to multiple resources and habitats and must have the option to switch. Flexibility is key to viability and depends on having access to a number of stocks to compensate for year-to-year fluctuations in abundance. The ability to follow a seasonal round of activities and the ability to switch fishing grounds and species—fishing more when a particular resource is abundant; switching when it is not—is also consistent with coastal ecosystem sustainability.

Hence, a pro-small-scale-sector policy helps maintain resource access, options and flexibility, in the process of accommodating other coastal uses. Appreciating the livelihood characteristics and needs of fisherfolk helps maintain a consistent policy that looks after the needs of small-scale fisheries. Focusing on entitlements, including public services, and following primary fisheries management, including attention to rights and food security, are the other elements of a policy informed by livelihood considerations. Incorporating social objectives into management requires an understanding of community objectives, values and knowledge. The next chapter expands on the issue of knowledge.

10
LOCAL AND TRADITIONAL KNOWLEDGE
BRIDGING WITH SCIENCE

> Conventional biological training has focused our attention so single-mindedly on the rigorous quantitative description of marine resources before committing ourselves to managing them, that we are liable to feel guilty if we diverge from this track—and worse still, we may even criticize others who do so. But when vital resources are rapidly degrading, as are reefs and other nearshore tropical habitats around the world, we often have neither the time nor the resources for such data-gathering. The choice is not between giving perfect or imperfect advice to managers. It is between giving imperfect advice or none at all.
>
> (Johannes 1998b, p. 245)

Introduction

Bob Johannes was writing about what he called the data-less management of tropical nearshore fisheries, using some combination of MPAs and traditional knowledge and management systems. His deliberately pro-vocative language did attract criticism from those who could not quite subscribe to the notion that "management should be judged by its fruits, not by its roots" (Johannes 1998b, p. 245). But, if traditional management can be characterized as "data-less," in the sense of lack of stock assess-ment and other numerical data, it is important to point out that it is information-rich in time-tested knowledge of the environment and rules for collective action to put that knowledge into play. What was unconventional in the 1990s is not so anymore. Appreciation of the value of local and traditional knowledge of coastal people has increased substantially since Johannes's time (Menzies 2006; Haggan et al. 2007; Lutz and Neis 2008).

There is no universally accepted definition of traditional ecological knowledge. For some, traditional means old and static—inflexible adherence to the past. For others, traditional does not mean that at all, but simply time-tested and wise. For many groups of indigenous people, the word tradition carries many positive meanings, and it defines a way of life. Traditional ecological knowledge begins at the level of local and empirical knowledge of species and the environment. It proceeds to the level of practice, which requires understanding local ecological processes and how to live and work with them. Practice requires rules-in-use or institutions to guide how a group of people relate to their environment and resources. For a given group of people, practice and institutions are embedded in a particular worldview or belief system, which guides the way that they interact with their environment. Here, traditional ecological knowledge is depicted as consisting of four interrelated levels of analysis, one embedded in the other (Figure 10.1).

Hence, an operational definition of *traditional ecological knowledge* is "a cumulative body of knowledge, practice, and belief, evolving by adaptive processes and handed down through generations by cultural transmission" (Berkes 2012b, p. 7). Traditional ecological knowledge is a way of knowing; it is dynamic, building on experience and adapting to changes. It has a learning-by-doing component that makes it similar to adaptive management (Berkes et al. 2000). It is an attribute of societies with historical continuity in resource use in a particular place. The term *local knowledge* is used when referring to recent knowledge that is not multi-generational or time-tested. The term *indigenous knowledge* is defined as the local knowledge held by indigenous peoples or local knowledge unique to a given culture or society (Berkes 2012b). As appropriate, one may refer to fisher knowledge. As not all traditional knowledge is ecological in nature, one may also use, as appropriate, the terms traditional knowledge or traditional environmental knowledge.

This chapter is about knowledge: what local and traditional knowledge signify, and how such knowledge can be bridged with science to increase

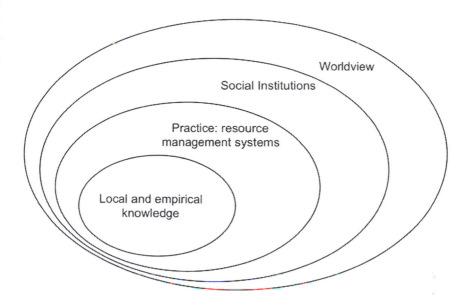

FIGURE 10.1 Levels of analysis of traditional knowledge and management systems
Source: Berkes 2012b

the range of information that can be brought to bear to solve practical problems. The argument is that too much time and effort have already been spent on criticizing or defending traditional knowledge (and, for that matter, Western science). The issue should be reframed instead as a science *and* traditional knowledge dialogue and partnership, with the overall aim of building bridges between the two kinds of knowledge and increasing the range of information available for problem solving (Berkes and Folke 1998). Figure 10.2 schematically illustrates this notion, which Tengö et al. (2014) refer to as the *multiple evidence base approach*, emphasizing the advantages of combining different kinds of knowledge (natural science, social science, local knowledge, indigenous knowledge) to produce an enriched picture.

The chapter first discusses indigenous knowledge as process, not merely as content. Second, it deals with the belief component of indigenous knowledge, to explore its nature and significance. Then the chapter illustrates the potential use of local and traditional knowledge with two examples, one from traditional knowledge (the First Salmon Ceremony) and the other from local knowledge (cod spawning areas in the Gulf of

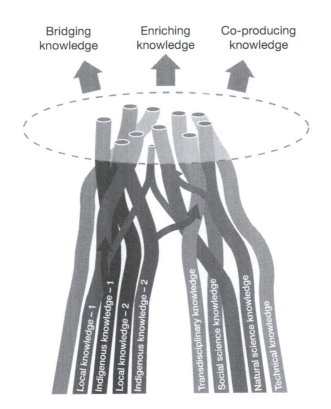

FIGURE 10.2 The multiple evidence base approach. Diverse knowledge systems (shown as knowledge roots) contribute to the generation of an enriched picture of a selected problem

Source: Adapted from Tengö et al. 2014

Maine). Finally, the chapter discusses the various ways in which indigenous knowledge and science can be bridged.

Indigenous Knowledge as Content, Indigenous Knowledge as Process

Take the example of climate change. Indigenous elders cannot transmit an actual knowledge of climate change, because many of the recent observations are beyond the range of historical experience (Berkes and Jolly 2001; Berkes 2012b). What they can do is to teach what to look for and how to look for what is important. The climate change example illustrates the distinction between traditional knowledge as content— information that can be passed on from one person to another—as opposed to traditional knowledge as process, a way of observing, discussing and making sense of information—indigenous ways of knowing (Berkes 2012b).

Fisher knowledge as content is the kind of traditional ecological knowledge that biologists and managers are most familiar with. Local resource users often have intimate knowledge of local species, their distributions and their habits. When Johannes was working in the tiny archipelago of Palau in the Pacific in the mid 1970s, he found that the local fishers knew the locations and timing of spawning aggregations of many species of fish. The species were well known to science but their reproductive habits and lunar spawning periodicity were not. So he obtained from local fishers the precise locations, months and timing of spawning aggregations of some 55 species of fish that followed the moon as a cue for spawning. Fishers' knowledge from just Palau amounted to more than twice as many species of fish exhibiting lunar spawning periodicity as had been described in the scientific literature for the *entire world* at that time (Johannes 1981).

Johannes noted one other thing. The fishers knew where the fish aggregations were and when they would occur. The aggregations of sluggish fish presented just the right conditions under which they could be most easily caught. Nevertheless, the fishers did not consider spawning time as an opportunity for uncontrolled harvest; it was simply looked upon as a time when the fish would be caught more easily than other times. This alerted Johannes to the local conservation ethic. His investigations in Palau and elsewhere in the Pacific in the 1970s found that reef and lagoon tenure systems had built-in harvest controls in the form of closed fishing areas and seasons; allowing escapement; bans on taking small individuals, nesting turtles and eggs; and restricting some fisheries for emergencies. "Almost every basic fisheries conservation measure devised in the West was in use in the tropical Pacific centuries ago," observed Johannes (1978, p. 352).

In fact, Pacific reef and lagoon tenure systems were so conservative (and conservation-oriented) that colonial powers forced open-access conditions on them to enable rapid exploitation, trade and revenue generation (Johannes 1978). Hence re-establishing conservation in the post-colonial Asia–Pacific has meant the revitalization of traditional management institutions, along with cultural revitalization (Johannes

1998a, 2002). But recovery has been slow. Re-instituting traditional controls in an area that is now integrated into the global economy has not been easy. However, enduring empirical knowledge of species and the environment is being put to good use toward conservation. Box 10.1 outlines one such effort in Fiji, a part of the LMMA Network.

Further on indigenous knowledge as process, one should point out the contested idea that indigenous knowledge may have its own unique processes. In the Western positivist tradition, there is only one kind of science—Western science. The conflict between science and indigenous knowledge is, to a major extent, related to claims of authority over knowledge. Understandings and insights that originate outside institutionalized Western science are not easily accepted. For this reason, one finds, for example, that the earlier reports of the Intergovernmental Panel on Climate Change (IPCC) included, almost exclusively, science from scientific papers and reports, with almost no mention of indigenous knowledge. As well, indigenous peoples themselves received mention only as "victims" of climate change (Salick and Ross 2009). The 2014 reports of the IPCC finally included some indigenous and local knowledge on the strength of accumulating evidence that indigenous observations were, in fact, contributing to the understanding of climate change (Nakashima et al. 2012).

Indigenous ways of knowing can be different from scientific ways of knowing, not only in terms of knowledge content but also in terms of what is observed. Elders or other knowledge-holders do not merely transmit knowledge, they also teach *what to observe and how to look for* what may be important. Such ways of knowing are relevant, not only for climate change, but also for biodiversity conservation. Hence, the IPBES that started in 2012–13 made a decision to incorporate traditional environmental knowledge in its work from the outset (UNESCO 2013). Both the material in Box 10.1 and the multiple evidence base approach (Tengö et al. 2014) are IPBES-related work.

Indigenous ways of knowing can be illustrated in a number of different ways. The example used here is the Inuit knowledge of the Greenland shark (*Somniosus microcephalus*), a deep-living species and the only shark normally resident in the eastern Arctic (Idrobo and Berkes 2012). The shark is chosen as the example because it is a species little known to

BOX 10.1 FIJI'S LMMA NETWORK: A BASIS FOR PROMOTING AND ASSESSING MARINE CONSERVATION SUCCESS

In the mid-1990s, local fishers and communities who had personally witnessed and been involved in the collapse of their fisheries, partnered with the Fiji national and provincial government agencies (including fisheries), NGOs, private industry, the University of the South Pacific (USP) and international funders, such as the Macarthur, Packard and Total Foundations to establish a Fiji Locally Managed Marine Areas Network (FLMMA). More than 200 villages now have LMMAs and have seen impressive improvements in reef ecosystems and gains in marine biodiversity. The success has been based on participatory management planning and involving communities in all phases, including monitoring.

Particularly exciting has been a taxon-by-taxon assessment of changes in the occurrence and abundance of over 1,000 species that have occurred over the past 50 years within the fishing grounds (*iqoliqoli*) of Vanua Navakavu in the Fiji Islands, based on a comparison of time–depth testimonies of surviving older male and female fishers with results from more recent surveys in an effort to record and correlate observed changes with factors such as intense overfishing, use of fish poisons, increased pollution, a 1953 tsunami and the establishment of the LMMA in 1991. At present, local vernacular names for over 1,000 species have been recorded and the recovery status of almost 900 assessed. Results show that the successful restriction of fish poisons, dynamite fishing, and small-mesh gill netting, combined with the establishment of a successful MPA, seem to be largely responsible for the return of many taxa not seen for decades and the increasing abundance and size of a wide range of fin fishes and invertebrates.

The results show that the combination of the best indigenous and modern scientific and taxonomic knowledge may be the only way of really determining how our efforts at marine conservation are impacting on, and will ultimately affect, marine biodiversity. The cumulative and ongoing results of the surveys highlight the incredible potential local and indigenous knowledge can play in sustainable fisheries management. These efforts are critical for documenting the un-written histories of the collapses and building ecological, economic and cultural sustainability in the face of global change.

(Randolph Thaman in UNESCO 2013, p. 15)

science and to the Inuit. However, the Inuit of Pangnirtung, southern Baffin Island, have had relatively greater exposure to this species, because it is a bycatch in their bottom long-line fishery, but their interactions are not about use or cultural meaning. The shark is little discussed and generally considered an undesirable species. When faced with a species that is seldom encountered or discussed, can indigenous ways of knowing help piece together accumulated observations of fragmentary knowledge to make inferences about the biology and ecology of that species?

In figuring out shark biology, the Inuit used heuristic rules in the form:

> IF—observation/appreciation—THEN—a possible explanation for what is observed

Variables related to habitat were used to understand feeding behavior. If sharks were bottom dwellers, then they were likely to be scavengers, but, if they were both bottom dwellers and free swimmers, the understanding of their feeding behavior expanded from exclusive scavenging to include predation. Stomach contents exclusively of seal and whale carrion established the shark as a scavenger. However, some Inuit had come across seal pups and apparently wounded animals in the stomach contents, and this increased the range of possibilities to include opportunistic predation. Further, a couple of hunters recalled hunting seals and whales with circular wounds and speculated that sharks could be active predators, capable of preying on healthy marine mammals (Figure 10.3).

The Inuit are well known as keen observers of species and ecological relationships, and some of their knowledge has provided insights for scientific research (Freeman 1993). Inuit marine ecology is not usually conceptualized in the form of food webs. However, the question posed to the Pangnirtung Inuit, "who eats who and who is not eaten by anybody else?" elicited species relationships that can be put in the form of food webs (Figure 10.4). Many of the relationships mapped in the figure are known to experienced Inuit knowledge-holders, but these are not consensus maps. Rather, they are the personal maps of two particularly knowledgeable Inuit. Each of them located the shark in the overall web of relationships as he sees them. The two maps are similar in broad outline

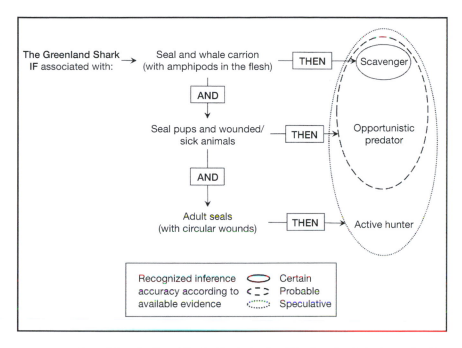

FIGURE 10.3 Pangnirtung Inuit and the feeding behavior of the Greenland shark: construction of traditional ecological knowledge based on heuristic reasoning

Source: Idrobo and Berkes 2012. Reprinted with permission from Springer

but different in detail. Hunter A showed more species detail, including opportunistic predation of sharks on bearded seals (*Eringnathus barbatus*). Hunter B showed fewer species and interactions, but notably included opportunistic cannibalism among sharks (Idrobo and Berkes 2012).

Indigenous knowledge does not necessarily encompass all of the species in the environment of a group of people. If a species does not have economic or cultural value, the knowledge about it may be fragmentary. Such is the case with the Greenland shark for the Inuit. However, existing fragments of information about a species can be brought together, shared and interpreted to produce community knowledge. This information can be further interpreted in the light of existing knowledge about other species and interrelationships in the marine ecosystem. However, such an understanding is likely to show variations among local experts. To the extent that interpretations overreach observational information, increasingly wider divergences may appear among knowledge-holders.

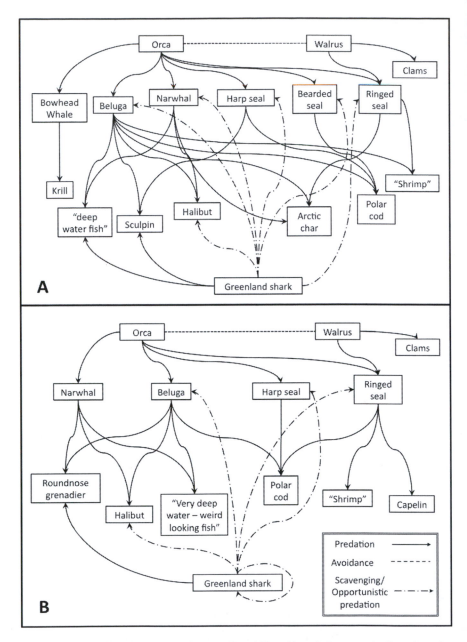

FIGURE 10.4 Two Pangnirtung Inuit hunters (A and B) and knowledge coproduction of species relationships. Species identifications based on photos and field guides. Inuit species correspond to scientific ones, except for those shown in quotation marks

Source: Idrobo and Berkes 2012. Reprinted with permission from Springer

The Belief Component of Traditional Knowledge

The Greenland shark example incorporates the type of knowledge, empirical knowledge, readily accepted cross-culturally. Given the same kind and amount of information about the shark, a group of marine ecologists may come up with very similar interpretations. In general, the first level of analysis in Figure 10.1, which is about species identifications, distributions, habitats and life cycles, concerns information that is likely to be acceptable to biological scientists (unless it is verifiably inaccurate— and of course there are such cases; Johannes 1981). The second and third levels, which are about management systems such as reef and lagoon tenure and the institutions that underpin them, are not as easily acceptable, because their outcomes are not readily observable in the short term. Nevertheless, for scientists and managers who can say, "Management should be judged by its fruits, not by its roots," indigenous management systems do work in some cases. Not only that, for some commons scholars, indigenous institutions provide novel arrangements and inspiration to help craft new institutions for dealing with contemporary commons problems (Berkes et al. 2003; Ostrom 2005).

It is the belief component of traditional knowledge that creates problems for many scientists and managers, the idea that the worldview of a group of people shapes the way they see human–environment relationships. The Greenland shark example was deliberately chosen to minimize the effect of the belief component of Inuit knowledge. If the example had been about seals instead, the belief component would have been significant: seals are culturally important species related to *Sedna*, the sea goddess in Inuit creation mythology. What does the cultural belief component add? Box 10.2 is a description of the First Salmon Ceremony in the traditional indigenous fisheries of the Pacific Northwest, the stretch of coast from northern California to Alaska. It is a management system (although the indigenous peoples themselves would not use the word management) that does have a belief component.

Belief systems are intrinsically important as part of a culture. In this context, however, beliefs and values regulate proper relations between people and environment. Stories and myths provide social mechanisms that help societies remember social rules, including traditions of conservation (Turner 2005). Indigenous narratives often serve as teachings

BOX 10.2 THE FIRST SALMON CEREMONY OF THE INDIGENOUS PEOPLES OF THE PACIFIC NORTHWEST

The First Salmon Ceremony was practiced by many indigenous groups in the Pacific Northwest of North America, from northern California to Alaska. When the migrating salmon appeared in the river, the people of these tribes were not free to fish. They had to wait for the First Salmon Ceremony and the permission of elders (Swezey and Heizer 1977). There were many variations of the system. In some tribes, the ceremony relied on families who were the designated salmon watchers, and on runners who would communicate up the river the news about the approaching salmon. The system hinged upon a tribal ritual leader who would make the decision about the timing of the ceremony that then marked the opening of salmon fishing.

As a part of indigenous culture, the First Salmon Ceremony is important in its own right, but it also seems to have served a resource management function. It is known that an experienced observer could make a qualitative assessment of the strength of a particular salmon run. This is similar to what contemporary biologists do, with population models and counting fences in salmon rivers, to establish daily harvest quotas and to allow sufficient escapement, a term that refers to making sure that a portion of the reproducing stock is able to get by the fishery and reach spawning grounds.

It is also known that ritual leaders in the First Salmon Ceremony were able to adjust the timing of the ceremony to allow for a portion of the run to escape upstream before declaring the fishery open. For example, if a particularly strong run was coming, the leader might wait only three days before opening the fishery. But, if the run was weak, he might delay the opening for ten days. The leader did not use a resource management discourse; he supervised a ritual consistent with cultural values encoded in stories about respecting salmon, allowing them to reproduce and not interfering with the migration leaders (Swezey and Heizer 1977; Williams and Hunn 1982).

The First Salmon Ceremony has been superseded by biological management in many areas, even where indigenous tribes manage their own salmon fisheries. In Oregon and Washington State, for example, the tribes are obliged, under their co-management treaties, to use scientific management (Singleton 1998). However, many tribal biologists still know the traditional system, and a few places still practice it—for example, the Karuk people on Klamath River in northwestern California. The Klamath has sites where the river narrows, and the migrating salmon can be visually assessed by experienced harvesters. The Karuk people have traditional fishing sites where the salmon and some other species are harvested, consistent with historic practice.

of respect and appreciation of the environment and resources. Many indigenous societies hold beliefs about animals having agency and acting purposefully (Dowsley and Wenzel 2008). Beliefs in the necessity of respect and reciprocity and mutual obligations in animal–human relations are common. Such beliefs and values are transmitted through oral traditions, including stories and ancestral sayings (Wehi et al. 2013; Turner 2014).

In the Pacific Northwest, the Saanich people's story of the Origin of Salmon starts at a time when people were starving. Two brave youths embarked in their canoe and went looking for salmon. After a long journey, they reached a strange country and stayed with some wise people who had good relations with salmon. After some time, their hosts arranged for them to travel with the salmon back toward home. Along the coast, they burned qex̱min (Indian celery, *Lomatium nudicaule*), for their hosts had said, "Burn qex̱min along the beach to feed the salmon that travel with you. Then, if you treat the salmon well, you will always have them in abundance." The story continues, relating how the Salmon People taught the young men fishing techniques and how to honor the First Salmon with a ceremony and prayer so that the salmon may always be plentiful (traditional, retold in Turner and Berkes 2006).

The First Salmon Ceremony serves to remind people that they need to treat salmon with respect. However, the ceremony has practical management value as well. The ritual allows the tribal leader to make adjustments for the year-to-year variation in the strength of the salmon run. In a bad year, the leader delays the opening of the fishery, allowing a sufficient number of individual fish to escape upstream to spawn. The system described in Box 10.2 is based on making good observations, accurate judgment of the strength of the run, and the ability to set the opening date flexibly. The management rule is enforced socially, backed up by traditional beliefs and values: one may not fish until the First Salmon Ceremony has been carried out, signalling the opening of the salmon fishery.

Can an indigenous leader, with knowledge and understanding of salmon migrations and populations but without scientific data in hand, produce results similar to those achieved by scientific management? According to some tribal biologists in Oregon who were posed this question, an experienced observer can, in fact, do a good qualitative visual assessment of the strength of a salmon run. Scientific management accomplishes something similar, but uses intrusive techniques, forcing migrating salmon through a counting fence to obtain data. By contrast, the ritual leader of the tribe presumably carries out data-less or qualitative assessment, estimating the strength of the run visually, based on experience. He also "eyeballs" a sufficient number of spawners that are allowed to escape upstream, before the fishery is ritually declared open and the event marked by the ceremony (Berkes 2012b).

Data-less management, based on local and traditional knowledge, is being carried out in some other parts of the world as well, both in indigenous and nonindigenous areas. For example, no-take fish sanctuaries on the Mekong River in Laos use a community-based fisheries co-management framework (Baird and Flaherty 2005). Managing the Mekong River basin and its fisheries is complex. Said to be the third most diverse freshwater fish fauna in the world, the basin is characterized by a diversity of aquatic habitats—rapids, wetlands, deep-water pools and flooded forests, and many species groups migrate across borders of the basin ecosystem. Further complicating management are regional conflicts in this six-country basin.

An innovative approach to conserve fish was initiated in Laos in the early 1990s by local fishers, in effect, an ICCA system locally known as *pha pa* or *pha nong*. A characteristic of these community-based sanctuaries was that they were often established in deep-water pools. Initially, fisheries biologists and managers were skeptical of the value of establishing fish sanctuaries in rivers (Baird 2006), but these locally chosen sanctuaries typically included deep-water pools, and studies showed that deep-water pools were a critical habitat, serving as important dry season refuges for many species, especially large fish. Established by villagers, but now enjoying government support, these fish sanctuaries are protected by "community rules that prohibit fishing in these areas during the dry season. Locals generally do not violate these rules, for fear of retribution from powerful spirits or from other villagers" (Baird 2006, p. 4).

Local and Traditional Knowledge in Practical Management

Some kinds of traditional knowledge and management exist only in the day-to-day practices of a group of people (Ingold 2000). Other kinds of traditional knowledge and management system are observable in the engineering works that people have used or structures that may be seen in the archaeological record. Coastal examples of physical structures include stone ponds for fish aquaculture in Polynesia (Costa-Pierce 1987); stone fish traps in Alaska (Langdon 2006) and in much of the Pacific Northwest; and *kata* (brush piles made of tree branches) in Bangladesh (Sultana and Thompson 2007) and in India, Sri Lanka and various places in West Africa.

Archaeological evidence and oral history indicate that many traditional peoples around the world actively managed and enhanced coastal ecosystems to increase productivity. Documented examples are few, perhaps because researchers have not been looking for them. Only in the 2000s, researchers in British Columbia discovered human-engineered intertidal terraces in coves and at the mouths and along the edges of embayments. Thought to have been constructed in the late Holocene, these terraces, called *clam gardens*, have been recorded from Alaska through to British Columbia and Washington State. Constructed by building rock walls in the low, intertidal areas of soft-sediment clam beaches, they are thought to stabilize sediments behind the wall, presumably to enhance shellfish productivity (Lepofsky and Caldwell 2013). Figure 10.5 shows a clam garden terrace, as compared with a non-walled beach.

Groesbeck et al. (2014) assessed the productivity of ancient clam gardens on Quadra Island, British Columbia. Clam gardens ranged in size and shape, but were characterized by shallow, sloping, intertidal terraces (as sketched in Figure 10.5), encompassing tidal heights of

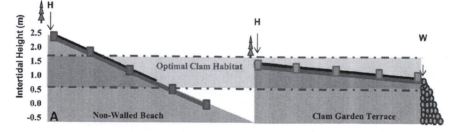

FIGURE 10.5 Clam garden: comparison of the profile of a non-walled beach vs. clam garden terrace. Groesbeck et al. (2014) surveyed clams across a vertical transect from the top of the clam habitat (H) to the edge of the rock wall (W) in clam gardens. Note the expansion of the optimal clam habitat in walled beaches

Source: Groesbeck et al. 2014

0.9–1.5 m above chart datum. The researchers used in situ transplant experiments supplemented with surveys, querying if clam gardens had higher clam densities, biomass and growth rates compared with non-walled beaches. They found that clam gardens had greater densities of littleneck clams (*Leukoma staminea*) and butter clams (*Saxidomus giganteus*), particularly at smaller size-classes. Overall, clam gardens contained four times as many butter clams and over twice as many littleneck clams as compared with non-walled beaches. Transplanted juvenile littleneck clams grew 1.7 times faster, and smaller size-classes were more likely to survive in clam gardens than in non-walled beaches, especially at the top and bottom of beaches. Groesbeck et al. (2014) concluded that clam gardens likely increased clam productivity by altering the beach slope and expanding optimal intertidal clam habitat, thereby enhancing growing conditions.

Quadra Island clam gardens had not been actively tended or managed for decades, but, in parts of the region, knowledge of clam gardens still exists. Box 10.3 is part of the account of a fieldtrip by ethnoecologist Nancy Turner and her colleagues with Clan Chief Adam Dick (Kwaxsistalla), an elder of the Tsawataineuk community of Kwakwaka'wakw people, Kingcome Inlet, British Columbia (Turner et al. 2013b). The objective of the fieldtrip was to visit a clam garden, learn about it and get a sense of traditional peoples' attachment to place and their detailed knowledge of the environment. In retrospect, it seems amazing that indigenous clam gardens escaped the notice of scientists for so long. All they had to do was to ask Chief Adam Dick, and he would have told them what they were. This is a telling story that illustrates why it is so important to foster a dialogue between science and traditional knowledge.

Not all traditional knowledge and management systems can be deduced from observable structures. Some exist only in the day-to-day knowledge and practice of a group of people, and not necessarily indigenous people. Some North Atlantic fishers come from families with multigenerational fishing experience and can, therefore, be said to hold traditional knowledge. One such fisher is Ted Ames of Maine. He first went to sea at the age of six, with his grandfather, and spent the better part of his life on the Maine coast, fishing for shrimp, scallop, lobster and groundfish (Clark 2006).

BOX 10.3 CLAM GARDENS OF THE KWAKWAKA'WAKW

One of the main features we wanted to learn more about was the *loqiweys*—the clam gardens—that Kwaxsistalla's ancestors had built, possibly 2,000 years ago or more. These gardens were created to enhance the production of clams, a keystone food for coastal peoples. As Kwaxsistalla said, "When you see clam shells up and down the coast, that's where people lived." Thousands of people lived in villages all around the Broughton Archipelago, Vancouver Island, and the opposite mainland, and the chiefs needed predictable food supplies for all the people and to keep their sophisticated and intricate economies moving.

The clams also served as an assured backup food for times when the salmon or other food resources were in short supply. For many years, the clam gardens were not recognized outside the Kwakwaka'wakw world, even by archaeologists. It was assumed that these exceptionally productive clam beaches were naturally formed, and that the line of boulders accumulated just above the lowest tide line somehow came to be there through natural forces. Yet, once Kwaxsistalla was consulted, the clam gardens as human-built features became clear. These were engineered beaches, created by rolling the rocks from the middle part of the beach down to the edge, freeing up more space for clams to live and grow.

There were four different kinds of clams: large, smooth, bluish gray butter clams, giant horse clams, small littleneck clams and the prized, plump striated cockles with their large, pointed foot. . . . Kwaxsistalla filled our imaginations with the memories of his childhood, and it was so amazing to be able to walk along the beach, and scramble around the same rocks that he climbed over as a little boy, 75 years or more ago. There, the *loqiwey* is still in evidence, with a vast expanse of beach still cleared of the large boulders, all still piled up by the thousands along the lower tide line. At low tide, the clams were all squirting out streams of water in a seeming choreographed visual symphony.

(Turner et al. 2013b)

In 1990, with the eastern Maine groundfish virtually gone, Ames reluctantly sold his 45-foot dragger (trawler). To make a living, he taught school, ran a lab and continued to fish for lobsters, which remained plentiful. State and federal agencies alike agreed that the groundfish (mainly cod and haddock) were gone, but there was no consensus on how to bring them back. Ames had a plan: he would interview retired fishers, those who had fished in the 1930s and the 1940s. They knew where the fish had once been: "If we could find out where the old spawning areas

PHOTO 10.1 Clam garden, Kingcome Inlet, British Columbia, Canada

Source: Nancy Turner

were, we could restock them," Ames said. He picked out 28 of the best inshore cod and haddock fishermen he knew and interviewed them, "Some of the most wonderful bunch of old codgers you could ever imagine" (Clark 2006).

Ames published the results of the interviews in 2004 in the journal *Fisheries* of the American Fisheries Society. He compared data from three periods: (1) data from the 1920s in the Gulf of Maine, when the cod were abundant; (2) his interview findings with information from the 1930s and 1940s; and (3) data from the 1980s. He mapped the cod spawning areas from these three periods and they "fit like a glove." Data from the 1920s and the detailed information from the "old codgers" showed some 90 patches of spawning areas, from the shallow coastal to the deeper offshore (Figure 10.6). However, active spawning grounds fell from 90 to no more than 46 by the 1980s, with many of the remaining grounds showing only sporadic spawning activity (Ames 2004). The loss of spawning grounds coincided with the depletion or collapse of coastal subpopulations of cod, starting in the 1940s. From interview data on fish

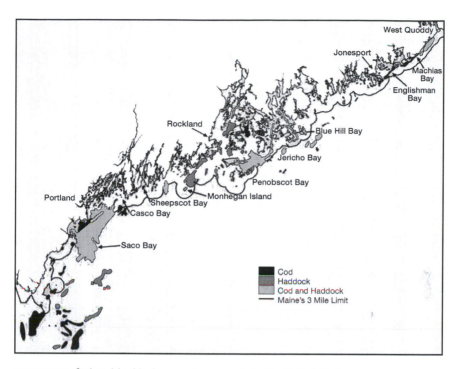

FIGURE 10.6 Cod and haddock spawning grounds in the Gulf of Maine

Source: Penobscot East Resource Center. Ted's publications: www.penobscoteast.org/research/ted-ames

distributions, Ames (2004) was further able to show the historical existence of four Gulf of Maine subpopulations of cod, each with several spawning components, some of them now extinct.

Ames (2004) set out to document the distributions and spawning movements of cod in the Gulf of Maine so that sustainable populations could be restored and maintained. In view of the fact that the Gulf of Maine has been transformed into a "lobster monoculture," this objective may not be so easy to achieve (Chapter 4; Steneck et al. 2011). However, in the process, he established some very important points. First, he showed that the local and traditional knowledge of "old codgers" could produce detailed maps of fishing areas, cod movements and spawning grounds that were not available in the scientific literature but complemented and fit with the data that were available. Second, he showed how cod disappearance likely came about: by slow erosion of each subpopulation, spawning component by component; loss of patches of spawning ground, starting from the coastal zone and moving to deeper areas, followed by loss of entire subpopulations.

Third, his findings showed the fatal flaw of centralized, system-wide stock assessments that missed the grand collapse of the Newfoundland cod (Chapter 1, Figure 1.1). As Ames (2007, p. 360) puts it, "Today's fisheries managers and fishers are trapped in a management system dependent on system-wide stock assessments that are not designed to detect local depletions." One could speculate further: many subpopulations, each with multiple spawning grounds, probably conferred resilience to the population as a whole. Local depletions eroded this resilience, until the system reached a tipping point, and the population could no longer absorb the impacts of multiple drivers and stresses (such as climate change). Then a regime shift occurred, from a groundfish-dominated ecosystem to a lobster-dominated one (Steneck et al. 2011).

Traditional Knowledge and Science: Bridging and Coproducing Knowledge

The clam garden example shows the usual state of affairs between traditional knowledge and science: a dialogue of the deaf. The Pacific Northwest probably has one of the highest "densities" of marine biologists and aquaculture specialists in the world, but it took some social scientists and indigenous elders to actually make the connection that the strange beach geomorphology throughout the area was but a human-made aquaculture system. The Gulf of Maine example paints a more optimistic picture (even if cod restoration does not). It shows a remarkable knowledge broker, a one-person bridging organization who is both a fisher and a traditional knowledge-holder/researcher, combining the two kinds of knowledge to make sense of the cod disappearance and to inform future management.

The work of Ames (2004, 2007) is an excellent example of the multiple evidence base approach (Tengö et al. 2014) producing an enriched picture with cross-fertilization and coproduction of knowledge. Humility is part of the challenge. As Harris (2007, p. 303) puts it, "Co-production of requisite knowledge requires all parties to recognize that all knowledge is partial and incomplete, that evidence is debatable, and that there are ways of knowing determined by culture, semiotics and values." Here, I focus on how the two kinds of knowledge can collaborate toward a multiple evidence base approach, and the methods or models that can be used to aid in this collaboration.

Combining the two kinds of knowledge is especially important in situations of insufficient information. Using the two knowledge paradigms together can improve problem solving. Such *coproduction of knowledge* has been defined by Armitage et al. (2011, p. 996) as, "the collaborative process of bringing a plurality of knowledge sources and types together to address a defined problem and build an integrated or systems-oriented understanding of that problem." Knowledge coproduction has been used most effectively in relation to questions about which neither knowledge system by itself has sufficient information to deal with the issue. Climate change is one such problem, and the complementarity of indigenous knowledge and Western science produces a better understanding of the issue than either would alone (Riedlinger and Berkes 2001; Nakashima et al. 2012).

Respecting the integrity of each knowledge system is no doubt preferable to trying to test one kind of knowledge against the other. The operative word, therefore, is *bridging knowledge systems* (Reid et al. 2006). Such an approach is more respectful (and, therefore, more effective) than "synthesizing" or "combining" or "integrating" knowledge systems. This is because "integrating" knowledge often works to the disadvantage of indigenous people or other resource-based communities, owing to differences in power. As many examples show, power imbalances make local and indigenous communities and their knowledge vulnerable to outside influences (Berkes 2012b). Hence, bridging knowledge systems is far preferable to integrating them. It certainly is preferable to "mining" traditional knowledge and using it, often out of context, as "data" for science.

Respecting each knowledge system and considering them on equal footing is a challenge. An appropriate analogy for bridging is the Two-Row Wampum (Doubleday 1993; McGregor 2004). This is:

> [a] beaded belt describing a friendship treaty between the Dutch and the Iroquois. The rows of beads on the belt represent Dutch vessels and Iroquois canoes, traveling side by side down "the river of life." The paths of the two kinds of vessels remain separate, but the people on the two kinds of boats are meant to interact and to assist one another as need be. Such a relationship comes

closest to respecting the integrity of both ways of knowing while maintaining the opportunities for the two kinds of knowledge to enrich one another.

(As summarized in Berkes 2012b, p. 263)

A number of approaches, techniques and areas of co-operation exist to bring together the two kinds of knowledge in ways that are respectful and generally acceptable to knowledge holders (Table 10.1). First, we consider some approaches that foster equal partnerships between the two kinds of knowledge. Participatory rural appraisal has a relatively long history of use (Chambers 1983). It provides a toolkit that has been adapted for using local and indigenous knowledge, along with agricultural and other kinds of science (Warren et al. 1995). Participatory action research is not a toolkit but an approach that emphasizes collective inquiry, reflection and social change (Fals-Borda 1987). Participatory education (critical pedagogy) comes out of a tradition of empowerment in which the learner is treated as the co-creator of knowledge (Freire 1970; Moller et al. 2009a; Trimble and Berkes 2013). Some of these ideas have been applied to Native American education by indigenous scholars (Cajete 2000; Pierotti and Wildcat 2000; Kimmerer 2002). Place-based learning communities refer to groups of people with a shared interest, learning through partnerships through regular interactions based in practice (Davidson-Hunt and O'Flaherty 2007).

Second, a number of techniques exist to elicit and understand local and indigenous views and knowledge. Participatory mapping, as in the Gulf of Maine (Ames 2004) is probably the best known of these techniques. Film, video and other visual arts can be used in a similar way for the dissemination of indigenous knowledge research to a variety of audiences, such as communities themselves, co-management boards, educators and other researchers (Bonny and Berkes 2008). Participatory workshops and modeling have been used successfully with various groups and can be adapted to different kinds of knowledge and different cultural backgrounds. Participatory scenario planning is a part of the toolkit of participatory workshops and modeling approaches. Scenarios, defined here as plausible and challenging sets of stories about how the future might unfold, were used widely by the Millennium Ecosystem Assessment (Bennett and Zurek 2006).

TABLE 10.1 Fostering collaboration and two-way learning between indigenous knowledge and Western science

Some approaches that foster equal partnerships between two kinds of knowledge:

- *Participatory rural appraisal*, a toolkit that has been in use for some decades. It has been adapted for using local and indigenous knowledge

- *Participatory action research*, an approach that emphasizes collective inquiry and social change; seeks to change the world collaboratively and reflectively

- *Participatory education* (critical pedagogy) comes out of a tradition of empowering learners to become co-creators of knowledge

- *Learning communities* refers to groups of people with a shared interest, learning through partnerships through regular interactions based in practice

Some techniques to elicit and understand local and indigenous views and knowledge:

- *Participatory mapping* is probably the best known of these. Film, video and other visual arts can also be used in a similar way

- *Participatory workshops and modeling* have been used successfully with both indigenous and nonindigenous rural knowledge-holders

- *Participatory scenario planning* is a part of the toolkit of participatory workshops and modeling approaches

Cooperating around a particular task at which local and indigenous communities may have specific expertise:

- *Participatory conservation planning* uses complementary knowledge from Western science and local/indigenous communities

- *Participatory environmental restoration* uses both kinds of knowledge; local knowledge can provide essential information not otherwise available to science

- *Community-based monitoring* involves reading signs and signals of environmental change based on the ways of knowing of a given group

Note: References in text

Third, co-operation of the two kinds of knowledge works well, especially where local and indigenous communities may have specific kinds of expertise to contribute. For example, local knowledge can provide essential information not otherwise available to science about the ecological restoration of a wetland (Robertson and McGee 2003). Effective collaboration often occurs around a particular problem to be solved, as in the Gulf of Maine case. In fact, ethnobiology as a field developed initially to use the two kinds of knowledge together in a systematic way, to deal with species identifications and classification, and later to study biocultural landscapes and waterscapes (Hunn and Selam 1990; Kimmerer and Lake 2001; Johnson and Hunn 2010).

Participatory conservation planning can take advantage of the complementary strengths of the two kinds of knowledge (Reid et al. 2006; Stephenson et al. 2014). The meeting photo in Chapter 8 (Photo 8.2) shows a participatory planning session with Wemindji Cree representatives and university researchers toward the protected area proposal in James Bay. Similarly, environmental restoration often relies heavily on local knowledge and stewardship, as seen in the Chapter 7 examples of Nisqually River and delta restoration and others. Community-based monitoring takes advantage of indigenous ways of knowing, often with complementarities of scale (Cash and Moser 2000). Applications include the Arctic Borderlands Ecological Knowledge Co-op, which facilitates scientists getting together annually with indigenous knowledge-holders, sharing their observations of environmental changes (Kofinas et al. 2002; Eamer 2006).

Conclusions

Many resource and environmental problems require new approaches and the inclusion of a wide range of information, considerations and values. Knowledge is a dynamic process; knowledge can be created, validated and adapted to changing circumstances. Local and indigenous knowledge is not in competition with science. The relationship between the two kinds of knowledge should be reframed as a science *and* traditional knowledge dialogue and partnership, with the overall aim of bridging the two to increase the range of information available (Berkes and Folke 1998; Reid et al. 2006). However, it is also important to remember that there are different kinds of local and traditional knowledge, just as there are different kinds of Western science (Figure 10.2).

Some aspects of each knowledge system pose problems for the other. The belief component and values of traditional ecological knowledge are often explicit, as in the First Salmon Ceremony and in sacred areas such as fish sanctuaries in Laos. Many scientists can understand the ecological value of these beliefs, but tend to be dismissive of cultural values. One can respond by pointing out that Western science too has its own (often implicit) beliefs about what constitutes proper evidence and proper knowledge (Berkes 2012b). For their part, many traditional knowledge-holders have a great deal of trouble with the Western scientific notion of controlling and "managing" nature. For many indigenous knowledge-holders, one can exercise stewardship (Moller et al. 2009a; Chapin et al. 2012) or "care for country" (Rose 2005; Muir et al. 2010), but animals and the environment cannot be managed in the sense of control.

The subject of local and indigenous knowledge has come up several times earlier in this volume, for example, in the context of commons management and co-management. In co-management, bridging organizations are those that bring together the two sides of a divide and provide a forum for interaction (Hahn et al. 2006; Berkes 2009b). Knowledge coproduction is a kind of bridging to arrive at a creative synthesis (Armitage et al. 2011). The Greenland shark case is a good example. The inquiries about this little-known species, brought to the Inuit by a research team of social and natural scientists, enticed the Inuit to think about sharks in ways beyond what they normally would, reaching deep into their observations and experiences. This allowed the reorganization of available fragmentary information to address bigger ecological questions, such as those sketched in Figure 10.4, the essence of knowledge coproduction (Idrobo and Berkes 2012). Such knowledge coproduction requires all partners to be willing and open, and to proceed with humility (Moller et al. 2009a).

Some of the ways to bridge knowledge systems are based on joint research methods and processes (participatory rural appraisal; workshops, modeling and scenario planning) and/or approaches that consider local and indigenous people as equal partners (participatory action research; participatory education). Some rely on co-operating around a particular task in which local and indigenous communities may have specific expertise (environmental monitoring, conservation planning, environmental restoration). Yet others are based on new institutions and governance arrangements such as co-management. Some of the ways of bridging take advantage of the similarities between indigenous knowledge and certain areas of Western science, including adaptive management and fuzzy logic (Berkes et al. 2000; Peloquin and Berkes 2009; Berkes 2012b).

Although a number of approaches and methods exist to foster bridging, this does not mean that there are well-established, sure-fire ways to bring together the two paradigms respectfully. General protocols for bridging would be difficult to formulate. In some cases (e.g., spiritual practices), it may not be appropriate to attempt any bridging at all. In other cases (e.g., knowledge coproduction for conservation), it may be appropriate to go beyond bridging to synthesize the two kinds of knowledge creatively.

11
SOCIAL–ECOLOGICAL SYSTEM-BASED MANAGEMENT

Introduction

Pitcher and Lam (2010) evaluated ten commonly advocated fisheries management solutions against five performance modalities (ecological, economic, social, ethical, institutional) and found that ecosystem-based management came out as one of the two best ones. (The top one was historically based restoration; see Chapter 7.) Ecosystem-based approaches involve adopting a holistic view of managing resources in the context of their environment. The approach involves the broadening of the scope of management from the conventional single-species focus toward a systems view, including food web considerations, habitat and system resilience. In the case of fishery science, there has been considerable progress in both theory and practice. Single-species models that ignore food web interactions have been replaced by increasingly more sophisticated multispecies models (e.g., Essington and Punt 2011). Better biological models may be necessary but not sufficient, as there are a number of additional considerations. In particular, biological models often lack the important human dimension.

The "ten commandments" offered by Francis and colleagues (2007) extend the list of elements of ecosystem-based fisheries management (Table 11.1).

The list goes considerably beyond conventional biological management and ends with a call for integrated, interdisciplinary and inclusive

TABLE 11.1 **Action items for bridging the gap between general principles of ecosystem-based management and specific methodologies**

Keep a perspective that is holistic, risk-averse and adaptive	A fundamental commandment providing a worldview and context for the commandments that follow
Question key assumptions, no matter how basic	Single-species stock assessment models include assumptions that are questionable, if not outright faulty
Maintain old-growth age structure in fish populations	An unfished population tends to include many year-classes and multiple reproductive age-groups, probably conferring population resilience. Fishing simplifies age structure
Characterize and maintain the natural spatial structure of fish stocks	Subpopulations that we call unit stocks are assumed to be reproductively closed, but in fact they are not, even though they may be spatially distinct
Characterize and maintain viable fish habitats	All species need appropriate habitats that meet their requirements. Management could include seafloor mapping and fish habitat characterization
Characterize and maintain ecosystem resilience	The concept of resilience is a useful scoping device to integrate ecosystem and social system complexity
Identify and maintain critical food web connections	Food webs create the fundamental organizing relationships in ecosystems. Therefore, any marine resource exploitation needs to take this into account
Account for ecosystem change through time	Ecosystem analysis is complicated by the fact that some variables are fast and others are slow
Account for evolutionary change caused by fishing	Conventional management often assumes away the potential of fishing mortality to cause directional selection in fish populations
Implement an approach that is integrated, inclusive and inter-disciplinary	Kinds of issues raised by moving to a holistic approach cannot be addressed by a single disciplinary perspective

Source: Adapted from Francis et al. 2007

approaches. The Malawi Principles consider ecosystem-based management more generally (not solely from a fisheries point of view) and start with the all-important observation that management objectives are a matter of societal choice, not a technical or scientific matter (Table 11.2). They focus on the conservation of ecosystem structure and function and

TABLE 11.2 Malawi Principles for the ecosystem approach

1. Management objectives are a matter of societal choice

2. Management should be decentralized to the lowest appropriate level

3. Ecosystem managers should consider the effects of their activities on adjacent and other ecosystems

4. Recognizing potential gains from management, there is a need to understand the ecosystem in an economic context, considering, e.g., mitigating market distortions, aligning incentives to promote sustainable use and internalizing costs and benefits

5. A key feature of the ecosystem approach includes conservation of ecosystem structure and functioning

6. Ecosystems must be managed within the limits to their functioning

7. The ecosystem approach should be undertaken at the appropriate scale

8. Recognizing the varying temporal scales and lag effects that characterize ecosystem processes, objectives for ecosystem management should be set for the long term

9. Management must recognize that change is inevitable

10. The ecosystem approach should seek the appropriate balance between conservation and use of biodiversity

11. The ecosystem approach should consider all forms of relevant information, including scientific and indigenous and local knowledge, innovations and practices

12. The ecosystem approach should involve all relevant sectors of society and scientific disciplines

Source: Folke et al. 2005

include a consideration of scale, time-lag effects and multiple sources of knowledge. There are gaps still. The Malawi Principles mention "change," but not potential regime shifts (Österblom et al. 2010). Neither list directly mentions drivers of local and global change, to address what Carpenter (2002) has called "the long now."

In the case of broader coastal management, an ecosystem approach means moving from a single-sector focus (e.g., fisheries) to multiple sectors (e.g., aquaculture, conservation, recreation, energy production and other). Ecosystem-based management needs to focus on a suite of human activities that interact with one another and affect particular places. As Norse (2010, p. 185) points out, "patterns of primary production and seafloor structures have dramatic effects on where fishes feed and spawn; cultural traditions and proximity to harbors have dramatic effects on where people fish." Such place-based management of marine and coastal eco-systems is a marked departure from the conventional sector-based approach. It involves ocean and coastal zoning to implement ecosystem-based management (Norse and Crowder 2005). Marine spatial planning with comprehensive ocean zoning can help address the problem of fragmented governance. In practical terms, zoning would not replace existing regulations by sector but would add a spatial dimension by defining areas within which compatible uses could occur (Crowder et al. 2006).

Marine ecosystem-based management is used here as the more comprehensive concept, and ecosystem-based fisheries management as a component of it. Generally used definitions of *ecosystem-based management* are rather broad in scope. According to NOAA (2005, p. 3), "An ecosystem approach to management is management that is adaptive, specified geographically, takes into account ecosystem knowledge and uncertainties, considers multiple external influences, and strives to balance diverse social objectives." Not many ecosystem-based management applications satisfy this definition. Some focus on geographical aspects, as in marine spatial planning. Others focus on ecosystem goods and services (MA 2005a; Carpenter et al. 2009), ecosystem resilience (Hughes et al. 2005; McLeod and Leslie 2009), adaptive management (Walters 1986) or governance (Kooiman et al. 2005; Fanning et al. 2011).

The challenge is to combine these various approaches to find the "right" mix for a particular situation. Moving from management to the broader frame of governance may require embracing multiple disciplines and multiple objectives (Cochrane and Garcia 2009), and broader interdisciplinary approaches to deal with marine ecosystems as integrated systems of people and environment—as social–ecological systems, rather than merely as ecosystems (Ommer et al. 2011). "Diverse social objectives" as mentioned in the NOAA definition and livelihood concerns are crucial for reasons of equity. Small-scale fisheries, which may be vulnerable to zoning and privatization, continue to be important in terms of employment and food security, as noted in Chapter 9 (Béné et al. 2007; De Young et al. 2008). Particularly in developing country contexts, local-level governance and institutions are central to effective ecosystem-based management (Christie et al. 2007, 2009).

The knowledge dimension mentioned in the NOAA definition has many aspects, including the question of the appropriate kinds of knowledge and the role of local and traditional knowledge: "ignore fishers' knowledge and miss the boat" (Johannes et al. 2000). Also important are monitoring and the gap between available research and the data needs of many small stocks that are part of the ecosystem management challenge (Johannes 1998b; Prince 2003). Can we implement ecosystem-based fisheries management without addressing multiple objectives and the full range of governance issues? After all, the sole objective of maximizing yields stock by stock is simply the legacy of mid-20th-century biologists addressing the overfishing problem (Saenz-Arroyo and Roberts 2008). As well, we know that single-species stock assessment rates poorly against other strategies in terms of composite policy performance (Pitcher and Lam 2010). The serious consideration of some of these points would require a major rethinking of ecosystem-based management—not minor tinkering with concepts and practice, but revolutionary change.

The argument in this chapter is that implementing ecosystem-based management in the coastal and marine environment requires a new interdisciplinary science. This new science can best be characterized as revolutionary, rather than evolutionary, because it breaks away from many of the assumptions and practices of conventional ecosystem-based man-agement (Berkes 2012a). It would require going into the realm of interdisciplinary approaches dealing with wicked problems in a context of ever-shifting drivers and intractable management problems; finding ways to grapple with social–ecological systems; and developing new kinds of governance unforeseen by the mid-20th-century fathers of resource management. This is governance that may involve co-operative, multilevel (rather than centralized) management, partnership approaches, social learning and knowledge coproduction.

In short, the chapter argues that ecosystem-based management has to come to terms with uncertainty and complexity (Charles 2001; Norberg and Cumming 2008), an interdisciplinary visioning of management objectives (Berkes et al. 2001; Cochrane and Garcia 2009), and putting humans back into the ecosystem (Glaser 2006; Ommer et al. 2011). First, I review some ecosystem-based management examples for lessons. Second, I make the case that ecosystem-based management is a wicked problem, and I discuss marine and coastal environments as complex social–ecological systems in which it is simply not possible to isolate the various uses and impacts from one another. Third, I explore a range of new, and some not so new, governance approaches to help implement ecosystem-based management. Finally, I explore some possible ways to deal with complexity, trying to cut down to size this messy and increasingly complex world.

Lessons from Ecosystem-based Management Cases

Ecosystem-based management is not a new scientific concept. To put it in historic context, ecosystem-like concepts exist in some traditional societies. Two characteristics help recognize these concepts as ecosystem-like. First, the unit of land and water is defined in terms of a geographic boundary, usually a watershed boundary. Second, the traditional concept holds that everything within this social–ecological unit is interrelated. There are differences as well as similarities between traditional and Western scientific concepts of ecosystems. It would not be correct to label these traditional concepts as prescientific ecosystem concepts, because they differ in context and conceptual underpinning (Berkes et al. 1998).

A relatively well-known example, first mentioned in Chapter 3 as an illustration of integrated social–ecological systems, is Hawai'i's *ahupua'a*, a mountain-to-sea ecosystem. Each *ahupua'a* is a roughly wedge-shaped catchment, starting from the mountaintop of these volcanic islands, often bordered on the sides by lava flows, and extending to the lagoon and fringing coral reefs. Typically, each *ahupua'a* was controlled by a chief and consisted of a forested mountain area, integrated farming zones in upland and coastal areas, a fringe of coconut palms along the coastline, and brackish water and seawater fishponds. The *ahupua'a* as a locally controlled, integrated resource management unit collapsed after colonization of Hawai'i. However, they are being restored, both ecologically and culturally, in recent years (Kaneshiro et al. 2005).

Hawai'i's *ahupua'a* is not unique. Many Pacific island societies have similar concepts (Ruddle and Akimichi 1984; Ruddle and Johannes 1990). For example, *vanua* in Fiji is an area seen as an integrated whole with its human occupants. *Vanua* has physical dimensions, a land–water area and all that grows on it. It also has social and cultural dimensions, "the human occupants with their traditions, customs beliefs, values and institutions . . . established for many generations from the time of a founding ancestor" (Baines 1989, p. 275). According to Hviding (1990, p. 23), in the Solomon Islands:

A *puava* is a defined, named area of land and in most cases sea. A *puava* in the widest sense includes all areas and resources associated with a *butubutu* (descent group) through ancestral rights, from the top of the mainland mountains to the open sea outside the barrier reef.

In each case, the intimate association of a group of people with land, reef and lagoon effectively constitutes the personal ecosystem of that group of people. Close association of societies with their lands and waters is found in many indigenous societies. Watershed-based management of salmon rivers was a common practice of the Native American people of the North American Pacific Northwest (Swezey and Heizer 1977; Williams and Hunn 1982) and the indigenous Ainu people of Japan (Watanabe 1973). All of these traditional ecosystem-like management systems rely on an understanding of the biology and ecology of the species involved and how the coastal ecosystem functions, inspiring modern versions such as Japan's *sato-umi* discussed in Chapter 7.

Detailed descriptions of contemporary applications of traditional ecosystem-like systems clearly show ecosystem-based management characteristics. For example, modern *vanua* applications in Fiji include the network of MPAs in the Kubulau District on Vanua Levu, the second largest island of Fiji. (See Figure 8.4 and the accompanying text in Chapter 8.) In 2005, communities in this district established a network of protected areas, including 17 locally managed *tabu* areas and three no-take district marine reserves. The design of the network was informed by socioeconomic and biological research carried out by the local resource management committee and its conservation partners, which were national, regional and international NGOs. With additional research and local and traditional knowledge input, the local resource management committee and its conservation partners set out in 2008 to develop an integrated "ridge-to-reef" management plan, consistent with the land-and-water ecosystem-based management characteristics of a traditional *vanua* (Clarke and Jupiter 2010).

The scientific literature on ecosystem-based management is immense and varied, and includes some cases that strive to take a social–ecological systems approach. I use two cases (from Australia and Chile) to illustrate the kinds of consideration and finding that emerge when the framing of the ecosystem is expanded to include the human dimension and the broader ecosystem. Both cases involve zoning, but use two different approaches.

Australia's Great Barrier Reef, introduced in Chapter 8, is one of the largest MPAs in the world, and it is managed as a spatial mosaic of fully protected areas and zones supporting a range of uses (McCook et al. 2010). Often cited as an example of comprehensive ecosystem-based management, it was developed step by step from humble beginnings. The transition from protection of selected individual reefs to the stewardship of the large-scale seascape occurred in 2004 and was accompanied by the transformation of the governance regime. Olsson et al. (2008) regard extensive rezoning as the main mechanism to achieve ecosystem-based management and adaptive co-management of the seascape. They identified five key strategies used by the Great Barrier Reef Marine Park Authority (GBRMPA), the main management agency, to transition to ecosystem-based management: internal organizational changes, bridging science and policy, changing people's perceptions, facilitating community participation, and generating political support for rezoning.

Rezoning emphasized protecting biodiversity and maintaining ecosystem function and services, rather than maximizing resource yields or revenue. The gaining of political support was made possible by the use of a critical window of opportunity to set the zoning timeframe to the timing of the sitting parliament. Mobilizing public awareness of the larger conservation issues, engaging a broader set of stakeholders, compensating user-groups impacted by expanding conservation, making a commitment to deliberative processes, and developing flexible governance systems by linking institutions across multiple levels of organization, from local to national levels, emerged out of these five strategies (Olsson et al. 2008). In doing so, the GBRMPA overcame many of the barriers, such as lack of public support and inflexible institutions, faced by zoning initiatives in other jurisdictions, such as southern California (Crowder et al. 2006).

The Great Barrier Reef provides an example of marine spatial planning with comprehensive zoning. Each of the seven zones manages a different set of users. The General Use Zone, for example, allows most uses, some through a permit process. The most restrictive three zones, by contrast, allow very few. Despite strict controls, however, the Great Barrier Reef is still susceptible to impacts that originate outside the protected area, such as sedimentation from river runoff and climate change, thought to be the cause of coral bleaching events in the Reef. Some of the human activity-related drivers, such as population increase, were predictable, but others were not. For example, few would have guessed that the State of Queensland would become a major producer and exporter of coal, with ports in the area of the Great Barrier Reef (Hughes 2014).

The Chile case deals with a coastal strip in which benthic invertebrate resources are allocated for exclusive use of fisher associations and governed under a co-management arrangement. Gelcich et al. (2010) trace the evolution of the system, from open-access declines through the 1980s of the gastropod *loco* (*Concholepas concholepas*), the most economically important shellfish in Chile. The collapse of *loco* in 1988 was followed by closure in 1989–92, leading to a transition and population rebuilding/restoration. The return to democracy in Chile provided a window of opportunity to draft new fishery legislation in 1991, allocating exclusive territorial user rights to fisher associations and establishing quota management for some species, including *loco*.

The Chilean system, like the Great Barrier Reef, uses principles of spatial management (Figure 11.1). A new fisheries law adopted in 1991 reformed fishing rights for industrial and artisanal fisheries by regulating fleet mobility through zoning. The artisanal fleet (vessels not exceeding 18 m and 50 gross tons) was allocated exclusive use of the five-mile coastal zone. Larger vessels were considered industrial fleet. The mid-scale artisanal fleet targets mainly finfish and small pelagic species and has since become a major sector (Castilla 2010). The small-scale artisanal sector, composed of shellfish divers, inshore fin-fishers and seaweed gatherers, uses open boats under 10 m. Within the five-mile coastal zone, associations of small-scale artisanal fishers were granted territorial use rights to demarcated fishing coves (*caletas*) for *loco* and other resources. The rights to use these *caletas*, some 700 in number, is subject to user fees, an initial baseline study and management plan, and annual monitoring by authorized experts to set TAC year by year (Gelcich et al. 2010).

The transformation to a sustainable benthic fishery was not quick and easy, but involved a series of steps and decisions to divert a system trapped in an undesirable management pathway (open-access *loco* fishing) toward

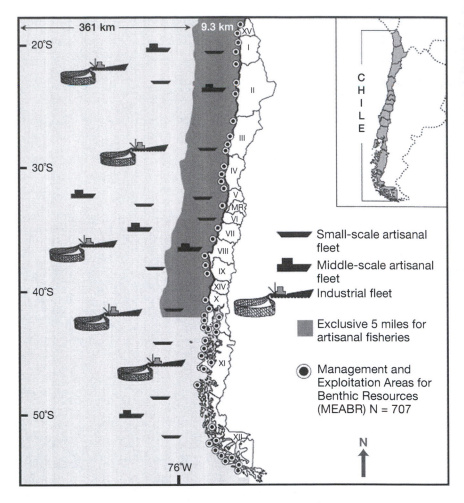

FIGURE 11.1 Schematic representation of fisheries zoning in Chile (not to scale). Roman numerals indicate administrative regions

Source: Gelcich et al. 2010

an alternative pathway. One of the key elements was experimental research involving scientists and fishers that led to a learning process about *loco* population recovery rates and ecosystem responses to management and conservation. For example, it was found that, when *loco* is depleted, the coastal ecosystem shifts to a low-value, mussel-dominated seascape (Gelcich et al. 2010). Such coproduced knowledge was built into new management, and practices developed by learning networks were connected to decision-making. It took some six years of debate and deliberation over

PHOTO 11.1 *Loco* fishers setting out to their fishing cove, Caleta Montemar, central Chile
Source: Andrés Marín

such information to create a governance transformation by 1997. Perhaps because the new governance regime was seen by some as an "end point" at that time, co-learning processes subsequently weakened. It appears that the Chilean system still needs to develop values to continue experimentation and adaptive learning (Gelcich et al. 2008; Marín and Berkes 2010).

Social–Ecological Systems and Wicked Problems

A discussion of ecosystem-based management requires reference to some cases and revisiting of some concepts considered earlier in this volume, in particular social–ecological systems and the wicked problems idea. The management issue is not about human-free ecosystems but about social–ecological systems. In some ancient ecosystem-like concepts that consider humans an integral part of the system, people are so much a part of their particular environments that their self-identity includes a description of their land. In the contemporary world, individuals and groups no longer have such strong bonds with their environment.

Nevertheless, our unit of analysis is the social–ecological system, a complex adaptive system that includes social (human) and ecological (biophysical) subsystems in a two-way feedback relationship. The two subsystems function as a coupled, interdependent and co-evolutionary system (Chapter 3). They are co-evolutionary in the sense that the human system is adapted to the characteristics of the environment through its institutions. For example, the First Salmon Ceremony in Chapter 10 is a mechanism to deal with the variability of annual salmon spawning migrations. Co-evolution is further illustrated by fishing livelihood systems in West Africa that seem to be adapted to the variability of their marine ecosystems (Perry and Sumaila 2007).

Scale issues also come into play in these social–ecological systems. There is a long list of drivers of change that may originate somewhere else and act on a given ecosystem (MA 2005a). Climate change is not the only example. Many of these drivers involve economic externalities, market demands, government policies, resource conflicts, and politics and economics in general. All of them are outside the realm of biological management. In regard to marine resources, Deutsch et al. (2011, p. 121) found that, "economic drivers are stronger than social and ecological drivers, and ecologically-relevant feedbacks are not only missing in the present market system, but are in fact blocked by current trade institutions."

As the roving bandits example in Chapter 5 shows, local marine tenure, national laws and international regulations are all insufficient to deal with problems related to global economic drivers of the kind referred to by Deutsch et al. (2011). Market demands and the resulting high-speed resource exploitation may overwhelm the ability of management institutions to respond. Local fishers are powerless, national-level regulation is too slow, and international controls are even slower. For small or highly localized stocks, the resource may be fished out before the problem is even detected. In the case of more widely distributed and relatively abundant species, catch statistics may blur local depletions, as exploitation shifts geographically. Even under a sound ecosystem-based resource management regime, managers may be ultimately powerless, because the problem (high market demand) is originating from outside the ecosystem. For example, the managers of the Great Barrier Reef are powerless to deal with climate change-related coral bleaching events, even if they can further expand their jurisdictions to deal with the other troublesome driver, sedimentation from river runoff.

As the Australian and Chilean cases illustrate, ecosystem-based management is an ongoing process and not an end point. No matter how well designed, the current management arrangements will need to be modified and reinterpreted to respond to new problems that will keep coming up. Revisiting the wicked problem idea first introduced in Chapter 1, one can say that ecosystem-based management is a wicked problem. When Ludwig (2001) declared that the era of management was over, he probably was alluding to the fact that managing such wicked problems requires an entirely different approach than managing some solvable scientific problem in a human-free ecosystem.

Many environmental problems are "wicked" in the sense that they could not be solved once and for all but continue to pose an ongoing challenge, as problems of the Great Barrier Reef and Chilean benthic co-management illustrate. Each wicked problem is unique and not amenable to technical and scientific solutions. Jentoft and Chuenpagdee (2009) suggested that coastal governance issues have many of the characteristics of wicked problems—they are difficult to define and delineate, they are persistent and they have no right or wrong solutions that can be determined objectively. Ecosystem-based fisheries management is a wicked problem for much the same reasons.

The biophysical boundaries of the ecosystem help frame the problem to be managed, but this provides only limited assistance. Within the ecosystem, there are various uses and activities that may compete with one another, such as Inuit beluga hunting and Arctic recreational kayaking (Dressler et al. 2001). Or they may be simply incompatible, such as wind farming and parasailing, to use Norse's (2010) colorful example; they cannot occur in the same place at the same time. Therefore, there is a need to evaluate trade-offs and priorities: "the best site for a wind farm might not be the best for a wave farm, a marine reserve, recreational fishing, or bottom trawling" (Norse 2010, p. 185). Priorities may shift over time, affecting trade-offs. For example, as biodiversity conservation attains higher priority than fish production or tourism revenue in the Great Barrier Reef, no-take areas will increase, and the revised zoning will reflect that. There is still a trade-off, but the balance has now shifted. In Chile, neoliberal resource management policies led to the collapse of *loco* in 1988.

Under a different political regime and policy priorities, new measures led to *loco* recovery and the establishment of territorial use rights for small-scale fishers (Gelcich et al. 2010).

The possibility of regime shifts in ecosystems (Chapter 4) makes wicked problems even more wicked. Consider, for example, the Gulf of Maine, a low species diversity ecosystem in which the American lobster has exploded in numbers, accounting for over 80 percent of Maine's landed value (Steneck et al. 2011). Many fishers and managers see this outcome as a success, but the Gulf's lucrative fishery is at risk because of the loss of functional diversity of the socioeconomic system and its ecological base. Steneck et al. (2011) characterize the Gulf as a "gilded trap," a social trap in which erosion of social–ecological system resilience and the risk of a regime shift are masked by short-term success.

Governance Approaches: Diverse and Creative

One important point stands out in each case of ecosystem-based management: the central role of governance. In each case, the outcomes are not determined by science but by a combination of the effects of drivers, exploitation strategies of users, management strategies and decisions, and science. The issue of governance is so important that some papers on ecosystem-based management focus largely on governance, almost to the exclusion of science, as in the study of the large marine ecosystem approach by Mahon et al. (2009). In their study of the Baltic as a case of ecosystem-based management, Österblom et al. (2010) focus on multilevel (local, national, basin-wide, European Union) governance, whereby bottom–up initiatives can lead to diffusion of innovation, assisted by enabling legislation at the international level.

Why has governance become such an important aspect of ecosystem-based management? The short answer is that management and policy directions in fisheries and marine resources are no longer as clear as they were in the era of command-and-control management (Holling and Meffe 1996) and under expert-knows-best decision-making (Ludwig 2001). Governance is no longer under the sole authority of governments in many countries around the world. From Chile to Fiji, shared governance involves many partners and co-operative interactions, and market solutions often take precedence over regulatory controls (Kooiman et al. 2005), not only in the West but also in developing countries (Wilson et al. 2006).

The problem is not that we lack management alternatives. There is a diversity of management strategies to choose from. The problem is in deciding which strategies are compatible with the issue in hand and which are not, and how to combine them. Each management case is unique. For example, community-based MPAs, developed in one region of the Philippines and then replicated in other parts of the country, but with little attention to local context, resulted in a high rate of failure (White et al. 2002). There is some guidance on how to deal with the local context (Ostrom 2007, 2009; Cox et al. 2010), and how to assess management alternatives.

Pitcher and Lam (2010) produced a study of ten commonly advocated fisheries management solutions, evaluated against five performance variables: ecological, economic and social viability, ethical status, and ease of institutional implementation. By their performance criteria and assessment, *laissez-faire*, privatization, MPAs and conventional stock assessment ended up as the bottom four out of ten strategies. The middle group consisted of selective fishing technology, community-based management, traditional ecological knowledge and total economic valuation. The two best strategies, historically based restoration and ecosystem-based management, have the advantage of being inherently composite. Further, historically based restoration is deep in time, and ecosystem-based management is broad in space:

> and thus better able to capture the complex human dimension of fisheries ... By examining historical ecosystems and customary practices and norms, by returning to traditional food sources and community-based management, by considering judicious use of plankton resources in an ecosystem-based context, and by the selective and efficient use of technology, we may intentionally shift global society to a more desirable future.
>
> (Pitcher and Lam 2010, p. 12)

The details of the Pitcher and Lam (2010) findings are perhaps not as important as the main message: improving the management of fisheries and coastal resources requires the judicious use of a mix of strategies. Ecosystem-based management is a key approach because it already is a composite strategy and considers broad spatial scales; it could be even

TABLE 11.3 **Aids to implementing ecosystem-based governance**

Integrative science	Methods and processes to support suitable institutional responses, a broader planning perspective, and development of resilience-building strategies. It seeks a shared understanding of problems while avoiding tunnel-vision arising from disciplinary training (Miller et al. 2010)
Knowledge coproduction	The collaborative process of bringing a plurality of knowledge sources and types together to build an understanding of the problem (Armitage et al. 2011). Incorporating the knowledge, skills, resources and perspectives of several actors (Lejano and Ingram 2009b)
Clumsy solutions	Exploratory solutions that include inputs from a broad range of stakeholders along the fish chain, from producers to consumers, and require information-sharing, knowledge synthesis and trust-building (Khan and Neis 2010)
Primary fisheries management	The minimum management goal, where adequate management does not exist, aimed at food security, poverty reduction and social and ecological resilience to avoid crossing undesirable thresholds (Cochrane et al. 2011)
Human rights-based fishing	The consideration of fishing rights as human rights. Embedding fisheries governance within a broader perspective of human rights to achieve both human development and resource sustainability outcomes (Allison et al. 2012)
Ecosystem stewardship	A strategy to shape social–ecological systems under conditions of uncertainty and change to sustain opportunities for use of ecosystem services for human well-being (Chapin et al. 2010). Governance that provides incentives that leads to behavior consistent with conservation (Hilborn et al. 2005)

more effective if it included time depth as well. Complementing Pitcher and Lam (2010), Table 11.3 sketches six ideas or concepts that may be considered companions to ecosystem-based management—potential aids to make it work. These six items are overlapping and cannot all be used at the same time. Some will be more appropriate for a given case than others, thinking diagnostically rather than in blueprint solutions (Ostrom 2007).

The notion of integrative science describes a "thing" and a "process" and is applied to building resilience under conditions of uncertainty, particularly in the face of climate change. The "thing" is a broad combination of natural science, social science and local knowledge applied to the study of social–ecological systems. The "process" is about the steps involved in bringing together this combination of knowledge to engage with research challenges and knowledge needs (Miller et al. 2010). Integrative science is systems-oriented and seeks to produce a shared understanding of the problem at hand. The idea is to avoid the tunnel-vision arising from disciplinary training, and the narrow set of standard fixes that arise from limited perspectives.

Knowledge coproduction is a strategy for combining knowledge to deal with research challenges and information needs. It can lead to data-less management (Johannes 1998b) where hard data are scarce, or to creative solutions by reorganizing available fragments of information to come up with new insights to tackle a management problem (Armitage et al. 2011; Idrobo and Berkes 2012). It is a collaborative process of bringing a plurality of knowledge sources and types together. To emphasize the importance of different sets of knowledge and skills that partners can bring to the table, Lejano and Ingram (2009b) refer to it as inclusive management.

Collaborative knowledge production among partners is important also for explorations of clumsy solutions. The term is used by Khan and Neis (2010) to refer to policies that creatively combine opposing perspectives on problem identification and solutions. In cases of fisheries collapse (as in Newfoundland cod), rebuilding is more than stock recovery. Treating fisheries as social–ecological systems, rebuilding aims at the entire fish chain, from the ecosystem to harvesting and processing sectors, and all the way to the consumer. Rebuilding, as a wicked problem, may need clumsy solutions and approximations to be able to move forward.

Table 11.3 has two items first discussed in Chapter 9 on livelihoods. Using the analogy with primary health care, Cochrane et al. (2011) suggested that we should be aiming for primary fisheries management, with goals of resilience, food security and poverty reduction. As many fisheries of the world are not managed at all, there is a need for such minimum benchmarks applicable to all fisheries, and presumably to other coastal resources. The longer-term goal should still be well-informed adaptive management. The argument for human rights-based fishing is that fishing rights are human rights. Fishers who are less vulnerable and more secure in basic entitlements, such as food and the right to a dignified livelihood, make more effective and motivated resource managers (Allison et al. 2012).

PHOTO 11.2 Food security as access to sufficient, safe and nutritious food: in many parts of the world, sanitation and environmental health are major issues in fish consumption. The dry fish in this market in Kutubdia Island, Bangladesh, have been sprayed heavily with pesticides, a common practice. Dr. Emdad Haque drew the attention of international researchers to the fact that there were no flies in the dry fish market!

Source: F. Berkes

Finally, ecosystem stewardship may be considered a distinct strategy or set of strategies to implement ecosystem-based management. The Chapin et al. (2010) definition of ecosystem stewardship is heavily based on resilience thinking (Norberg and Cumming 2008; Scheffer 2009), emphasizing uncertainty and change. Consistent with the more conventional definitions of stewardship, this new synthesis of ecosystem stewardship may also include attachment to place. Institutional incentives would be important to encourage responsibility for long-term conservation (Hilborn et al. 2005).

Table 11.3 is indicative of the amount of thinking and discussion that is going on among academics and practitioners. It is perhaps not surprising that many of the items address human dimensions of fisheries and other coastal resources management, as these areas have been poorly developed in the past (Ban et al. 2013). The table can be expanded to include more explicitly many of the ideas and practices covered in detail elsewhere in this volume: social learning (Armitage et al. 2007); governance based on learning approaches (Olsson et al. 2004a; Walters 2007); polycentric governance (Ostrom 2010); co-management and adaptive co-management (Armitage et al. 2007, 2009); and use of local and traditional knowledge and the multiple evidence base approach (Tengö et al. 2014).

Implementing Governance: Cutting Complexity Down to Size

The conventional (biological) tools of ecosystem-based management are no longer sufficient to deal with the three generally accepted objectives of 21st-century resource governance: ecological, economic and social sustainability. Interdisciplinary approaches are needed (Cochrane and Garcia 2009; Ommer et al. 2011). The consideration of multiple sectors and impacts of drivers creates an additional heavy burden on ecosystem-based management. As problems are complex enough already, are we perhaps making the task impossible by tackling complex adaptive systems, complete with the human dimension?

The intuitive view is that, the more complex the system being managed, the more complex the rules of management should be. However, there is evidence for a counterintuitive answer: simple rules may deal with complexity better than complex rules in some situations (Gadgil et al. 1993; Hilborn et al. 2003). One way to explore this phenomenon is through the subdiscipline of fuzzy logic and Zadeh's (1973) principle of incompatibility. The principle holds that, "as the complexity of a system increases, our ability to make precise and yet significant statements about its behavior diminishes until a threshold is reached beyond which precision and significance (or relevance) become almost mutually exclusive characteristics" (Zadeh 1973, p. 28). There is an inverse relationship between the complexity of a system and the degree of precision that can be used meaningfully to describe it.

Many researchers buried under data know this principle only too well. Walters (1986) discovered decades ago that, in quantifying food chain relationships, even in a lake with relatively few species, precision became less and less meaningful, as more and more data were collected to describe the ecosystem. With more and more variables, the entire model of the ecosystem, as Walters described it, "sagged" like a loose Meccano set.

But does one give up modeling ecosystems? Every ecosystem scientist dreams of improving on Lindeman's (1942) classic ecosystem measurements. Researchers cannot afford not to collect data on variables that they know are important. The use of few variables, no matter how well chosen, may be inadequate in capturing complexity. However, the dilemma is, more and more data collected from a complex system will run up against the principle of incompatibility, and quantitative precision will eventually cease to be meaningful.

The counterintuitive solution proposed by Zadeh's fuzzy logic is that things need not be precisely defined or quantified before they can be considered mathematically. Fuzzy logic models do not need precise data inputs. Like the human mind, fuzzy logic puts together related objects into categories in such a way as to reduce the complexity of the processing task. Fuzzy logic, used in engineering and in many applied areas, from "smart" high-speed trains to rice cookers, provides the tools to classify information into broad groupings, simulating the workings of the human mind.

Berkes and Berkes (2009) used fuzzy logic to make sense of indigenous ways of knowing. The Inuit are concerned about Arctic ecosystem contamination from organic pollutants, carried to the Arctic by atmospheric transport and concentrated there (Donaldson et al. 2010). The Inuit have developed their own ways to determine if an animal is healthy or not and make decisions, for example, about the suitability of a particular seal for human consumption (O'Neil et al. 1997). They seem to be using what we might call fuzzy logic thinking in these decisions. Observations of the fatness/thinness of the seal, its behavior in the water, the color of its bones and liver are some of the many variables that the Inuit observe on a qualitative scale to make a decision about its edibility, without need for quantitative data.

Berkes and Berkes (2009) speculated on how Inuit ways of knowing might work. Suppose that experienced hunters have been hunting seals for a long time (a large sample size) and finding that some of them have abnormalities. Over several hunting seasons (longitudinal data), hunters have noticed that some seals are thin, some have abnormal livers, and some have discolored bones. Hunters share their observations (data pooling). They already know what a healthy seal looks like. After some time, they would also begin to make some generalizations (formulate a model) of what an unhealthy seal looks like, and what to look for to make a distinction between a healthy and an unhealthy animal (formulate a hypothesis about key variables). Note that quantitative data are not necessary for such an analysis; qualitative data on perceived ranks (e.g., fat, thin, very thin seal) serve perfectly well.

The ability of the Inuit and some other indigenous groups to make observations on multiple variables and to identify key variables seems to hold for different kinds of environmental knowledge. For example, Inuit observations of climate change in the western Canadian Arctic encompass a large number of variables (Berkes and Jolly 2001), but the key variables they recognize (an increase in extreme weather events, increased unpredictability of *sila*, the day-to-day weather, and sea-ice conditions) are few in number. They have no interest whatsoever in the "average annual temperature change" on which scientific models of the early 2000s spent large budgets, nor do they have any interest in quantifying their observations or other climate data (Berkes 2012b).

Such examples suggest that building holistic pictures of the environment by considering a large number of variables qualitatively (as opposed to using a small number of variables quantitatively) might be an appropriate way to deal with complexity. Combining the two might be even better, suggesting a synergistic effect of the use of science and traditional knowledge together (Berkes and Berkes 2009). Hence, the wisdom of the multiple evidence base approach (Chapter 10).

Fuzzy logic may help understand how indigenous knowledge systems might work. A related approach is the use of expert systems. Many fishers and coastal resource users hold applied knowledge that can be described as an *expert system*:

> a branch of artificial intelligence, providing theories and methods
> for automating intelligent behavior. They are computer programs
> that use heuristic rules to store knowledge, which is used to infer
> solutions and help provide assistance in solving complex problems
> normally handled by human experts.
>
> (Mackinson 2001, p. 534)

Expert systems are based on the assumption that humans use heuristic rules to solve problems. The knowledge used for decision-making is not quantitative but qualitative and consists of fuzzy sets (Mackinson 2001).

Grant and Berkes (2007) studied the use of local knowledge among long-line fishers of Gouyave, Grenada, West Indies, and treated it as an expert system. Long-lines are used for large pelagic fish, such as yellowfin tuna (*Thunnus albacares*) and Atlantic sailfish (*Istiophorus albicans*). The decision-making system begins with the knowledge of the fishing season and the type of bait to be used, followed by the long-line weight type. Once at sea, they use "folk oceanography" (presence/absence of sea birds, seawater color, current strength and direction) to decide where to fish. Fishers experiment with the variables they can control (e.g., bait), while learning from the variables they cannot (e.g., weather, fish behavior). An expert system can be built as a decision tree in the form, IF *a certain situation occurs*, THEN *a particular outcome is likely* (similar in structure to the Greenland shark example in Chapter 10). Fishers reflect on their observations, evaluate their performance against other fisheries and (if not successful) try again with modifications (Grant and Berkes 2007).

Another example that fits with fuzzy logic kind of thinking is the data-less management of Johannes (1998b). Observing that it would be nearly impossible to collect the biological data needed for managing innumerable small stocks in the vast expanse of Oceania, Johannes proposed using a combination of local fisher knowledge and a network of MPAs. Such a management system, he argued, would not depend on conventional quantitative data but could, nevertheless, satisfy information needs for management. As by far the great majority of fisheries in the world are data-poor (e.g., Arce-Ibarra and Charles 2008), such creative solutions may have wide applicability.

A number of studies suggest that simple decision rules may in some cases be appropriate to manage complex fisheries. In the Bristol Bay, Alaska, sockeye salmon (*Onchorhynchus nerka*) fishery, two very simple rules have been used for decades: (1) a minimum number of salmon should be allowed to escape to any given watershed before fishing is allowed, and (2) within any watershed, escapement should be distributed over time in as "natural" a pattern as possible. This policy has helped maintain the biocomplexity of the fish stocks and has provided resilience to environmental change (Hilborn et al. 2003).

Several cases suggest that simple rules of thumb may work better than complex government regulations. Given its biological success (Chapter 4), the Gulf of Maine lobster fishery, with its fisher-enforced v-notch rule, backed up by size limits and other regulations, is one example (Chaper 4, Box 4.1). The rule of thumb could involve resource tenure. Orensanz et al. (2005) observed that government regulations such as closed seasons and catch quotas could never be enforced in benthic invertebrate fisheries in South America. However, territorial use rights, as in Chile (Castilla and Defeo 2001; Hilborn et al. 2005), co-ordinated at a larger spatial scale, could work. Combined with qualitative monitoring and feedback, such a system would rely on simple feedback decision rules to adjust harvesting practices from year to year.

The important lesson from fuzzy logic is that qualitative data and approximations may be appropriate in situations that seem to require an impossibly large data set. Complexity brings out the complementarity of science and local/traditional knowledge: combining quantitative scientific data on a small number of key variables with fuzzy/qualitative data on many variables, as "eyeballed" by local experts, fishers and experienced field people. This is not such a difficult approach to use, especially in a knowledge coproduction and integrative science context. A number of approaches and theories, such as resilience, are developing shortcuts into complexity by identifying key variables at different temporal and spatial scales (Gunderson and Holling 2002; Chapin et al. 2009). The Millennium Ecosystem Assessment (MA 2005a, 2005b) took a similar approach through the identification of key drivers. Those cases that seem to lend themselves to management by simple rules, such as Bristol Bay salmon and Chilean shellfish, hold the promise that creative solutions may be possible for a larger number of problems than we might think.

Conclusions

Ecosystem-based management, an increasingly dominant approach, has to come to terms with uncertainty and complexity, an interdisciplinary visioning of management objectives, and putting humans back into the ecosystem. All approaches inevitably fall short of expectations, and ecosystem-based management is no exception. Pitcher and Lam (2010, p. 6) observe that, "despite highly optimistic claims by its proponents, we know of no cases where applying [ecosystem-based management] has yielded its expected benefits." Nevertheless, by the performance criteria used by Pitcher and Lam (2010), ecosystem-based management came out as one of the two best management strategies out of the ten evaluated.

Can ecosystem-based management do even better? Lessons from the Australian and Chilean cases indicate that marine spatial planning has a great deal of potential. However, one caution is that, judging by both cases, the gestation period may be long. In the Great Barrier Reef case, the major adjustment with zoning took place some three decades after the protected area was first established, and the list of tasks has not yet been exhausted. In the Chilean benthic resources case, the governance transformation from formulating new legislation to *loco* stock recovery and a working implementation of territorial use rights took some six years. A second caution is that spatial use rights have the potential of leading to privatization of resources, benefiting the rich and powerful and dispossessing the poorer and weaker users of the coastal resources, as the human rights-based fishing argument holds (Allison et al. 2012). Hence, inclusive and participatory management with full deliberation of equity issues becomes important (Lejano and Ingram 2009b).

I argued in this chapter that conceptualizing and implementing ecosystem-based management should be thought of as revolutionary, and not evolutionary. It is revolutionary, because the scope has expanded from ecosystem-based management to social and ecological system-based management, dealing with multiple disciplines and multiple objectives (Cochrane and Garcia 2009; Ommer et al. 2011). The scope has expanded also from management to governance (Kooiman et al. 2005) that includes co-operative, multilevel approaches involving partnerships, social learning and knowledge coproduction. In addition to incorporating relatively well-known resilience, adaptive management and co-management approaches, taking ecosystem-based management to the next stage may include conceptualizing ecosystem-based management as a wicked problem that has no single solution once and for all; picking and choosing from an assortment of new governance ideas as appropriate to the case; and finding creative ways of dealing with complexity.

AN INTERDISCIPLINARY
SCIENCE FOR THE COAST

The common scientific and media narrative in fisheries is one of failure: poor governance, collapsed stocks, and vanishing livelihoods. Yet, there are successful fisheries—instances where governments and/or communities have maintained or rebuilt stocks, where fishers have robust livelihoods, and where institutions are strong.

(Cinner et al. 2013)

Looking Back and Looking Forward

Many scientists and managers who work on fishery and coastal issues are deeply pessimistic. In many cases, both fish stocks and fishing communities are in poor health, and coastal ecosystems are in decline. Yet other scientists and managers are able to point to cases of healthy stocks, communities and ecosystems (Orensanz et al. 2005; Hilborn 2006; Cinner et al. 2013). In this volume, I make the argument that the decline of coastal resources and ecosystems is not inevitable. There is an accumulated body of theory and practice that should allow us to improve on the record of the last half-century or so. However, solutions are not clear-cut, and there are no global blueprints or widely applicable recipes to follow. More likely, solutions need to be worked out case by case, collaboratively and adaptively. This chapter starts by revisiting the historical approach taken in this volume, followed by a recap of the eight subdisciplines to build an interdisciplinary science of resource management for coastal and marine environments. Finally, the chapter explores two divergent strategies that may be used to build such an interdisciplinary science.

A historical approach is always a good place to start, as history puts current problems in perspective. Looking deep into changing philosophies of human–environment interactions, three broad changes or trends stand out in shaping the background for a new interdisciplinary science of the coast. All three can be characterized as paradigm change in the sense of Thomas Kuhn (1962). The first is a paradigm change from reductionism to a systems view. It has far-reaching implications because it forces the abandonment of stock-by-stock and sector-by-sector management approaches. It also undermines all the management tools designed under the assumption of a predictable and controllable nature that can be analytically pulled apart and put back together again. We know with a fair degree of confidence that such reductionism does not work. Instead, we need to work with unpredictable and uncontrollable human and natural systems, using learning-based approaches such as adaptive management and resilience (Gunderson and Holling 2002).

The second is a paradigm change in the way we consider commons. Conceptually, we have moved from equating "commons" with a "tragedy," to developing a theory of commons that tries to explain the conditions under which commons can be governed successfully or not. Nobel laureate Elinor Ostrom's 1990 book, *Governing the Commons*, provides perhaps the clearest statement of the paradigm change. The Kuhnian paradigm change is complete among commons scholars, but perhaps not so among practitioners. The paradigm change has been slow to impact entrenched management practices for coastal resources.

The third paradigm change is in governance. There has been a sea change in the way governing is perceived—no longer a task only for government managers. Many countries are recognizing the need for participatory governance, involving public and private actors. The last two decades have seen a sharp increase in co-management and multi-stakeholder bodies, along with an increasing role for market mechanisms. Dividing lines between public and private sectors have become blurred, as indicated by the phrase public–private partnerships. This paradigm change signals a new role for government resource managers as facilitators, as well as a new role (and new responsibilities) for user-groups, businesses and civil society.

These historical developments in management philosophy regarding the adoption of a systems view, a new vision of commons and a shift to participatory governance are developed in Chapter 1 as cross-cutting themes for the volume. Continuing with the historical approach and extending the three paradigm shifts, Chapter 2 discusses the evolution of the notions of natural resources and management.

Historically, natural resources were considered "free gifts of nature," disconnected from their roles in the ecosystem and even disconnected from local economies and livelihoods. "Natural resources, exploited for markets abroad, in the first instance, were, and sometimes still are, seen as the engine for growth, leading over time to domestic economic development" (Ommer and Paterson 2014, p. 1). The natural resources in question include minerals and energy, and not just the marine and coastal living resources that we are primarily concerned with in this volume.

As manufacturing became the engine for economic growth and as developed countries moved increasingly to the service sector:

> [natural resource exploitation] went global, and thus it became increasingly possible to avoid mostly national, or at best regional, regulatory controls . . . The end result has been our inability to effectively control the pillaging of the oceans and many of the other natural resources of this planet.
>
> (Ommer and Paterson 2014, p. 1)

Does this mean coastal living resources have become irrelevant? They have become less relevant than before as the "engine" of economic growth. But they remain as important as ever as integral parts of eco-systems and biodiversity, and as ecosystem services for human well-being (MA 2005a).

The old concept of natural resources carries a sense of free goods, solely human-centric use, and commodification of nature. The definition of the term natural resource needs to be adjusted to reflect emerging views, changing priorities and historic realities. Natural resources cannot be seen merely as engines for national economic growth; they are important for local economies and livelihoods, producing ecosystem services for human well-being, while maintaining biodiversity and social–ecological system resilience. Figure 9.1, from MA (2005a), concisely captures the idea of linkages between ecosystem services and human well-being.

Similarly, the old concept of management carries implications of domination of nature, efficiency, social and ecological simplification, and expert-knows-best, command-and-control approaches. As detailed in Chapter 2, many of the assumptions behind conventional management have been abandoned or are in the process of being abandoned. Hence, the term management can be updated to emphasize stewardship in place of domination and control of nature. Economic efficiency objectives need to be balanced against ecological (e.g., biodiversity) and social (e.g., equity) objectives. Top-down, expert-knows-best management has to be replaced by participatory approaches that are adaptive and take a wider range of objectives into account (Cochrane and Garcia 2009).

In seeking an approach consistent with paradigm shifts and the emerging views of people-and-environment relationships, I propose in Chapter 3 that the unit of analysis should be integrated social–ecological systems. Social and ecological systems are closely interconnected; for example, the biophysical characteristics of an MPA are affected by the local social system, and the social system, with its governance and socioeconomic characteristics, is affected by the biophysical system. The historic disconnection of the study of social versus natural systems creates a major challenge in trying to reconnect natural science and social science perspectives.

Ancient philosophers probably did a better job of this than our best-trained natural scientists and social scientists. In particular, the perceived need for the search for universal truths and thus universal applications, what Ostrom (2007) would call panaceas, is a major impediment. Reconnecting the two perspectives can be thought of as a balancing act. As Jentoft (2006) puts it, it is a balancing act that can draw on both *episteme* of the natural sciences and *phronesis* of the social sciences and humanities. Jentoft (2006, p. 678) goes on to quote Aristotle: "*Phronesis* is not concerned with universals only; it must also take cognizance of particulars, because it is concerned with conduct, and conduct has its spheres in particular circumstances." Managing social–ecological systems is an interdisciplinary science of the particular. There are no blueprint solutions and no deterministic outcomes.

Mobilizing New Concepts and Theories

The emergence of new subdisciplinary fields concerned with human and environment interrelationships is one of the reasons that we have witnessed remarkable changes in dealing with coastal and marine resources in the last two or three decades. A full list of these fields can be very long. Pretty et al. (2009) assembled a list of some 40 fields (Table 1.2). Many, if not all, of these fields provide insights for coastal resource management and contribute to an understanding of social–ecological systems. But, of course, no single volume can deal with all of these concepts. In this volume, I focus on eight fields, or subdisciplines, to build an interdisciplinary science of resource management for coastal and marine environments: resilience, commons, co-management, coastal zone management, conservation and marine protected areas, livelihoods and development, local and traditional knowledge, and ecosystem-based management.

These eight fields, each with its own chapter, constitute the elements of a new interdisciplinary science, but there is nothing definitive about this particular set of fields. A different author might have picked a different set. For example, one could easily have picked ecological economics as one of the fields (now spread into several chapters, including Chapter 9), or political ecology (also spread into various chapters, including the aquaculture discussion in Chapter 3). Neither do I make a claim that any of these fields, as elements of the new interdisciplinary science, is new. There is a substantial literature in all of them. What is new is that the chapters of this volume are attempting to produce an original synthesis.

Social–ecological resilience is a key element of the new interdisciplinary science, as it introduces a higher-order management objective. Coastal resources need to be managed, not for commodities but for resilience, the capacity of a system to absorb disturbance and reorganize while under-going change. Resilience thinking takes change as a given, and multiple equilibria and multiple stable states as a common condition. The management task, therefore, is to stay in a desirable stable state (for example, a cod- and groundfish-dominated marine ecosystem) or to explore alternative stable states (for example, a lobster fishery-dominated Gulf of Maine social–ecological system vs. a recreation-dominated one). The resilience of a system can be strengthened so that it stays in a desirable state, or transformation from one state to another can be navigated, at least in some cases (Olsson et al. 2008; Folke et al. 2010).

Resilience thinking is useful in alerting managers and policymakers to the realities of drivers, nonlinear effects and thresholds of change from one state to another. However, thresholds cannot be predicted. Resilience cautions against trying to eliminate natural variability, because this may impair the renewal capacity of social–ecological systems and, thus, their ability to absorb shocks and stresses. It encourages management to retain and restore some types of natural and social variability and diversity. The emphasis on panarchy, or embedded systems, provides a good fit with multilevel governance. Perhaps the most basic message of resilience thinking is to use a learning-based approach, respond flexibly and keep options open, all of them common-sense management suggestions.

Another key element of the new interdisciplinary science is the field of commons, as it deals with resources in which the exclusion of potential users is difficult, and exploitation by one user reduces resource availability for others. Most coastal resources have these two characteristics. Historically, coastal communities have devised a rich diversity of common-property solutions to deal with these two characteristics of commons, including Johannes's (1981) "words of the lagoon" or the more formal rules-in-use or institutions of modern states (North 1990). Community-based solutions, government regulation and market regulation through privatization are the three property rights regimes or the three broad categories of potential solutions to the commons problem (Ostrom 2005). The key issue is to decide which of these three property rights regimes works best for a particular situation.

In some cases, multiple solutions are possible. For example, Basurto et al. (2013) showed that two nearby communities in the Gulf of California, Mexico, achieved sustainability objectives using very different techniques. One of them, Seri, developed territorial use areas; the other, Peñasco, developed a network of marine reserves. (A third one, Kino, could develop neither.) The results show that there can be different pathways to effective governance. In other cases, commons users are employing a mix of regimes. Galappaththi and Berkes (2014) found just such a mixing or layering of property rights regimes in shrimp aquaculture in Sri Lanka, a surprising finding, because aquaculture, like agriculture, tends to be private property. These shrimp farms were individually owned by small producers but managed under community-level rules, because they all used water from the same lagoon-and-canal source. The system was characterized by three layers of institution: community-level shrimp farmers' associations, zone-level associations and a national-level shrimp farming sector association.

Such relationships characterize co-management, which involves the sharing of management power and responsibility between users and governments. Even though there are local systems that operate under the radar of government management or those that use delegated powers, such as Japan's fishery co-operative associations (Makino 2011), pure community-based management is not possible in today's interconnected world. By definition, co-management involves vertical linkages between at least two levels, such as the local level and one or more government levels. The essence of co-management comprises social learning and joint problem solving through multiple linkages in the form of networks. Hence, partnerships and networks are critically important (Pinkerton et al. 2014).

Co-management often proceeds through social learning in these networks. Conventional theories in education hold that learning occurs at the level of the individual. Yet individual learning seems inadequate to account for group-centered and multilevel social learning processes that often seem to operate in co-management. As Pahl-Wostl and Hare (2004, p. 193) put it:

> Management is not a search for the optimal solution to one problem but an ongoing learning and negotiation process where a high priority is given to questions of communication, perspective sharing, and the development of adaptive group strategies for problem solving.

In the process, social learning may proceed from simple, single-loop learning to double-loop learning (learning-to-learn), which characterizes adaptive co-management (Armitage et al. 2009).

As the above quote indicates, negotiation and deliberation are important for developing working partnerships between managers and resource users, in both co-management (Chapter 6) and in other multi-stakeholder processes dealing with coastal resources (Chapter 7). Adaptive management, scenario building and learning networks are three approaches that use deliberation. Adaptive management recognizes, as a starting point, that information will always be imperfect. It brings stakeholders and managers together and aims to use a planning cycle approach in which policies can be used as experiments from which managers can learn (Holling 1978). Scenario-building exercises bring together the relevant parties to consider a limited number of future options as a way to deliberate policy options (Bennett and Zurek 2006). Learning networks, also called communities of practice, operate with the idea of learning-as-participation to create problem-solving partnerships (Olsson et al. 2004a).

The use of imperfect information necessitates close co-operation and risk sharing between management agency and local people. Such a process requires collaboration, transparency, accountability and legitimacy (Pinkerton and John 2008), so that trust can be created in the learning environment, and practice can build on experience. The approach of bringing the community actively into the management process is fundamentally different from command-and-control management. As Chapter 7 discusses, we are also increasingly seeing the opposite approach: especially with restoration projects, communities are initiating action and bringing government agencies, NGOs and universities into the management process. The Nisqually River and delta restoration project in Washington State is one example where the tribe initiated the project and partnered with a number of agencies and groups. Such partnerships occur widely throughout the world in conservation–development projects (Berkes 2007a), including the Chapter 11 example of locally designed, neo-traditional protected area networks in Fiji (Clarke and Jupiter 2010).

Conservation of biodiversity in the coastal and marine environment is attracting a great deal of international attention. On the one hand, there is an urgent need for increased conservation effort. On the other, coastal waters are fully used and increasingly contested, with relatively new uses such as aquaculture impacting existing uses such as small-scale fisheries. There are a few examples of large, well-governed MPAs, such as Australia's Great Barrier Reef Marine Park, but many and perhaps the vast majority of government MPAs throughout the world are "paper parks." The exception seems to be MPA networks created by local peoples themselves and enforced by them, using government legislation but relying largely on locally effective social sanctions. They are important, because local control helps build and maintain traditions of stewardship.

This creates a dilemma for conservation purists, whose mental model of a protected area is one administered (preferably) by the national government and free of human activity. The competing model is an MPA that may be partially closed, in space and time, and partially open for local use. Studies indicate that, in such co-managed areas (in this case, coral reefs), fish biomass is higher than that in open-access areas, but lower than that in no-take protected areas (Cinner et al. 2012). Such an outcome indicates a trade-off to achieve (imperfect) conservation and the protection of local livelihoods. Community-based conservation, "by, for, and with the local community" (Western and Wright 1994, p. 7), has the great advantage that biodiversity conservation benefits can be directly linked to livelihood benefits, thus creating incentives for stewardship. Well-to-do urban people can afford to hold stewardship values without the need for livelihood benefits (Dasmann 2002), but rural people, dependent on local coastal resources, need incentives. The tools are largely in place. ICCAs and biocultural approaches can help achieve "the coexistence of people and nature, as distinct from protectionism and the segregation of people and nature" (Western and Wright 1994, p. 8).

Livelihoods are a key consideration for the use of multifunctional coastal resources, and reconciling conservation and livelihoods is only one of a number of issues. The broader issues concern human development, poverty and the nature of coastal livelihoods. Amartya Sen, who was awarded the Nobel Memorial Prize in Economic Sciences in 1998 for his work in welfare economics, developed the notion of entitlements and the capabilities approach. In Sen's view, famines did not only occur owing to shortages, they could also occur owing to food entitlement failure, that is, a failure of means of command over food, because of a range of economic, political and social factors. The capabilities approach, a reaction to development models that focused entirely on income growth, considers the notion of freedom as both the outcome and the instrument for development. Freedom from poverty is the ultimate goal of development, but it is also the essential means by which it is achieved.

A key point regarding coastal livelihoods is the multidimensional definition of poverty, inspired by Sen and others, as encompassing "different dimensions of deprivation that relate to human capabilities including consumption and food security, health, education, rights, voice, security, dignity and decent work" (OECD 2001, p. 8). How do fishers and other coastal resource users stay out of poverty? Livelihood diversification is the answer: both within fisheries and outside fisheries. The vast majority of fishers in the world are not full-time fishers. In the developing world, as well as in many industrialized countries, fishing is often part of a complex of livelihood activities. The availability of livelihood options outside of fisheries and the ability to follow a seasonal round of fishing activities—switching gears, fishing grounds and target species—are necessary for livelihood resilience, providing options and flexibility.

Another key element of the new interdisciplinary science concerns knowledge. Traditional knowledge is time-tested, multigenerational, local knowledge. It is relevant for the issues discussed in this volume because many resource and environmental problems require mobilizing a wide range of information, considerations and values. Local and traditional knowledge is clearly an underutilized and underappreciated source of management know-how. A dialogue of science and traditional knowledge, with the overall aim of bridging the two, helps increase management capabilities. Although there are some areas of incompatibility between the two, the multiple evidence base approach emphasizes the advantages of combining different kinds of knowledge (natural science, social science, local knowledge, indigenous knowledge) to produce an enriched picture of the problem to be solved (Tengö et al. 2014).

Bridging knowledge systems is different from combining them, and it requires using the two in parallel, and with respect, each within its own rules. Bridging may be accomplished through joint research methods and processes (such as participatory rural appraisal, workshops, modeling and scenario planning). It may also be accomplished through practices and approaches that consider local and indigenous people as equal partners (participatory action research, participatory education). One effective way of bridging is to co-operate around a particular task in which local and indigenous communities may have their own specific expertise, such as environmental monitoring, conservation planning and environmental restoration. Some of the ways of bridging take advantage of the similarities between indigenous knowledge and certain areas of Western science, such as adaptive management and fuzzy logic.

Ecosystem-based management is the holistic view of managing resources in the context of their environment. According to NOAA (2005, p. 3), "An ecosystem approach to management is management that is adaptive, specified geographically, takes into account ecosystem knowledge and uncertainties, considers multiple external influences, and strives to balance diverse social objectives." It is an approach, as opposed to a widely applicable methodology, and is often constrained by the disciplinary backgrounds of the practitioners (Miller et al. 2010). Different kinds of ecosystem-based management exist, including ecosystem-based fisheries and marine spatial planning. The latter is a way to move from a single-sector focus (e.g., fisheries) to multiple sectors (e.g., aquaculture, fisheries, conservation, recreation, energy production, mining and others).

In the context of the present volume, ecosystem-based management should be thought of as revolutionary, and not evolutionary (Berkes 2012a). It is revolutionary in the sense that the scope has to be expanded from ecosystem-based management to social and ecological system-based management, dealing with multiple disciplines and multiple objectives (Cochrane and Garcia 2009). The scope has to be expanded also from single sector to multiple sectors, and from management to governance (Kooiman et al. 2005). That means the inclusion of co-operative, multi-level approaches involving partnerships, social learning and knowledge coproduction. In addition to using relatively well-known resilience, adaptive management and co-management approaches, taking ecosystem-based management to the next stage may include conceptualizing ecosystem-based management as a wicked problem that has no final solution, and finding creative ways of dealing with complexity.

Neoliberalism on the Coast: Privatization Strategies

Looking to the future, there seem to be two divergent strategies to build an interdisciplinary science for marine and coastal resources. Anthony Scott, who was writing about the commons more than a decade before Garrett Hardin (Scott 1955), observed that, a few decades ago, most papers in a conference on fisheries and coastal resources would have been about regulation. That is not the case anymore.

First, government rules began to regulate the time, gear, vessels, and size and species selection in particular ocean harvesting areas. In the century that followed, these were made less absolute and more quantitative. The past 40 years saw them being transformed into individual quotas, and the past 20 saw these quotas become tradable. Today, as McCay explains, fisher associations or "communities" are emerging and taking over much of the government's regulatory function. McCay's three key words for this progression are that the commons property ocean fishery became, in effect, "enclosed" by regulation; enclosed fisheries became "privatized" by license limitation and the distribution of individual quotas; and "communities" are now being assembled out of quota holders.

(Scott 2012, p. 252)

Scott's insightful summary, backed up by some 60 years of professional experience, captures concisely the progression in the United States (with exceptions to be sure), and to a large extent in Canada, New Zealand, Australia and the European Community. It does not capture the situation in much of the rest of the world, where species-by-species quotas cannot be determined for the lack of data, much less privatized into ITQs. However, some ITQ management may well be coming to some of the larger international fisheries, including those in the waters of developing countries (Global Partnership for Oceans 2014). "Some," because turning all of the multispecies coastal fisheries into ITQ fisheries would be nearly impossible for biological reasons (Mahon 1997), as well as for reasons of cost, administration and enforcement.

There is general agreement that government regulation, as Scott (2012) observed, has retreated to the background. Privatization is in vogue and is being pushed by some large international organizations and favored by many national governments. However, the community solution seems not so much part of a progression as Scott makes it, but rather an alternative approach to privatization. First, I briefly recap basic commons theory, looking for a fit between the common-pool resource and the property rights regime, and then I discuss some of the arguments for and against the privatization alternative.

Government regulation is one of the three property rights regimes for the commons. It can work with judicious top-down management (or, better still, with co-management). Once the unquestioned solution, pure government regulation has fallen out of favor, because it has a poor track record, not only with coastal resources, but with many different kinds of natural resource. As well, costs of management have skyrocketed at a time when many governments are trying to cut back on costs and services. The rapid retreat of the state in the last two decades or so has created problems. The withdrawal of certain essential services, such as basic research on marine and coastal resources, has left a governance gap, where civil society and the private sector are often unable to provide those functions. The Port Mouton Bay case in Chapter 7, where the community ended up carrying out its own research project to document the deleterious impacts of salmon aquaculture on the local lobster fishery, is an example of the failure of government responsibility.

The second property rights regime, privatization, works best when a commons can be controlled by a private individual or corporate owner. There are many ways to privatize a commons, often referred to as enclosing the commons. Aquaculture rights given to a company can turn a bay or a lagoon into de facto private property. Transferable fish quotas that can be bought or sold can create a market in exclusive rights to capture fish. These quotas seem to work best with offshore, single-stock fisheries. They can create user-group conflicts where they involve resources and areas already being used by groups who hold long-standing rights. Although there is a trend to zone coastal uses (Norse and Crowder 2005), there are limits to privatizing coastal resources, simply because uses and users interact more, and are more interdependent, than those on land.

Community-based solutions, the third property rights regime, work best when a case meets collective action criteria, that is, when Ostrom's (1990) principles are met. In most cases, these are commons management problems, in which the resource is locally important, and the user community is able to exclude outsiders and make and enforce collective action rules for the insiders. In such situations, community-based solutions are cost-effective; they do not require expensive technical solutions from the government. There is another reason in favor of community-based solutions: as Jentoft (2007, p. 265) puts it, "the state has no fingers, only thumbs."

The two divergent alternatives seem to be the privatization emphasis or the community-based emphasis, keeping in mind that we should not be seeking panaceas (Ostrom 2007) and that some resources may be more suitable for management under one property rights regime than the other. The issue is not about fisheries only, but covers the whole suite of coastal resources, including aquaculture, protected areas, recreation, energy production and others. The following puts privatization under the spotlight because community-based management has already been covered in several chapters of this volume, but privatization has not.

The theory and logic of privatization programs are well known. Privatization measures such as the ITQs are thought to cause a reduction in overcapitalization and regulated inefficiencies, and they often do. Privatization brings into the picture Adam Smith's "invisible hand," letting market processes help adjust investments to resources. Efficient quota holders buy out inefficient ones, preventing the dissipation of the resource rent. Reduction in investments and the harvesting effort brings back profitability. Privatization also helps conservation, the theory goes, because both the costs and benefits go to the same owner. That is, the owner has incentives to stay within sustainability limits and not create externalities by overharvesting. As both costs and benefits accrue to the same entity, externalities are internalized (Grafton et al. 2008; Charles 2009; Sumaila 2010).

Some of the major critiques of resource privatization measures such as the ITQs are social, rather than economic. ITQs help economic rationalization and result in the concentration of fishing quotas in fewer and fewer hands. Thus, the dissipation of the resource rent is prevented by the invisible hand of the market. This results in an initial consolidation and downsizing, with fewer owners and fewer crew members. For example, in the economic rationalization of the US mid-Atlantic surf clam fishery, it made no economic sense to assign quotas to the original 120 vessels, because each of them would end up with too small a quota to produce an economic return to the owner. Despite much opposition from the smaller fishers, the regional fishery management council decided, in 1988, to allow the fishery to be managed by ITQs, rather than by boat quotas. The new system began in 1990 and resulted in the rapid decline of the number of boats (down to 35 vessels), as quotas were consolidated by some operators buying out others (McCay 2012).

A full critique of the ITQ or other resource privatization schemes is beyond the scope of this volume. Suffice to say, there is a downside to these schemes. ITQs can have negative effects on employment, independent small-scale owners, fishing practices, households and communities (Olson 2011). Socially inequitable outcomes may include redistribution of access to fishing and fish-processing opportunities, favoring some enterprises and communities and disadvantaging others (McCay 2012). Socio-economic impacts include the windfall profits (by initial allocation) to the first generation of ITQ holders, and the subsequent difficulty for new generations of fishers to pay for access to fishing rights (Copes 1986). In many fishing communities, the youth cannot enter the fishery as owner–operators because they cannot afford it, and can only look forward to a life as crew on boats owned by large fishers and companies.

One of the interesting controversies over privatization concerns conservation. Does privatization lead to self-interested conservation? In a classic paper in 1973, the bioeconomist Colin Clark said, yes, in some cases. However, when the growth or replenishment rate of the renewable resource, in percent per year terms, was lower than the prevailing bank interest rate, then it was economically rational to exploit the resource to extinction, and then take out the present value and move on to some other resource and re-invest it. Clark (1973) showed mathematically that a resource such as the blue whale, with very slow replenishment rates, would never be used sustainably under privatized harvesting rights.

For many ecologists and environmentalists, the analysis showed that privatization could never be the ultimate solution. However, for those economists who were arguing that the problem of the commons was defined by the lack of private property, Clark's (1973) analysis was damaging for the cause. There were attempts to marginalize it by arguing that it was merely a theoretical possibility. In response, Clark and colleagues extended the 1973 analysis to show that the original results "cannot be safely dismissed as being no more than a theoretical possibility. There [are] a nontrivial number of resources that cannot be safely entrusted to complete private control and management. There are indeed limits to private resource ownership" (Clark et al. 2010, p. 216). The authors went on to give examples of ITQ systems that worked well, but pointed out that the ultimate management powers must rest with the public sector.

As with most management measures, one can probably say that ITQs work in some cases but not in others. However, even where the effect of ITQs on the sustainability of the target fish stock is positive, its effect on the ecosystem as a whole and the bycatch of non-target species is unknown (Branch 2009). In other cases, such as in roving bandit fisheries (Chapter 5), the question of ITQ management is irrelevant, because these fisheries may go through their boom-and-bust cycles before a quota is even calculated (Berkes et al. 2006). However, there is another aspect of ITQ fisheries that is worrisome in a different way. For some, privatization of fisheries and other coastal and marine resources has become a matter of ideology, rather than effective management. Pinkerton (2013, p. 5) has documented, "how an alternative fishermen-designed and operated system of spreading fishing effort to avoid the race for fish—called the lay-up system—worked effectively and equitably for four decades in the British Columbia halibut fishery," before it was allowed to collapse and was replaced by an ITQ system. Pinkerton (2013) finds evidence of the role played by conflicting ideologies in the replacement of a working system by ITQ management.

More broadly, the halibut case and arguments over ITQs are part of a larger debate over neoliberal and pro-business versus grassroots and communitarian approaches. The trend toward ITQ management is consistent with the neoliberal agenda to favor private enterprise solutions, with an emphasis on privatization, marketization and globalization. Mansfield (2004, p. 313) writes that neoliberalism is becoming a dominant mode of ocean governance in which proponents "take property as their central problematic and contribute to the idea that creating market incentives, by specifying property rights, is the foundation upon which proper use of ocean resources rests." Three examples help illustrate the issues: the first is over rent dissipation, the second over "rights-based" approaches, and the third over eco-certification.

The "wealth-based approach" in World Bank documents seems to be referring to the prevention of wealth dissipation in fisheries (Global Partnership for Oceans 2014). Privatization of fishing rights can help maximize the resource rent. But, Ben-Yami (2014), an experienced researcher in developing country fisheries, asks who would benefit from this? He quotes the economist Daniel Bromley as saying, "avoiding 'rent dissipation' is nothing but the creation of excess profits for the fortunate firms not evicted under rationalization schemes." Creating more resource rent will benefit some firms, Ben-Yami (2014) notes, but what about the value of fishing for sustaining livelihoods and food security? He then quotes another economist, Christophe Béné, as saying that generating no economic rent does not necessarily mean that these fisheries are worth nothing: "the wealth-based approach singularly misrepresents the real contribution that small-scale fisheries [make] for the livelihood and food security of millions in Africa" (p. 39). Ben-Yami (2014) suggests the principle that all fish that can be caught by artisanal fishers should be caught only by artisanal fishers; only such resources not accessible to artisanal fishers should be allocated to large-scale, industrial fisheries.

The World Bank-initiated Global Partnership for Oceans (2014) has also been advocating for "rights-based fishing" reforms to provide incentives for good management. The World Forum for Fisher Peoples (WFFP) and the World Forum of Fish Harvesters and Fish Workers (WFF) have interpreted this as a policy position to privatize ocean and coastal resources. To expand on a point raised in Chapter 11, these two groups have countered the call for rights-based fishing with a call for human rights-based fishing (WFFP–WFF 2013). For the non-industrial fishers represented by these two groups, the notion of rights concerns not merely fishing rights but basic entitlements: food security, decent work, freedom from oppression and the right to a dignified livelihood (Allison et al. 2012). Hence, fishing rights grade into human rights, as articulated in the statement from a workshop in Zanzibar:

> Fishing rights should not be treated as a tradable commodity and they should be seen as an integral part of human rights. A rights-based approach to fisheries should not lead to the privatization of fisheries resources . . . For the effectiveness of a rights-based fisheries approach we recognize the indivisibility of: (i) fishery access and user rights, (ii) post-harvest rights and (iii) human rights.
>
> (Kumar 2008, p. 14/15)

Eco-certification is another area in which the interests of small producers seem to be diverging from those of large companies. Environmental certification and eco-labeling are an effective way to provide consumers with awareness of the products they buy. In theory, the premium price paid by the consumers rewards sustainability and fair prices to producers. The system has worked well for small-scale agricultural producers (e.g., shade grown fair-trade coffee). Does it work for coastal resource producers? The Marine Stewardship Council (MSC) is the global leader in sustainability certification for wild caught seafood. MSC's data requirements and whole stock definition of sustainability make it very difficult for small producers to get certification. Nevertheless, Foley and McCay (2014) found that a group of nine co-operatives on the Pacific coast of Baja California, Mexico, and the Fogo Island Co-operative Society in Newfoundland, Canada, were able to get MSC certification. However, certification institutions seem to privatize resources in largely unexamined ways, through the injection of new forms of exclusive rights or privileges. This creates conditions for exclusion, confusion and conflict, but potentially also for inclusion, co-operation and collective action. Unlike fair-trade programs, MSC certification does not reward social sustainability or contain mechanisms to guarantee tangible material benefits to producers. Overall, implications of certification for community-based fisheries are problematic (Foley and McCay 2014).

Divergent Strategies for the Way Ahead

The above discussion indicates two divergent alternatives for the way ahead: the neoliberal strategy and the community-based management strategy. The neoliberal option is a kind of managerial approach to coastal resources management, except that the manager is no longer the government but rather large corporations. Those resources that can be privatized are privatized, a problematic situation where sectors can conflict (e.g., capture fisheries vs. aquaculture), and one kind of resource use can create externalities for the other, without a strong government presence to regulate uses and implement societal objectives. With a weak public sector to look after societal objectives, economic efficiency could become the resource allocation criterion, and societal objectives could be assumed to coincide with corporate objectives. Valorization of economic efficiency and the commodification of nature would reverse historic trends (Chapter 2). In such a world, any measure that impedes trade globalization would be blocked (Deutsch et al. 2011), and governance would be global and top-down, with large-scale, control-oriented approaches to problem solving.

The community-based management option includes some sharply different ways of doing things. This option could entail grassroots networks, alliances and partnerships in dealing with conservation–development issues and solving commons problems by adaptive co-management. Social learning would include democratic deliberation, and collective action would be used for solutions in the Ostrom (1990) sense. Polycentric, multilevel, adaptive approaches would foster local institutions, experience and knowledge, in a range of areas from MPA management to the siting of aquaculture and wind farms. Plurality of participation and deliberative approaches would be used to establish, and periodically revise, societal goals. Local stewardship and sense of place would be valued, both for conservation and for sustainable resource use. This may result in giving priority to artisanal fisheries, which are place-based, socially important and which contribute to local food security; the more distant resources may be allocated to large-scale, industrial fisheries, so they can exercise their corporate creativity (Ben-Yami 2014).

As wildly divergent as these two options might seem, both are proceeding in the contemporary world. On the one hand, many large, single-stock fisheries in industrialized countries now use the ITQ approach. The state is retreating, and many resources and services are privatized. On the other hand, the community-based management option is alive and vibrant.

For example, co-management arrangements have proliferated throughout the world (Evans et al. 2011; Gutiérrez et al. 2011). Locally administered MPA networks that balance conservation with livelihoods show great promise for biodiversity conservation (Chapter 8). Communities and local associations are beginning to develop their own visions (Charles et al. 2010) and tools (Graham et al. 2006). They are also carrying out their own research with partners of their own choice (Chapters 6 and 7). University researchers work closely with resource users in many parts of the world (Sowman 2009; Loucks et al. 2011; Trimble and Berkes 2013), and people-centered perspectives are moving to the mainstream of resource management (McConney and Charles 2009). Citizen science has become empowering, and community and indigenous groups have had notable successes, especially in the area of ecological restoration, in partnership with government agencies and private groups (Chapter 7). Using market-based tools, innovative grassroots action connects consumers to producers and to information about the source of seafood. Movements such as Slow Fish, borne out of the Slow Food movement and active in over 20 countries, favor good, clean and fair fisheries (Beaton 2014).

It seems neither option is likely to wither away anytime soon. The above characterization of the two options is deliberately black and white, a method used in the scenario planning exercise of the Millennium Ecosystem Assessment (MA 2005a) as a means of triggering debate and deliberation regarding the kind of future that people would like to see. Nevertheless, the two options do remain in sharp contrast in terms of priorities, directions and tools. Perhaps some creative trade-offs and syntheses can eventually come out of the dialectic or the dynamic tension between the two options.

REFERENCES

Acheson, J.M. 2003. *Capturing the Commons: Devising Institutions to Manage the Maine Lobster Industry.* University Press of New England, Lebanon, NH.

Adger, W.N., T.P. Hughes, C. Folke, S.R. Carpenter and J. Rockström 2005. Social–ecological resilience to coastal disasters. *Science* 309: 1036–1039.

Agrawal, A. 2002. Common resources and institutional sustainability. In: *The Drama of the Commons* (E. Ostrom, T. Dietz, N. Dolsak, P.C. Stern, S. Stonich and E.U. Weber, eds.). National Academy Press, Washington, DC, pp. 41–85.

Agrawal, A. 2005. *Environmentality. Technologies of Government and the Making of Subjects.* Duke University Press, Durham, NC, and London.

Agrawal, A. and C.C. Gibson 1999. Enchantment and disenchantment: The role of community in natural resource conservation. *World Development* 27: 629–649.

Ahl, V. and T.F.H. Allen 1996. *Hierarchy Theory, a Vision, Vocabulary and Epistemology.* Columbia University Press, New York.

Alegret, J.L. 1996. Ancient institutions confronting change: the Catalan fishermen's Cofradías. In: *Fisheries Management in Crisis* (K. Crean and D. Symes, eds.). Fishing New Books, Oxford, UK.

Allison, E.H., and F. Ellis 2001. The livelihoods approach and management of small-scale fisheries. *Marine Policy* 25: 377–388.

Allison, E.H. and B. Horemans 2006. Putting the principles of sustainable livelihoods approach into fisheries development policy and practice. *Marine Policy* 30: 757–766.

Allison, E.H., B.D. Ratner, B. Asgard et al. 2012. Rights-based fisheries governance: from fishing rights to human rights. *Fish and Fisheries* 13: 14–29.

Allison, E.H. and J.A. Seeley 2004. HIV and AIDS among fisherfolk: a threat to "responsible fisheries"? *Fish and Fisheries* 5: 215–234.

Almudi, T. and F. Berkes 2010. Barriers to empowerment: fighting eviction for conservation in a southern Brazilian protected area. *Local Environment* 15: 217–232.

Ames, E.P. 2004. Atlantic cod stock structure in the Gulf of Maine. *Fisheries* 29(1): 10–28.

Ames, E., S. Watson and J. Wilson 2000. Rethinking overfishing: insights from oral histories of retired groundfishermen. In *Finding Our Sea Legs* (B. Neis and L. Felt, eds.). Institute of Social and Economic Research. St. John's, Newfoundland, Canada, pp. 153–164.

Ames, T. 2007. Putting fishers' knowledge to work. In: *Fishers' Knowledge in Fisheries Science and Management* (N. Haggan, B. Neis and I.G. Baird, eds.). UNESCO, Paris, pp. 353–363.

Amundsen, H. 2012. Illusions of resilience? An analysis of community responses to change in northern Norway. *Ecology and Society* 17(4): 46. http://dx.doi.org/10.5751/ES-05142-170446

Anderson, P.W. 1972. More is different. *Science* 177: 393–396.

Anderson, R.B., L.P. Dana and T.E. Dana 2006. Indigenous land rights, entrepreneurship, and economic development in Canada: "opting-in" to the global economy. *Journal of World Business* 41: 45–55.

Anderson, S.C., J.M. Flemming, R. Watson and H.K. Lotze 2011. Serial exploitation of global sea cucumber fisheries. *Fish and Fisheries* 12: 317–339.

Andrew, N.L., Y. Agatsuma, E. Ballesteros et al. 2002. Status and management of world sea urchin fisheries. *Oceanography and Marine Biology Annual Review* 40: 343–425.

Andrew, N.L., C. Béné, S.J. Hall et al. 2007. Diagnosis and management of small-scale fisheries in developing countries. *Fish and Fisheries* 8: 227–240.

Anon. 2014. Books in brief. *Nature* 507: 305.

Arce-Ibarra, A.M. and A. Charles 2008. Inland fisheries of the Mayan Zone in Quintana Roo, Mexico: using a combined approach to fishery assessment for data-sparse fisheries. *Fisheries Research* 91: 151–159.

Armitage, D. 2008. Governance and the commons in a multi-level world. *International Journal of the Commons* 2(1): 7–32.

Armitage, D., F. Berkes, A. Dale, E. Kocho-Schellenberg and E. Patton 2011. Co-management and the co-production of knowledge: learning to adapt in Canada's Arctic. *Global Environmental Change* 21: 995–1004.

Armitage, D., F. Berkes and N. Doubleday, editors 2007. *Adaptive Co-Management: Collaboration, Learning, and Multi-Level Governance*. University of British Columbia Press, Vancouver, Canada.

Armitage, D., M. Marschke and R. Plummer 2008. Adaptive co-management and the paradox of learning. *Global Environmental Change* 18: 86–98.

Armitage, D. and R. Plummer, editors 2010. *Adaptive Capacity and Environmental Governance*. Springer, Heidelberg, Germany.

Armitage, D., R. Plummer, F. Berkes et al. 2009. Adaptive co-management for social–ecological complexity. *Frontiers in Ecology and the Environment* 7: 95–102.

Arctic Council 2013. Arctic Resilience Interim Report 2013. Stockholm Environment Institute and Stockholm Resilience Centre, Stockholm.

Aswani, S. and R. J. Hamilton 2004. Integrating indigenous ecological knowledge and customary sea tenure with marine and social science for conservation of bumphead parrotfish (*Bolbometopon muricatum*) in the Roviana Lagoon, Solomon Islands. *Environmental Conservation* 31: 69–82.

Ayles, B.G., R. Bell and A. Hoyt 2007. Adaptive fisheries co-management in the western Canadian Arctic. In: *Adaptive Co-management* (D. Armitage, F. Berkes,

N. Doubleday, eds.). University of British Columbia Press, Vancouver, Canada, pp. 125–150.

Baines, G.B.K. 1989. Traditional resource management in the Melanesian South Pacific: a development dilemma. In: *Common Property Resources* (F. Berkes, ed.). Belhaven, London, pp. 273–295.

Baird, I.G. 2006. Strength in diversity: fish sanctuaries and deep-water pools in Lao PDR. *Fisheries Management and Ecology* 13: 1–8.

Baird, I.G. and M.S. Flaherty 2005. Mekong River fish conservation zones in southern Laos: assessing effectiveness using local ecological knowledge. *Environmental Management* 36: 439–454.

Ban, N.C., M. Mills, J. Tam et al. 2013. A social–ecological approach to conservation planning: embedding social considerations. *Frontiers in Ecology and the Environment* 11: 194–202.

Basurto, X., S. Gelcich and E. Ostrom 2013. The social–ecological system framework as a knowledge classificatory system for benthic small-scale fisheries. *Global Environmental Change* 23: 1366–1380.

Bateson, G. 1979. *Mind and Nature: A Necessary Unity.* Dutton, New York.

Bavinck, M. 2001. *Marine Resource Management. Conflict and Regulations in the Fisheries of the Coromandel Coast.* Sage, New Delhi.

Bavinck, M., R. Chuenpagdee, S. Jentoft and J. Kooiman, editors 2013. *Governability of Fisheries and Aquaculture: Theory and Applications.* Springer, Dordrecht, Netherlands.

Bavington, D. 2002. Managerial ecology and its discontents: exploring the complexities of control, careful use and coping in resource and environmental management. *Environments* 30(3): 3–21.

Bawa, K.S., R. Seidler and P.H. Raven 2004. Reconciling conservation paradigms. *Conservation Biology* 18: 859–860.

Beaton, S. 2014. Making fishing fair. *Samudra Report* No. 67: 16–18.

Bebbington, A. 1999. Capitals and capabilities: a framework for analyzing peasant viability, rural livelihoods and poverty. *World Development* 27: 2021–2044.

Beem, B. 2007. Co-management from the top? The roles of policy entrepreneurs and distributive conflict in development co-management arrangements. *Marine Policy* 31: 540–549.

Begossi, A. 1995. Fishing spots and sea tenure: incipient forms of local management in Atlantic Forest coastal communities. *Human Ecology* 23: 387–406.

Begossi, A. 2010. Small-scale fisheries in Latin America: management models and challenges. *MAST Maritime Studies* 9: 7–31.

Begossi, A. 2014. Ecological, cultural, and economic approaches to managing fisheries. *Environment, Development and Sustainability* 16: 5–34.

Begossi, A., P.H. May, P.F. Lopes, L.E.C. Oliveira et al. 2011. Compensation of environmental services from artisanal fisheries in SE Brazil: policy and technical strategies. *Ecological Economics* 71: 25–32.

Begossi, A., S. Salivonchyk, V. Nora, P.F. Lopes and R.A.M. Silvano 2012. The Paraty artisanal fishery (southeastern Brazilian coast): ethnoecology and management of a social–ecological system (SES). *Journal of Ethnobiology and Ethnomedicine* 8: 22.

Béné, C. 2003. When fishery rhymes with poverty: a first step beyond the old paradigm of poverty in small-scale fisheries. *World Development* 31: 949–975.

Béné, C. and R.M. Friend 2011. Poverty in small-scale fisheries: old issue, new analysis. *Progress in Development Studies* 11: 119–144.

Béné, C., G. Macfadyen and E.H. Alison 2007. Increasing the contribution of small-scale fisheries to poverty alleviation and food security. FAO Fisheries Technical Paper 481.

Béné, C. and A. E. Neiland 2004. Empowerment reform, yes ... but empowerment of whom? Fisheries decentralization reforms in developing countries: a critical assessment with specific reference to poverty reduction. *Aquatic Resources, Culture and Development* 1: 35–49.

Béné, C. and A. E. Neiland 2006. From participation to governance. WorldFish Center, Penang, and CGIAR Challenge Program on Water and Food, Colombo.

Béné, C, A. Newsham, M. Davies, M. Ulrichs and R. Godfrey-Wood 2014. Resilience, poverty and development. *Journal of International Development* DOI: 10.1002/jid.2992

Bennett, E. and M. Zurek 2006. Integrating epistemologies through scenarios. In: *Bridging Scales and Knowledge Systems* (W.V. Reid, F. Berkes, T. Wilbanks, and D. Capistrano, eds.). Island Press, Washington, DC, pp. 275–294.

Ben-Yami, M. 2014. Banking on wealth? *Samudra Report* No. 67: 36–39.

Berkes, F. 1985. The common property resource problem and the creation of limited property rights. *Human Ecology* 13: 187–208.

Berkes, F. 1986. Local-level management and the commons problem: a comparative study of Turkish coastal fisheries. *Marine Policy* 10: 215–229.

Berkes, F., editor 1989. *Common Property Resources: Ecology and Community-Based Sustainable Development*. Belhaven Press, London.

Berkes, F. 2002. Cross-scale institutional linkages: perspectives from the bottom up. In: *The Drama of the Commons* (E. Ostrom, T. Dietz, N. Dolsak, P.C. Stern, S. Stonich and E.U. Weber, eds.). National Academy Press, Washington, DC, pp. 293–321.

Berkes, F. 2004. Rethinking community-based conservation. *Conservation Biology* 18: 621–630.

Berkes, F. 2007a. Community-based conservation in a globalized world. *Proceedings of the National Academy of Sciences* 104: 15188–15193.

Berkes, F. 2007b. Understanding uncertainty and reducing vulnerability: lessons from resilience thinking. *Natural Hazards* 41: 283–295.

Berkes, F. 2009a. Social aspects of fisheries management. In: *A Fishery Manager's Guidebook*. 2nd edition (K.L. Cochrane and S.M. Garcia, eds.) FAO/Wiley-Blackwell, Chichester, UK, pp. 52–74.

Berkes, F. 2009b. Evolution of co-management: role of knowledge generation, bridging organizations and social learning. *Journal of Environmental Management* 90: 1692–1702.

Berkes, F. 2010a. Devolution and natural resources governance: trends and future. *Environmental Conservation* 37: 489–500.

Berkes, F. 2010b. Linkages and multi-level systems for matching governance and ecology: lessons from roving bandits. *Bulletin of Marine Science* 86: 235–250.

Berkes, F. 2010c. Shifting perspectives on resource management: resilience and the reconceptualization of "natural resources" and "management." *MAST Maritime Studies* 9: 11–38.

Berkes, F. 2011. Restoring unity: the concept of social–ecological systems. In: *World Fisheries: A Social–Ecological Analysis* (R.E. Ommer, R.I. Perry, K. Cochrane and P. Cury, eds.). Wiley-Blackwell, Oxford, UK, pp. 9–28.

Berkes, F. 2012a. Implementing ecosystem-based management: Evolution or revolution? *Fish and Fisheries* 13: 465–476.

Berkes, F. 2012b. *Sacred Ecology*. 3rd edition. Routledge, New York.

Berkes, F. 2013. Poverty reduction isn't just about money: community perceptions of conservation benefits. In: *Biodiversity Conservation and Poverty Alleviation* (D. Roe, J. Elliott, C. Sandbrook and M. Walpole, eds.). Wiley, London, pp. 270–285.

Berkes, F., D. Armitage and N. Doubleday 2007. Synthesis: adapting, innovating, evolving. In: *Adaptive Co-Management* (D. Armitage, F. Berkes and N. Doubleday, eds.). University of British Columbia Press, Vancouver, Canada, pp. 308–327.

Berkes, F. and M.K. Berkes 2009. Ecological complexity, fuzzy logic and holism in indigenous knowledge. *Futures* 41: 6–12.

Berkes, F., J. Colding and C. Folke 2000. Rediscovery of traditional ecological knowledge as adaptive management. *Ecological Applications* 10: 1251–1262.

Berkes, F., J. Colding and C. Folke, editors 2003. *Navigating Social–Ecological Systems: Building Resilience for Complexity and Change.* Cambridge University Press, Cambridge, UK.

Berkes, F. and I.J. Davidson-Hunt 2007. Communities and social enterprises in the age of globalization. *Journal of Enterprising Communities* 1: 209–221.

Berkes, F., N.C. Doubleday and G.S. Cumming 2012. Aldo Leopold's land health from a resilience point of view: self-renewal capacity of social–ecological systems. *EcoHealth* 9: 278–287.

Berkes, F. and H. Fast 2005. Introduction. In: *Breaking Ice: Renewable Resource and Ocean Management in the Canadian North* (F. Berkes, R. Huebert, H. Fast, M. Manseau and A. Diduck, eds.). University of Calgary Press, Calgary, Canada, pp. 1–19.

Berkes, F. and C. Folke, editors 1998. *Linking Social and Ecological Systems. Management Practices and Social Mechanisms for Building Resilience.* Cambridge University Press, Cambridge, UK.

Berkes, F. and C. Folke 2002. Back to the future: ecosystem dynamics and local knowledge. In: *Panarchy* (L.H. Gunderson and C.S. Holling, eds.). Island Press, Washington, DC, pp. 121–146.

Berkes, F., T.P. Hughes, R.S. Steneck et al. 2006. Globalization, roving bandits and marine resources. *Science* 311: 1557–1558.

Berkes, F. and D. Jolly 2001. Adapting to climate change: social–ecological resilience in a Canadian western Arctic community. *Conservation Ecology* 5 (2): 18. www.consecol.org/vol5/iss2/art18/ (accessed June 2014).

Berkes, F., M. Kislalioglu, C. Folke and M. Gadgil 1998. Exploring the basic ecological unit: ecosystem-like concepts in traditional societies. *Ecosystems* 1: 409–415.

Berkes, F., R. Mahon, P. McConney, R.C. Pollnac and R.S. Pomeroy 2001. *Managing Small-Scale Fisheries: Alternative Directions and Methods.* International Development Research Centre, Ottawa.

Berkes, F. and H. Ross 2013. Community resilience: toward an integrated approach. *Society and Natural Resources* 26: 5–20.

Bhatta, R. and M. Bhat 1998. Impacts of aquaculture on the management of estuaries in India. *Environmental Conservation* 25: 109–121.

Biggs, D., N. Abel, A.T. Knight, A. Leitch, A. Langston and N. Ban 2011. The implementation crisis in conservation planning: could "mental models" help? *Conservation Letters* 4: 169–183.

BNP 2009. Big number program. Intermediate Report. Food and Agriculture Organization of the United Nations and WorldFish Center, Rome and Penang, Malaysia.

Bocking, S. 2004. *Nature's Experts. Science, Politics and the Environment*. Rutgers University Press, New Brunswick, NJ.

Bonny, E. and F. Berkes 2008. Communicating traditional environmental knowledge: addressing the diversity of knowledge, audiences and media types. *Polar Record* 44: 243–253.

Borrini-Feyerabend, G., N. Dudley, T. Jaeger, B. Lassen, N. Pathak Broome, A. Phillips and T. Sandwith 2013. Governance of protected areas: from understanding to action. Best Practice Protected Area Guidelines Series No. 20, IUCN, Gland, Switzerland.

Borrini-Feyerabend, G., M. Pimbert, M.T. Farvar, A. Kothari and Y. Renard 2004. *Sharing Power. Learning-by-doing in Co-management of Natural Resources throughout the World*. Cenesta, in cooperation with IIED and IUCN, Tehran.

Branch, T.A. 2009. How do individual transferable quotas affect marine ecosystems? *Fish and Fisheries* 10: 39–56.

Brechin S.R., P.R. Wilshusen, C.L. Fortwangler et al. 2002. Beyond the square wheel: toward a more comprehensive understanding of biodiversity conservation as social and political process. *Society and Natural Resources* 15: 41–64.

Brinkerhoff, J.M. 2002. Government–nonprofit partnership: a defining framework. *Public Administration and Development* 22: 19–30.

Bromley, D.W., editor 1992. *Making the Commons Work. Theory, Practice and Policy*. Institute for Contemporary Studies Press, San Francisco, CA.

Brondizio, E.S., E. Ostrom and O.R. Young 2009. Connectivity and the governance of multilevel social–ecological systems: the role of social capital. *Annual Review of Environment and Resources* 34: 253–278.

Brown, K. 2002. Innovations for conservation and development. *The Geographical Journal* 168: 6–17.

Brown, K., J. Mackensen, S. Rosendo et al. 2005. *Ecosystems and Human Well-being: Policy Responses*. Vol. 3, Chapter 15, Integrated responses. Millennium Ecosystem Assessment and Island Press, Washington, DC, pp. 425–465.

Brown, K., E.L. Tompkins and W.N. Adger 2002. *Making Waves. Integrating Coastal Conservation and Development*. Earthscan, London.

Brown, K. and E. Westaway 2011. Agency, capacity, and resilience to environmental change: lessons from human development, well-being, and disasters. *Annual Review of Environment and Resources* 36: 321–342.

Brugere, C. 2006. Can integrated coastal management solve agriculture–fisheries–aquaculture conflicts at the land–water interface? In: *Environment and Livelihoods in Tropical Coastal Zones* (C.T. Hoanh, T.P. Tuong, J.W. Gowing and B. Hardy, eds.). CAB International, Wallingford, UK, pp. 258–273.

Brunner, R., T. Steelman, L. Coe-Juell, C. Cromley, C. Edwards, and D. Tucker 2005. *Adaptive Governance: Integrating Science, Policy and Decision Making*. Columbia University Press, New York.

Cajete, G. 2000. *Native Science: Natural Laws of Interdependence*. Clear Light Publishers, Santa Fe, NM.

Callicott, J.B. 2003. The implication of the "shifting paradigm" in ecology for paradigm shifts in the philosophy of conservation. In: *Reconstructing Conservation* (B.A. Minteer and R.E. Manning, eds.). Island Press, Washington, DC, pp. 239–261.

Campbell, L.M., J.J. Silver, N.J. Gray et al. 2008. Co-management of sea turtle fisheries: biogeography versus geopolitics. *Marine Policy* 33: 137–145.

Capistrano, D. and C.J.P. Colfer 2005. Decentralization: issues, lessons and reflections. In: *The Politics of Decentralization. Forests, People and Power* (C.J.P. Colfer and D. Capistrano, eds.). Earthscan, London, pp. 296–313.

Capistrano, D., K. Samper, M.J. Lee, and C. Raudsepp-Hearne, editors 2005. *Ecosystems and Human Well-being: Multiscale Assessments*. Vol. 4. Millennium Ecosystem Assessment and Island Press, Washington, DC.

Carlsson, L. 2000. Policy networks as collective action. *Policy Studies Journal* 28: 502–520.

Carlsson, L. and F. Berkes 2005. Co-management: concepts and methodological implications. *Journal of Environmental Management* 75: 65–76.

Carpenter, S.R. 2002. Ecological futures: building an ecology of the long now. *Ecology* 83: 2069–2083.

Carpenter, S., W. Brock and P. Hanson 1999. Ecological and social dynamics in simple models of ecosystem management. *Conservation Ecology* 3(2): 4. www.consecol.org/vol3/iss2/art4/ (accessed June 2014).

Carpenter, S.R., Mooney, H.A., Agard, J. et al. 2009. Science for managing ecosystem services: beyond the Millennium Ecosystem Assessment. *Proceedings of the National Academy of Sciences* 106: 1305–1312.

Carpenter, S.R., B.H. Walker, J.M. Anderies and N. Abel 2001. From metaphor to measurement: resilience of what to what? *Ecosystems* 4: 765–781.

Carpenter S.R., F. Westley and M.G. Turner 2005. Surrogates for resilience of social–ecological systems. *Ecosystems* 8: 941–944.

Cash, D.W., W.N. Adger, F. Berkes et al. 2006. Scale and cross-scale dynamics: governance and information in a multilevel world. *Ecology and Society* 11(2): 8. www.ecologyandsociety.org/vol11/iss2/art8/

Cash, D.W. and S.C. Moser 2000. Linking global and local scales: designing dynamic assessment and management processes. *Global Environmental Change* 10: 109–120.

Castello, L., J.P. Viana, G. Watkins et al. 2009. Lessons from integrating fishers of Arapaima in small-scale fisheries management at the Mamirauá Reserve, Amazon. *Environmental Management* 43: 197–209.

Castilla, J.C. 2010. Fisheries in Chile: small pelagics, management, rights and sea zoning. *Bulletin of Marine Science* 86: 221–234.

Castilla, J.C. and O. Defeo 2001. Latin American benthic shellfisheries: emphasis on co-management and experimental practices. *Reviews in Fish Biology and Fisheries* 11: 1–30.

Castro, F. 2002. From myths to rules: the evolution of local management system in the Amazonian floodplain. *Environment and History* 8: 197–216.

Castro, F. and D.G. McGrath 2003. Moving toward sustainability in the local management of floodplain lake fisheries in the Brazilian Amazon. *Human Organization* 62: 123–133.

CBD 2014. Convention on Biological Diversity. www.cbd.int/

Chambers, R. 1983. *Rural Development: Putting the Last First*. Longman, London.

Chambers, R. 1997. *Whose Reality Counts: Putting the First Last*. Intermediate Technology Publications, London.

Chambers, R. and G. Conway 1992. Sustainable rural livelihoods: practical concepts for the 21st century. Institute for Development Studies Discussion Paper No. 296.

Chan, K.M.A., T. Satterfield and J. Goldstein 2012. Rethinking ecosystem services to better address and navigate cultural values. *Ecological Economics* 74: 8–18.

Chantraine, P. 1993. *The Last Cod-Fish*. Robert Davies, Montreal, Canada.

Chapin, F.S. III, S.R. Carpenter, G.P. Kofinas et al. 2010. Ecosystem stewardship: sustainability strategies for a rapidly changing planet. *Trends in Ecology and Evolution* 25: 241–249.

Chapin, F.S. III, G.P. Kofinas and C. Folke, editors 2009. *Principles of Ecosystem Stewardship: Resilience-based Resource Management in a Changing World*. Springer-Verlag, New York.

Chapin, F.S. III, A.F. Mark, R.A. Mitchell and K.J.M. Dickinson 2012. Design principles for social–ecological transformation toward sustainability: lessons from New Zealand sense of place. *Ecosphere* 3(5): article 40. www.esajournals.org (accessed June 2014).

Chapman, M.D. 1987. Women's fishing in Oceania. *Human Ecology* 15: 267–288.

Charles, A. 2009. Rights-based fisheries management: the role of use rights in managing access and harvesting. In: *A Fishery Manager's Guidebook*. 2nd edition (K.L. Cochrane and S.M. Garcia, eds.) FAO/Wiley-Blackwell, Chichester, UK, pp. 253–282.

Charles, A. 2011. Good practices for governance of small-scale fisheries. In: *World Small-Scale Fisheries. Contemporary Visions* (R. Chuenpagdee, ed.). Eburon, Delft, Netherlands, pp. 285–298.

Charles, A., M. Wiber, K. Bigney et al. 2010. Integrated management: a coastal community perspective. *Horizons* 10(4): 26–34.

Charles, A.T. 2001. *Sustainable Fishery Systems*. Fishing News Books, Blackwell Science, Oxford, UK.

Charles, A.T. 2007. Adaptive co-management for resilient resource systems. In *Adaptive Co-Management* (D. Armitage, F. Berkes and N. Doubleday, eds.). British Columbia Press, Vancouver, Canada, pp. 83–102.

Chhatre, A. and A. Agrawal 2008. Forest commons and local enforcement. *Proceedings of the National Academy of Sciences* 105: 13286–13291.

Christie, P., D.L. Fluharty, A.T. White, L. Eisma-Osorio and W. Jatulan 2007. Assessing the feasibility of ecosystem-based fishery management in tropical contexts. *Marine Policy* 31: 239–250.

Christie, P., R.B. Pollnac, E.G. Oracion et al. 2009. Back to basics: an empirical study demonstrating the importance of local-level dynamics for the success of tropical marine ecosystem-based management. *Coastal Management* 37: 349–373.

Chuenpagdee, R. editor 2011. *World Small-Scale Fisheries. Contemporary Visions*. Eburon, Delft, Netherlands.

Chuenpagdee, R. and S. Jentoft 2007. Step zero for fisheries co-management: what precedes implementation. *Marine Policy* 31: 657–668.

Cicin-Sain, B and R.W. Knecht 1998. *Integrated Coastal and Ocean Management*. Island Press, Washington, DC.

Cinner, C.E., N.A.J. Graham, C. Hutchery and M.A. McNeil 2013. Global effects of local human population density and distance to markets on the condition of coral reef fisheries. *Conservation Biology* 27: 453–458.

Cinner, C.E. and T.R. McClanahan 2006. Socioeconomic factors that lead to overfishing in small-scale coral reef fisheries of Papua New Guinea. *Environmental Conservation* 33: 73–80.

Cinner, C.E., T. R. McClanahan and M.A. McNeil et al. 2012. Comanagement of coral reef social–ecological systems. *Proceedings of the National Academy of Sciences* 109: 5219–5222.

Clark, C.W. 1973. The economics of over-exploitation. *Science* 181: 630–634.

Clark, C.W. 1985. *Bioeconomic Modelling and Fisheries Management.* Wiley, New York.

Clark, C.W., G.R. Munro and U.R. Sumaila 2010. Limits to privatization of fishery resources. *Land Economics* 86: 209–218.

Clark, E. 2006. Ted Ames and the recovery of Maine fisheries. *Yankee*, November. www.yankeemagazine.com (accessed June 2014).

Clarke, P. and S.D. Jupiter 2010. Law, custom and community-based natural resource management in Kubulau District (Fiji). *Environmental Conservation* 37: 98–106.

COASST 2014. Coastal observation and seabird survey team. http://depts.washington.edu/coasst/ (accessed June 2014).

Cochrane, K. and S. Garcia, editors 2009. *A Fishery Manager's Guidebook,* 2nd edition. FAO/Wiley-Blackwell, London.

Cochrane, K.L., N.L. Andrew and A.M. Parma 2011. Primary fisheries management: a minimum requirement for provision of sustainable human benefits in small-scale fisheries. *Fish and Fisheries* 12: 275–288.

Cohen, F. 1986. *Treaties on Trial: The Continuing Controversy over Northwest Indian Fishing Rights.* University of Washington Press, Seattle, WA.

Coleman, W.D. and A. Perl 1999. Internationalized policy environments and policy network analysis. *Political Studies* 47: 691–709.

Colfer, C.J.P. 2005. *The Complex Forest: Communities, Uncertainty, and Adaptive Collaborative Management.* Resources for the Future/CIFOR, Washington DC.

Colfer, C.J.P. and D. Capistrano 2005. *The Politics of Decentralization. Forests, People and Power.* Earthscan, London.

Coomes, O.T., Y. Takasaki, C. Abizid, and B.L. Barham 2010. Floodplain fisheries as natural insurance for the rural poor in tropical forest environments: evidence from Amazonia. *Fisheries Management and Ecology* 17: 513–521.

Copes, P. 1986. A critical review of the individual quota as a device in fisheries management. *Land Economics* 62: 278–291.

Costanza, R., R. d'Arge, R. de Groot et al. 1997. The value of world's ecosystem services and natural capital. *Nature* 387: 253–260.

Costanza, R., R. d'Arge, R. de Groot et al. 1998. The value of ecosystem services: putting the issues in perspective. *Ecological Economics* 25: 67–72.

Costanza, R., R. de Groot, P. Sutton et al. 2014. Changes in the global value of ecosystem services. *Global Environmental Change* 26: 152–158.

Costello, C.J. and D. Kaffine 2008. Natural Resource use with limited-tenure property rights. *Journal of Environmental Economics and Management* 55: 20–36.

Costa-Pierce, B.A. 1987. Aquaculture in ancient Hawai'i. *BioScience* 37: 320–330.

Costa-Pierce, B.A. 1988. Traditional fisheries and dualism in Indonesia. *Naga* 11(2): 34.

Coulthard, S. 2008. Adapting to environmental change in artisanal fisheries: insights from a south Indian lagoon. *Global Environmental Change* 18: 479–489.

Cox, M., G. Arnold and S. Villamayor Tomás 2010. A review of design principles for community-based natural resource management. *Ecology and Society* 15(4): 38. www.ecologyandsociety.org/vol15/iss4/art38/

Crance, C. and D. Draper 1996. Socially co-operative choices: an approach to achieving resource sustainability in the coastal zone. *Environmental Management* 20: 175–184.

Crona, B. and O. Bodin 2006. What you know is who you know? Communication patterns among resource users as a prerequisite for co-management. *Ecology and Society* 11(2): 7. www.ecologyandsociety.org/vol11/iss2/art7/

Crona, B.I. and J.N. Parker 2012. Learning in support of governance: theories, methods, and a framework to assess how bridging organizations contribute to adaptive resource governance. *Ecology and Society* 17(1): 32. http://dx.doi.org/10.5751/ES-04534-170132

Cronon, W. 1983. *Changes in the Land: Indians, Colonists, and the Ecology of New England.* Hill and Wang, New York.

Crowder, L.B., G. Osherenko, O.R. Young et al. 2006. Resolving mismatches in U.S. ocean governance. *Science* 313: 617–618.

Cumming, G.S. 2011. *Spatial Resilience in Social–Ecological Systems.* Springer, New York.

Dahlman, C. 1980. *The Open Field System and Beyond: A Property Rights Analysis of an Economic Institution.* Cambridge University Press, Cambridge, UK.

Dasmann, R.F. 2002. *Called by the Wild. The Autobiography of a Conservationist.* University of California Press, Berkeley, CA.

Davidson-Hunt, I.J. and O'Flaherty, R.M. 2007. Researchers, indigenous peoples and place-based learning communities. *Society and Natural Resources* 20: 291–305.

Davies, J., R. Hill, F.J. Walsh, M. Sandford, D. Smyth and M.C. Holmes 2013. Innovation in management plans for community conserved areas: experiences from Australian indigenous protected areas. *Ecology and Society* 18(2): 14. http://dx. doi.org/10.5751/ES-05404-180214

de Haan, L. and A. Zoomers 2005. Exploring the frontier of livelihoods research. *Development and Change* 36: 27–47.

De Silva, S.S. and F.B. Davy, editors 2010. *Success Stories in Asian Aquaculture.* Springer and International Development Research Centre, Ottawa.

De Young, C., A. Charles and A. Hjort 2008. Human dimensions of the ecosystem approach to fisheries: an overview of context, concepts, tools and methods. FAO Fisheries Technical Paper 489: 152 pp.

Deutsch, L., M. Troell, K. Limburg and M. Huitric 2011. Global trade of fisheries products: implications for marine ecosystems and their services. In: *Ecosystem Services and Global Trade of Natural Resources* (T. Köllner, ed.). Routledge, London, pp. 120–147.

Deutsch, L., Gräslund, S., Folke, C. et al 2007. Feeding aquaculture growth through globalization: exploitation of marine ecosystems for fishmeal. *Global Environmental Change* 17: 238–249.

DFO 2002. *Canada's Oceans Strategy. Our Oceans, Our Future. Policy and Operational Framework for Integrated Management of Estuarine, Coastal and Marine Environments of Canada.* Department of Fisheries and Oceans, Ottawa.

Dick, J., R. Turner, J. Stephenson, R. Kirikiri and H. Moller 2012. *Mana moana, mana tangata: testimonies on depletion and restoration of mahinga kai*. Tirohia he Huarahi Research Report #1, Centre for Sustainability, Otago University, Dunedin, New Zealand.

Diduck, A. 2004. Incorporating participatory approaches and social learning. In: *Resource and Environmental Management in Canada*, third edition (B. Mitchell, ed.). Oxford University Press, Don Mills, Ontario, Canada, pp. 497–527.

Diduck, A., J. Sinclair, G. Hostetler and P. Fitzpatrick 2012. Transformative learning theory, public involvement, and natural resource and environmental management. *Journal of Environmental Planning and Management* 55: 1311–1330.

Dietz, T., E. Ostrom and P.C. Stern 2003. The struggle to govern the commons. *Science* 302, 1907–1912.

DFID 1999. Sustainable livelihoods guidance sheets. Department for International Development, UK.

Donaldson, S.G., J. Van Oostdam, C. Tikhonov et al. 2010. Environmental contaminants and human health in the Canadian Arctic. *Science of the Total Environment* 406: 5165–5234.

Doubleday, N.C. 1993. Finding common ground: natural law and collective wisdom. In: *Traditional Ecological Knowledge: Concepts and Cases* (J, T. Inglis, ed.). Canadian Museum of Nature and the International Development Research Centre, Ottawa, pp. 41–53.

Dowie, M. 2009. *Conservation Refugees: The Hundred-year Conflict between Global Conservation and Native Peoples*. MIT Press, Cambridge, MA.

Downs, A. 1998. *Political Theory and Public Choice: The Selected Essays of Anthony Downs*. Vol. 1. Edward Elgar, Northampton, MA.

Dowsley, M. and G. Wenzel 2008. "The time of the most polar bears": a co-management conflict in Nunavut. *Arctic* 61: 177–189.

Dressler, W., F. Berkes and J. Mathias 2001. Beluga hunters in a mixed economy: managing the impacts of nature-based tourism in the Canadian Western Arctic. *Polar Record* 37: 35–48.

Dressler, W., B. Buscher, M. Schoon et al. 2010. From hope to crisis and back again? A critical history of the global CBNRM narrative. *Environmental Conservation* 37: 5–15.

Eamer, J. 2006. Keep it simple and be relevant: the first ten years of the Arctic Borderlands Ecological Knowledge Co-op. In: *Bridging Scales and Knowledge Systems* (W.V. Reid, F. Berkes, T. Wilbanks and D. Capistrano, eds.). Millennium Ecosystem Assessment and Island Press, Washington, DC, pp. 185–206.

Eckert, R. 1979. *The Enclosure of Ocean Resources: Economics and the Law of the Sea*. Hoover Institution Press, Stanford, CA.

Ellis, F. 2000. *Rural Livelihoods and Diversity in Developing Countries*. Oxford University Press, Oxford, UK.

Essington, T.E. and A.E. Punt 2011. Editorial. Implementing ecosystem-based fisheries management: advances, challenges and emerging tools. *Fish and Fisheries* 12: 123–124.

Evans, L., N. Cherrett and D. Pemsl 2011. Assessing the impact of fisheries co-management interventions in developing countries. *Journal of Environmental Management* 92: 1938–1949.

FAO 1995. *Code of Conduct for Responsible Fisheries.* Food and Agricultural Organization of the United Nations, Rome.

FAO 2014. *The State of World Fisheries and Aquaculture.* Food and Agricultural Organization of the United Nations, Rome.

Fabinyi, M. 2010. The intensification of fishing and the rise of tourism: competing coastal livelihoods in the Calamianes Islands, Philippines. *Human Ecology* 38: 415–427.

Fabricius, C., E. Koch, H. Magome and S. Turner, editors 2004. *Rights, Resources and Rural Development: Community-based Natural Resource Management in Southern Africa.* Earthscan, London.

Fals-Borda, O. 1987. The application of participatory action-research in Latin America. *International Sociology* 2: 329–347.

Fanning, L., R. Mahon and P. McConney, editors 2011. *Towards Marine Ecosystem-based Management in the Wider Caribbean.* Amsterdam University Press, Amsterdam.

Feeny, D., F. Berkes, B.J. McCay and J.M. Acheson 1990. The tragedy of the commons: twenty-two years later. *Human Ecology* 18: 1–19.

Fernandes, D. 2004. Community-Based Arapaima Conservation in the North Rupununi, Guyana. Equator Initiative Technical Report. www.umanitoba.ca/institutes/natural_ resources/nri_cbrm_projects_eiprojects.html (accessed June 2014).

Fernandes, D. 2005. TIDE Port Honduras Marine Reserve, Belize. Equator Initiative Technical Report. www.umanitoba.ca/institutes/natural_resources/nri_cbrm_projects_ eiprojects.html (accessed June 2014).

Fernandes, L., J. Day, A. Lewis et al. 2005. Establishing representative no-take areas in the Great Barrier Reef: large-scale implementation of theory on marine protected areas. *Conservation Biology* 19: 1733–1744.

Finlayson, A.C. and B.J. McCay 1998. Crossing the thresholds of ecosystem resilience: the commercial extinction of northern cod. In: *Linking Social and Ecological Systems* (F. Berkes and C. Folke, eds.). Cambridge University Press, Cambridge, UK, pp. 311–337.

Fisher, R., R. Prabhu, C. McDougall, editors 2007. Adaptive collaborative management of community forests in Asia. Center for International Forestry Research, Bogor, Indonesia.

Foley, P. and B. McCay 2014. Certifying the commons: eco-certification, privatization, and collective action. *Ecology and Society* 19(2): 28. http://dx.doi.org/10.5751/ES-06459–190228

Folke C. 2006. Resilience: the emergence of a perspective for social–ecological systems analyses. *Global Environmental Change* 16: 253–267.

Folke, C., S.R. Carpenter, B. Walker et al. 2010. Resilience thinking: integrating resilience, adaptability and transformability. *Ecology and Society* 15(4): 20. www.ecologyand society.org/vol15/iss4/art20/

Folke, C., J. Colding and F. Berkes 2003. Building resilience and adaptive capacity in social–ecological systems. In: *Navigating Social–Ecological Systems* (F. Berkes, J. Colding and C. Folke, eds.). Cambridge University Press, Cambridge, UK, pp. 352–387.

Folke, C., T. Hahn, P. Olsson and J. Norberg 2005. Adaptive governance of social–ecological systems. *Annual Review of Environment and Resources* 30: 441–473.

Folke, C., Jansson, A., Rockström, J. et al. 2011. Reconnecting to the biosphere. *Ambio* 40: 719–738.

Folke, C., L. Pritchard Jr., F. Berkes, J. Colding and U. Svedin 2007. The problem of fit between ecosystems and institutions: ten years later. *Ecology and Society* 12(1): 30. www.ecologyandsociety.org/vol12/iss1/art30/

Francis, R.C., M.A. Hixon, M.E. Clarke, S.A. Murawski and S. Ralston 2007. Ten commandments for ecosystem-based fishery scientists. *Fisheries* 32(5): 217–233.

Freeman, M.M.R. 1984. Contemporary Inuit exploitation of the sea-ice environment. In: *Sikumiut: "The People Who Use the Sea Ice."* Canadian Arctic Resources Committee, Ottawa, pp. 73–96.

Freeman, M.M.R. 1993. Traditional land users as a legitimate source of environmental expertise. In: *Traditional Ecological Knowledge: Wisdom for Sustainable Development* (N.M. Williams and G. Baines, eds.). Centre for Resource and Environmental Studies, Australian National University, Canberra, pp. 153–161.

Freire, P. 1970. *Pedagogy of the Oppressed.* Continuum, New York.

Frey, J. and F. Berkes 2014. Can partnerships and community-based conservation reverse the decline of coral reef social–ecological systems? *International Journal of the Commons* 8(1): 26–46.

Gadgil, M., F. Berkes and C. Folke 1993. Indigenous knowledge for biodiversity conservation. *Ambio* 22: 151–156.

Gadgil, M. and R. Guha 1992. *This Fissured Land: An Ecological History of India.* Oxford University Press, Delhi.

Gadgil, M., P. Olsson, F. Berkes and C. Folke 2003. Exploring the role of local ecological knowledge in ecosystem management: three case studies. In: *Navigating Social–Ecological Systems* (F. Berkes, J. Colding and C. Folke, eds.). Cambridge University Press, Cambridge, UK, pp. 189–209.

Gadgil, M., P.R.S. Rao, G. Utkarsh et al. 2000. New meanings for old knowledge: the People`s Biodiversity Registers Programme. *Ecological Applications* 10: 1307–1317.

Galaz, V., T. Hahn, P. Olsson, C. Folke and U. Svedin 2008. The problem of fit among biophysical systems, environmental regimes and broader governance systems. In: *Institutions and Environmental Change* (O. Young, L.A. King and H. Schroeder, eds.). MIT Press, Cambridge, MA, pp. 147–186.

Galappaththi, E.K. and F. Berkes 2014. Institutions for managing common-pool resources: the case of community-based shrimp aquaculture in northwestern Sri Lanka. *Maritime Studies* 13: 3.

Gallopin, G.C. 2006. Linkages between vulnerability, resilience and adaptive capacity. *Global Environmental Change* 16: 293–303.

Gallopin, G.C., S. Funtowicz, M. O'Connor and J. Ravetz 2001. Science for the 21st century: from social contract to the scientific core. *International Social Science Journal* 168: 219–229.

Garcia, S.M. and K.L. Cochrane 2009. From past management to future governance: a perspective view. In: *A Fishery Manager's Guidebook.* 2nd edition (K.L. Cochrane and S.M. Garcia, eds.). FAO/Wiley-Blackwell, Chichester, UK, pp. 447–472.

Gelcich, S., T.P. Hughes, P. Olsson et al. 2010. Navigating transformations in governance of Chilean marine coastal resources. *Proceedings of the National Academy of Sciences* 107: 16794–16799.

Gelcich, S., M.J. Kaiser, J.C. Castilla and G. Edward-Jones 2008. Engagement in co-management of marine benthic resources influences environmental perceptions of artisanal fishers. *Environmental Conservation* 35: 36–45.

Gibson, C., E. Ostrom, and T.-K. Ahn 2000. The concept of scale and the human dimensions of global change: a survey. *Ecological Economics* 32: 217–239.

Glaser, M. 2006. The social dimension in ecosystem management: strengths and weaknesses of human-nature mind maps. *Human Ecology Review* 13: 122–142.

Glavovic, B.C. and S. Boonzaier 2007. Confronting coastal poverty: building sustainable coastal livelihoods in South Africa. *Ocean and Coastal Management* 50: 1–23.

Global Partnership for Oceans 2014. www.globalpartnershipforoceans.org/about (accessed June 2014).

Goldstein, B.E. 2008. Skunkworks in the embers of the Cedar fire: enhancing resilience in the aftermath of disaster. *Human Ecology* 36: 15–28.

Goldstein, B.E. 2009. Resilience to surprises through communicative planning. *Ecology and Society* 14(2): 33. www.ecologyandsociety.org/vol14/iss2/art33/

Goldstein, B.E., editor 2012. *Collaborative Resilience*. MIT Press, Cambridge, MA.

Gordon, H.S. 1954. The economic theory of a common property resource: the fishery. *Journal of Political Economy* 62: 124–142.

Grafton, R.Q., R. Hilborn, L. Ridgeway et al. 2008. Positioning fisheries in a changing world. *Marine Policy* 32: 630–634.

Graham, J., A. Charles and A. Bull. 2006. *Community Fisheries Management Handbook*. Gorsebrook Research Institute, Saint Mary's University, Halifax, Canada. www.coastalcura.ca/ (accessed June 2014).

Grant, S. and F. Berkes 2007. Fisher knowledge as expert system: a case from the longline fishery of Grenada, the Eastern Caribbean. *Fisheries Research* 84: 162–170.

Grant, S., F. Berkes and J. Brierley 2007. Understanding the local livelihood system in resource management: the pelagic longline fishery in Gouyave, Grenada. *Gulf and Caribbean Research* 19: 113–122.

Groesbeck, A.S., K. Rowell, D. Lepofsky and A.K. Salomon 2014. Ancient clam gardens increased shellfish production. Adaptive strategies from the past can inform food security today. *PLoS ONE* 9(3): e91235.

Grossman, Z. 2010. The native renaissance of Washington's tribal nations. *American Association of Geographers Newsletter* 45 (10): 1–11.

Gunderson, L.H. and C.S. Holling, editors 2002. *Panarchy: Understanding Transformations in Human and Natural Systems*. Island Press, Washington, DC.

Gutiérrez, N., R. Hilborn and O. Defeo 2011. Leadership, social capital and incentives promote successful fisheries. *Nature* 470: 386–389.

Haas, P.M. 1990. *Saving the Mediterranean: The Politics of International Environmental Cooperation*. Columbia University Press, New York.

Habermas, J. 1981. *Theorie des Kommunikativen Handelns*. 2 Volumes. Suhrkamp, Frankfurt, Germany.

Haggan, N., B. Neis and I.G. Baird, editors 2007. *Fishers' Knowledge in Fisheries Science and Management*. UNESCO Publishing, Paris.

Hahn, T., P. Olsson, C. Folke and K. Johansson 2006. Trust building, knowledge generation and organizational innovations: the role of a bridging organization for adaptive co-management of a wetland landscape around Kristianstad, Sweden. *Human Ecology* 34: 573–592.

Hall, C.M. 2001. Trends in ocean and coastal tourism: the end of the last frontier? *Ocean and Coastal Management* 44: 615–620.

Halpern, B.S., C. Longo, D. Hardy et al. 2012. An index to assess the health and benefits of the global ocean. *Nature* 488: 615–620.

Hanazaki, N. and A. Begossi 2003. Does fish still matter? Changes in the diet of two Brazilian fishing communities. *Ecology of Food and Nutrition* 42: 279–301.

Hanazaki, N., F. Berkes, C.S. Seixas and N. Peroni 2013. Livelihood diversity, food security and resilience among the Caiçara of coastal Brazil. *Human Ecology* 41: 152–164.

Hanazaki, N., F. de Castro, V.G. Oliveira and N. Peroni 2007. Between the sea and the land: the livelihood of estuarine people in southeastern Brazil. *Ambiente e Sociedade* 10: 121–136.

Haque, C.E. 1998. *Hazards in a Fickle Environment: Bangladesh.* Kluwer, Dordrecht, Netherlands.

Haque, C.E., A.K. Deb and D. Medeiros 2009. Integrating conservation with livelihood improvement for sustainable development: the experiment of an oyster producers' cooperative in southeast Brazil. *Society and Natural Resources* 22: 554–570.

Hardin, G. 1968. The tragedy of the commons. *Science* 162: 1243–1248.

Harper, S., D. Zeller, M. Hauzer, D. Pauly and U.R. Sumeila 2013. Women and fisheries: contribution to food security and local economies. *Marine Policy* 39: 56–63.

Harris, G. 2007. *Seeking Sustainability in an Age of Complexity.* Cambridge University Press, Cambridge, UK.

Heaslip, R. 2008. Monitoring salmon aquaculture waste: the contribution of First Nations' rights, knowledge and practices in British Columbia, Canada. *Marine Policy* 32: 988–996.

Hilborn, R. 2006. Faith-based fisheries. *Fisheries* 31(11): 554–555.

Hilborn, R. and Walters, C.J. 1992. *Quantitative Fisheries Stock Assessment.* Chapman and Hall, London.

Hilborn, R., T.P. Quinn, D.E. Schindler and D.E. Rogers 2003. Biocomplexity and fisheries sustainability. *Proceedings of the National Academy of Sciences* 100: 6564–6568.

Hilborn, R., J.M. Orensanz and A.M. Parma 2005. Institutions, incentives and the future of fisheries. *Philosophical Transactions of the Royal Society B* 360: 47–57.

HLPE 2014. Sustainable fisheries and aquaculture for food security and nutrition. A report by the High Level Panel of Experts on Food Security and Nutrition of the Committee on World Food Security, Rome. www.fao.org/3/a-i3844e.pdf (accessed June 2014).

Holling, C.S. 1973. Resilience and stability of ecological systems. *Annual Review of Ecology and Systematics* 4: 1–23.

Holling, C.S., editor 1978. *Adaptive Environmental Assessment and Management.* Wiley, London.

Holling, C. S. 2001. Understanding the complexity of economic, ecological, and social systems. *Ecosystems* 4: 390–405.

Holling, C.S., F. Berkes and C.Folke 1998. Science, sustainability and resource management. In: *Linking Social and Ecological Systems* (F. Berkes and C. Folke, eds.). Cambridge University Press, Cambridge, UK, pp. 342–362.

Holling, C.S. and G.K. Meffe 1996. Command and control and the pathology of natural resource management. *Conservation Biology* 10: 328–337.

Hovelsrud, G.K. and B. Smit, editors 2010. *Community Adaptation and Vulnerability in Arctic Regions*. Springer, Dordrecht, Netherlands.

Hughes, T.P. 2014. Marine social and ecological systems between global stewardship and community management. Paper presented at Resilience 2014, Third International Science and Policy Conference, May 2014, Montpellier, France.

Hughes, T.P., A.H. Baird, D.R. Bellwood et al. 2003. Climate change, human impacts and the resilience of coral reefs. *Science* 301: 929–933.

Hughes, T.R., D.R. Bellwood, C. Folke, R.S. Steneck and J. Wilson 2005. New paradigm for supporting the resilience of marine ecosystems. *Trends in Ecology and Evolution* 20: 380–386.

Huitric, M., C. Folke and N. Kautsky 2002. Development and government policies of the shrimp farming industry in Thailand in relation to mangrove ecosystems. *Ecological Economics* 40: 441–455.

Hunn, E. S. and J. Selam 1990. *Nch'i-Wana "The Big River": Mid-Columbia Indians and their Land*. University of Washington Press, Seattle, WA.

Huong, T.T.T. and F. Berkes 2011. Diversity of resource use and property rights in Tam Giang Lagoon, Vietnam. *International Journal of the Commons* 5(1): 130–149.

Hviding, E. 1990. Keeping the sea: aspects of marine tenure in Marovo Lagoon, Solomon Islands. In: *Traditional Marine Resource Management in the Pacific Basin: An Anthology* (K. Ruddle and R.E. Johannes, eds.). UNESCO, Jakarta.

ICCA 2014. Indigenous peoples' and community conserved territories and areas (ICCAs). www.iccaconsortium.org (accessed June 2014).

Idrobo, C.J. and F. Berkes 2012. Pangnirtung Inuit and the Greenland shark: co-producing knowledge of a little discussed species. *Human Ecology* 40: 405–414.

Idrobo, C.J. and I.J. Davidson-Hunt 2012. Adaptive learning, technological innovation and livelihood diversification: the adoption of pound nets in Rio de Janeiro State, Brazil. *Maritime Studies* 11: 3.

Ingold, T. 2000. *The Perception of the Environment: Essays in Livelihood, Dwelling and Skill*. Routledge, New York.

Innis, H.A. 1930. *The Fur Trade in Canada. An Introduction to Canadian Economic History*. 2nd edition. University of Toronto Press, Toronto, Canada.

Japan Satoyama Satoumi Assessment 2010. Japan Satoyama Satoumi Assessment. Experiences and Lessons from Clusters. United Nations University, Tokyo. http://archive.ias.unu.edu/sub_page.aspx?catID=111&ddlID=1485 (accessed June 2014).

Jentoft, S. 1999. Beyond the veil. *Samudra Report* No. 23.

Jentoft, S. 2000. The community: a missing link of fisheries management. *Marine Policy* 24: 53–59.

Jentoft, S. 2005. Fisheries co-management as empowerment. *Marine Policy* 29: 1–7.

Jentoft, S. 2006. Beyond fisheries management: the *phronetic* dimension. *Marine Policy* 30: 671–680.

Jentoft, S. 2007. Limits to governability: institutional implications for fisheries and coastal governance. *Marine Policy* 31: 360–370.

Jentoft, S. and R. Chuenpagdee 2009. Fisheries and coastal governance as a wicked problem. *Marine Policy* 33: 553–560.

Jentoft, S. and A. Eide, editors 2011. *Poverty Mosaics: Realities and Prospects in Small-Scale Fisheries*. Springer, New York.

Jentoft, S. and B.J. McCay 1995. User participation in fisheries management. Lessons drawn from international experiences. *Marine Policy* 19: 227–246.

Johannes, R.E. 1978. Traditional marine conservation methods in Oceania and their demise. *Annual Review of Ecology and Systematics* 9: 349–364.

Johannes, R.E. 1981. *Words of the Lagoon: Fishing and Marine Lore in the Palau District of Micronesia*. University of California Press, Berkeley, CA.

Johannes, R.E. 1998a. Government-supported, village-based management of marine resources in Vanuatu. *Ocean and Coastal Management* 40: 165–186.

Johannes, R.E. 1998b. The case for data-less marine resource management: examples from tropical nearshore fisheries. *Trends in Ecology and Evolution* 13: 243–246.

Johannes, R.E. 2002. The renaissance of community-based marine resource management in Oceania. *Annual Review of Ecology and Systematics* 33: 317–340.

Johannes, R.E., M.M.R. Freeman and R.J. Hamilton 2000. Ignore fishers' knowledge and miss the boat. *Fish and Fisheries* 1: 257–271.

Johannes, R.E., P. Lasserre, S.W. Nixon, J. Pliya and K. Ruddle 1983. Traditional knowledge and management of marine coastal systems. *Biology International*, Special Issue 4.

Johnson, D.S. 2006. Category, narrative and value in the governance of small-scale fisheries. *Marine Policy* 30: 747–756.

Johnson, L.M. and E.S. Hunn, editors 2010. *Landscape Ethnoecology*. Berghahn, New York and Oxford, UK.

Jones, P.S.J. 2013. Governing protected areas to fulfil biodiversity conservation obligations: from Habermasian ideals to a more instrumental reality. *Environment, Development and Sustainability* 15: 39–50.

Jones, P.S.J. 2014. *Governing Marine Protected Areas. Resilience through Diversity*. Earthscan Routledge, London and New York.

Jones, R., C. Rigg and L. Lee 2010. Haida marine planning: First Nations as a partner in marine conservation. *Ecology and Society* 15(1): 12. www.ecologyandsociety.org/vol15/iss1/art12/

Kaimowitz, D. and D. Sheil 2007. Conserving what and for whom? Why conservation should help meet basic human needs in the tropics. *Biotropica* 39: 567–574.

Kaneshiro, K.Y., P. Chinn, K.N. Duin, A.P. Hood, K. Maly and B.A. Wilcox 2005. Hawai'i's mountain-to-sea ecosystems: social–ecological microcosms for sustainability science and practice. *EcoHealth* 2: 349–360.

Kates, R.W., W.C. Clark, R. Corell et al. 2001. Sustainability science. *Science* 292: 641–642.

Kautsky, N., C. Folke, P. Ronnback, M. Troell, M. Beveridge and J. Primavera 2001. Aquaculture and biodiversity. In: S. Levin (ed.) *Encyclopedia of Biodiversity*, Vol. I (S. Levin, ed.). Academic Press, San Diego, CA, pp. 185–198.

Kay, R.C. and J. Alder 2005. *Coastal Planning and Management*. Taylor and Francis, New York.

Kearney, J. and F. Berkes 2007. The importance of community for adaptive co-management. In: *Adaptive Co-Management* (D. Armitage, F. Berkes and N. Doubleday, eds.). University of British Columbia Press, Vancouver, Canada, pp. 191–207.

Khan, A.S. and B. Neis 2010. The rebuilding imperative in fisheries: clumsy solution for a wicked problem? *Progress in Oceanography* 87: 347–356.

Kimmerer, R.W. 2002. Weaving traditional ecological knowledge into biological education: a call for action. *BioScience* 52: 432–8.

Kimmerer, R.W. and F.K. Lake. 2001. The role of indigenous burning in land management. *Journal of Forestry* 99(11): 36–41.

Kinzig, A.P., P. Ryan, M. Etienne et al. 2006. Resilience and regime shifts: assessing cascading effects. *Ecology and Society* 11(1): 20. www.ecologyandsociety.org/vol11/iss1/art20/

Kittinger, J.N., A. Dowling, A.R. Purves, N.A. Milne and P. Olsson 2011. Marine protected areas, multiple-agency management, and monumental surprise in the northwestern Hawaiian Islands. *Journal of Marine Biology* Vol. 2011, Article ID 241374, 17 pages.

Klooster, D. 2000. Institutional choice, community, and struggle: a case study of forest co-management in Mexico. *World Development* 28(1): 1–20.

Kocho-Schellenberg, J.-E. and F. Berkes 2014. Tracking the development of co-management: using network analysis in a case from the Canadian Arctic. *Polar Record*. doi:10.1017/50032247414000435.

Kofinas, G. with the communities of Aklavik, Arctic Village, Old Crow and Fort McPherson 2002. Community contributions to ecological monitoring. In: *The Earth is Faster Now* (I. Krupnik and D. Jolly, eds.). Arctic Research Consortium of the United States, Fairbanks, AK, pp. 54–91.

Kooiman, J. 2003. *Governing as Governance*. Sage, London.

Kooiman, J., M. Bavinck, S. Jentoft and R. Pulin, editors 2005. *Fish for Life: Interactive Governance for Fisheries*. Amsterdam University Press, Amsterdam.

Kotchen, M.J. and O.R. Young 2007. Meeting the challenges of the anthropocene: towards a science of coupled human–biophysical systems. *Global Environmental Change* 17: 149–151.

Kothari, A. 2006. Community-conserved areas: towards ecological and livelihood security. *Parks* 16: 3–13.

Krupnik, I. and D. Jolly, editors 2002. *The Earth is Faster Now*. Arctic Research Consortium of the United States, Fairbanks, AK.

Kuhn, T. 1962. *The Structure of Scientific Revolutions*. University of Chicago Press, Chicago, IL.

Kumar, K.G. editor 2008. *Asserting Rights, Defining Responsibilities: Perspectives from Small-scale Fishing Communities on Coastal and Fisheries Management in Eastern and Southern Africa*. The Zanzibar Workshop Proceedings. International Collective in Support of Fishworkers, Chennai. www.icsf.net/images/proceedings/pdf/english/issue_100/100_all.pdf (accessed June 2014).

Kurien, J. 1992. Ruining the commons and responses of the commoners: coastal overfishing and fishworkers' actions in South India. In: *Grassroots Environmental Action* (D. Ghai and J. Vivian, eds.). Routledge, London, pp. 221–258.

Lam, M.E. and D. Pauly 2010. Who is right to fish? Evolving a social contract for ethical fisheries. *Ecology and Society* 15(3): 16. www.ecologyandsociety.org/vol15/iss3/art16/

Langdon, S.J. 2006. Tidal pulse fishing: selective traditional Tlingit salmon fishing techniques on the west coast of the Prince of Wales Archipelago. In: *Traditional Ecological Knowledge and Natural Resource Management* (N.C. Menzies, ed.). University of Nebraska Press, Lincoln, NE, pp. 21–46.

Lannan 2014. InterTribal Sinkyone Wilderness Council, NE Mendocino County, CA. www.lannan.org/indigenous-communities/special-projects/intertribal-sinkyone-wilderness-council-ne-mendocino-county-ca/ (accessed June 2014).

Lansing, J.S. 2002. Complex adaptive systems. *Annual Review of Anthropology* 32: 183–204.

Larkin, P.A. 1977. An epitaph for the concept of maximum sustained yield. *Transactions of the American Fisheries Society* 106: 1–11.

Larson, A.M. and F. Soto. 2008. Decentralization of natural resource governance regimes. *Annual Review of Environment and Resources* 33: 213–239.

Leach, M., R. Mearns and I. Scoones 1999. Environmental entitlements: dynamics and institutions in community-based natural resource management. *World Development* 27: 225–247.

Lebel, L., J. Anderies, M. Campbell et al. 2006. Governance and the capacity to manage resilience in regional social–ecological systems. *Ecology and Society* 11(1): 19. www.ecologyandsociety.org/vol11/iss1/art19/

Lee, K. 1993. *Compass and the Gyroscope.* Island Press, Washington, DC.

Lees, S.H. and D.G. Bates 1990. The ecology of cumulative change. In: *The Ecosystem Approach in Anthropology* (E.F. Moran, ed.). University of Michigan Press, Ann Arbor, MI, pp. 247–277.

Leichenko, R.M. and K.L. O'Brien 2008. *Environmental Change and Globalization. Double Exposures.* Oxford University Press, Oxford, UK, and New York.

Lejano, R.P. and Ingram, H. 2009a. Place-based conservation: lessons from the Turtle islands. *Environment* 49(9): 19–26.

Lejano, R.P. and H. Ingram 2009b. Collaborative networks and new ways of knowing. *Environmental Science and Policy* 12: 653–662.

Lele, S., P. Wilshusen, D. Brockington, R. Seidler and K. Bawa 2010. Beyond exclusion: alternative approaches to biodiversity conservation in the developing tropics. *Current Opinion in Environmental Sustainability* 2: 94–100.

Leopold, A. 1949 [1966] *A Sand County Almanac with Essays on Conservation from Round River.* Random House, New York.

Lepofsky, D. and M.E. Caldwell 2013. Indigenous marine resource management on the northwest coast of North America. *Ecological Processes* 2(1): 12.

Levin, S.A. 1999. *Fragile Dominion: Complexity and the Commons.* Perseus Books, Reading, MA.

Levin, S.A. 2005. Self-organization and the emergence of complexity in ecological systems. *BioScience* 55: 1075–1079.

Lim, C.P., Y. Matsuda and Y. Shigemi 1995. Co-management in marine fisheries: the Japanese experience. *Coastal Management* 23: 195–221.

Lindeman, R.L. 1942. The trophic–dynamic aspect of ecology. *Ecology* 23: 399–417.

Liu, J., T. Dietz, S.R. Carpenter et al. 2007. Complexity of human and natural systems. *Science* 317: 1513–1516.

LMMA Network 2014. The Locally-Managed Marine Area Network. www.lmmanetwork.org/ (accessed June 2014).

Lobe, K. and F. Berkes 2004. The *padu* system of community-based fisheries management: change and local institutional innovation in south India. *Marine Policy* 28: 271–281.

Lopes, P.F.M., E.M. Rosa, S. Salyvonchyk, V. Nora and A. Begossi 2013. Suggestions for fixing top-down coastal fisheries management through participatory approaches. *Marine Policy* 40: 100–110.

Loucks, L. 2007. Patterns of fisheries institutional failure and success: experience from the southern gulf of St. Lawrence snow crab fishery in Nova Scotia, Canada. *Marine Policy* 31: 320–326.

Loucks, L., A. Charles, D. Armitage and F. Berkes (in prep.). The emergence of community science in Port Mouton Bay: a process of transformative learning.

Loucks, L., R. Gunn, J. Spencer, A. Day and D. Dalmer. 2011. *A Socio-economic Overview of West Coast Vancouver Island Communities and Marine-use Sectors.* The Tsawalk partnership, West Coast Aquatic, Port Alberni, Canada.

Lowry, G.K., A.T. White and P. Christie 2009. Scaling up to networks of marine protected areas in the Philippines: biophysical, legal, institutional and social considerations. *Coastal Management* 37: 274–290.

Ludwig, D. 2001. The era of management is over. *Ecosystems* 4: 758–764.

Lutz, J.S. and B. Neis, editors 2008. *Making and Moving Knowledge.* McGill-Queen's University Press, Montreal, Canada.

Lyytimäki, J. and M. Hildén 2007. Thresholds of sustainability: policy challenges of regime shifts in coastal areas. *Sustainability: Science, Practice, and Policy* 3(2): 61–69. http://ejournal.nbii.org/archives/vol3iss2/communityessay.lyytimaki.html (accessed June 2014).

MA 2005a. *Ecosystems and Human Well-Being: Synthesis.* Millennium Ecosystem Assessment, Island Press, Washington, DC.

MA 2005b. *Ecosystems and Human Well-Being: Current State and Trends*, Vol. 1, Chapter 19, Coastal systems. Millennium Ecosystem Assessment, Island Press, Washington, DC.

MA 2005c. *Ecosystems and Human Well-Being: Policy Responses*, Vol. 3, Chapter 15, Integrated responses. Millennium Ecosystem Assessment, Island Press, Washington, DC.

McCay, B.J. 1998. *Oyster Wars and Public Trust. Property, Law and Ecology in New Jersey.* University of Arizona Press, Tucson, AZ.

McCay, B.J. 2008. The littoral and the liminal: or why it is hard and critical to answer the question "who owns the coast?"? MAST 7(1): 7–30.

McCay, B.J. 2012. Enclosing the fishery commons from individuals to communities. In: *Property in Land and Other Resources* (D.H. Cole and E. Ostrom, eds.). Lincoln Institute of Land Policy, Cambridge, MA, pp. 219–251.

McCay, B.J. and J.M. Acheson, editors 1987. *The Question of the Commons: The Culture and Ecology of Communal Resources.* University of Arizona Press, Tucson, AZ.

McCay, B.J. and S. Jentoft 1996. From the bottom up: participatory issues in fisheries management. *Society and Natural Resources* 9: 237–250.

McCay, B.J and P.J.S. Jones 2011. Marine protected areas and the governance of marine ecosystems and fisheries. *Conservation Biology* 25: 1130–1133.

McConney, P. and A. Charles 2009. Managing small-scale fisheries: moving toward people-centred perspectives. In: *Handbook of Marine Fisheries Conservation and Management* (R.Q. Grafton, R. Hilborn, D. Squires, M. Tait and M. Williams, eds.). Oxford University Press, Oxford, UK, pp. 532–545.

McConney, P., H.A. Oxenford and M. Haughton 2007. Management in the Gulf and Caribbean: mosaic or melting pot? *Gulf and Caribbean Research* 19: 103–112.

McCook, L.J., T. Ayling, M. Cappo et al. 2010. Adaptive management of the Great Barrier Reef: a globally significant demonstration of the benefits of networks of marine reserves. *Proceedings of the National Academy of Sciences* 107: 18278–18285.

McEvoy, A.F. 1986. *The Fishermen's Problem: Ecology and the Law in the California Fisheries, 1850–1980.* Cambridge University Press, New York.

McEvoy, A.F. 1996. Historical interdependence between ecology, production, and management in the California fisheries. In: *Sustainability Issues for Resource Managers.* US Department of Agriculture, Pacific Northwest Research Station, General Technical Report PNW-GTR-370, pp. 45–53.

McGinnis, M.D., editor 2000. *Polycentric Games and Institutions.* University of Michigan Press, Ann Arbor, MI.

McGoodwin, J.R. 1990. *Crisis in the World's Fisheries.* Stanford University Press, Stanford, CA.

McGrath, D.G., A. Cardoso, O.T. Almeida and J. Pezzuti 2008. Constructing a policy and institutional framework for an ecosystem-based approach to managing the Lower Amazon floodplain. *Environment, Development and Sustainability* 10: 677–695.

McGregor, D. 2004. Traditional ecological knowledge and sustainable development: towards co-existence. In: *In the Way of Development. Indigenous Peoples, Life Projects and Globalization* (M. Blaser, H.A. Feit and G. McRae, eds.). Zed Books, London and New York, pp. 72–91.

McIntosh, R.J. 2000. Social memory in Mande. In: *The Way the Wind Blows: Climate, History, and Human Action* (R.J. McIntosh, J.A. Tainter and S.K. McIntosh, eds.). Columbia University Press, New York, pp. 141–180.

Mackinson, S. 2001. Integrating local and scientific knowledge: an example in fisheries science. *Environmental Management* 27: 533–545.

McLeod, K. and H. Leslie, editors 2009. *Ecosystem-based Management for the Oceans: Resilience Approaches.* Island Press, Washington, DC.

McPherson, J.M. and A.C.J. Vincent 2004. Assessing East African trade in seahorse species as a basis for conservation under international controls. *Aquatic Conservation: Marine and Freshwater Ecosystems* 14: 521–538.

McShane. T.O., P.D. Hirsch, T.C. Trung et al. 2011. Hard choices: making trade-offs between biodiversity conservation and human well-being. *Biological Conservation* 144: 966–972.

Maffi, L. and E. Woodley 2010. *Biocultural Diversity Conservation. A Global Sourcebook.* Earthscan, London.

Mahon, R. 1997. Does fisheries science serve the needs of managers of small stocks in developing countries? *Canadian Journal of Fisheries and Aquatic Sciences* 54: 2207–2213.

Mahon, R., L. Fanning and P. McConney 2009. A governance perspective on the large marine ecosystem approach. *Marine Policy* 33: 317–321.

Mahon, R., P. McConney and R.N. Roy 2008. Governing fisheries as complex adaptive systems. *Marine Policy* 32: 104–112.

Makino, M. 2011. *Fisheries Management in Japan: Its Institutional Features and Case Studies.* Springer, London.

Maliao, R.J., R.S. Pomeroy and R.G. Turingan 2009. Performance of community-based coastal resource management (CBCRM) programs in the Philippines: a meta-analysis. *Marine Policy* 33: 818–825.

Manor, J. 1999. *The Political Economy of Decentralization*. World Bank, Washington, DC.

Mansfield, B. 2004. Neoliberalism in the oceans: "rationalization," property rights, and the commons question. *Geoforum* 35: 313–326.

Marín, A. and F. Berkes 2010. Network approach for understanding small-scale fisheries governance: the case of the Chilean coastal co-management system. *Marine Policy* 34: 851–858.

Marschke, M. 2012. *Life, Fish and Mangroves. Resource Governance in Coastal Cambodia*. University of Ottawa Press, Ottawa.

Marschke, M. and F. Berkes 2005. Local level sustainability planning for livelihoods: a Cambodian experience. *International Journal of Sustainable Development and World Ecology* 12: 21–33.

Marschke, M. and F. Berkes 2006. Exploring strategies that build livelihood resilience: a case from Cambodia. *Ecology and Society* 11(1): 42. www.ecologyandsociety.org/vol11/iss1/art42/ (accessed June 2014).

Marine Stewardship Council 2014. Certified sustainable seafood. www.msc.org/ (accessed June 2014).

Mascia, M.B. and C.A. Claus 2008. A property rights approach to understanding human displacement from protected areas: the case of marine protected areas. *Conservation Biology* 23: 16–23.

Mascia, M.B., C.A. Claus and R. Naidoo 2010. Impacts of marine protected areas in fishing communities. *Conservation Biology* 24: 1424–1429.

Martin, G.J., C.I. Camacho Benavides, C.A. Del Campo Garcia et al. 2011. Indigenous and community-conserved areas in Oaxaca, Mexico. *Management of Environmental Quality* 22: 250–266.

Menzies, N.C., editor 2006. *Traditional Ecological Knowledge and Natural Resource Management*. University of Nebraska Press, Lincoln, NE.

Miller, K., T. Charles, M. Barange et al. 2010. Climate change, uncertainty, and resilient fisheries: institutional responses through integrative science. *Progress in Oceanography* 87: 338–346.

Moller, H., P. O'B. Lyver, C. Bragg et al. 2009a. Guidelines for cross-cultural participatory action research partnerships: a case study of a customary seabird harvest in New Zealand. *New Zealand Journal of Zoology* 36: 211–241.

Moller, H., K. Charleton, B. Knight and P.O'B. Lyver 2009b. Traditional ecological knowledge and scientific inference of prey availability: harvests of sooty shearwater (*Puffinus griseus*) chicks by Rakiura Maori. *New Zealand Journal of Zoology* 36: 259–274.

Muir C, D.R. Rose and P. Sullivan 2010. From the other side of the knowledge frontier: indigenous knowledge, social–ecological relationships and new perspectives. *The Rangeland Journal* 32: 259–265.

Murphree, M.W. 2009. The strategic pillars of communal natural resource management: benefit, empowerment and conservation. *Biodiversity Conservation* 18: 2551–2562.

Murray, G. and L. King 2012. First Nations values in protected area governance: Tla-o-qui-aht Tribal Parks and Pacific Rim National Park Reserve. *Human Ecology* 40: 385–395.

Myers, R.A. and B. Worm 2003. Rapid worldwide decline of predatory fish communities. *Nature* 423: 280–283.

Nagendra, H. 2007. Drivers of reforestation in human-dominated forests. *Proceedings of the National Academy of Sciences* 104: 15218–15223.

Nakashima, D.J., K. Galloway McLean, H.D. Thrulstrup, A. Ramos Castillo and J. Rubis 2012. *Weathering Uncertainty: Traditional Knowledge for Climate Change Assessment and Adaptation.* UNESCO, Paris.

Napier, V.R., G.M. Branch and J.M. Harris 2005. Evaluating conditions for successful co-management of subsistence fisheries in KwaZulu-Natal, South Africa. *Environmental Conservation* 32: 165–177.

Narayan, D., R. Chambers, M.K. Shah and P. Petesch 2000. *Voices of the Poor: Crying Out for Change.* Oxford University Press, New York.

NAS 1986. *Proceedings of the Conference on Common Property Resource Management.* National Research Council/National Academy Press, Washington, DC.

Natcher, D.C., S. Davis and C.G. Hickey 2005. Co-management: managing relationships, not resources. *Human Organization* 64: 240–250.

Nayak, P. and F. Berkes 2008. Politics of co-optation: community forest management vs. Joint Forest Management in Orissa, India. *Environmental Management* 41: 707–718.

Nayak, P.K. and F. Berkes 2010. Whose marginalization? Politics around environmental injustices in India's Chilika Lagoon. *Local Environment* 15: 553–567.

Nayak, P.K. and F. Berkes 2011. Commonisation and decommonisation: understanding the processes of change in Chilika Lagoon, India. *Conservation & Society* 9: 132–145.

Nayak, P. and F. Berkes 2014. Linking global drivers with local and regional change: a social–ecological system approach in Chilika Lagoon, Bay of Bengal. *Regional Environmental Change* 14: 2067–2078.

Nayak, P.K., L.E. Oliveira and F. Berkes 2014. Resource degradation, marginalization, and poverty in small-scale fisheries: threats to social–ecological resilience in India and Brazil. *Ecology and Society* 19(2): 73. http://dx.doi.org/10.5751/ES-06656-190273

Naylor, R.L., R.J. Goldburg, J.H. Primavera et al. 2000. Effect of aquaculture on world fish supplies. *Nature* 405: 1017–1024.

Neis, B. and L. Felt, editors 2000. *Finding our Sea Legs. Linking Fishery People and Their Knowledge with Science and Management.* Institute of Social and Economic Research, St. John's, Newfoundland, Canada.

Nisqually Delta Restoration 2014. http://nisquallydeltarestoration.org/index.php (accessed June 2014).

NOAA 2005. *New Priorities for the 21st Century: NOAA's Strategic Plan.* National Oceanographic and Atmospheric Administration, Washington, DC.

NOAA 2014. NOAA, partners predict possible record-setting dead zone for Gulf of Mexico. www.noaanews.noaa.gov/stories2013/20130618_deadzone.html (accessed June 2014).

Norberg, J. and G. Cumming, editors 2008. *Complexity Theory for a Sustainable Future.* Columbia University Press, New York.

Norse, E.A. 2010. Ecosystem-based spatial planning and management in marine fisheries: why and how? *Bulletin of Marine Science* 86: 179–195.

Norse, E.A. and L.B. Crowder, editors 2005. *Marine Conservation Biology.* Island Press, Washington, DC.

North, D. 1990. *Institutions, Institutional Change, and Economic Performance.* Cambridge University Press, New York.

Norton, B. 2005. *Sustainability. A Philosophy of Adaptive Ecosystem Management.* University of Chicago Press, Chicago, IL.

O'Brien, K. 2008. Thinking globally and thinking locally: ecology, subsidiarity, and a multiscalar environmentalism. *Journal for the Study of Religion, Nature and Culture* 2: 218–236.

O'Brien, K., B. Hayward and F. Berkes 2009. Rethinking social contracts: building resilience in a changing climate. *Ecology and Society* 14(2): 12. http://www.ecologyand society.org/vol14/iss2/art12/

OECD 1997. Evaluation of programs promoting participatory development and good governance: synthesis report. Organization for Economic Cooperation and Development, Paris.

OECD 2001. Development action committee's guidelines on poverty reduction. Organization for Economic Cooperation and Development, Paris. www.oecd.org (accessed June 2014).

OECD 2004. Fish piracy: combating illegal, unreported and unregulated fishing. Organisation for Economic Co-operation and Development, Paris.

Olsen, S.B., J. Tobey and L.Z. Hale 1998. A learning-based approach to coastal management. *Ambio* 27: 611–619.

Olson, J. 2011. Understanding and contextualizing social impacts from the privatization of fisheries: an overview. *Ocean and Coastal Management* 54: 353–363.

Olson, M. 1965. *The Logic of Collective Action: Public Goods and the Theory of Groups.* Harvard University Press, Cambridge, MA.

Olson, M. 2000. *Power and Prosperity.* Basic Books, New York.

Olsson, P. and C. Folke 2001. Local ecological knowledge and institutional dynamics for ecosystem management: a study of Lake Racken watershed, Sweden. *Ecosystems* 4: 85–104.

Olsson, P., C. Folke and F. Berkes 2004a. Adaptive co-management for building resilience in social–ecological systems. *Environmental Management* 34: 75–90.

Olsson, P., C. Folke, V. Galaz, T. Hahn, L. Schultz 2007. Enhancing the fit through adaptive co-management: creating and maintaining bridging functions for matching scales in the Kristianstads Vattenrike Biosphere Reserve Sweden. *Ecology and Society* 12(1), 28. www.ecologyandsociety.org/vol12/iss1/art28/

Olsson, P., C. Folke and T. Hahn 2004b. Social–ecological transformation for ecosystem management: the development of adaptive co-management of a wetland landscape in southern Sweden. *Ecology and Society* 9(4): 2. www.ecologyandsociety.org/vol9/iss4/art2/

Olsson, P., C. Folke and T.P. Hughes 2008. Navigating the transition to ecosystem-based management of the Great Barrier Reef, Australia. *Proceedings of the National Academy of Sciences* 105: 9489–9494.

Ommer, R.E., H. Coward and C.C. Parrish 2008. Knowledge, uncertainty and wisdom. In: *Making and Moving Knowledge* (J.S. Lutz and B. Neis, eds.). McGill-Queen's University Press, Montreal, Canada, pp. 20–41.

Ommer, R.E. and B. Paterson 2014. Conclusions: reframing the possibilities for natural and social science dialogue on the economic history of natural resources. *Ecology and Society* 19(1): 17. http://dx.doi.org/10.5751/ES-05972-190117

Ommer, R.E., R.I. Perry, K. Cochrane and P. Cury, editors 2011. *World Fisheries: A Social–Ecological Analysis*. Wiley-Blackwell, Oxford.

Ommer, R.E. and team 2007. *Coasts under Stress. Restructuring and Social–Ecological Health*. McGill-Queen's University Press, Montreal, Canada.

O'Neil, J., B. Elias and A. Yassi 1997. Poisoned food: cultural resistance to the contaminants discourse. *Arctic Anthropology* 34: 29–40.

Orensanz , J.M., A.M. Parma, G. Jerez et al. 2005. What are the key elements for the sustainability of "S-fisheries"? Insights from South America. *Bulletin of Marine Science* 76: 527–556.

Ostrom, E. 1990. *Governing the Commons. The Evolution of Institutions for Collective Action*. Cambridge University Press, Cambridge, UK.

Ostrom, E. 2000. Collective action and the evolution of social norms. *The Journal of Economic Perspectives* 14: 137–158.

Ostrom, E. 2005. *Understanding Institutional Diversity*. Princeton University Press, Princeton, NJ.

Ostrom, E. 2007. A diagnostic approach for going beyond panaceas. *Proceedings of the National Academy of Sciences* 104: 15181–15187.

Ostrom, E. 2009. A general framework for analyzing sustainability of social–ecological systems. *Science* 325: 419–422.

Ostrom, E. 2010. Beyond markets and states: polycentric governance of complex economic systems. *American Economic Review* 100: 641–672.

Ostrom, E., J. Burger, C.B. Field, R.B. Norgaard and D. Policansky 1999. Revisiting the commons: local lessons, global challenges. *Science* 284: 278–282.

Ostrom, E., T. Dietz, N. Dolsak, P.C. Stern, S. Stonich and E.U. Weber, editors 2002. *The Drama of the Commons*. National Academy Press, Washington, DC.

Oviedo, G. 2006. Community-conserved areas in South America. *Parks* 16: 49–55.

Österblom, H., A. Gardmark, L. Bergström et al. 2010. Making the ecosystem approach operational—can regime shifts in ecological and governance systems facilitate the transition? *Marine Policy* 34: 1290–1299.

Pahl-Wostl, C. 2009. A conceptual framework for analyzing adaptive capacity and multi-level learning processes in resource governance regimes. *Global Environmental Change* 19: 354–365.

Pahl-Wostl, C., M. Craps, A. Dewulf, E.Mostert, D.Tabara and T. Taillieu 2007. Social learning and water resources management. *Ecology and Society* 12(2): 5. www.ecologyandsociety.org/vol12/iss2/art5/

Pahl-Wostl, C. and H. Hare 2004. Process of social learning in integrated resources management. *Journal of Community and Applied Social Psychology* 14: 193–206.

Park, R.E. 1936. Human ecology. *American Journal of Sociology* 42: 1–14.

Pearce, D.W. and A. Markandya 1989. *Environmental Policy Benefits: Monetary Valuation*. OECD, Paris.

Peloquin, C. and F. Berkes 2009. Local knowledge, subsistence harvests, and social–ecological complexity in James Bay. *Human Ecology* 37: 533–545.

Perry, R.I., R.E. Ommer, M. Barange and F. Werner 2010. The challenge of adapting marine social–ecological systems to the additional stress of climate change. *Current Opinion on Environmental Sustainability* 2: 356–363.

Perry, R.I. and U.R. Sumaila 2007. Marine ecosystem variability and human community responses: the example of Ghana, West Africa. *Marine Policy* 31: 125–134.

Phillips, A. 2003. Turning ideas on their head—the new paradigm for protected areas. *The George Wright Forum* 20(2): 8–32.

Pierotti, R. and D. Wildcat 2000. Traditional ecological knowledge: the third alternative. *Ecological Applications* 10: 1333–1340.

Pinkerton, E., editor 1989. *Co-operative Management of Local Fisheries.* University of British Columbia Press, Vancouver, Canada.

Pinkerton, E. 1992. Translating legal rights into management practice: overcoming barriers to the exercise of co-management. *Human Organization* 51: 330–341.

Pinkerton, E. 2003. Toward specificity in complexity: understanding co-management from a social science perspective. In: *The Fisheries Co-management Experience* (C.C. Wilson, J.R. Nielson and P. Degnbol, eds.). Kluwer, Dordrecht, Netherlands, pp. 61–77.

Pinkerton, E. 2007. Integrating holism and segmentalism: overcoming barriers to adaptive co-management between management agencies and multi-sector bodies. In: *Adaptive Co-Management* (D. Armitage, F. Berkes and N. Doubleday, eds.). University of British Columbia Press, Vancouver, Canada, pp. 151–171.

Pinkerton, E. 2009. Partnerships in management. In: *A Fishery Manager's Guidebook.* 2nd edition (K.L. Cochrane and S.M. Garcia, eds.). FAO/Wiley-Blackwell, Chichester, UK, pp. 283–300.

Pinkerton, E. 2013. Alternatives to ITQs in equity–efficiency–effectiveness trade-offs: how the lay-up system spread effort in the BC halibut fishery. *Marine Policy* 42: 5–13.

Pinkerton, E., E. Angel, N. Ladell et al. 2014. Local and regional strategies for rebuilding fisheries management institutions in coastal British Columbia: what components of comanagement are most critical? *Ecology and Society* 19(2): 72. http://dx.doi.org/10.5751/ES-06489–190272

Pinkerton, E. and L. John 2008. Creating local management legitimacy. *Marine Policy* 32: 680–691.

Pitcher, T.J., P.J.B. Hart and D. Pauly, editors 1998. *Reinventing Fisheries Management.* Chapman and Hall Fish and Fisheries Series 23. Kluwer, Dordrecht, Netherlands.

Pitcher, T.J. and M.E. Lam 2010. Fishful thinking: rhetoric, reality, and the sea before us. *Ecology and Society* 15(2): 12. www.ecologyandsociety.org/vol15/iss2/art12/

Plummer, R. 2009. The adaptive co-management process: an initial synthesis of representative models and influential variables. *Ecology and Society* 14(2): 24. www.ecologyandsociety.org/vol14/iss2/art24/

Plummer, R., B. Crona, D.R. Armitage, P. Olsson, M. Tengö and O. Yudina 2012. Adaptive comanagement: a systematic review and analysis. *Ecology and Society* 17(3): 11. http://dx.doi.org/10.5751/ES-04952–170311

Plummer, R. and J. FitzGibbon 2004. Some observations on the terminology in co-operative environmental management. *Journal of Environmental Management* 70: 63–72.

Pollnac, R. and T. Seara 2011. Factors influencing success of marine protected areas in the Visayas, Philippines, as related to increasing protected area coverage. *Environmental Management* 47: 584–592.

Pomeroy, R.S., editor 1994. *Community Management and Common Property of Coastal Fisheries in Asia and the Pacific.* ICLARM Conference Proceedings 45. ICLARM, Manila.

Pomeroy, R.S. and F. Berkes 1997. Two to tango: the role of government in fisheries co-management. *Marine Policy* 21: 465–480.

Pomeroy, R.S., L. Garces, M. Pido and G. Silvestre 2010. Ecosystem-based fisheries management in small-scale tropical marine fisheries: emerging models of governance arrangements in the Philippines. *Marine Policy* 34: 298–308.

Pomeroy, R.S., R.B. Pollnac, B.M. Katon and C.D. Predo 1997. Evaluating factors contributing to the success of community-based coastal resource management: the Central Visayas regional Project-1, Philippines. *Ocean and Coastal Management* 36: 97–120.

Prabhu, R., C. McDougall and R. Fisher 2007. Adaptive collaborative management: a conceptual model. In: *Adaptive Collaborative Management of Community Forests in Asia* (R. Fisher, R. Prabhu and C. McDougall eds.). Center for International Forestry Research, Bogor, Indonesia, pp. 16–49.

Pretty, J., W. Adams, F. Berkes et al. 2009. The intersections of biological diversity and cultural diversity: towards integration. *Conservation & Society* 7(2): 100–112.

Pretty, J. and H. Ward 2001. Social capital and the environment. *World Development* 29: 209–227.

Primavera, J.H. 1997. Socio-economic impacts of shrimp culture. *Aquaculture Research* 28: 815–827.

Primavera, J.H. 2005. Mangroves, fishponds and the quest for sustainability. *Science* 310: 57–59.

Prince, J. 2003. The barefoot ecologist goes fishing. *Fish and Fisheries* 4: 359–371.

Prince, J. 2010. Rescaling fisheries assessment and management: a generic approach, access rights, change agents and toolboxes. *Bulletin of Marine Science* 86: 197–219.

Pritchard, D.W. 1967. What is an estuary: physical viewpoint. In: *Estuaries* (G.H. Lauf, ed.). AAAS Publication 83, Washington, DC, pp. 3–5.

Pullin, R.S.V. 2013. Food security in the context of fisheries and aquaculture—a governability challenge. In: *Governability of Fisheries and Aquaculture* (M. Bavinck, R. Chuenpagdee, S. Jentoft and J. Kooiman, eds.). Springer, Dordrecht, Netherlands, pp. 87–109.

Raemaekers, S., M. Hauck, M. Burgener et al. 2011. Review of the causes of the rise of the illegal South African abalone fishery and consequent closure of the rights-based fishery. *Ocean and Coastal Management* 54: 433–445.

Ravuvu, A.D. 1987. *The Fijian Ethos*. University of the South Pacific, Suva, Fiji.

Reed, M., P. Courtney, J. Urquhart and N. Ross 2013. Beyond fish as commodities: understanding the socio-cultural role of inshore fisheries in England. *Marine Policy* 37: 62–68.

Regier, H.A. and K.H. Loftus 1972. Effects of fisheries exploitation on salmonid communities in oligotrophic lakes. *Journal of the Fisheries Research Board of Canada* 29: 959–968.

Regier, H.A., R.V. Mason and F. Berkes 1989. Reforming the use of natural resources. In: *Common Property Resources* (F. Berkes, ed.). Belhaven, London, pp. 110–126.

Reid, W.V., F. Berkes, T. Wilbanks and D. Capistrano, editors 2006. *Bridging Scales and Knowledge Systems*. Millennium Ecosystem Assessment and Island Press, Washington, DC. www.millenniumassessment.org/en/Bridging.aspx (accessed June 2014).

Resilience Alliance 2010. *Assessing Resilience in Social–Ecological Systems: Workbook for Practitioners* (revised version 2.0). www.resalliance.org/index.php/resilience_assessment (accessed June 2014).

Ribot, J.C. 2002. *Democratic Decentralization of Natural Resources: Institutionalizing Popular Participation*. World Resources Institute, Washington, DC.

Ribot, J.C., A. Agrawal and A.M. Larson 2006. Recentralizing while decentralizing: how national governments reappropriate forest resources. *World Development* 34: 1864–1886.

Riedlinger, D. and F. Berkes 2001. Contributions of traditional knowledge to understanding climate change in the Canadian Arctic. *Polar Record* 37: 315–328.

Rittel, H. and M. Webber 1973. Dilemmas in a general theory of planning. *Policy Sciences* 4: 155–169.

Robards, M.D. and J.A. Greenberg 2007. Global constraints on rural fishing communities: whose resilience is it anyway? *Fish and Fisheries* 8: 14–30.

Robertson, H.A. and T.K. McGee 2003. Applying local knowledge: the contribution of oral history to wetland rehabilitation at Kanyapella Basin, Australia. *Journal of Environmental Management* 69: 275–287.

Robinson, L.W. and F. Berkes 2011. Multi-level participation for building adaptive capacity: formal agency-community interactions in northern Kenya. *Global Environmental Change* 21: 1185–1194.

Rockström, J., W. Steffen, K. Noone et al. 2009. A safe operating space for humanity. *Nature* 461: 472–475.

Roe, D., J. Elliott, C. Sandbrook and M. Walpole, editors 2013. *Biodiversity Conservation and Poverty Alleviation*. Wiley-Blackwell, Oxford, UK.

Roe, D., D. Mayers, M. Grieg-Gran, A. Kothari, C. Fabricius and R. Hughes 2000. *Evaluating Eden: Exploring the Myths and Realities of Community-Based Wildlife Management*. Evaluating Eden Series No. 8, IIED, London.

Rogers, G.W. 1979. Alaska's limited entry program: another view. *Journal of the Fisheries Research Board of Canada* 36: 783–788.

Rosales, H. 2010. The Intertribal Sinkyone Wilderness. Tribes reclaiming, stewarding and restoring ancient lands. *International Journal of Wilderness* 16(1): 8–12.

Rose, D. 2005. An indigenous philosophical ecology: situating the human. *Australian Journal of Anthropology* 16: 294–305.

Ross, H., C. Grant, C.J. Robinson, A. Izurieta, D. Smyth and P. Rist 2009. Co-management and indigenous protected areas in Australia: achievements and ways forward. *Australasian Journal of Environmental Management* 16: 242–252.

Ross, H. and J. Innes 2005. A framework for designing co-operative management of the Great Barrier Reef World Heritage Area. IASCP Conference Paper. Delegación Coyoacán, México.

Rubec, P.J., F. Cruz, V. Pratt, R. Oellers, B. McCullough and F. Lallo. 2001. Cyanide-free net-caught fish for the marine aquarium trade. *Aquarium Science and Conservation* 3: 37–51.

Ruddle, K. and T. Akimichi, editors 1984. *Maritime Institutions in the Western Pacific*. Senri Ethnological Studies 17, National Museum of Ethnology, Osaka, Japan.

Ruddle, K. and R.E. Johannes, editors 1990. *Traditional Marine Resource Management in the Pacific Basin: An Anthology*. UNESCO, Jakarta.

Saenz-Arroyo, A. and Roberts, C.M. 2008. Consilience in fisheries science. *Fish and Fisheries* 9: 316–327.

Salafsky, N. and E. Wollenberg 2000. Linking livelihoods and conservation: a conceptual framework and scale for assessing the integration of human needs and biodiversity. *World Development* 28: 1421–1438.

Salick, J. and N. Ross 2009. Traditional peoples and climate change (Introduction to Special Issue). *Global Environmental Change* 19: 137–139.

Scales, H., A. Balmford, M. Liu, Y. Sadovy and A. Manica 2006. Keeping bandits at bay? *Science* 313: 612–613.

Scheffer, M. 2009. *Critical Transitions in Nature and Society*. Princeton University Press, Princeton, NJ.

Scheffer, M. and S.R. Carpenter 2003. Catastrophic regime shifts in ecosystems: linking theory to observation. *Trends in Ecology and Evolution* 18: 648–656.

Scheffer, M., S.R. Carpenter and B. de Young 2005. Cascading effects of overfishing marine systems. *Trends in Ecology and Evolution* 20: 579–581.

Schlager, E. and E. Ostrom 1992. Property-rights regimes and natural resources: a conceptual analysis. *Land Economics* 68: 249–262.

Schwartzman, S. and B. Zimmerman 2005. Conservation alliances with indigenous peoples of the Amazon. *Conservation Biology* 19: 721–727.

Scott, A.D. 1955. The fishery: the objectives of sole ownership. *Journal of Political Economy* 63: 116–129.

Scott, A. 2012. Commentary. In: *Property in Land and Other Resources* (D.H. Cole and E. Ostrom, eds.). Lincoln Institute of Land Policy, Cambridge, MA, pp. 252–255.

Scott, C. 2014. Proposed Tawich (Marine) Protected Area: an update and prospectus. Paper Presented at the Symposium on Science and Traditional Knowledge in the Eeyou Marine Region, March 2014, Montreal, Canada.

Scott, J. 1998. *Seeing Like a State*. Yale University Press, New Haven, CT.

Seixas, C.S. and F. Berkes 2010. Community-based enterprises: the significance of partnerships and institutional linkages. *International Journal of the Commons* 4: 183–212.

Seixas, C.S. and B. Davy 2008. Self-organization in integrated conservation and development initiatives. *International Journal of the Commons* 2: 99–125.

Sen, A. 1981. *Poverty and Famine: An Essay on Entitlement and Deprivation*. Clarendon Press, Oxford, UK.

Sen, A. 1999. *Development as Freedom*. Random House, New York.

Senyk, J. 2006. Pred Nai community forestry group and mangrove rehabilitation, Thailand. Equator Initiative Technical Report. www.umanitoba.ca/institutes/natural_resources/nri_cbrm_projects_eiprojects.html (accessed June 2014).

Shirk, J.L., H.L. Ballard, C.C. Wilderman et al. 2012. Public participation in scientific research: a framework for deliberate design. *Ecology and Society* 17(2): 29. http://dx.doi.org/10.5751/ES-04705-170229

Shuman, C.S., G. Hodgson and R.F. Ambrose 2004. Managing the marine aquarium trade: is eco-certification the answer? *Environmental Conservation* 31: 339–348.

Sims, L. and A.J. Sinclair 2008. Learning through participatory resource management programs: case studies from Costa Rica. *Adult Education Quarterly* 58: 151–168.

Sinclair, A.J., S.A. Collins and H. Spaling 2011. The role of participant learning in community conservation in the Arabuko-Sokoke forest, Kenya. *Conservation and Society* 9(1): 42–53.

Singleton, S. 1998. *Constructing Cooperation: The Evolution of Institutions of Comanagement.* University of Michigan Press, Ann Arbor, MI.

Singleton, S. and M. Taylor 1992. Common property, collective action and community. *Journal of Theoretical Politics* 4: 309–324.

Smyth, D. 2006. Indigenous protected areas in Australia. *Parks* 16: 14–20.

Sodhi, N.S. and P.R. Ehrlich, editors 2010. *Conservation Biology for All.* Oxford University Press, Oxford and New York. www.conbio.org/images/content_publications/ConservationBiologyforAll_reducedsize.pdf (accessed June 2014).

Sowman, M. 2009. An evolving partnership: collaboration between university "experts" and net-fishers. *Gateways: International Journal of Community Research and Engagement* 2: 119–143.

Sowman, M. 2011. New perspectives in small-scale fisheries management: challenges and prospects for implementation in South Africa. *African Journal of Marine Science* 33: 297–311.

Sowman, M. and P. Cardoso 2010. Small-scale fisheries and food security strategies in countries in the Benguela Current Large Marine Ecosystem (BCLME) region: Angola, Namibia and South Africa. *Marine Policy* 34: 1163–1170.

Steneck, R.S., T.P. Hughes, J.E. Cinner et al. 2011. Creation of a gilded trap by the high economic value of the Maine lobster fishery. *Conservation Biology* 25: 904–912.

Stephenson, J. and H. Moller 2009. Cross-cultural environmental research and management: challenges and progress. *Journal of the Royal Society of New Zealand* 39: 139–149.

Stephenson, J., F. Berkes, N.J. Turner and J. Dick 2014. Biocultural conservation of marine ecosystems: examples from New Zealand and Canada. *Indian Journal of Traditional Knowledge* 13: 257–265.

Stern, P. 2005. Deliberative methods for understanding environmental systems. *BioScience* 55: 976–982.

Steward, J.H. 1955. *Theory of Culture Change.* University of Illinois Press, Urbana, IL.

St. Martin, K. and M. Hall-Arber 2008. Creating a place for "community" in New England fisheries. *Human Ecology Review* 15: 161–170.

Sultana, P. and P. Thompson 2007. Use of fishers' knowledge in community management of fisheries in Bangladesh. In: *Fishers' Knowledge in Fisheries Science and Management* (N. Haggan, B. Neis and I.G. Baird, eds.). UNESCO, Paris, pp. 267–287.

Sumaila, U.R. 2010. A cautionary note on individual transferable quotas. *Ecology and Society* 15(3): 36. www.ecologyandsociety.org/vol15/iss3/art36/

Swezey, S.L. and R.F. Heizer 1977. Ritual management of salmonid fish resources in California. *Journal of California Anthropology* 4: 6–29.

TBTI 2014. Too Big to Ignore. Global Partnership for Small-scale Fisheries Research. http://toobigtoignore.net/ (accessed June 2014).

Taiepa, T., P. Lyver, P. Horsley, J. Davis, M. Bragg and H. Moller 1997. Co-management of New Zealand's conservation estate by Māori and Pakeha: a review. *Environmental Conservation* 24: 236–250.

Takahashi, S., B.J. McCay and O. Baba 2006. The good, the bad, or the ugly? Advantages and challenges of Japanese costal fisheries management. *Bulletin of Marine Science* 78: 575–591.

Takeuchi, K. 2013. Integrating local and indigenous knowledge (LINK) in scientific assessments in IPBES. Workshop on the Contribution of Indigenous and Local Knowledge Systems to IPBES, United Nations University, Tokyo.

Tengö, M., E.S. Brondizio, T. Elmqvist, P. Malmer and M. Spierenburg 2014. Connecting diverse knowledge systems for enhanced ecosystem governance: the multiple evidence base approach. *Ambio.* DOI 10.1007/s13280–014–0501–3

Trimble, M. and F. Berkes 2013. Participatory research towards co-management: lessons from artisanal fisheries in coastal Uruguay. *Journal of Environmental Management* 128: 768–778.

Turner, B.L. II, R.E. Kasperson, P.A. Matson et al. 2003. A framework for vulnerability analysis in sustainability science. *Proceedings of the National Academy of Sciences of the United States* 100: 8074–8079.

Turner, K.L., F. Berkes and N.J. Turner 2012. Indigenous perspectives on ecotourism development: a British Columbia case study. *Journal of Enterprising Communities* 6: 213–229.

Turner, K.L. and C.P.H. Bitonti 2011. Conservancies in British Columbia, Canada: bringing together protected areas and First Nations' interest. *International Indigenous Policy Journal* 2(2). http://ir.lib.uwo.ca/iipj/vol2/iss2/3 (accessed June 2014).

Turner, N.J. 2005. *The Earth's Blanket. Traditional Teachings for Sustainable Living.* Douglas and McIntyre, Vancouver, Canada, and University of Washington Press, Seattle, WA.

Turner, N.J. 2014. *Ancient Pathways, Ancestral Knowledge: Ethnobotany and Ecological Wisdom of Indigenous Peoples of Northwestern North America.* McGill-Queen's University Press, Montreal, Canada.

Turner, N.J. and F. Berkes 2006. Coming to understanding: developing conservation through incremental learning in the Pacific Northwest. *Human Ecology* 34: 495–513.

Turner, N.J., F. Berkes, J. Stephenson and J. Dick 2013a. Blundering intruders: extraneous impacts on two indigenous food systems. *Human Ecology* 41: 563–574.

Turner, N.J., K. Recalma-Clutesi and D. Deur 2013b. Back to the clam gardens. www.ecotrust.org/indigenousaffairs/Back-to-the-Clam-Gardens.pdf (accessed June 2014).

UN 2008. What Is Good Governance? United Nations ESCAP. www.unescap.org/pdd/prs/ProjectActivities/Ongoing/gg/governance.asp (accessed June 2014).

UN 2014. We Can End Poverty. Millennium Development Goals and beyond 2015. www.un.org/millenniumgoals/ (accessed June 2014).

UNESCO 2013. The Contribution of Indigenous and Local Knowledge Systems to IPBES: Building Synergies with Science. IPBES Expert Meeting Report, June 2013, Tokyo. www.unesco.org/links (accessed June 2014).

UNESCO 2014. World Heritage listing for Papahānaumokuākea. http://whc.unesco.org/en/list/1326 (accessed June 2014).

US Army Corps of Engineers 2014. Seminole Big Cypress Reservation Water Conservation Plan. www.saj.usace.army.mil/Portals/44/docs/FactSheets/Seminole BigCypress_FS_February2014.pdf (accessed June 2014).

Walker, B., C.S. Holling, S.R. Carpenter and A. Kinzig 2004. Resilience, adaptability and transformability in social–ecological systems. *Ecology and Society* 9(2): 5. www.ecologyandsociety.org/vol9/iss2/art5/

Walker, B. and J.A. Meyers 2004. Thresholds in ecological and social–ecological systems: a developing database. *Ecology and Society* 9(2): 3. www.ecologyandsociety.org/vol9/iss2/art3/

Walker, J. and M. Cooper 2011. Genealogies of resilience: from systems ecology to political economy of crisis adaptation. *Security Dialogue* 42: 143–160.

Walters, C. 1986. *Adaptive Management of Renewable Resources*. MacMillan, New York.

Walters, C.J. 2007. Is adaptive management helping to solve fisheries problems? *Ambio* 36: 304–307.

Warren, D.M., L.J. Slikkerveer and D. Brokensha, editors 1995. *The Cultural Dimension of Development: Indigenous Knowledge Systems*. Intermediate Technology Publications, London.

Washington Tribes 2014. www.washingtontribes.org/default.aspx (accessed June 2014).

Watanabe, H. 1973. *The Ainu Ecosystem, Environment and Group Structure*. University of Washington Press, Seattle, WA.

Wehi, P.M. 2009. Indigenous ancestral sayings contribute to modern conservation partnerships: examples using *Phormium tenax*. *Ecological Applications* 19: 267–275.

Wehi, P., M. Cox, T. Roa and H. Whaanga 2013. Marine resources in Maori oral tradition: *he kai moana, he kai ma te hinengaro*. *Journal of Marine and Island Cultures* 2: 59–68.

Wenger, E. 1998. *Communities of Practice: Learning, Meaning and Identity*. Cambridge University Press, Cambridge, UK.

Westaway, E., J. Seeley and E. Allison 2007. Feckless and reckless or forbearing and resourceful? Looking behind the stereotypes of HIV and AIDS in "fishing communities." *African Affairs* 106: 663–679.

Western, D. and R. M.Wright, editors 1994. *Natural Connections*. Island Press, Washington, DC.

WFFP–WFF 2013. A call for governments to stop supporting the Global Partnership for Oceans (GPO) and rights-based fishing (RBF) reforms. The World Forum of Fisher Peoples and the World Forum of Fish Harvesters and Fish Workers. http://masifundise.org.za/wp-content/uploads/2013/03/WFFP-WFF-Call-on-Governments_GPO_200313.pdf (accessed June 2014).

White, A.T., C.A. Courtney and A. Salamanca 2002. Experience with marine protected area planning and management in the Philippines. *Coastal Management* 30: 1–26.

Wiber, M., F. Berkes, A. Charles and J. Kearney 2004. Participatory research supporting community-based fishery management. *Marine Policy* 28: 459–468.

Wiber, M., A. Charles, J. Kearney and F. Berkes 2009. Enhancing community empowerment through participatory fisheries research. *Marine Policy* 33: 172–179.

Williams, N.M. and E.S. Hunn, editors 1982. *Resource Managers: North American and Australian Hunter-Gatherers*. American Association for the Advancement of Science, Washington, DC.

Wilson, D.C., M. Ahmed, S.V. Siar and U. Kanagaratnam 2006. Cross-scale linkages and adaptive management: fisheries co-management in Asia. *Marine Policy* 30: 523–533.

Wilson, D.C., J.R. Nielson and P. Degnbol, editors 2003. *The Fisheries Co-management Experience*. Kluwer, Dordrecht, Netherlands.

Wilson, G. 2012. *Community Resilience and Environmental Transitions*. Earthscan, Oxford, UK.

Wilson, J.A. 2006. Matching social and ecological systems in complex ocean fisheries. *Ecology and Society* 11(1): 9. www.ecologyandsociety.org/vol11/iss1/art9/

Wilson, J.A., J.M. Acheson, M. Metcalfe and P. Kleban 1994. Chaos, complexity and communal management of fisheries. *Marine Policy* 18: 291–305.

Wollenberg, E., R. Iwan, G. Limberg et al. 2007. Facilitating cooperation during times of chaos: spontaneous orders and muddling through in Malinau District, Indonesia. *Ecology and Society* 12(1): 3. www.ecologyandsociety.org/vol12/iss1/art3/

Worm, B., E.B. Barbier, N. Beaumont et al. 2006. Impacts of biodiversity loss on ocean ecosystem services. *Science* 314: 787–790.

Worster, D. 1977. *Nature's Economy: A History of Ecological Ideas*. Cambridge University Press, Cambridge, UK.

Worster, D., editor 1988. *The Ends of the Earth: Perspectives on Modern Environmental History*. Cambridge University Press, Cambridge, UK.

WRI 2005. *World Resources 2005. The Wealth of the Poor—Managing Ecosystems to Fight Poverty*. World Resources Institute, Washington, DC.

Yanagi, T. 2008. "Sato-umi"—a new concept for sustainable fisheries. In: *Fisheries for Global Welfare and Environment*. 5th World Fisheries Congress. Terrapub, pp. 351–358.

Young, O.R. 2002. *The Institutional Dimensions of Environmental Change: Fit, Interplay, and Scale*. MIT Press, Cambridge, MA.

Young, O.R., F. Berkhout, G.C. Gallopin et al. 2006. The globalization of socio-ecological systems: an agenda for scientific research. *Global Environmental Change* 16: 304–316.

Young, O.R., L.A. King and H. Schroeder, editors 2008. *Institutions and Environmental Change*. MIT Press, Cambridge, MA, and London.

Yuerlita, S.R. Perret and G.P. Shivakoti 2013. Fishing farmers or farming fishers? *Environmental Management* 52: 85–98.

Zadeh, L.A. 1973. Outline of a new approach to the analysis of complex systems and decision process. *Transactions on Systems, Man and Cybernetics* SMC-3: 28–44.

Zimmerman, E.W. 1951. *World Resources and Industries* (first published in 1933). Harper, New York.

Zurba, M. and F. Berkes 2014. Caring for country through participatory art: creating a boundary object for communicating indigenous knowledge and values. *Local Environment* 19: 821–836.

APPENDIX
WEB LINKS AND TEACHING TIPS

Chapter 1: Introduction: The Ongoing Agenda

The chapter provides a web-based background to concepts, definitions, and institutions/organizations involved in marine and coastal resource management in the US and around the world. It will focus on the people, organizations, and institutions that have played key roles in developing the concepts, theories, and practices of ocean and marine resource management.

- **Encyclopedia of the Earth: Definitions Ecology Theory—Coastal Zone:**
  www.eoearth.org/view/article/151298
  This site contains definitions and information on defining the coastal zone. The continental shelf, continental margin, coastal ocean and coastal zone are fuzzy concepts for which various definitions have been proposed.

- **UN Global Issues—Oceans and Law of the Sea:**
  www.un.org/en/globalissues/oceans/links.shtml
  A website for UN and related bodies dealing with oceans and coasts.

- **UN Sustainable Development Knowledge Platform:**
  http://sustainabledevelopment.un.org/index.php?menu=1680
  Eighth session of the Open Working Group on Sustainable Development Goals—Oceans, Seas Forests, Biodiversity.

- **Ocean and Seas:**
  http://sustainabledevelopment.un.org/index.php?menu=232

- **Issues Brief 4—Oceans:**
  http://sustainabledevelopment.un.org/index.php?page=view&type=400&nr=325&menu=35
  This brief is aimed at providing an overview of international commitments, implementation successes, remaining gaps, challenges, and emerging issues.

- **Global Economic Forum:**
  www.weforum.org/content/global-agenda-council-oceans-2012–2014
  Global Agenda Council on Oceans 2012–2014.

- **FAO: UN Atlas of the Oceans:**
  www.fao.org/fishery/topic/14838/en
  An excellent resource for all issues pertaining to the use of ocean resources. The UN Atlas of the Oceans is an Internet portal developed jointly by the UN agencies responsible for matters relevant to the sustainable development of the oceans and the advancement of ocean science.

- **FAO at Rio+20—Oceans:**
  www.fao.org/rioplus20/77633/en
  Online FAO documents regarding ocean issues from the Rio+20 conference.

- **FAO State of the World's Fisheries and Aquaculture:**
  www.fao.org/fishery/sofia/en
  Homepage for the report produced every 2 years by FAO.

- **World Ocean Review:**
  http://worldoceanreview.com/en/wor-2
  A website dedicated to covering issues of resource management in the seas via two extensive overviews.

- **European Commission-Fisheries:**
  http://ec.europa.eu/fisheries/index_en.htm

- **Reforming the Common Fisheries Program (EC):**
  http://ec.europa.eu/fisheries/reform/index_en.htm

- **MarBEF Marine Biodiversity Wiki:**
  www.marbef.org/wiki/The_Integrated_approach_to_Coastal_Zone_Management_(ICZM)
  A portal for marine biodiversity issues and information for an integrated approach to coastal zone management (EU).

- **The White House Draft National Ocean Policy:**
  www.whitehouse.gov/sites/default/files/microsites/ceq/national_ocean_policy_draft_implementation_plan_01–12–12.pdf

- **White House Council on Environmental Quality:**
  www.whitehouse.gov/administration/eop/ceq/initiatives/oceans
  Final recommendations of the Interagency Ocean Policy Task Force.

- **U.S. Commission on Ocean Policy:**
  http://govinfo.library.unt.edu/oceancommission/welcome.html

- **Living near and making a living from the nation's coasts and oceans Appendix C:**
  http://govinfo.library.unt.edu/oceancommission/documents/prelimreport/append_c.pdf

- **Joint Ocean Commission Initiative:**
  www.jointoceancommission.org/rc-reports.html
  Securing America's ocean future.

- **Environmental Protection Agency (USA), Coastal Zone Management Act (CZMA):**
  www.epa.gov/oecaagct/lzma.html

- **Center for Coastal Monitoring and Assessment:**
  http://ccma.nos.noaa.gov

- **Ocean Exploration 2020:**
  http://oceanexplorer.noaa.gov/oceanexploration2020/welcome.html

- **Magnuson–Stevens Fishery Conservation and Management Act (1976):**
  www.nmfs.noaa.gov/msa2005
  Key piece of legislation for management of coastal fisheries and environments.

- The M-S FCM Act:
  www.nmfs.noaa.gov/sfa/magact
  The actual, legal text.

- National Marine Fisheries Service, NMFS NOAA:
  www.nmfs.noaa.gov

- U.S. Department of State, Ocean and Polar Affairs:
  www.state.gov/e/oes/ocns/opa

- U.S. Regional Fisheries Management Councils:
  www.fisherycouncils.org

- U.S. Deparment of Defense, climate change and impacts of sea level rise:
  www.serdp.org/Featured-Initiatives/Climate-Change-and-Impacts-of-Sea-Level-Rise

- Florida Ocean Alliance:
  www.floridaoceanalliance.org

- Paul G. Allen Foundation:
  www.pgafamilyfoundation.org/oceanchallenge
  Ocean challenge—mitigating acidification impacts.

- Sea Around Us Project, EEZ—analyses and visualization:
  www.seaaroundus.org/eez

- National Geographic, The Ocean:
  http://ocean.nationalgeographic.com/ocean

- Sustainable Ocean Summit:
  www.oceancouncil.org/site/summit_2013

- Blue Ocean Institute:
  http://blueocean.org/programs

- MarineBio Conservation Society:
  http://marinebio.org

- Dumping:
  http://marinebio.org/oceans/ocean-dumping.asp

- **World Ocean Observatory:**
  www.worldoceanobservatory.org

- **Millennium Assessment:**
  www.worldoceanobservatory.com/content/millennium-ecosystem-assessment

- **Center for the Blue Economy, Monterey Institute of International Studies, Ocean and Coastal Resource Management:**
  www.miis.edu/academics/researchcenters/blue-economy/academics/ocean-management

- **The Coastal Society:**
  www.thecoastalsociety.org

- **Compass:**
  www.compassonline.org/about

- **Oceans:**
  www.compassonline.org/search/node/Oceans

- **Ocean Health Index:**
  www.oceanhealthindex.org

- **Supplemental material and comments:**
  www.nature.com/nature/journal/v488/n7413/full/nature11397.html#supplementary-information

- **Global Oceans:**
  http://global-oceans.org/site

  Science support for ocean research.

- **10 Proposals for the Oceans (UNESCO):**
  www.unesco.org/new/en/natural-sciences/ioc-oceans/priority-areas/rio-20-ocean/10-proposals-for-the-ocean

- **Global Ocean Commission:**
  www.globaloceancommission.org
  The Global Ocean Commission originated as an initiative of the Pew Charitable Trusts, in partnership with Somerville College, University of Oxford, Adessium Foundation, and Oceans 5.

- **Ocean Literacy Framework:**
  http://oceanliteracy.wp2.coexploration.org/ocean-literacy-framework
  Ocean literacy is defined as an understanding of the ocean's influence
  on you and your influence on the ocean.

- **International Waters Learning Exchange and Resource Network:**
  http://iwlearn.net

- **Project Seahorse—Community-Based MPA:**
  http://seahorse.fisheries.ubc.ca/marine-protected-areas

- **ROLE [rivers, oceans, lands, education] Foundation—CB MPA:**
  www.rolefoundation.org/community-based-marine-protected-areas

- **MARINET:**
  www.marinet.org.uk
  The voluntary network of Friends of the Earth local groups tasked
  with managing marine conservation issues.

- **Environmental Evaluation Unit University of Cape Town, Coastal
  and Fisheries Governance:**
  www.eeu.org.za/thematic-areas/coastal-and-fisheries-governance

- **Stockholm Environment Institute, Valuing the Ocean:**
  www.sei-international.org/publications?pid=2064
  This study, the work of an international, multidisciplinary team of
  experts coordinated by SEI, will be published to inform preparations
  for the Rio+20 Earth Summit.

- **Managing Ocean Environments:**
  www.sei-international.org/publications?pid=2422

- **Costing Climate Impacts and Adaptation:**
  www.sei-international.org/publications?pid=1960
  A Canadian study on coastal zones.

- **Philippine Integrated Coastal Management:**
  www.sei-international.org/publications?pid=1861
  The need for improved accountability and local ownership.

- **Education: How to Become a Natural Resource Manager:**
  www.academicinvest.com/science-careers/environmental-science-
  careers/how-to-become-a-natural-resources-manager

- **Career Portal: Natural Resource Manager:**
  http://education-portal.com/articles/Natural_Resource_Manager_Career_Summary.html

---

EXERCISE

- List some of the key global and US-based organizations involved in oceans and coastal issues. Describe any key interorganizational linkages fostering International—U.S. commitments to sustainable ocean development.

Chapter 2: Natural Resources and Management: Emerging Views

Web links for this chapter help set the stage by describing the historical development of conventional natural resources management and begin to describe the "end of management," the shortcomings of these approaches, and the redefining of how resources can be better managed within a more complex social–political context. Wikipedia is useful for some of the technical terms, but care should be taken to look up other sources as well.

- **Interdisciplinary Science Reviews:**
  http://isr-journal.blogspot.ca

- **Worster, Historians and Nature:**
  http://theamericanscholar.org/historians-and-nature/#.U9-2S2NeL5M

- **What is environmental history?**
  www.cnr.berkeley.edu/departments/espm/env-hist/studyguide/chap1.htm

- **Environmental history timeline:**
  www.environmentalhistory.org

- **Holling and Meffe, The pathology of natural resource management:**
  www.ecology.ethz.ch/education/Ecosystem_Files/Holling_and_Meffe__1996__Pathology_of_Natural_Resource_Management.pdf

- **Age of Enlightenment:**
  http://en.wikipedia.org/wiki/Age_of_Enlightenment

- Maximum sustainable yield (MSY):
  http://en.wikipedia.org/wiki/Maximum_sustainable_yield

- Sustainable yield in fisheries:
  http://en.wikipedia.org/wiki/Sustainable_yield_in_fisheries

- W. Cronon, *Changes in the Land*, 1983:
  http://en.wikipedia.org/wiki/Changes_in_the_Land:_Indians,_
  Colonists,_and_the_Ecology_of_New_England

- Gifford Pinchot:
  http://en.wikipedia.org/wiki/Gifford_Pinchot

- Gesellschaft and Gemeinschaft:
  http://en.wikipedia.org/wiki/Gemeinschaft_and_Gesellschaft

- Cod fisheries:
  http://en.wikipedia.org/wiki/Cod_fisheries

- B.J. McCay and C. Finlayson: The Political Ecology of Crisis—
  Case of Northern Cod, 1995:
  http://arcticcircle.uconn.edu/NatResources/cod/mckay.html

- CBC: Remembering the Mighty Cod—20 years after the
  Moratorium:
  www.cbc.ca/news/canada/remembering-the-mighty-cod-fishery-
  20-years-after-moratorium-1.1214172

- Boldt Decision, 1975 upheld:
  Boldt Decision (legal doc), Center for Columbia River History:
  www.ccrh.org/comm/river/legal/boldt.htm

- The Encyclopedia of Puget Sound:
  www.eopugetsound.org/content/selected-papers
  A collection of online papers relating to the community and ecology
  of Puget Sound.

- M. Bavinck, MARE Centre, University of Amsterdam:
  www.marecentre.nl/organisation/bavinck.html

- D. Armitage and ECGG Waterloo, Environmental Change and
  Governance Group:
  http://ecgg.uwaterloo.ca

- **U.S. Department of the Interior: What is Adaptive Management?**
  www.doi.gov/initiatives/AdaptiveManagement/TechGuide/
  Chapter1.pdf

- **DoI Adaptive Management Working Group—Applications Guide:**
  www.usgs.gov/sdc/doc/DOI-Adaptive-Management-Applications-
  Guide-27.pdf

EXERCISE

- The collapse of the northern cod stocks off Newfoundland is said to be one of the greatest human-made resource management disasters. How did this happen? How was this collapse related to the five assumptions related to shifting perspectives on the environmental philosophy of resource management?

Chapter 3: Social–Ecological Systems

Chapter 3 looks at the emerging concept of linked social–ecological systems as a new paradigm in which to observe, study, and manage human–nature systems. The SES framework is used to look at the multiple linkages that make up the interacting and mutually dependent social and ecological components of marine and coastal systems.

- **GLOBEC: Global Ecosystem Ocean Dynamics:**
  www.globec.org

- **Ian R. Perry: Adapting Marine SES to a World of Change—GLOBEC Experience:**
  www.pices.int/publications/presentations/2010-Climate-Change/
  C1/C1–6210-Perry.pdf

- **Model Scenarios for Marine Social Ecological Systems:**
  www.stockholmresilience.org/21/research/research-news/
  10-24-2013-model-behaviour.html

- **Henrik Osterblom, Stockholm Resilience Centre: Marine Social Ecological Systems—Whiteboard Session:**
  www.youtube.com/watch?v=37EznBl5WrU

- Ecosystem-Based Management Scientific Consensus Statement for the Oceans:
  www.compassonline.org/science/EBM_CMSP/EBMconsensus
  Comprehensive ecosystem-based management (EBM) was called for by both U.S. ocean commissions.

- The Top 10 Publications on EBM (as listed by T. Agardy):
  http://openchannels.org/literature-library-top-lists/top-10-publications-ecosystem-based-management

- Millennium Ecosystem Assessment (MEA):
  www.maweb.org/en/condition.aspx
  Current state and trends, marine and coastal systems.

- Acadja:
  www.ajol.info/index.php/jasr/article/view/2882
  Community-based fishing.

- Marova Puava Wiki:
  http://en.marovo.org/index.php?title=About

- Northern Highland Lakes District, Wisconsin:
  http://lter.limnology.wisc.edu/nhld

- Pokkali Rice Farming:
  www.youtube.com/watch?v=q6fArQJSp_E

- Penaeids: South Pacific Commission Aquaculture Portal:
  www.spc.int/aquaculture/index.php?option=com_commodities
  &view=commodity&id=16

- Oceans, drivers of change:
  www.driversofchange.com/oceans

- Global Policy Forum—Globalization:
  www.globalpolicy.org/globalization.html

- SUNY Levin Institute, Globalization 101:
  www.globalization101.org

- International Forum on Globalization:
  http://ifg.org

- **Aquaculture—The Benefits of Aquaculture:**
  http://fishery.about.com/od/BenefitsofAquaculture/a/Aquaculture
  Benefits.htm

- **9 Things Everyone Should Know About Farmed Fish:**
  www.mindbodygreen.com/0–11561/9-things-everyone-should-
  know-about-farmed-fish.html

- **Farmed vs Wild Salmon:**
  www.davidsuzuki.org/publications/resources/2010/think-twice-
  about-eating-farmed-salmon

- **Jurgenne Primavera, mangrove expert and aquaculture critic:**
  www.femalenetwork.com/news-features/dr-jurgenne-honculada
  primavera-environmental-champion-and-heroine
  - https://personalmemoir.wordpress.com/tag/dr-jurgenne-h-
    primavera
  - www.youtube.com/watch?v=A3dI4_xw4aE

- **Bristol Bay salmon fishery:**
  www.worldfishing.net/news101/industry-news/bristol-bay-
  commends-epa-proposal
  - www.alaskajournal.com/Alaska-Journal-of-Commerce/July-
    Issue-4–2014/FISH-FACTOR-Bristol-Bay-sockeye-salmon-
    run-strong-but-prices-arent
  - www.thearcticsounder.com/article/1430bristol_bay_sockeye_
    run_tops_records

- **Fishmeal:**
  www.iffo.net/benefits-fishmeal-and-fish-oil-use
  - www.worldwildlife.org/industries/fishmeal-and-fish-oil

- **Bycatch Reduction Techniques Database:**
  www.bycatch.org

- **FAO Code of Conduct for Responsible Fishing (CCRF):**
  www.fao.org/fishery/code/en

- **UNDP MDGs: Water and Ocean Governance:**
  www.undp.org/content/undp/en/home/ourwork/environment
  andenergy/focus_areas/water_and_ocean_governance.html

- International Institute for Sustainable Development, MDG web sites:
  www.iisd.ca/process/weblinks.htm

- Committee on World Food Security, High Level Panel of Experts (HLPE):
  www.fao.org/cfs/cfs-hlpe/en

EXERCISE

- Table 3.2 lists some examples of drivers of change related to globalization. Can you think of others? Make up your own list.
- Some critics say that the "ecological" ends up being downplayed in the paradigm of the SES as the unit of analysis. Discuss.
- What are the pros and cons of the rapid growth of aquaculture?
- Look up fish farming, aquaculture, and mariculture. Check the sources or sponsors of the web sites. What are the points of agreement and points of disagreement?

Chapter 4: Resilience: Health of Social–Ecological Systems

This chapter describes the history, content and application of resilience theory. Examples are provided of resilience concepts and dynamics from U.S. and other coastal systems in which human impacts are having lasting effects on resource use and sustainability. The chapter begins to answer the question, how do we manage for resilience?

- **Sand County Foundation:**
  http://sandcounty.net

- **Resilience Alliance:**
  www.resalliance.org

- **Resilience Alliance, key concepts:**
  www.resalliance.org/index.php/key_concepts

- **Resilience heuristics:**
  Walker et al. *Ecology and Society* 11(1): 13 [online]:
  www.ecologyandsociety.org/vol11/iss1/art13

- **Resilience: Building Resilient Communities (US)**:
  www.resilience.org

- **The Sustainable Scale Project: Panarchy**:
  www.sustainablescale.org/ConceptualFramework/Understanding
  Scale/MeasuringScale/Panarchy.aspx

- **Pulicat's Padu System**:
  http://community.icsf.net/en/yemaya/detail/EN/1825-Asia-/-India.
  html?detpag=mapart

- **Gulf of Maine Lobster Foundation**:
  www.gomlf.org

- **Gulf of Maine Research Institute**: lobsters:
  www.gma.org/lobsters

- **Gulf of Maine Lobster**:
  www.pressherald.com/2012/11/29/states-lobster-explosion-an-
  economic-boon-biodiversity-bust_2012–11–29

- **Caught in a Gilded Trap: Lobsters and the Gulf of Maine**:
  www.stockholmresilience.org/21/research/research-news/9–30–
  2011-caught-in-a-gilded-trap.html

- *NY Times*: **Lobsters find Utopia where Biologists see Trouble**:
  www.nytimes.com/2011/08/23/science/23lobster.html?_r=0

- **Lobster v-notch**:
  www.eregulations.com/massachusetts/fishing/saltwater/v-notching-
  regulations

- **Resilience + The Beach (Rutgers, New Jersey): Coastal Typologies
  of the Jersey Shore**:
  www.rebuildbydesign.org/project/sasaki-project

- **Coastal Resilience**:
  www.coastalresilience.org

- **Clear Village—Resilient Islands Initiative**:
  www.clear-village.org/projects/galapagos

- **Coastal Resilience Decision-Support Framework**:
  www.csc.noaa.gov/digitalcoast/tools/coastalresilience

- Social Learning and NRM: R. Rodela:
  www.ecologyandsociety.org/vol16/iss4/art30

- BC Ministry of Forests and Range: Defining Adaptive
  Management:
  www.for.gov.bc.ca/hfp/amhome/Admin/index.htm

- National Climate Change Adaptation Research Facility
  (NCCARF) Australia:
  www.nccarf.edu.au

- Adaptation Research Network—Marine Biodiversity and
  Resources:
  http://arnmbr.org/content/index.php/site/aboutus

- Climate Adaptation Knowledge Exchange (CAKE) Coastal
  Resilience, Long Island Sound:
  www.cakex.org/case-studies/2778

- Surging Seas: Plans, Actions Resources, Preparing for Sea level
  Rise, Coastal USA:
  http://sealevel.climatecentral.org/responses/plans

EXERCISE

- Explore different kinds of resilience and provide relevant examples of feedbacks
  in aquatic systems leading to the building or weakening of resilience in coastal
  SES.

- Gulf of Maine: What are the different possible states of the social–ecological
  system? Can human intervention cause a transformation from one state to
  another? What considerations might go into a decision to favor one state over
  another?

Chapter 5: Can Commons be Managed?

Chapter 5 shows that many of the marine and coastal resource issues we
face are commons problems, and that, in many cases, the "tragedy" can
be averted by various governance and management approaches. Web sites
cover commons theory, approaches, and case studies.

- **Elinor Ostrom: Defender of the Commons:**
  www.economist.com/node/21557717

- **E. Ostrom, Collective Action and The Commons: What have we Learned?** (September 17, 2009):
  www.cornell.edu/video/elinor-ostrom-collective-action-and-the-commons

- **No Panaceas! Elinor Ostrom Talks with Fran Korten:**
  www.shareable.net/blog/no-panaceas-elinor-ostrom-talks-with-fran-korten

- **International Association for the Study of the Commons (IASC):**
  www.iasc-commons.org
  The leading professional associating dealing with the commons.

- **IASC: Digital resources:**
  www.iasc-commons.org/library-resources

- **Environmental Justice Organizations Liabilities and Trade. Mapping Environmental Justice (EU): Common Pool Resources:**
  www.ejolt.org/2013/02/common-pool-resources

- **Intergovernmental Platform on Biodiversity Ecosystem Services (IPBES):**
  www.ipbes.net

- **University of Illinois: Introduction to Property Rights:**
  http://urbanext.illinois.edu/lcr/propertyrights.cfm

- **Property Rights and Environment Research Center (PERC): Helping Property Rights Evolve in Marine Fisheries:**
  http://perc.org/articles/helping-property-rights-evolve-marine-fisheries

- **The International Commission for the Conservation of Atlantic Tunas (ICCAT):**
  www.iccat.es/en
  An intergovernmental fishery organization responsible for the conservation of tunas and tuna-like species in the Atlantic Ocean and its adjacent seas.

- Fisheries and Oceans Canada: Snow Crab:
  www.dfo-mpo.gc.ca/fm-gp/sustainable-durable/fisheries-peches/
  snow-crab-eng.htm

- Sea Choice: Snow Crab Fishery:
  www.seachoice.org/fish/snow-crab

- Institutional Capacity Building Framework:
  http://afrosai-e.org.za/institutional-capacity-building-framework

- ARC Centre of Excellence: Coral Reef Studies:
  www.coralcoe.org.au

- Subsidiarity: From Maastricht to Lisbon:
  www.iasc-commons.org/library-resources

- Institutional Capacity Building: Coastal Wiki:
  www.coastalwiki.org/wiki/Institutional_Capacity_Building

- UN—LOS: Capacity-building links:
  www.un.org/depts/los/Links/Capacity-links.htm

- Capacity Building: Global Ocean Forum:
  http://globaloceanforum.com/areas-of-focus/capacity-development

- Institutions for Collective Action: Common Rules:
  www.collective-action.info/_PRO_NWO_CommonRules_Main

- National Geographic: Roving Bandits Depleting Fisheries.
  Experts say.
  http://news.nationalgeographic.com/news/2006/03/0316_060316_
  ocean_bandits.html

- WWF: Building a Sustainable Live Reef Fish Trade:
  wwf.panda.org/what_we_do/where_we_work/coraltriangle/solutions/
  live_reef_fish_trade

- WWF: Coral Triangle and the Live Reef Food Fish Trade:
  wwf.org.hk/en/whatwedo/footprint/seafood/ctni

- Bandits and "Fishing Down the Price List":
  http://scienceline.org/2010/11/fishing-%E2%80%9Cdown-the-
  pricelist%E2%80%9D-threatens-ocean-ecosystems

- Reef2Rainforest: Aquarium Trade Provides Incentives to Protect Wild Reefs:
www.reef2rainforest.com/2012/12/11/aquarium-trade-provides-incentives-to-protect-wild-reefs

---

EXERCISE

- Detail the concept of "roving bandits" and how they impact commons. Give an example from your area, along with possible governance solutions.

Chapter 6: Co-management: Searching for Multilevel Solutions

Web sites for this chapter provide additional information on the theory, applications, actors and organizations involved with developing co-management as a potentially valuable approach. Co-management is also a way of getting people and communities involved in their resource management process.

- University of Washington: Co-management holds promise of Sustainable Fisheries Worldwide 2011:
www.washington.edu/news/2011/01/05/co-management-holds-promise-of-sustainable-fisheries-worldwide

- Community-based management and co-management, OMRN workshop backgrounders:
www.maritimeawards.ca/OMRN/pinkerton.html

- NOAA: Co-Management of Marine Mammals in Alaska:
http://alaskafisheries.noaa.gov/protectedresources/comanagement.htm

- IDRC: Practical Fishery Co-Management:
www.idrc.ca/EN/Resources/Publications/Pages/IDRCBookDetails.aspx?PublicationID=185

- Adaptive Co-Management:
www.resalliance.org/index.php/adaptive_comanagement

- Polycentric governance:
www.press.umich.edu/16055/polycentric_governance_and_development

- Polycentric approach for climate change:
  www10.iadb.org/intal/intalcdi/pe/2009/04268.pdf

- Asia–Pacific Adaptation Network—Coastal Management:
  www.apan-gan.net

- UNESCO MAB: Kristianstad Vattenrike:
  www.unesco.org/mabdb/br/brdir/directory/biores.asp?mode=
  all&code=SWE+02

- MEA: Kristianstad Wetlands:
  www.maweb.org/en/SGA.SwedenKristianstad.aspx

- Introduction into Communities of Practice:
  http://wenger-trayner.com/theory

- Infed: Lean Lave, Etienne Wenger: Communities of Practice:
  http://infed.org/mobi/jean-lave-etienne-wenger-and-communities-
  of-practice

- Lofoten's Legendary Seasonal Fishery:
  www.lofoten.info/en/history

- Norwegian Fishing Village Museum: The Lofoten Fishery:
  http://d1011110–1219.avaboo.net/nfmuseum/history/fishery.htm

- Lofoten Islands, Norway:
  www.grida.no/photolib/collection/fish-farming-and-processing-on-
  the-lofoten-islands

- University of Idaho: Salmon and The Columbia River—Boldt
  Implications:
  www.webpages.uidaho.edu/~rfrey/422salmon.htm

- Cultural Survival: The Unintended Consequences of the Boldt
  Decision:
  www.culturalsurvival.org/publications/cultural-survival-
  quarterly/united-states/unintended-consequences-boldt-decision

- Co-management of Land in Australia: Kakadu National Park,
  N. Territory:
  http://caringforthelandtogether.weebly.com/case-study-1-kakadu-
  northern-territory.html

- Australian Government: Kakadu National Park Management Plan: www.environment.gov.au/resource/management-plan-2007–2014-kakadu-national-park

- Bridging organizations: http://ecgg.uwaterloo.ca/bridging-organizations-play-key-role-in-connecting-social-networks-with-ecosystem-services

- Boundary organizations: www.atmos.washington.edu/~breth/PCC/guston_2001_Boundary Org.pdf

- Woodrow Wilson Centre: J. Ribot, Uma Lele, and Panel on Democratic Decentralization and NRM: www.wilsoncenter.org/event/decentralization-and-democratization-natural-resource-management

- FiS Seafood Technology: Chiloe seeks to disrupt the illegal trade of Chilean abalone, February 17, 2014: www.fis.com/fis/worldnews/worldnews.asp?monthyear=&day=17&id=66523&l=e&special=&ndb=1%20target=

- Catch Share Design Centre: Chilean National Benthic Resources Territorial Use Rights for Fishing Program: http://catchshares.edf.org/design-stories/chilean-national-benthic-resources-territorial-use-rights-fishing-program

- Arctic Borderlands Ecological Knowledge Co-op: www.taiga.net/coop/index.html
  The Borderlands Co-op monitors and assesses change in the range of the porcupine caribou herd and adjacent Mackenzie Delta area in NWT, Yukon, and Alaska.

- Commercial Fisheries News: http://fish-news.com/cfn

- NOAA: Chesapeake blue crab: http://chesapeakebay.noaa.gov/fish-facts/blue-crab

- Stockholm Resilience Centre: Adaptive Governance: www.stockholmresilience.org/21/research/research-themes/stewardship/adaptive-governance-.html

- International Institute for Sustainable Development: Adaptive Governance and Policy-Making:
  www.iisd.org/foresightgroup/gov.aspx

- World Bank Social Development: What is social capital?
  http://web.worldbank.org/WBSITE/EXTERNAL/TOPICS/
  EXTSOCIALDEVELOPMENT/EXTTSOCIALCAPITAL/0,,
  contentMDK:20185164~menuPK:418217~pagePK:148956
  ~piPK:216618~theSitePK:401015,00.html

- Social Capital Markets: Marine Conservation:
  http://socialcapitalmarkets.net/tag/marine-conservation

EXERCISE

- Describe some of the key aspects of a co-management regime and provide a coastal case study in which some or all of these characteristics are in play. Why aren't co-management arrangements more common than they are?

Chapter 7: Coastal Zone: Reconciling Multiple Uses

This chapter shows why the coastal zone is considered a complex SES. In order to manage these environments, strategies are needed to involve the direct participation of resource users and communities. These web links elaborate on theory and provide examples of participatory coastal zone use.

- Images for integrated coastal zone management:
  www.google.ca/search?q=integrated+coastal+zone+management
  &client=firefox-a&hs=1Os&rls=org.mozilla:en-US:official&channel
  =fflb&tbm=isch&tbo=u&source=univ&sa=X&ei=FtvXU6-fN4-
  HyATb14CICw&ved=0CEkQsAQ&biw=1400&bih=916

- Coastal zone management planning:
  www.unesco.org/csi/act/russia/intman1.htm

- INCOFISH: Integrating Multiple Demands:
  www.incofish.org/index.php

- **Law of the Sea:**
  http://worldoceanreview.com/en/wor-1/law-of-the-sea
  Definitions, issues and challenges surrounding the implementation of
  UNCLOS.

- **The EEZ: What is it?**
  http://oceanservice.noaa.gov/facts/eez.html

- **UNCLOS Academic Links: Division of Ocean Affairs and
  Law of the Sea:**
  www.un.org/depts/los/Links/Academic-links.htm
  Links to organizations dealing with LOS.

- **Canada's Ocean Act:**
  http://laws-lois.justice.gc.ca/eng/acts/O-2.4

- **U.S. Maritime Limits and Boundaries:**
  www.nauticalcharts.noaa.gov/csdl/mbound.htm
  – www.gc.noaa.gov/gcil_maritime.html

- **Partnership for Interdisciplinary Study of Coastal Oceans
  (PISCO):**
  www.piscoweb.org/what

- **NOAA: Office of Sustainable Fisheries (OSF):**
  www.nmfs.noaa.gov/sfa
  OSF is a headquarters program office of NOAA's National Marine
  Fisheries Service (NMFS).

- **Marine Affairs Research and Education (MARE):**
  www.marineaffairs.org/index.html

- **OpenChannels:**
  http://openchannels.org
  Forum for ocean planning and management.

- **Coastal Community University Research Alliance (CURA):**
  www.coastalcura.ca

- **Incofish: Coastal Transects Analysis Model (CTAM):**
  www.incofish.org/CTAM/index2.htm

- **Mangroves for the Future:**
  www.mangrovesforthefuture.org/topics/empower-civil-society/
  sustainable-livelihoods
  Investing in sustainable coastal livelihoods, empowering civil society
  with a vision for healthier, more prosperous, and more secure future
  for all coastal communities.

- **Partnerships in Environmental Management for the Seas of
  East Asia (PEMSEA):**
  http://pemsea.org/knowledge-center/links-to-coastal-and-marine-
  topics
  Links to coastal and marine topics.

- **International Collective in Support of Fishworkers (ICSF):**
  http://community.icsf.net
  Community-based coastal management.

- **UNEP: African Environment Outlook: Coastal and Marine
  Systems:**
  www.unep.org/dewa/africa/publications/aeo-1/094.htm

- **Sato-Umi:**
  www.env.go.jp/water/heisa/satoumi/en/01_e.html
  Social capital for Japanese coastal communities.

- **UNU: Satoumi: The link between humans and the sea:**
  http://ourworld.unu.edu/en/satoumi-the-link-between-humans-
  and-the-sea

- **MAVA (*Fondation pour la nature*):**
  http://en.mava-foundation.org/our-programmes/coastal-west-africa
  The wealth of nature along West Africa's coastal fringe comes from
  an upwelling of nutrients into the warm, shallow seas that mark the
  Sahara's embrace of Atlantic swells.

- **The Society for Ecological Restoration—Programs:**
  www.ser.org/programs/online-networks

- **Indigenous Peoples Restoration Network:**
  www.ser.org/iprn/iprn-home/welcome

- **Community Restoration Network:**
  www.communityrestorationnetwork.com

- **Global Restoration Network, Society for Ecological Restoration:**
  www.globalrestorationnetwork.org/restoration/guidelines/articles/
  ser-international-collaborations

- **The Nature Education Knowledge Project:**
  www.nature.com/scitable/knowledge/library/restoration-ecology-
  13339059

- **U.S. Environmental Protection Agency, Definitions and
  Distinctions: What is restoration?**
  http://water.epa.gov/type/wetlands/restore/defs.cfm

- **Wetlands: Community-Based Coastal Restoration
  (Mangroves for Coastal Resilience):**
  www.wetlands.org/Whatwedo/Mangrovesforcoastalresilience/Green
  Coastscommunity-basedrestoration/tabid/436/Default.aspx

- **Intertribal Sinkyone Wilderness Council:**
  www.lannan.org/indigenous-communities/special-projects/
  intertribal-sinkyone-wilderness-council-ne-mendocino-county-ca

- **Nisqually River and Delta Restoration, Olympia, WA:**
  http://nisquallydeltarestoration.org/
  – www.washingtontribes.org/default.aspx?ID=39

- **Everglades Comprehensive Restoration:**
  www.evergladesplan.org

- **Citizen science:**
  www.scientificamerican.com/citizen-science

- **Citizen science for CA naturalists:**
  http://calnat.ucanr.edu/California_PPSR

- **People's biodiversity registers, India:**
  www.ces.iisc.ernet.in/biodiversity/sahyadri_enews/newsletter/
  issue15/index.htm

EXERCISE

- Integrated coastal zone management: how would marine spatial planning help?
- Social–ecological restoration: What are some of the lessons? Why is community involvement so important in restoration projects?
- At what level of participation does citizen science become empowering?

Chapter 8: Conserving Biodiversity: MPAs and Stewardship

Concepts and ideas around conservation and their relationships to development are outlined, and the potential areas for conflict and co-operation are discussed in this chapter and associated web links. The ideas of integrated conservation and development, and the use of marine protected areas (MPAs) are explored: How can their use be tailored to create more inclusive, stewardship-oriented conservation?

- **Community-based conservation:**
  www.wcs.org/conservation-challenges/local-livelihoods/community-based-conservation.aspx

- **Community-based conservation, Wiley online library:**
  http://onlinelibrary.wiley.com/doi/10.1111/j.1523–1739.2004.00077.x/pdf

- **Local Communities Playing Vital Role in Marine Conservation:**
  http://ourworld.unu.edu/en/local-communities-playing-vital-role-in-marine-conservation

- **Integrated Conservation–Development Projects (ICDPs):**
  http://en.wikipedia.org/wiki/Integrated_Conservation_and_Development_Project

- **Convention on Biological Diversity: Marine and Coastal:**
  www.cbd.int/marine

- **Convention of the Parties (COP) Decisions on Marine and Coastal Biodiversity:**
  www.cbd.int/marine/decisions.shtml

- Large Marine Management Area (LMMA) Network:
  www.lmmanetwork.org
  – Fiji: http://lmmanetwork.dreamhosters.com/fiji

- Reef Check—Indonesia:
  http://reefcheck.or.id

- South Pacific Community, Traditional Marine Resource
  Management and Knowledge Information Bulletin:
  www.spc.int/coastfish/News/Trad/trad.htm

- ICCA Consortium Home:
  www.iccaconsortium.org

- ICCA Living Oceans:
  www.livingoceans.org/initiatives/ocean-planning/issues/indigenous-
  peoples-and-community-conserved-territories-and-areas

- IUCN: ICCAs:
  http://iucn.org/about/union/commissions/ceesp/topics/governance/
  icca

- IUCN: Marine and Polar Conservation Program:
  www.iucn.org/about/work/programmes/marine/marine_our_work/
  livelihoods

- Great Barrier Reef:
  www.greatbarrierreef.org

- Great Barrier Reef Marine Park Authority:
  www.gbrmpa.gov.au

- Papahānaumokuākea Marine National Monument (PMNM):
  www.papahanaumokuakea.gov

- PMNM (NOAA):
  www.fpir.noaa.gov/DIR/dir_nwhimnm.html

- Marine Conservation Institute: Papahānaumokuākea Marine
  National Monument:
  www.marine-conservation.org/what-we-do/program-areas/mpas/
  pacific-islands-conservation/papahanaumokuakea

- UNESCO: Papahānaumokuākea:
  http://whc.unesco.org/en/list/1326

- New Zealand Marine Protected Areas:
  www.doc.govt.nz/conservation/marine-and-coastal/marine-protected-areas

- NZ Government—MPA Listing:
  www.doc.govt.nz/conservation/marine-and-coastal/marine-protected-areas/marine-reserves-a-z

- The WSA 1992:
  www.legislation.govt.nz/act/public/1992/0121/latest/whole.html

- The Fisheries Settlement (Maori web):
  www.nmow.co.nz/Fisheries-Settlement

- Terralingua: Biocultural Diversity Conservation:
  www.terralingua.org/bcdconservation

- Conservation Gateway: R. Hamilton, Local Knowledge Report
  on Roviana Lagoon:
  www.conservationgateway.org/Files/Pages/spawning-aggregations-coraspx92.aspx

- Parks Canada Gwaii Haanas:
  www.pc.gc.ca/eng/pn-np/bc/gwaiihaanas/index.aspx

- Marine Stewardship Group Haida Gwaii:
  www.marinematters.org/programs/abalone.html

- Coastal First Nations Guardians:
  http://coastalguardianwatchmen.ca

- Equator Initiative:
  www.equatorinitiative.org/index.php?lang=en

- Marine Conservation Institute: Chief Scientist, Dr. Elliot Norse:
  www.marine-conservation.org

- U.S. Fish and Wildlife Service: Coastal Program:
  www.fws.gov/coastal

- **Center for Coastal Conservation (US)**:
  www.coastalconservation.us/index.php

- **The Nature Conservancy: Protecting Oceans and Coasts**:
  www.nature.org/ourinitiatives/habitats/oceanscoasts

- **Network of Conservation Educators and Practitioners**:
  http://ncep.amnh.org

- **FAO: About MPAs**:
  www.fao.org/fishery/topic/4400/en

- **MPA News**:
  http://depts.washington.edu/mpanews/conflist.html

- **Coral Triangle Initiative**:
  www.coraltriangleinitiative.org

- **How do we manage MPAs in a way that makes them more effective and resilient?**
  http://openchannels.org/blog/pjsjones/how-do-we-manage-marine-protected-areas-mpas-way-makes-them-more-effective-and

- **The Commonwealth Secretariat: Protecting Coastal Habitats to Mitigate Impacts of Climate Change—Vanuatu**:
  http://thecommonwealth.org/project/protecting-coastal-habitats-mitigate-against-climate-change-vanuatu

- **Fishbase**:
  www.fishbase.org
  A global information system.

- **Reefbase**:
  www.reefbase.org/main.aspx
  A global information system for coral reefs.

- **IGBP: Ocean Governance in the Anthropocene**:
  www.igbp.net/news/features/features/oceangovernanceinthe anthropocene.5.64c294101429ba9184d483.html
  First published in IGBP's *Global Change* magazine, issue 81, October 2013.

- **Comunidad y Biodiversidad (CoBi):**
  http://cobi.org.mx/en
  A nonprofit organization dedicated to promoting the conservation of marine biodiversity in coastal communities of Mexico.

- **Coastal Conservation in Pacific Northwest, Eco-tourism:**
  http://bluewateradventures.ca/site/bluewater-culture/coastal-conservation.html

- **Coastal Conservation Network:**
  www.coastalconservation.net

- **European Environmental Agency: Europe's Coasts: Reconciling Development and Conservation:**
  www.eea.europa.eu/highlights/europe2019s-coasts-reconciling-development-and-conservation

- **Lake Huron Centre for Coastal Conservation:**
  http://lakehuron.ca

- **Wetlands Institute: Coastal Conservation Research Program:**
  http://wetlandsinstitute.org/research/ccrp

EXERCISE

- List and describe the some of the key conservation issues facing coastal areas. For each issue, try to identify key drivers.

- If you were involved in an ICCA, would you want your ICCA to become part of a government conserved-areas network?

- What are some of the factors that can help community-based conservation work? What are some of the barriers?

Chapter 9: Coastal Livelihoods: Resources and Development

Natural resource-based livelihoods from coastal areas are explored via the sustainable livelihoods approach (SLA), coupled with cases that look at the importance of developing participatory management. How can governance foster resilient marine and coastal SESs that provide creative space for both social and technical innovation?

- **Sustainable livelihoods in a nutshell:**
  www.poverty-wellbeing.net/media/sla/docs/2–1.htm

- **Sustainable livelihoods approach:**
  www.ifad.org/sla

- **Sustainable livelihoods guidance sheets:**
  www.efls.ca/webresources/DFID_Sustainable_livelihoods_guidance_
  sheet.pdf

- **Images for sustainable livelihoods:**
  www.google.ca/search?q=sustainable+livelihoods&tbm=isch&tbo=
  u&source=univ&sa=X&ei=nAfYU86KEcityASghICABA&ved=
  0CCIQsAQ&biw=1400&bih=916

- **Images for grassroots development:**
  www.google.ca/search?q=grassroots+development&tbm=isch&tbo=
  u&source=univ&sa=X&ei=jAzYU5GdFcubyASq7oHACw&sqi=
  2&ved=0CFIQsAQ&biw=1400&bih=916

- **Samudra ICSF publications:**
  www.icsf.net/en/page/436-Publications.html

- **Amartya Sen:**
  www.nobelprize.org/nobel_prizes/economic-
  sciences/laureates/1998/sen-bio.html

- *The Economist* **on Amartya Sen:**
  www.economist.com/topics/amartya-sen

- **A.M. Sackler Colloquia and the National Academy of Sciences:
  Linking Knowledge and Action for Sustainable Development:**
  www.nasonline.org/programs/sackler-colloquia/completed_colloquia/
  linking-knowledge-with-action-for-sustainable-development.html

- **Ocean Wise:**
  www.oceanwise.ca
  A Vancouver aquarium conservation program created to educate and
  empower consumers about the issues surrounding sustainable seafood.

- **Ecology Action Centre, Halifax:**
  www.ecologyaction.ca/issue-area/coastal-livelihoods
  Coastal livelihoods for vibrant and healthy coastal communities.

- **Too Big to Ignore:**
  http://toobigtoignore.net
  Exploring research and development issues for global small-scale
  fisheries and their communities.

- **Regional Fisheries Livelihoods Program (FAO RFLP):**
  www.fao.org/asiapacific/rap/nre/links/regional-fisheries-livelihoods-
  programme/en
  Sets out to strengthen capacity among participating small-scale fishing
  communities in a number of developing countries.

- **NOAA's State of the Coast: Vulnerability:**
  http://stateofthecoast.noaa.gov/vulnerability/welcome.html

- **Maryland CoastSmart Communities:**
  www.dnr.state.md.us/coastsmart

- **Ecostrust—North Pacific Fisheries Trust:**
  www.ecotrust.org/npft
  Supports the efforts of coastal communities and local fishing families.

- **Cape Cod Fisheries Trust:**
  http://capecodfishermen.org/fisheries-trust
  Cape Cod's smaller-scale fishing tradition is vibrant, sustainable, and
  a model for other fishing communities.

- **Coastal Enterprises of Maine:**
  www.ceimaine.org
  CEI's philosophy and mission are rooted in the civil rights movement.

- **Environmental Defence Fund (EDF): Catch Share Design
  Centre—A Fisheries Tool Kit:**
  http://catchshares.edf.org

- **Natural Capital Project:**
  www.naturalcapitalproject.org/InVEST.html
  NatCap aims to integrate the values of nature into all major decisions
  affecting the environment and human well-being.

- **Global Oceans Action Summit—Food Security:**
  www.globaloceansactionsummit.com

- Coastal Tourism: PPPs USA:
  www.publicaffairs.noaa.gov/oceanreport/tourism.html

- GPO Indispensable Oceans—PPP, 2013:
  www.globalpartnershipforoceans.org/indispensable-ocean

- Northwest Atlantic Marine Alliance (NAMA):
  http://namanet.org
  NAMA works with community-based fishermen on market and policy alternatives that protect and maintain marine biodiversity while ensuring healthy local fishing economies.

- Cape Cod Commercial Hook Fisherman's Association (CCCHFA):
  http://namanet.org/csf/cape-cod-commercial-hook-fishermens-association-community-supported-fishery

- Penobscot East Resource Center—NE Coastal Communities Sector:
  www.penobscoteast.org/programs/northeast-coastal-communities-sector

- C-Fish, Caribbean Fish Sanctuary Program—Alternative Livelihoods:
  http://c-fish.org/what-we-do/alternative-livelihoods

- South Africa's subsistence fishers:
  www.irinnews.org/report/98617/more-support-needed-for-south-africa-apos-s-subsistence-fishermen

- Fishing in South Africa:
  www.wwf.org.za/what_we_do/marine/sustainable_fisheries/oceans_in_trouble/fishing_in_sa

- Food security:
  www.who.int/trade/glossary/story028/en

- Food security—indigenous peoples' food systems:
  www.fao.org/docrep/018/i3144e/i3144e.pdf

- Gender and fishing:
  www.fao.org/gender/gender-home/gender-programme/gender-fisheries/en

- Gender and small-scale fisheries:
  http://seahorse.fisheries.ubc.ca/node/702

- Social enterprise:
  http://en.wikipedia.org/wiki/Social_enterprise

- Social enterprise:
  www.socialenterprisecanada.ca/learn/nav/whatisasocialenterprise.html

---

EXERCISE

- Describe what is meant by *alternative* livelihoods and give clear examples of how fishing contributes to sustainable livelihoods in coastal systems.
- Gender considerations and food security are part of the social objectives of fishery and coastal resource management systems. Explain.

Chapter 10: Local and Traditional Knowledge: Bridging the Science

Web links support the chapter's description of the origins, use, and importance of local and traditional ecological knowledge (TEK). Fisher knowledge is highlighted as an important and necessary input into developing more robust, conventional science-based approaches. A number of methods exist for bridging the two knowledge systems.

- **Indigenous Knowledge:**
  www.dlist.org/book/export/html/1024

  Introduction and case studies.

- **Robert Johannes—A Tribute, Florida State University:**
  www.bio.fsu.edu/mote/bob_johannes.php

- **Envacapstone: TEK Lesson Plan:**
  http://envacapstone.wiki.usfca.edu/Traditional+Ecological+Knowledge+(TEK)+-+Lesson+Plan

- **"Coming full circle":**
  http://muse.jhu.edu/login?auth=0&type=summary&url=/journals/american_indian_quarterly/v028/28.3mcgregor.html

- **Local Futures—International Society for Ecology & Culture:**
  www.localfutures.org www.theeconomicsofhappiness.org

- **First Salmon Ceremony:**
  www.opb.org/television/programs/ofg/segment/first-salmon-
  ceremony

- **Massachusetts Government: Cod Conservation Zone:**
  www.mass.gov/eea/agencies/dfg/dmf/programs-and-projects/
  cod-conservation-zone.html

- **Conservation Law Foundation: Tagging and catch limits set
  for Gulf of Maine cod:**
  www.clf.org/blog/tag/gulf-of-maine-cod

- **CBC: Scientist plans to tag Greenland Sharks, University of
  Windsor:**
  www.cbc.ca/news/canada/north/scientist-plans-to-tag-greenland-
  sharks-1.1183241

- **Simon Fraser University: Ancient clam gardens nurture food
  security:**
  www.sfu.ca/pamr/media-releases/2014/ancient-clam-gardens-
  nurture-food-security.html

- **Aboriginal Aquaculture Association: Gallery—Clam Gardens:**
  www.aboriginalaquaculture.com/new-page

- **Maine Rivers, Estuaries, and Coastal Fisheries:**
  http://research.bowdoin.edu/rivers-estuaries-and-coastal-fisheries
  Ecological and economic connections.

- **Atlas of Community-Based Monitoring for a Changing Arctic:**
  www.arcticcbm.org/index.html

- **Two Row (Wampum) History:**
  http://honorthetworow.org/learn-more/history

- **Participatory Rural Appraisal:**
  www.iisd.org/casl/caslguide/pra.htm

- **Participatory Education:**
  http://twbonline.pbworks.com/w/page/29052439/Participatory
  %20Education

- Participatory Workshops: The Learning Design Grid:
  www.ld-grid.org/resources/methods-and-methodologies/
  participatory-pattern-workshops

- Participatory Resource Mapping: Forest Peoples Program:
  www.forestpeoples.org/topics/environmental-governance/
  participatory-resource-mapping

- Participatory Conservation Planning: Conservation Gateway,
  Nature Conservancy:
  www.conservationgateway.org/Files/Pages/participatory-conservatio.
  aspx

- Participatory Ecological Restoration: Watershed, Rio Blanco
  Colombia:
  www.forestlandscaperestoration.org/resource/participatory-
  ecological-restoration-rio-blanco-watershed-ecosystem-based-
  adaptation-action

- Weaving Indigenous and Sustainability Sciences (workshop report
  for the NSF):
  www.ipsr.ku.edu/igrc/wis2dom/WorkshopReport2013.pdf

EXERCISE

- How can traditional fisher knowledge foster adaptive capacity in the face of a diverse set of change agents?
- Provide an example of traditional fisher knowledge and conventional scientific management working together in some area of coastal resources.

Chapter 11: Social–Ecological System-Based Management

These web links are mainly about ecosystem-based management, but with due consideration also of the social component of SES.

- Ecological Society of America, Scientific Basis for Ecosystem
  Management:
  http://infohouse.p2ric.org/ref/31/30848.pdf

- **Francis et al., Ten Commandments for Ecosystem-Based Fisheries Scientists:**
  http://hixon.science.oregonstate.edu/files/hixon/publications/069%20-%20Francis%20et%20al%2007%20Fisheries.pdf

- **Using the Ecosystem Approach (and Malawi Principles):**
  https://testportals.iucn.org/library/sites/library/files/documents/CEM-002.pdf

- **Ecosystem Approach to Fisheries (EAF)—Principles Including Subsidiarity** (FAP Document Repository):
  www.fao.org/docrep/006/y4773e/y4773e09.htm

- **CBNRM Listing of Case Studies:**
  http://srdis.ciesin.columbia.edu/cases/caselist.html

- **Stockholm Resilience Center (SRC)—Social–Ecological Systems:**
  www.stockholmresilience.org/21/research/what-is-resilience/research-background/research-framework/social-ecological-systems.html

- **University of Southampton: Complex Social–Ecological Systems:**
  www.southampton.ac.uk/sustainability_science/researchgroups/socio_ecological_systems.page

- **Center of Ocean Solutions (Stanford University):**
  www.centerforoceansolutions.org/initiatives/social-ecological-resilience-small-scale

- **Ecosystem-Based Management (EBM) Tools Network:**
  www.ebmtools.org
  The EBM Tools Network, co-ordinated by NatureServe as part of its Coastal and Marine Strategy, is one of the premier sources of information about coastal and marine planning and management tools in the United States and internationally.

- **Marine Ecosystems and Management (MEAM):**
  http://depts.washington.edu/meam/index.html
  Bimonthly information service.

- **SeaWeb: Ecosystem-Based Management:**
  www.seaweb.org/resources/ebm.php

- NOAA: Ecosystem-Based Management—Chesapeake Office:
  http://chesapeakebay.noaa.gov/ecosystem-based-management/
  ecosystem-based-fisheries-management

- ICES: Vision and Mission:
  www.ices.dk/Pages/default.aspx

- iMarine: Data e-Infrastructure Initiative for Fisheries Management
  and Conservation of Marine Living Resources:
  www.i-marine.eu/pages/Home.aspx

- ESRI Ocean GIS Forum:
  www.esri.com/events/oceans
  The new ESRI GIS for Ocean Forum is about you and the work you
  do for marine and coast.

- Geological Society of America: Managing U.S. Coastal Hazards:
  www.geosociety.org/positions/position22.htm

- Tambuyog Development Center:
  http://legal.icsf.net/icsflegal/uploads/pdf/instruments/phi3.pdf

- ECGG (University of Waterloo): Uncovering a Social–Ecological
  Transformation in Coastal Vietnam:
  http://ecgg.uwaterloo.ca/uncovering-a-social-ecological-
  transformation-in-coastal-vietnam

- Fuzzy logic:
  http://en.wikipedia.org/wiki/Fuzzy_logic

- How rice cookers work:
  http://home.howstuffworks.com/rice-cooker2.htm

- Fuzzy logic tutorial:
  www.seattlerobotics.org/encoder/mar98/fuz/flindex.html

- Expert system:
  http://en.wikipedia.org/wiki/Expert_system

- MARES:
  www.mares-eu.org/index.asp?p=1614&a=1224&mod=cursus
  &id=3918
  Applications of fuzzy logic to marine environmental research.

> **EXERCISE**
>
> - What are some of the key advantages and disadvantages of expanding the concept of ecosystem-based management to SES-based management? To multiple sectors? To governance?

Chapter 12: An Interdisciplinary Science for the Coast

The summary chapter reviews the key concepts, theories, and frameworks put forward in earlier chapters. It starts to look at how to move into the future, with divergent strategies for the way ahead. Web links start with some U.S. educational web sites.

- **School of Marine and Environmental Affairs: University of Washington:**
  http://depts.washington.edu/smea

- **Coastal Resource Center: University of Rhode Island:**
  www.crc.uri.edu

- **U.S. Oceans and Coastal Law: Gallagher Law Library, University of Washington:**
  https://lib.law.washington.edu/content/guides/oceancoastal

- **Centre for Oceans Law and Policy, University of Virginia:**
  www.virginia.edu/colp

- **Bren School of Environmental Science and Management, University of California, Santa Barbara, Sustainable Fisheries Group:**
  http://sfg.msi.ucsb.edu

- **Oregon State University: Pacific Fishing History Project:**
  http://carmelfinley.wordpress.com

- **Blog: California Sardines/Pilchards:**
  http://carmelfinley.wordpress.com/2010/04/29/oregon-pilchards-and-california-sardines

- **Integration and Application Network (IAN): University of Maryland—Center for Environmental Science:**
  http://ian.umces.edu

- Alliance for Sustainability and Prosperity: Leaving GDP Behind: www.asap4all.com

- The White House: Council on Environmental Quality—Preparing Now for Our Climate Future, 2014: www.whitehouse.gov/blog/2014/03/04/preparing-now-our-climate-future

- APFIC: November 5, 2013: www.apfic.org GEF-funded, FAO project forms part of global effort to improve fisheries management in the common oceans.

- Marine Activities, Resources and Education (MARE): Ocean Science Curriculum Sequences: http://mare.lawrencehallofscience.org/curriculum/ocean-science-sequence

- Universities Council on Water Resources: http://ucowr.org

- The Great Transition Initiative: www.gtinitiative.org

- The Social Planning and Research Council of BC (SPARC BC): www.sparc.bc.ca/about-sparc-bc

- Global Partnership for Oceans: www.globalpartnershipforoceans.org

- Global Ocean Refuge System: Building Ocean Resilience: http://globaloceanrefuge.org/2014/05/08/glores-and-ocean-resilience

- Pew Charitable Trusts: Future of America's Oceans—Better or Worse? www.pewenvironment.org/news-room/other-resources/future-of-americas-oceans-better-or-worse-85899479449

- M. Ben-Yami, Fisheries Management: Hijacked by Neoliberal Economics: www.paecon.net/PAEReview/issue27/BenYami27.htm

- **B. Mansfield, Neoliberal Fisheries:**
  http://citeseerx.ist.psu.edu/viewdoc/summary?doi=10.1.1.330.4266

- **New England Fisheries Build New Business Model:**
  www.pbs.org/newshour/bb/north_america-july-dec10-pledge_08–02

- **Local Catch Org:**
  www.localcatch.org/resources.html
  Network of community-supported fisheries.

- **Fishermen Direct-Marketing Manual:**
  http://wsg.washington.edu/communications/online/FishDirect
  MarMan.pdf

- **Rhode Island's Direct Fisheries Marketing:**
  www.riclimatechange.org/reports/Fisheries.pdf

- **ThisFish: Finding Traceable Seafood:**
  http://thisfish.info

- **Slow Fish:**
  www.slowfood.com/slowfish
  Good, clean, and fair fish.

- **Fish Wise:**
  http://fishwise.org
  A sustainable seafood consultancy.

EXERCISE

- Divergent strategies for the way ahead: Evaluate the pros and cons of the options and give your reasoned view for the preferred way ahead.

INDEX